WITS
THE EARLY YEARS

Wits Press RE/PRESENTS

Wits University Press celebrates its centenary in 2022. Since its inception, the Press has been curating and publishing innovative research that informs debate to drive impactful change in society. Drawing on an extensive backlist dating from 1922, **Wits Press Re/Presents** is a new series that makes important research accessible to readers once again. While much of the content demonstrates its historical provenance, it remains of interest to researchers and students, and is re-published in e-book and print-on-demand formats.

WITS
THE EARLY YEARS

A HISTORY OF THE UNIVERSITY OF THE
WITWATERSRAND, JOHANNESBURG, AND ITS
PRECURSORS 1896 – 1939

BRUCE K. MURRAY
Foreword by Keith Breckenridge

Published in South Africa by:
Wits University Press
1 Jan Smuts Avenue
Johannesburg 2001

www.witspress.co.za

Copyright © Bruce Murray 1982
Foreword © Keith Breckenridge 2022
Published edition © Wits University Press 2022

First published 1982

http://dx.doi.org.10.18772/12022088080

978-1-77614-808-0 (Paperback)
978-1-77614-809-7 (Hardback)
978-1-77614-810-3 (Web PDF)
978-1-77614-811-0 (EPUB)

All rights reserved. No part of this publication may be reproduced, stored in a retrieval system, or transmitted in any form or by any means, electronic, mechanical, photocopying, recording or otherwise, without the written permission of the publisher, except in accordance with the provisions of the Copyright Act, Act 98 of 1978.

Cover image: Wits in 1937, courtesy of Wits Central Records and Archives

To
Robert, Margaret
and
my friends and colleagues at
WITS

CONTENTS

Foreword to this edition by Keith Breckenridge ... ix
Foreword by D.J. du Plessis ... xvii
Acknowledgements ... xix
Abbreviations ... xxi

Part I: Prelude to a University
1. False Start: Milner, Beit, and Smuts ... 3
2. From School of Mines to University ... 39

Part II: The New University
3. A Turbulent Beginning ... 71
4. Administration, Finance, and Buildings ... 93
5. Arts and Science ... 125
6. The Professional Faculties ... 162

Part III: Raikes: The First Decade
7. Depression and Recovery ... 199
8. Ascendancy of the Professions ... 234

Part IV: Students and Special Issues
9. Questions of Discrimination ... 297
10. Student Life ... 337

A Note on Sources ... 379
Index ... 381

FOREWORD

Bruce Murray may be the least celebrated of the many important South African historians of the 1980s. One reason for this neglect is that his research specialisation – drawn from his mid-1960s theses at the University of Kansas – was on Lloyd George's famous 1909 Budget. The first *People's Budget* increased land and income taxes to fund the Liberal Party's new pension, health and employment schemes and it set the fiscal lines of class conflict in modern Britain. It also triggered a revolt in the Lords, led by Alfred Milner, the former Imperial Proconsul in southern Africa, which hastened the decline of liberalism and the rise of the Labour Party. These long-term political consequences were more, as Murray shows, an accidental consequence of George's fiery rhetoric than of a deliberate plan to lift the poor and fleece the middle class. Yet all of these questions around the fair distribution of tax and welfare remain powerful and unresolved in British politics, leading scholars back to the 1909 reforms and to Bruce Murray's work. Sadly, their links to imperial, and especially South African, politics, have largely been forgotten, as much here as they have been in Britain.

In the republication of the history of Wits, two volumes of which were written by Murray, readers have an opportunity to explore the often dramatic and contested story of this university, and his two volumes, Murray's distinctive style as writer. Perhaps to make up for the neglect of his excellent work on Lloyd George, Murray produced an intimate, almost scandalous intellectual history of the institution that served as his home for practically half a century. The first volume – this book – was published in 1982 (shortly after the modest and careful prose of the *People's Budget*), and the second almost a generation later, in 1997. Both share the skilled archival historian's interest in the high drama and low stakes of personalised emotional conflicts. Murray was always, without being nasty about it, a serious institutional and scholarly gossip, irresistibly attracted to the small-beer political conflicts within departments and levels of the university, and between the different South African institutions. This interest in the personal character of scholarly conflicts, combined with his elegant and engaging writing style, give both books an engaging quality that most readers would not expect from a history – and especially from an institutional history.

This book is an expanded family history of the university, with the personal conflicts and political disagreements foregrounded in Murray's narrative. Perhaps inevitably for a university struggling to establish itself as a serious and well-regarded centre of higher education in the middle of a wild and disorderly mining city, these disagreements turned, very often, on the private and political problems of its academic staff. The university's first gifted and radical historian, W.M. Macmillan, was forced into resignation by the principal in 1933 because of an extra-marital affair. Margaret Ballinger, another brave and charismatic liberal lecturer in the department, was forced into retirement two years later after marrying her activist husband. My favourite example of the gentle, continuous scandal that defines the history of my university comes in his discussion, in the second volume, of the Economics Department's 'unanimous' decision to fail Charles Feinstein's Honours dissertation as suitable only 'for Moscow University'. Feinstein would go on to become the most celebrated and influential economic historian of modern Britain. Many former Wits students will feel some sympathy for him, I suspect.

This first volume of the history of the University takes this story from the early years of the twentieth century, when Milner and his most ambitious followers began to consider the establishment of a university in Johannesburg, to the outbreak of World War II. In this short period the institution grew from being little more than a shack into a prodigious engine of globally influential professionalisation. One of the remarkable features of this transformation was its organisation around the education of a new generation of Jewish professionals. Throughout these years the university's overall student body was nearly one-third Jewish, while the Medical School enrolment – to the state's chagrin – was close to half, the vast majority of whom came from working class families in the city's retailing economy. The great achievement of the institution in this period, as Murray shows, was its success in fostering a 'large Jewish professional class on the Rand'. Less obvious, but as important, was the parallel transformation of the city's white Afrikaans-speaking families, whose children made up nearly a quarter of the student body by the 1930s.

If Wits's first generation was unmistakably a product of the city's poorest white families' boot-straps determination to access professional education (often delivered chaotically by the university), it was also deeply controversial and contested. Murray's book is structured by six of these conflicts, which ran through the period from 1900 to 1940. The first, and unarguably the most long-lasting, was the bitter conflict between the city's white electorate and the Smuts government, over its suitability as the site for a university. The second, strongly connected to the first problem, was the institution's *raison d'être* as an instrument for the educational advancement of white people, in competition with the initially better-educated black residents of the city. Race was at the core of the university's intellectual project from the outset, and the third theme, perhaps inevitably, was that the sciences of race and of race relations had profound effects on the kinds of teaching and research it professed. A fourth problematic, also alive and well into the present, was the persistent requirement to deliver tertiary education without proportionate resources. Making a globally respectable university on the smell of an oil rag was required in part because the university's endowment had been usurped by the more arcadian campuses in Pretoria and Cape Town, but also because of the provincial constraints on competent lecturers, the demographic pressures from the city, and families' demands for professionalisation. Murray's careful examination of the drivers of success, and failure, in this earlier period, of sustained austerity is particularly interesting and instructive in the modern era, as Wits finds itself competing with hundreds of Anglophone universities overseas fuelled by hedge-fund endowments. The fifth theme that drives this history is an uneven story of local scholarly competence and achievement. Murray does a truly remarkable job in examining the strengths and failures, and eccentricities, of the disciplines at Wits, from Afrikaans poetry to physics. It is not a simple story: what we might call the development of the university seems to have emerged from outside, from the wider politics, its students' families, and the regional economy. The final theme – which encapsulates these individual threads of academic labour within the disciplines and the faculties – draws out the contrasting economic moments of the 1920s (where the country faced a post-war and post-pandemic crisis not unlike our own) with the post-1932 mining boom that ushered into being the city's (and the university's) golden age. These last two themes are developed through the book, and cannot easily be summarised. But let me turn, briefly, to some instances of the first four to give the reader a sense of the flavour and stakes of Murray's history.

To begin with, consider the problem of the city's suitability as a site for a research university. The original idea for a university in the manic and disorderly mining city came from the social imperialists Chamberlain and Milner, with support from the American mining engineers, including Gardiner Williams, who managed De Beers (and the first School of Mines) in Kimberley. It was Percy Fitzpatrick who persuaded the reluctant, childless Rand Mines plutocrat, Alfred Beit, to leave the city £200 000 for a university from his enormous £8 million estate. (Amongst academic generous bequests in England to Oxford, Cambridge and Imperial, Beit also left £100 000 to help establish the combined University of Hamburg.) From the outset, however, the local elites organised in Het Volk took a dim view of the idea that a university could succeed in the disorderly city, which spent much of the first quarter of the century in a state of serious tumult. With Stellenbosch and Christ's College Cambridge in his own experience, Jan Smuts, as Murray shows, was a particular opponent of the idea of the University of the Witwatersrand. He pushed Pretoria as the location of the Transvaal's provincial university, and cleverly redirected the Beit bequest to our academic friends building the university on the slopes of Table Mountain. As was often the case with Smuts, his brutal realism had strong roots in his acute understanding of the society, and he was quickly vindicated. Just one week after the university eventually opened the doors of its Milner Park campus for the first time (against his carefully worked out, long-term plans) in March 1922, Smuts was forced to return to the city to direct the military – with artillery and bomber aircraft – to subdue the white miners' uprising in the adjacent suburb of Fordsburg. It is fair to say that the disorder and tumult of city life in Johannesburg remains both an animator and a burden on the research university; but it is also, undeniably, what motivates the institution's distinctively intense forms of enquiry and vituperative argument.

Another distinguishing element of the university's intellectual history was its obsessive and constitutive focus on the instruments and problems of racial hierarchy and racism. From the early public meetings in 1917, the city's leaders justified the project of building an institution of higher education, against the plans of the central government, as a key element in the project of 'preserving "European" ascendancy'. This racist project also imposed an unusual democratising motivation for white people, as Murray shows, 'offering a ladder upwards to the sons of the poor'. The university also quickly took the 'scientific study of the Natives' as a – arguably *the* – major interdisciplinary research ambition. The international reputation of the university's Medical School turned in this period, as is well known, on Raymond Dart's palaeoanthropology, which had potent effects on racism, locally and internationally. Murray shows a similar paradoxical movement in the social sciences. With support from the Chamber of Mines, Bantu Studies became an unusual and influential research expertise, and the home to some of the most influential and important researchers at Wits – studying African society and white attitudes about it – from the anthropologist Winifred Hoernlé, through the linguist Clement Doke, to the social psychologist I.D. Macrone.

All of the departments at Wits, from the Medical School to the Humanities, worked with extreme resource constraints in this period. The university received some support from the mining companies, and from the municipality, but the general model was to admit as many students as were prepared to pay the generally 'remarkably low fees'. The early university made no meaningful effort to select its students. Black students were generally (but not always) refused entry, and their numbers were pitifully small, only rising to around 100 during World War II. Murray shows that, in the 1920s, students were paying £20 per annum in the Humanities, rising to £40 per annum in the Medical School. The main result was very large classes, brutally low faculty numbers, lecturer-focused teaching and assessment (a striking contrast with the one-to-one tutorial system of the ancient universities in Britain) and, again distinctively, eye-watering failure rates. Yet, if measuring the success of the alumni is a useful measure, this clinical model seems to have worked very well for the white families who could afford the modest fees.

How the city's African families related to the university in this period has been harder to explore, because the numbers were so low before World War II. One exception was Nelson Mandela's experience as the first African law student admitted to the university in 1943. Murray recently published a detailed reconstruction of his interaction with the Law Faculty, both in the period before he abandoned his studies in 1949, and much later, in the 1970s, when he appealed to be allowed to complete his Wits degree. After his application was intercepted by the security police, Mandela went on to complete his degree through Unisa in the late 1980s; Wits attempted to undo some of the damage by granting the first president of the democratic era an honorary doctorate in 1991. In both eras Mandela faced the unyielding and legalistic response from the university that many students will say is basic to its nature. As Murray notes, 'that Mandela constituted an exceptional case and was worthy of special encouragement, was beyond the imagination of the Faculty of Law'.[1] Yet it is also a distinguishing feature of the university

---

1   B. Murray, 'Nelson Mandela and Wits University,' *The Journal of African History* 57, no. 2 (July 2016): 271–92, https://doi.org/10.1017/S002185371500078X.

that its own researchers, in this case its institutional historian, have such an unflinchingly critical view of its history.

One of the most interesting conclusions of Murray's intimate history of Wits is that the real driver of the university's success seems to have come not from changes of curriculum or governance within the institution (the problems so beloved of the indefatigable higher education reformers of my own lifetime), but from the outside economy. While the numbers (and viability) of the Humanities departments remained madly high through this period – with hundreds of enrolled students in each department and one or two employed lecturers (and the women, especially, on insecure contracts) – the numbers of professionals, especially in the engineering-related fields, grew dramatically after the abolition of the gold standard ushered in the long mining boom. In the five years immediately after the university opened its Milner Park campus, the mining-supported Engineering Faculty graduated a total of 110 students, most of them in civil engineering, and only nine in the field closest to the mines' heart, mining and metallurgy. The reason for this glacial throughput was the absence of positions in the gold mines, which were suffering from the brutal deflationary effects of the restored gold standard (and an unsympathetic Nationalist-Labour government). The Medical School also worried about the 'oversupply of doctors' in this period, although again, managing throughput with the failure rate had some benefits for the value of professional training: through the entire 1920s the Dental School graduated only six students!

All of this changed dramatically during the 1930s. The student enrolment in the Faculty of Medicine grew from 231 to 740 between 1928 and 1939, and a similar expansion, from 267 to 829, occurred in the Engineering Faculty. Even Dentistry doubled its student intake. Law and the Humanities, the stalwarts of the deflationary twenties, declined significantly during the boom era. As Murray shows, the primary cause of this professional transformation of the university was the investment in secondary industry (some of it planned, but not funded, in the 1920s). It was the growth of Iscor, Eskom, AECI, the Railways, and the National Road Board that prompted young people (most of them men, and all of them white) to opt for the demanding degrees that became the foundation for Wits's global reputation as an engineering university. Again, however, the numbers of graduates were relatively low, especially in comparison with our own time (the Wits faculty of Engineering graduated about 200 students in 2022). By 1939 the university had produced a total of 720 graduates in engineering, with 214 in mining and metallurgy. As Murray shows, it was these graduates who would go on to drive the muscular engineering firms that dominated the twentieth century South African economy: parastatals like Escom and Iscor, private corporations like AngloVaal, the Post Office, and the very large engineering divisions of the municipalities.

It was the Wits professionals in these firms – fuelled by the strange half-century Bretton Woods gold mining boom that lasted until the end of the 1960s – that built the dense urban infrastructures of transport, power and production that mark out the highveld cities from Witbank to Welkom. The university also produced several generations of fierce political critics of the same economic order, culminating in the work of radical historians in Bruce Murray's own department. Today the university faces a new kind of political crisis as the local and central state and the state-owned enterprises fail to sustain and repair these twentieth century infrastructures. Often, in 2022, solving these problems seems depressingly insurmountable. Yet looking back at the history that Murray recounts in this book, it is striking how small the numbers of professional students were in the boom period, how limited the university's resources, and how quick the turnaround in both atmosphere and achievement between the middle of the 1920s and the middle of the 1930s. The history he offers here suggests that the predicament we confront right now may be more malleable than it seems.

Keith Breckenridge, Professor of History and Deputy Director at the Wits Institute for Social and Economic Research
July 2022

FOREWORD

Early in 1978 the Council of the University decided to mark the diamond jubilee of the University in 1982 by the publication of a history of its early years — the greening of Wits.

A committee was formed, consisting of Professor Ellison Kahn, Deputy Vice-Chancellor, as convener; Professor Noel G. Garson, Head of the Department of History; Professor Reuben Musiker, the University Librarian; Professor Phyllis Lewsen, of the Department of History; and Dr A.J. de V. Herholdt, Administrative Adviser to the Office of the Vice-Chancellor, to set the project afoot and recommend the appointment of an author. The committee was indeed fortunate in finding Professor Bruce K. Murray, of the Department of History, prepared to undertake this formidable task. He is an historian of distinction, and this work shows the measure of his scholarship.

Historians, in general, shy away from writing an institutional history, but Professor Murray has produced no mere chronicle of the growth of Wits; it is a critical assessment of the University's approach to higher education, its contribution to the evolution of the professions of the country, the role it played in the particular society to which it belongs, and its contribution to the advancement of knowledge. We are presented with an enthralling work, embracing a chronological account and an analysis of specific facets.

The University gave Professor Murray unrestricted access to its records; it imposed no censorship of any sort. Everything that appears in these pages has been authenticated. Not only did the author winnow the publications and files in our archives; he explored the Government archives and the papers of other institutions and of individuals; and he conducted many interviews with those who were participants in the events of those early days.

This book is the splendid product of high endeavour and the cost of publication has been generously underwritten by the Trustees of the University of the Witwatersrand. It should have a wide appeal: not only to all those who have attended Wits, but to all who are interested in the history of education and, indeed, in South African history and political development in general.

D.J. DU PLESSIS
Vice-Chancellor and Principal

January 1982

ACKNOWLEDGEMENTS

We are grateful to the copyright holders for permission to quote from the following:

Beit, O. Letter to Sir John Carruthers Beattie. In the Beattie Collection BC 215 20.9 in the University of Cape Town Libraries. The University Librarian.
Bosman, H.C. *A Cask of Jerepigo* (ed. L. Abrahams). Human & Rousseau and Mrs Helena Lake.
British Medical Journal. Extract from issue dated 13.8.1921. The Editor.
Brookes, E. *The Colour Problems of South Africa.* The Lovedale Press. *R.J.: John David Rheinallt Jones.* South African Institute of Race Relations.
Craib, W.H. My removal from Wits 1946. *Bulletin of the Adler Museum of the History of Medicine.* The Hon. Editor, *Adler Museum Bulletin.*
Dalton, J.P. *Our Changing World View.* ©Witwatersrand University Press 1932.
Dart, R.A. *Adventures with the Missing Link.* The Author and the Director, The Institutes of the Achievement of Human Potential. Also an extract reprinted by permission from *Nature,* Vol. 115, No. 2884, p. 195. Copyright ©1925 Macmillan Journals Limited.
De Kiewiet, C.W. *The Anatomy of South African Misery.* Oxford University Press.
Doke, C.M. Extract from the *Rand Daily Mail* 1.11.1923. The Editor and Mrs E.A. Cooper.
Fouché, L. (ed.). *Diary of Adam Tas, 1705–1706.* Longmans.
Frankel, S.H. *The Railway Policy in South Africa.* Hortors.
Headlam, C. *The Milner Papers* (1931–3). Cassell.
Herbert, G. *Martienssen and the International Style: The Modern Movement in South African Architecture.* The Author.

HOERNLÉ, R.F.A. *Race and Reason* (ed. I.D. MacCrone). ©Witwatersrand University Press 1945. *South African Native Policy and the Liberal Spirit.* University of Cape Town.

HUTCHINSON, G. EVELYN. *The Kindly Fruits of the Earth.* Yale University Press.

KANNEMEYER, J.C. *Geskiedenis van die Afrikaanse Literatuur.* Human & Rousseau.

KEITH, SIR ARTHUR. Letter to the Editor. Reprinted by permission from *Nature,* Vol. 116, No. 2905, p. 11. Copyright ©1925 Macmillan Journals Limited.

KERR, A. *Fort Hare 1915–1948.* University of Fort Hare.

KIRBY, P.R. *Wits End.* Howard B. Timmins.

MACCRONE, I.D. *Race Attitudes in South Africa.* ©Witwatersrand University Press 1957.

MACMILLAN, W.M. *Complex South Africa.* Faber and Faber. *My South African Years.* David Philip.

RAIKES, H.R. Presidential Address, 'Liquid Fuel from Coal'. The Associated Scientific and Technical Societies of South Africa.

RAND DAILY MAIL. Illustrations and extracts from reports. The Editor.

RHEINALLT JONES, J.D. The need for a scientific basis for South African Native policy. *South African Journal of Science.* The Editor.

SOUTH AFRICAN ARCHITECTURAL RECORD. Extract from issue dated March 1927. The Editor.

SOUTH AFRICAN DENTAL JOURNAL. The Editor, *Journal of the Dental Association of South Africa.*

SOUTH AFRICAN MEDICAL RECORD, MEDICAL JOURNAL OF SOUTH AFRICA and the JOURNAL OF THE MEDICAL ASSOCIATION OF SOUTH AFRICA. The Editor, *South African Medical Journal.*

SOUTH AFRICAN MINING JOURNAL. Extracts from issues dated 26.8.1893 and 1.9.1894. Thomson Publications.

SOUTH AFRICAN MINING AND ENGINEERING JOURNAL. Extract from issue dated 28.8.1926. Thomson Publications.

STAR. Extracts from reports. The Editor.

TOBIAS, P.V. From Linné to Leakey: Six Signposts in Human Evolution. In Königsson, L-K. (ed.), *Current Argument on Early Man.* The Author and Pergamon Press.

VADERLAND. Extracts from reports. The Editor.

WALKER, W.J. Presidential Address. The South African Institution of Mechanical Engineers.

WATT, J.W. The history of the Medical School of the University of the Witwatersrand. *Leech.* The Editor.

ACKNOWLEDGEMENTS

Extracts from official publications reproduced under Government Printer's Copyright Authority 7751 of 19.11.1981:
Secretary for education to Principal Hofmeyer 11.5.1922 U.O.D. E33/13.
Report of the Committee Appointed to Inquire into the Training of Natives in Medicine and Public Health U.G. 35, 1928.
Annual Report of the Department of Education for the year ending December 1928 U.G. 51, 1929.
Report of the Committee of Enquiry into Subsidies to Universities, University Colleges, and Technical Colleges U.G. 8, 1934.

Abbreviations

E.R.P.M.	East Rand Proprietary Mines
N.U.S.A.S.	National Union of South African Students
R.D.M.	*Rand Daily Mail*
S.A.M.J.	*South African Mining Journal*
S.A.S.M.T.	South African School of Mines and Technology
S.R.C.	Students' Representative Council
T.T.I.	Transvaal Technical Institute
T.U.C.	Transvaal University College
U.O.D.	Union Education Department

PART I
Prelude to a University

1

FALSE START: MILNER, BEIT, AND SMUTS

I

THE PROPOSAL to establish a university on the Witwatersrand was first made by the new British regime in the Transvaal immediately after the Anglo-Boer War of 1899–1902. Both Lord Milner, the Governor of the Transvaal and Orange River Colony and High Commissioner for southern Africa, and Joseph Chamberlain, the British Colonial Secretary, wanted the establishment of a teaching university on the Rand. In his celebrated speech at the Wanderers Club on 17 January 1903 Chamberlain stated:

> If I were to point at this time to what, in my opinion, is the most urgent need of this community, I should say it was the immediate provision of a High School, efficient in every respect; and of a Scientific University specialised according to the needs of the great industries of the community. I can hardly doubt that an appeal to local patriotism to those who have made their fortune here will not be without its effect, and that before long Johannesburg will possess a University, which in its own lines will be superior to anything that now exists in the world.[1]

In 1904 the Transvaal Technical Institute opened in Johannesburg, and two years later the mining magnate, Alfred Beit, left £200 000 in his will for a 'University of Johannesburg'. But the Beit bequest was never to be used for a university in Johannesburg, and not until 1922 was a university finally established there. In 1906, the year of the Beit bequest, the Transvaal was given responsible government. This proved a fatal set-back to the initial movement to found a university in Johannesburg. Jan Christiaan Smuts, the Colonial Secretary and Minister of Education in General Louis Botha's Het Volk government, saw to it that, save for the provision of technical education in Johannesburg, Pretoria was preferred as the centre for higher education in the Transvaal. In 1910, on the eve of Union, Pretoria was made the seat of the

Transvaal University College, and Johannesburg of the South African School of Mines and Technology.

II

The opening of the Transvaal Technical Institute in 1904 marks the birth of the institution that was to become the University of the Witwatersrand, Johannesburg, nearly two decades later. The Transvaal Technical Institute was itself the heir to the South African School of Mines established at Kimberley in the Cape Colony in 1896.

The idea of creating a school of mines for South Africa had first been seriously mooted in 1890, and it was done so in Cape Town rather than in Kimberley or on the Rand. Cape Town was then the dominant city in southern Africa, the centre of education and culture, whereas Kimberley and Johannesburg were mining camps. It was the home of the University of the Cape of Good Hope, founded in 1873 as an examining university for the Cape and authorized two years later to operate beyond the borders of the colony. It was also the home of the South African College, established in 1829, the leading teaching institution in southern Africa which prepared students both for the matriculation and university examinations of the University of the Cape of Good Hope.

In 1890 the Council of the South African College proposed to establish a school of mines in Cape Town, but this was opposed by Cecil John Rhodes, who became Prime Minister of the Cape in July of that year. Rhodes informed the Cape Parliament that he believed Kimberley rather than Cape Town should serve as the seat of any new school of mines.[2] His ambitions for Cape Town were more grandiose; that it should become the home of a residential teaching university for all southern Africa, where both English and Dutch-speaking whites would study and live together, and forge the basis for a new unity. As a 'Cape Colonist' his purpose was 'to make Cape Town the centre of South Africa'.[3] In 1891 he set aside a site at Groote Schuur for the residential university he envisaged. The proposal for a school of mines in Cape Town was shelved, and the eighteen students who had entered the South African College with a view to preparing themselves for the new school were left in the lurch. Three proceeded to England to complete their studies, the other fifteen 'drifted away'.[4]

The prime mover behind the proposal to establish a school of mines in the Cape Colony had been P.D. Hahn, Professor of Chemistry at the South African College, later generally recognized as the 'father' of the Kimberley

School of Mines. He was concerned to open up professional opportunities in the mines to South Africans. With the growing complexity of diamond mining at Kimberley, leading to the formation of De Beers Consolidated in 1888, and more particularly with the discovery of gold on the Witwatersrand in 1886, Hahn had been impressed by the increasing number of students at the South African College who sought instruction in the chemistry of metallurgy and assaying, and by the fact that the mining industry in South Africa remained wholly dependent on overseas sources for trained mining engineers.[5] The introduction of deep-level mining on the Witwatersrand in 1892–4 underlined the growing need for mining engineers in South Africa.

In 1894 the proposal to establish a school of mines in the Cape was carried with the co-operation of the Cape government and De Beers in Kimberley. The scheme approved in 1894 was in the nature of a compromise. The South African College in Cape Town was to be responsible for the preliminary theoretical instruction, while Kimberley, and possibly Johannesburg as well, was to undertake the practical instruction. Rhodes, the board of De Beers, and the Kimberley M.P.s, J.L. Lawrence and Dr Frederick Rutherfoord Harris, all approved the scheme. Their support was encouraged by the fact that Rhodes's hopes for a 'non-racial' university at Groote Schuur had been set back, primarily because Cape Afrikaners were not prepared to sacrifice the Victoria College at Stellenbosch.[6] They also realized that, if the Cape failed to act, the initiative in establishing a school of mines might fall to the South African Republic.

In the debate in the Cape House of Assembly on Lawrence's motion of 17 July 1894, which called upon the government to take into consideration 'the expediency of establishing a School of Mines', both Lawrence and Rutherfoord Harris stressed the career opportunities offered by the mines to those 'born and bred in this country'. Rutherfoord Harris, a close associate of Rhodes, maintained that as the permanency of the mines in South Africa was now 'more than established', mining engineering offered an important new career opportunity for South Africans. Only two professions in the country, law and surveying, were at that time open to South Africans without going overseas for their training: 'The proposal now was to add a third profession to the list.' He estimated that within a few years there would be 600 leading posts on the gold mines of the Witwatersrand 'to which students trained in South Africa might aspire, providing only they had a School of Mines for the training of young men'. The motion was supported by the maverick M.P. for Victoria West, A.P. Le Roux. Such a school would provide a new opportunity for Afrikaners: 'He believed that if Afrikaners had only the chance, this country would be behind no other in the world.' C.W. Hutton, the M.P. for Fort

Beaufort, who pointed out that 'the Kafirs' had paid £2 600 during the past year in fees for the education of their children at Lovedale, also supported the motion 'in the belief that the school would be open to every Kafir who could afford to go there as well as to any Afrikander'. Cries of 'Hear, hear', but also of 'Oh, oh', met his assertion.[7] Several Afrikaners were to attend the South African School of Mines, but no blacks.

Responding to the motion, Rhodes stated that the government already favoured the commencement of a 'theoretical school' in connection with the South African College, and that it felt that the people of Johannesburg as well as Kimberley might wish to assist in providing facilities for practical instruction. The consequence was that a select committee was appointed to consider the establishment of a school of mines and to secure the co-operation of the University of the Cape of Good Hope in conducting the necessary examinations and conferring the 'proper' degrees. In September the select committee reported that the scheme was practicable, and requested the government to carry out its recommendations.

The scheme approved by the Rhodes government and the South African College to train mining engineers locally provided for two years of preliminary theoretical instruction at the South African College or any other college with suitable facilities, a third year of combined theoretical and practical instruction at Kimberley, and a final year of practical instruction at Johannesburg on a gold mine. Entrance requirements were to be 'more or less at matriculation standard'. Those who successfully completed the course would be awarded a diploma in mining engineering by the University of the Cape of Good Hope, as the examining body. In February 1895 the scheme was formally presented for approval to the Council of the University of the Cape of Good Hope.

The scheme was designed to ensure that a school of mines for South Africa would be controlled from the Cape and not the Transvaal, thus preserving the University of the Cape of Good Hope's monopoly over examining and the award of degrees. It was also expected to expand instruction in the sciences at the South African College. In Johannesburg the *South African Mining Journal* denounced the scheme as 'crude and hasty'. It had long thought that to establish a school of mines in the Cape rather than the Witwatersrand was rather ridiculous: 'The absurdity of starting a School of Mines in a place like Capetown is only second to the almost equally absurd proposition to make Kimberley the centre from which the science of mining the precious metals is to emanate.' But what particularly alarmed the *Mining Journal* was that the Cape had not secured the co-operation of the Transvaal government in its planning, and Pretoria was threatening to launch a rival school of mines. The scheme was patently designed to establish a Cape rather than a truly South

African school of mines supported by the various states of South Africa. The *Mining Journal* feared that 'if the Cape University carries out its present proposals and makes its certificates of proficiency in engineering of the same value as its present certificates in surveying, and if the Transvaal also establishes a School, the certificates of which will be of an even lower value, then the title of South African engineer, instead of being an honourable title, will be a by-word for laughter and scorn'. The *Mining Journal* wanted the whole issue of a school of mines to be treated as an educational question separate from 'the disturbing influence of political feeling'.[8]

The inter-state co-operation called for by the *Mining Journal* did not materialize, the Jameson Raid on the Transvaal in 1895 rendering such co-operation quite impossible. Indeed, the idea of students proceeding from Kimberley to Johannesburg for their final year proved impracticable, and the period spent by students on the Rand was consequently curtailed. The first class had to contend with 'chaos in Johannesburg'.[9]

The South African School of Mines in Kimberley, as a separate institution fed by the South African College and later also by the Victoria College, opened in August 1896. It received from the South African College five students who in July had passed the first mining examination of the University of the Cape of Good Hope. The five pioneers were welcomed in Kimberley by Professor J.G. Lawn, a graduate of the Royal School of Mines, London, and at 28 years of age, the first Professor of Mining in South Africa. He was also Principal of the South African School of Mines and its sole teacher. A local committee under Gardner F. Williams, the American-born general manager of De Beers, was responsible for the management of the Kimberley School.

As Gardner Williams later conceded, the Kimberley School of Mines never really got off the ground. 'We started the School of Mines', he admitted in 1902, 'on the worst possible basis and with the least amount of money that any school ever started, and we have dragged along from year to year.'[10] Throughout its brief career, the School was short alike of finance, staff, and students. In 1898 it acquired its second full-time teacher in John Orr, the iron and woodwork master at the South African College and a product of Glasgow University, who at the age of 28 was appointed Professor of Mechanical Engineering. No further full-time appointments were made. Student numbers fluctuated between twenty and thirty, except in July 1900 when thirty-eight students enrolled. This exceptional enrolment was because in the previous year the School had been obliged to close down temporarily with the outbreak of the Anglo-Boer War and the ensuing siege of Kimberley.

A particular problem that confronted the pioneer class of 1896 was that no discernible provision had been made for their final year in Johannesburg. In

J.G. Lawn

John Orr

South African School of Mines, Kimberley

desperation on 28 April 1897 they wrote to the Council of the South African College, 'We apply to you because we know of no central authority, and it was as students of your College that we were induced to enter upon this course and we trust therefore that you will be able to take steps to secure the necessary arrangements for us to complete our course with advantage.'[11]

As a result, in July, Lawn was sent to Johannesburg to ascertain 'the best method of carrying out the original scheme for the School of Mines, which was that the Fourth Year's course should consist of practical work on the Rand'. Though he had no difficulty in arranging for the students to continue their work at 'very good mines', he concluded that the idea of a final year on the Rand was impracticable:

> The chief objection to this scheme is the great expense which would be entailed on the School authorities and on individual students. It would be necessary that some suitable person be appointed at Johannesburg; and, on account of the expense of living there, a high salary would be necessary to provide which there are no funds available. Besides which, the theoretical instruction could not be given either conveniently or very efficiently because of the scattered positions of the mines at which the students would be working. The speculative atmosphere of Johannesburg is also against study.
>
> Students could not get board and lodgings for less than ten pounds per month, and if, in addition to this, heavy fees were charged, the cost of a year's course would be very considerable.[12]

As a consequence of Lawn's urgings, the period spent on practical work at Johannesburg was reduced to six months.

The defeat of the Boer republics in the Anglo-Boer War proved fatal to the Kimberley School of Mines. The war had already ended the brief life of a mining school established in Pretoria by the Kruger government in 1897. With the Boer republics reduced to colonial status, the political incentive for maintaining a school of mines in the Cape collapsed. At last the training of mining engineers in South Africa could be treated as essentially an educational question. In these circumstances the logic for basing a school of mines in Johannesburg, the centre of South Africa's gold mining, became irresistible, as even Kimberley recognized. Professor Lawn, at a special conference of representatives of the South African College and of the Kimberley School with the Transvaal Technical Education Committee in Johannesburg in December 1902, indicated that the current sharp demarcation between the two years of theoretical instruction and the two years of technical training was most unsatisfactory, and that what was required was a single properly co-ordinated

The first five students of the School of Mines, Kimberley
Standing: Val E. Scaer, H.B. Maggs and Max Baumann   Seated: R.M. Keyser and W. Versfeld

Students leaving Kimberley after the siege

course at a single institution located in Johannesburg. Gardner Williams also supported the opening of a school of mines in Johannesburg, and the closure of the Kimberley School, recognizing that, in addition to its other advantages, Johannesburg had the greater financial resources with which to maintain a modern school of mines.[13]

The Kimberley School had none the less played an important pioneering role. It had begun the training of mining engineers in South Africa; it had drawn its students from a wide range of South African society, from the Free State and the Transvaal as well as the Cape, and from the sons of farmers and clerks as well as the sons of professional and commercial men.[14] A large proportion of its graduates were to attain positions of responsibility and leadership in the mining industry of South Africa. Too few graduated from the Kimberley School to satisfy the demands of the industry, which continued to recruit extensively from abroad, but a new career opportunity had been opened to the white youth of southern Africa.

III

Almost as soon as the Treaty of Vereeniging had been signed on 31 May 1902, steps were taken by the British regime in the Transvaal, under the command of Lord Milner, to establish Johannesburg as the centre for mining and technical education in South Africa, and possibly even of university education as well. Johannesburg and the Rand were crucial to the British South Africa that Milner wished to create. From the gold mines would pour the wealth that would enrich all South Africa, that would stimulate its entire economy, including agriculture, and that would attract British settlers to the country, both to the land and the towns. Milner envisaged Johannesburg as the heart of the new society, and it was in Johannesburg that he established his own headquarters. As he put it on 9 January 1902 at a banquet given for him by the Johannesburg Town Council, Chamber of Mines, and Chamber of Commerce:

> A great Johannesburg—great not only in the number but in the character of its inhabitants, in their intelligence, cultivation, their public spirit—means a British Transvaal. A British Transvaal will turn the scale in favour of a British South Africa, and a British South Africa may go a long way to consolidate the British Empire.[15]

It was for these imperial reasons that Milner favoured Johannesburg as the centre for technical and higher education in South Africa.

Milner's vision for South Africa and the Empire was shared by Joseph Chamberlain, and it was this that led Chamberlain during his visit to South Africa in 1902–3 to urge the foundation of a 'scientific university' in Johannesburg. Both Milner and Chamberlain perceived that Johannesburg would have to attract a large settled British population, as opposed to the cosmopolitan, floating population of the pre-war years, if it was to play the historic role they had chosen for it. Chamberlain saw two major obstacles barring the attraction of such a population – the Rand's 'excessive' cost of living, and its want of adequate educational facilities.

Lord Milner

Before the Anglo-Boer War the Witwatersrand mines had been worked overwhelmingly by a migrant labour force, white as well as black. After the war, Milner and the mining capitalists sought to create a stable British workforce in Johannesburg and on the rest of the Rand. This strategy, which was based on the assumption that the gold mines had a substantial life ahead of them and that the profits from gold might finance the industrialization of the Witwatersrand, was of enormous consequence for Johannesburg's development, greatly speeding up its transition from a rough-and-ready mining town to a modern industrial, commercial, and residential city. In the 'municipal revolution' after the war, Johannesburg acquired an elected town council with effective powers of local government, a waterborne sewage system, a municipal electric tramway system to replace the horse-drawn trams of the City and Suburban Tramways Company, and new townships were proclaimed. At the same time, a systematic attempt was made by the British authorities to clear Johannesburg of the myriads of pimps, prostitutes, and illicit liquor sellers who had helped cater for the needs of the bachelor workforce of the pre-war years.[16]

In 1904, the year of the first census after the war, the white population of Johannesburg and the Witwatersrand was given as 119 000, including 74 000 males. The white population of Johannesburg itself was 65 000, of whom

47 000 were males, 22 000 British-born, 16 000 South African-born, and 9 000 European-born. Boer defeat in the war had helped to make Johannesburg, the Witwatersrand, and even Pretoria, much more British, and rather less cosmopolitan, in population. In the decade after the war, the balance of the sexes became more even as men were encouraged to settle with their families. In 1911, the year of the next census, Johannesburg's white population was given as 122 000, of whom 69 000 were male.

Between the two censuses the white population of Johannesburg and the Transvaal had grown remarkably, but it was neither as large nor as British as Milner had planned at the end of the war. Milner had been hopelessly over-optimistic in his demographic projections, and in his calculations of the increased industrialization of the Witwatersrand. Consequently, his goal of a pro-imperial Transvaal proved to be 'A Grand Illusion'.[17]

Milner's plan for a university in or near Johannesburg reflected his over-optimistic projections for Johannesburg and the Transvaal. He and his educational advisers envisaged a basically technical university, designed to promote economic growth and professional opportunity. This, it was hoped, would stabilize the British population and promote the assimilation of the Afrikaner. The plan included provision for a school of agriculture to encourage the 'scientific' farming which Milnerites regarded as essential to rescue agriculture from 'the rut of stagnation in which the Boer farmers had been content to allow it to remain'.[18] But what was missing at the end of the Anglo-Boer War was a system of secondary education in the Transvaal capable of sustaining anything approaching a university.

Before the war, schooling for whites in the Transvaal in general and in Johannesburg in particular, had been notoriously inadequate. In October 1895 John Robinson, the secretary of the Witwatersrand Council of Education, drew up a report on education in Johannesburg and the Rand which indicated how appalling conditions were for children in the area. The poverty of the western suburbs of Johannesburg, notably Fordsburg, Ferreirastown, and the Brickfields, shocked Robinson, as did the unkempt, insanitary, and undisciplined nature of 'the private adventure type' schools that predominated, and the poor salaries given to teachers: 'Many teachers are at present working for smaller salaries than is earned by a good kafir on the mines.' In Johannesburg itself, Robinson estimated that 2 000 out of 6 500 white children of school-going age were not at school. It was to help meet a genuine need for elementary education on the Rand, as well as to counter the emphasis placed on Dutch in state-supported schools, that the Witwatersrand Council of Education was created by prominent Uitlanders earlier in 1895.[19] In 1899, in response to an appeal among London finance houses connected with the gold mining industry on the Rand, the Council succeeded in raising almost £100 000, and had been poised to embark upon a large-scale programme for the establishment of schools, when war had broken out.

British rule revolutionized the school system in the Transvaal, in part so as to promote the anglicization of the Afrikaner. Under E.B. Sargant, Milner's Director of Education, a closely controlled system of free elementary and secondary education, with English as the medium of instruction, was established. The curriculum was given a strong imperial bias. 'Language is important', Milner urged, 'but the tone and spirit of the teaching conveyed in it is even more important.'[20] Between 1902 and 1905 six high schools were established in the Transvaal, two in Pretoria, one in Potchefstroom, and three in Johannesburg. These high schools extended from standards four to ten, and by 1907 had an enrolment of 828 pupils. With a mere 84 pupils in standard 10, and with the quality of education still appallingly low, the system could not sustain a university.

Almost immediately after the peace treaty had been signed, Sargant appointed a committee, which included representatives of the Witwatersrand Council of Education, to examine the best means of promoting technical education in the Transvaal. In October the committee recommended the creation of a technical institute in the vicinity of Johannesburg and proposed further that the institute should 'form an integral part of a Teaching University'. At the beginning of 1903 a commission was consequently established to consider the larger question of a teaching university. Its chairman was Fabian Ware, Deputy Director of Education and a staunch imperialist, and its membership included representatives of the mining industry and the Council of Education.

By 1902–3 the Council of Education had outlived its original purpose to provide English-language elementary schooling in the Transvaal, a function now performed by the government.[21] The Council had, however, also pioneered technical education on the Rand, and had established, in 1897, evening classes in physics, chemistry, and assaying. Dominated by mining and professional interests, the Council saw its future role primarily as that of helping to meet the demand for more advanced education on the Witwatersrand. As it possessed a fund of £100 000, and as its leading members, like Percy Fitzpatrick, shared Milner's over-all objectives, the Milner government naturally was anxious that it should participate in the Transvaal Technical Education Commission.

The Ware Commission's report of July 1903 made three substantive recommendations. First, was that temporary premises be acquired in Johannesburg for the immediate provision of a mining course, embracing four years, 'of a standard at least as high as that of the course of mining engineering of the South African School of Mines at Kimberley'. Second, was that the Transvaal government set aside Plein Square, adjacent to Park Station, as the site of a permanent technical teaching institution, in the nature of a polytechnic, which would include accommodation for evening classes, scientific collections, a technical library, and perhaps even the public library. Third, was to establish a teaching university for the Transvaal, which would have as its most important branch a school of mines, and to which would be attached the technical institute, an agricultural school, a 'normal school' for teachers, and the state laboratories. The site for the proposed teaching university was to be located within a convenient distance of Johannesburg and Pretoria, and within easy reach of the mines.[22]

The Commission's deliberations on the establishment of a teaching university for the Transvaal provide a fascinating glimpse into the social engineering of the Milner regime. They are also striking for their essential pragmatism, and their entire lack of high-flown statements about a university dedicated to scholarship and the advancement of learning and knowledge. Such ideals, or such rhetoric, had no part in the beginning of the movement to establish a university that would serve Johannesburg and the Transvaal. The motivating ideas were to cater for the needs of industry, particularly mining, by providing a regular supply of trained recruits; to give white South African youth the opportunity of a professional training and career; and to ensure British hegemony in the Transvaal, and with it South Africa.

The Commission made no attempt to provide a detailed blueprint for the organization of a university in Johannesburg; its concern was rather with the wider social design of higher education on the Rand. The Commission insisted that technical training in Johannesburg would have to cater for the interests of the artisan class as well as of the well-to-do. This was why evening classes were proposed. White artisans were required to be given an opportunity to improve their skills, and even an opportunity for them or their sons to rise into the professional middle class, otherwise they might never recognize their permanent stake in the society. Where exactly to locate a teaching university for the Transvaal was a question of great social and moral concern to the Commission. Johannesburg possessed many and obvious advantages. Easy of access, it would provide many of the university's students. It was near to the mines, in Hospital Hill it possessed a natural site for a medical school, and last but not least the atmosphere of Johannesburg was British. But some thought Johannesburg disadvantaged as a potential seat for a university. The cost of living was inordinately high, and there was the danger that Johannesburg would provide students with too many distractions and temptations. It was a haven of pimps and prostitutes, speculators and sharp dealers, liquor and violence. For some it was the last place that any right-minded person would wish to establish a university intended to mould the minds and morals of impressionable young men.

In considering the question of location, the members of the Commission entertained two contrasting models of a university, typified for them by Oxford and Birmingham. The former was represented as a residential community of scholars and students, located in a small town rather than a major urban centre, and where the objective was to strike a fine balance between training a student in a particular profession and a subtler exercise where the measure of the product was as much quality of mind as content. The balance between these two components might differ from 'school' to 'school', but a non-utilitarian core of studies still tended to dominate. The Birmingham model, by contrast, was of a utilitarian, civic university, and this in many respects seemed the more appropriate for Johannesburg. Technicians, not scholars and gentlemen, were at a premium. Birmingham was certainly the model Chamberlain had in mind when he urged the creation of a 'scientific university' in Johannesburg. Chamberlain, who had made his money as a screw manufacturer, was a former Lord Mayor of Birmingham, and had played a major part in the founding of the city's university in 1900. Birmingham University was intended to be 'democratic' in the sense of being accessible to anyone with ability. It should serve to link scholarship and knowledge with industry, trade, and transport, and should be situated centrally in the community it served. In 1904 Birmingham appeared to represent the university of the future, and it was this model which recommended itself to the members of the Ware Commission. None the less the Commission's members revealed a certain ambivalence for they also favoured a residential university, less exposed to the distractions and grosser influences of urban life, and providing a setting for Boer and Briton to live as well as study together, and so perhaps further the assimilation of the Afrikaner.

The compromise solution reached by the Commission was to recommend that the technical institute should be located in the Johannesburg municipal area, while the teaching university be situated on a large farm outside Johannesburg. There was one dissentient to this recommendation, Dr Charles Porter, the Medical Officer of Health. He ridiculed the suggestion that 'an Oxford or Cambridge, without the endowment, social atmosphere or traditions of either, is going to be successfully created and maintained on the veldt', and urged that, as the type of university education required in the Transvaal was largely technical and utilitarian, the model of Birmingham

University should be more closely followed, and the university located in the town itself. With a view to the assimilation of the Afrikaner he further contended that 'students from rural districts, accustomed to a somewhat narrow and primitive daily environment, should be brought into contact with the wider circumstances and refining influence of modern urban social life'. He rejected the notion that 'university students are of weaker moral fibre than their contemporaries engaged in business pursuits in towns, and must therefore be specially safeguarded by rural seclusion from the temptations of the world they must afterwards work in', indicating that this was 'not borne out by the experience of the great towns of England, Scotland and Ireland, where Universities exist'.[23]

The Commission paid scant attention to suggestions that it was premature to consider establishing a university in or near Johannesburg, that it would be a very long time before the Transvaal might be justified in embarking on so expensive a project as a university, and that the colony's system of secondary education would have to make enormous strides before it could ever sustain a university. For the sake of a new South Africa, the Commission emphasized the need for rapid action. As Dr Manfred Nathan, a Johannesburg advocate, had urged in his evidence to the Commission: 'I consider in view of the fact that the war is over and that education is one of the great factors for bringing the races together, that the present is an opportune time for starting a university, inasmuch as the Government has now special opportunities which may not later arise when there is a representative form of Government.' Events were to confirm Nathan's forebodings about the consequences of delay, for the award of responsible government to the Transvaal in 1906 was to prove a major set-back to the introduction of university education in Johannesburg.

The Johannesburg press recognized that the proposal for a teaching university for the Transvaal was 'encouraged by the highest authority of the land', and generally welcomed the initiative. In the opinion of a columnist in the *Rand Daily Mail*, such a university would become 'a repository of a genuine South African culture yet to be created, a special training-ground for the honest and careful development of the country, and a leavening centre of loyalty'. He added that a university 'would go far to provide for one crying want of the Transvaal—a stable population, ready to undergo their education, to find their pleasure, and to live their lives contentedly here'. The *Star* also approved the idea of a teaching university, but ridiculed 'the fantastic recommendation that the university should be planted down on the veld between Johannesburg and Pretoria'. The *Star* from the first had doubted the Commission's competence to deal with the question of a teaching university, and attributed to its American-bred members 'the recurrence of the old vicious

Original headquarters of the Transvaal Technical Institute, corner Gold and Kerk Streets

theory that Governments and Universities should exercise their functions as far from the great centres of population as possible'.[24] But without exception the press supported the immediate establishment of a technical institute in Johannesburg.

In August 1903, within weeks of the Ware Commission reporting, Sir Arthur Lawley, the Lieutenant-Governor for the Transvaal, formally established the Transvaal Technical Institute and appointed a governing Council under the chairmanship of Fabian Ware. Temporary premises for the Institute were secured in an old cigar factory at the corner of Gold and Kerk streets, and in the old Lost Property Building, Von Brandis Square. The former of these buildings had served as the Government High School for Boys, the forerunner of King Edward VII School, the latter had catered for the recovery of property lost in the war. Henry Hele-Shaw, the first Professor of Engineering at Liverpool University College and later inventor of the multiplate clutch, was seconded as senior professor, and by mid-February 1904 five assistant professors had been appointed. They were John Orr in engineering, J.H. Dobson in mathematics and electrotechnics, R.B. Young in geology, T.E. Robertson in mining and metallurgy, and J.A. Wilkinson in chemistry and physics. Classes at the Institute started on 7 March 1904.

Initially it had been intended that the Institute should begin by providing those third- and fourth-year mining courses previously offered by the Kimberley School of Mines and examined by the University of the Cape of Good Hope. Hele-Shaw was more ambitious. At his instigation the Institute's Council agreed to initiate courses of its own during the first year of operation. The Institute was to provide a three-years' general course in engineering, followed by a fourth year of specialization in mining, mechanical, electrical or civil engineering. The Institute would examine its own courses and award its own certificates and diplomas. Thus, it would be independent of the University of the Cape of Good Hope, its teaching freed from the constraints imposed by the demands of an external examination. Nevertheless, should students desire a degree rather than a diploma they were at liberty to write the Cape examinations.

For 1904, thirty-six students enrolled for the third- and fourth-year mining courses, and another nine for the Institute's own general course. The fee for a course was £32 per annum, payable half yearly in advance. Lectures were formal, and members of the teaching staff were expected to wear 'academical dress whilst lecturing, when it does not interfere with their work'. In addition to the full-time courses, the Institute also opened evening classes in Pretoria, Johannesburg, Germiston, the East Rand Proprietory Mines, Krugersdorp, and Roodepoort. In 1904, 426 students enrolled for the evening classes.

The evening classes, designed primarily for apprentices on the mines, ranged from the very elementary for those who were almost completely illiterate to technical courses of an equivalent standard to those offered during the day. Evening classes performed a variety of functions. In some instances, as in carpentry and joinery, they taught particular skills; in others they sought to give apprentices an elementary understanding of the theory behind their practical work; and yet others again provided a part-time route to professional qualification. Their general social and economic purpose was to help create a stable, skilled white workforce on the mines, a point emphasized by Hele-Shaw in the *South African Mining Journal:* 'The skilled workman class is likely to be the chief factor in a permanent white population, and the only really effective way to keep the ascendancy in the hands of that white population lies in higher scientific education.'[25]

Early in 1905 the Technical Institute moved to Plein Square, and occupied temporary wood and iron buildings at the Eloff Street or eastern end. The Transvaal Government provided £30 000, and the Council of Education £60 000, for a building programme for the square, of which the remainder was occupied by municipal buildings, hurriedly erected in 1903, and the Telephone Tower. In 1905 the Institute offered in Johannesburg and Pretoria its first part-time courses in law, and decided to begin courses in the arts and pure science in the following year. As was urged by people like Theodore Reunert, who became chairman of the Witwatersrand Council of Education in 1906, a technical education could not wisely be divorced from the humanities.

The Institute had the aim of advancing to university status firmly in view, and in July 1906 persuaded the Acting Lieutenant-Governor of the Transvaal to change its name to the Transvaal University College. That same month, Alfred Beit, a partner in the Rand's largest gold mining house of Wernher, Beit, and Company, died in London, providing in his will £200 000 for a 'University of Johannesburg'. It might now have been expected that Johannesburg would move rapidly to establish a university of its own. This was not to happen.

IV

From the outset it had been appreciated that lack of finance was a major barrier to the foundation of a fully fledged university in or near Johannesburg. The Transvaal government certainly did not possess the resources to fund a university, and the mining houses, beset by depression and labour difficulties, showed little enthusiasm for financing higher education. The Ware Commission had conceded: 'Owing to the present financial depression there is not much likelihood of attracting private funds for starting a scheme of Technical Education.'

One major fund for educaton did already exist: the £100 000 held by the Witwatersrand Council of Education. Milner's original idea had been that this fund should be reserved to help finance the university scheme on the edge of Johannesburg, but the Technical Institute soon laid claim to it for developments within Johannesburg. In September 1903, the Institute's Council 'invited' the Council of Education to 'entrust the funds held by it for educational purposes to the Council of the Transvaal Technical Institute'.[26] Despite the inter-locking membership of the two councils, the invitation was declined, though in 1905 the Council of Education agreed to vote £60 000 for the building programme at Plein Square, in addition to its annual contribution of £4 500 towards the current operating expenses of the Institute. The upshot was that there was no capital available for proceeding with the scheme to establish a university on the outskirts of Johannesburg.

It was universally accepted at the time that only the 'Randlords', the multi-millionaires created by the gold of the Rand, were in a position to provide the considerable sums required to establish a university, either within or outside Johannesburg. Joseph Chamberlain in his Wanderers Club speech had expressed the hope that some Rand millionaires would put forward the capital for a local university, but there was no immediate evidence of this hope being realized for most of the Randlords displayed remarkably little interest in the development of a school of mines and a university on the Rand.

Milner and others were troubled by the apparent reluctance of the Randlords to devote money and attention to local affairs. Milner is sometimes seen as a creature of the Randlords, but he had considerable contempt for the short-sightedness of a good many of them and their failure to identify themselves with the community that had enriched them. They lived in splendour in Parktown or Park Lane and ignored their responsibilities or, worse still, their own long-term interest. 'I want to interest you people in municipal affairs', he told Percy Fitzpatrick, of Wernher, Beit and Company, in March 1902, and stated that he had 'not much sympathy with those firms who made from half a million to a million a year' and did little or nothing for civic development: 'He referred by name to Farrar, Neumann, Robinson, Barnato and Bailey.'[27] On the question of financing a local university, Milner's scepticism about the Randlords was shared by the columnist P.C.G. in the *Rand Daily Mail:* 'A Carnegie-like resolution "to die poor" would come as a refreshing surprise from some of our Colonies' richest. The rarity of the species should be in itself an incentive for those who care to join its numbers.'[28]

In July 1906 Alfred Beit did not exactly 'die poor', but in his will he bequeathed £200 000 to 'the University of Johannesburg'. At the end of 1904 he had donated his magnificent plantation at Frankenwald, some twenty kilometres from the centre of Johannesburg on the Pretoria road, to 'the Government of the Transvaal or their successors for use in perpetuity for educational purposes of all kinds and solely and only for such purposes'. The estate, then valued at £80 000, fitted perfectly the requirements for a site for the teaching university envisaged by the Ware Commission. Although Beit, who visited South Africa in 1904, was personally sceptical as to whether the educational system in the Transvaal was adequate to sustain a university in the foreseeable future, he was nevertheless persuaded by Fitzpatrick, then a key figure in the Council of Education, to provide £200 000 in his will to construct and equip university buildings at Frankenwald, and to build a tramway connecting Frankenwald with Johannesburg. Beit's will further provided that the income from the £200 000 was 'to be applied meanwhile for educational projects as the Board of Education at Johannesburg may determine, but if at the expiration of ten years after my death the said £200 000 shall not have been applied in such building and equipment as aforesaid, then this legacy shall lapse and fall into my residuary estate'. The residuary legatee was his brother, Otto Beit.[29]

The Beit bequest was never used to establish a university in Johannesburg. In April 1916 it was given, by act of the Union Parliament, to the University of Cape Town. This diversion of the bequest provoked a storm of protest on the Rand, which felt cheated, though for nearly a decade the Rand had failed to use the bequest for the purposes for which it had originally been given. The explanation for this failure is twofold. First, the Transvaal University College possessed no definite plan for proceeding to full university status; rather than seek to force the pace of its own development it had approached the whole question of university education from a southern African and not a narrowly Johannesburg standpoint. Second, the attitude of government to the idea of a university in Johannesburg underwent a complete transformation. Up to 1905–6 the creation of a university in or near Johannesburg had been actively championed by government, in Whitehall and in the Transvaal itself, but from 1906 onwards government opposition proved one of the main obstacles to a university for the Rand. Milner's departure in April 1905 and his replacement by Lord Selborne as High Commissioner, the formation of a Liberal government in Britain at the end of 1905, the award of responsible government to the Transvaal in 1906, and the attainment of Union in 1910, were all political milestones in the history of South Africa, and each in turn helped to obstruct the introduction of a university in Johannesburg. The decisive set-back was to occur during the period of responsible government for the Transvaal.

Alfred Beit

The Beit bequest was made at a time when what was called 'the University Question' was emerging as an issue of inter-colonial or southern African significance. Simultaneously but independently in late 1905, the Councils of the South African College and the Transvaal Technical Institute examined the question of securing full university status for themselves. This was prompted by their dissatisfaction with the University of the Cape of Good Hope as the only degree-awarding body in southern Africa. Because the University of the Cape of Good Hope controlled the examination system it effectively dictated syllabi and thus transformed the teaching colleges into mere 'cram' schools. In practice, the Johannesburg institution could in part escape this 'tyranny' of the external examination by examining and awarding its own diplomas. It was the desire to award its students not merely diplomas but degrees on the basis of its own examinations that underlay the Transvaal Technical Institute's concern to achieve university status. But there was a fundamental divergence within the Council as to whether the Institute should immediately seek to become an independent university or whether it should associate with other institutions of higher learning in a federal university. Sir Richard Solomon, the Acting Lieutenant-Governor of the Transvaal, advised Lord Selborne, 'the more ambitious and optimistic' members of the Council were in favour of immediate legislation giving them degree-conferring powers, but the more cautious majority inclined to participate in some sort of federal university.[30] The South African College, for its part, firmly rejected the federal solution. After an investigation of university systems round the world, the Council of the South African College concluded that federal universities did not work particularly well, and decided to seek full powers as an independent teaching university, to be incorporated as 'the University of Cape Town'.[31]

The Council of the Johannesburg institution, both immediately before and after the Beit bequest, gave considerable thought to its own future, and that of higher education in South Africa generally. Even with the Beit money at its disposal it favoured a federal approach to the university question. In December 1905 the chairman of the Council, W.F. Lance, and the Registrar, John Robinson, had drawn up a report for the Transvaal government urging that the Technical Institute be given university status. They had contended that a 'vigorous teaching university' in Johannesburg would give unity and purpose to the entire education system in the Transvaal, check the exodus of students to the Cape and Europe, equip Transvaal youths for a range of professions, and be 'a means of bringing together for a common purpose, the various sections of the people who, outside of academical matters, may hold divergent views'.[32] The Council, appreciating the inherent dangers of independent and premature action, particularly that of calling into being in South Africa a series of 'tinpot universities' offering worthless degrees, voted instead to request the Transvaal government to arrange an inter-colonial conference 'to bring about co-operation among certain institutions doing higher educational work in the various South African Colonies'. Should the conference fail to devise a co-operative system for the granting of degrees in South Africa, which would involve teachers in the examining process, the Council would recommend that the Transvaal government go ahead and give the Technical Institute degree-conferring powers.[33] At the end of 1906, after Beit had made his bequest, the Council reiterated its preference for a federal university that would allow considerable autonomy to its constituent colleges. In a memorandum prepared in December 1906, the Council of the Transvaal University College asserted that, given the limited population in South Africa and the danger to standards that would be posed by separate degree-giving institutions, it would 'seem desirable, if possible, to have one university for the whole of the sub-Continent'. Its functions were nevertheless to be severely limited. Essentially, it was to serve as a guardian of standards, and was to do nothing that could 'possibly be left to the Colleges'. It would differ from the Cape University in that it would be composed of the constituent colleges, and that lecturers would have a major say in examinations and awards, but its functions were to be no greater.[34]

In response to the proposals of the Johannesburg institution for an intercolonial conference to consider setting up a federal university, and the urgings of Theodore Reunert, who became chairman of the Witwatersrand Council of Education in 1906, Selborne sounded out the colonial governments of southern Africa. After some negotiation an inter-colonial conference was summoned to meet in Cape Town at the beginning of 1907 to discuss university education.[35] The move disconcerted several groups in the Cape. Champions of the South African College saw the conference as an attempt to prevent it from gaining university status, and defenders of the University of the Cape of Good Hope likewise saw it as a threat. John X. Merriman, leader of the opposition South African Party in the Cape, in a letter of 17 February 1907 advised Jan Smuts in the Transvaal that the University of the Cape of Good Hope had drawn up its own plans for reform, and these were now being jeopardized. 'Your friend Selborne', Merriman protested to Smuts, 'must have a finger in this as in every pie.' Merriman suggested that Selborne and his officials in the north were desperately anxious to settle the university question before the new responsible governments of the Transvaal and Orange River Colony got to work, and this argument was in fact used to secure the postponement of the conference until February 1908.[36]

The University of the Cape of Good Hope's own plans for reform, and for associating teachers with the examining process, were regarded as inadequate by almost all the colleges of South Africa, but only the South African College favoured 'single college' or independent universities as opposed to some sort of federal scheme. When the inter-colonial conference finally met in February 1908, it accepted that the time was not yet ripe for 'single college universities', and advocated 'the establishment of a South African University with constituent or affiliated colleges'.[37] It also concluded that examinations should continue to be exclusively in the English language, thereby provoking a storm of protest among Afrikaners.[38] Thereafter the movement towards establishing a federal university for South Africa was overtaken by the wider movement for political unification, and it was left to the government of the new Union to establish a university system for all South Africa. In the intervening period, decisive steps were taken in the Transvaal that ensured Johannesburg would get neither the Beit bequest nor one of the Union's first teaching universities.

In the Transvaal the attitude of government to a university in or near Johannesburg had become positively hostile. The previously favourable attitude had cooled immediately after Milner's departure from South Africa. Although Alfred Lyttelton, Chamberlain's successor as Colonial Secretary in the Conservative government, continued to favour a residential university near Johannesburg, largely with a view to promoting the assimilation of the Afrikaner, Selborne, as Milner's successor, regarded the idea of a university in the Transvaal as rather preposterous. As he explained in a report to Lyttelton in December 1905, the Transvaal simply did not possess the educational infrastructure necessary to sustain a university. 'The general standard of education in the Transvaal', he wrote, 'is such as to make university work properly so called practically impossible for a considerable time to come.' The system of secondary education in the Transvaal was still 'retarded', and more of a handicap than a help in preparing students for higher education, and anyhow the demand for university education among the youth of the Transvaal was minimal. 'In the circumstances stated', Selborne advised, 'I think it would be unwise in the Government to force on the establishment of a residential university near Johannesburg much as I feel the weight of the considerations adduced by you as to the beneficial effect on the young men of both races of living a collegiate life together and growing up under a common university education.'[39] Thereafter the British authorities ceased to promote the idea of a university on the Rand. The extension of responsible government to the Transvaal, and the victory of Het Volk in the subsequent general election of February 1907, effectively wrecked the prospects for a university in Johannesburg by establishing a government in Pretoria actively hostile to the idea. Far from continuing to make progress in the field of higher education, Johannesburg was decisively set back by the government of Louis Botha.

As his Colonial Secretary and Minister of Education, Botha appointed Jan Smuts who proceeded to sabotage the development of Johannesburg as a centre for higher learning by transferring teaching in the liberal arts and pure science to Pretoria. Again it was to be Smuts who, with the coming of Union, was to play a key role in diverting the Beit bequest to Cape Town.

In his history of the Witwatersrand Council of Education, Professor J.W. Horton suggests that Smuts's opposition to a university in Johannesburg might have been rooted in a hostility to Johannesburg—Boer distrust of Uitlander Johannesburg, puritan dislike of a town which was a centre of vice and violence, and political rivalry with the Progressives, who drew their strength from the mining magnates of Johannesburg.[40] Professor H.M. Robertson, the historian of the University of Cape Town, believes that this is to ascribe to Smuts 'some rather more petty motives than seem to be consistent with the character of a man so markedly uninfluenced by petty and parochial views'.[41] What is clear is that in seeking in 1909–10 to divert the Beit bequest to a national university in Cape Town, Smuts was acting in what he deemed to be the national interest, but it is equally clear that he was strongly opposed to Johannesburg as a university centre. He bluntly informed the Transvaal Legislative Assembly in August 1907, Johannesburg was not a 'suitable place' for a university.[42] What is remarkable is the tenacity with which Smuts was to oppose the idea of a university in or near Johannesburg, and the lengths to which he was prepared to go in order to frustrate the development of Johannesburg as a potential university centre.

With regard to higher education in the Transvaal, Smuts's basic achievement between 1907 and 1910 was to transfer the teaching of the liberal arts and pure science, and the Transvaal University College itself, from Johannesburg to Pretoria, and to leave Johannesburg with a school of mines. From the first Smuts was determined that Pretoria rather than Johannesburg or Frankenwald should serve as a centre for university education in the Transvaal, and he immediately set about trying to devise a scheme whereby this might be achieved without sacrificing the Beit bequest. In 1910 he finally succeeded in transferring the Transvaal University College to Pretoria, but at the cost of the Beit bequest for higher education in the Transvaal. For the Beit bequest Smuts had developed another idea. With the formation of the Union, he wished to see the bequest diverted to the foundation of a national university for South Africa in Cape Town.

In 1907, the scheme that Smuts devised was for a tripartite division of the Transvaal University College. Mining and technical instruction was to remain in Johannesburg; teaching in the liberal arts and pure science was to be transferred to Pretoria; and an agricultural school was to be established at Frankenwald. He had hoped that the trustees of the Beit bequest would allow it to be devoted to the agricultural school, but they would not hear of the proposal. Beit had intended his bequest for a university, not an agricultural school. As Sir Percy Fitzpatrick informed Smuts in December 1907, 'In regard to Mr. Beit's Bequest—in regard to the clearly expressed wishes of a dead man, he had no right to compromise, and he never would compromise.'[43]

When first announcing his scheme in the Legislative Assembly, in the debate on the estimates in August 1907, Smuts made it clear that he would never consent to either Frankenwald or Johannesburg as the centre for higher education in the Transvaal. Frankenwald, 'as a place far from town . . . a place on the veld', was unsuited for anything other than an agricultural school precisely because of its isolated position. Johannesburg was unsuitable for 'our experience in the Transvaal is that parents will not send their children to Johannesburg'. They preferred instead to send their children to the Cape for higher education, and by making provision for the teaching of the arts and pure science in Pretoria Smuts said he hoped to check this exodus to 'the coast'. He saw Pretoria, the capital, as the ideal place for a university for the arts and science, and was determined it should 'become the centre of education in the Transvaal'.[44]

Jan Smuts

In the last months of 1907 Smuts pushed the main part of his scheme through in a highly autocratic fashion, offering little explanation why he considered a tripartite division necessary. In September 1907 a departmental committee, on which the Transvaal University College was represented, reported in favour of Smuts's scheme, but only under pressure and with the greatest reluctance. According to what Charles Ward, a member of the committee and chairman of the Council of the Transvaal University College, told his Council, 'when the committee convened its deliberations, the removal of the Arts branch to Pretoria had been decided upon by the Government'.[45] The committee reported that it supported the Smuts scheme 'only because we understand that the difficulties in the way of finding one place where the three branches can be developed side by side are insurmountable'; but what these 'insurmountable' difficulties were was not specified.[46] In November and December, when the Council of the Transvaal University College sought to delay the implementation of the scheme for 1908, Smuts simply went ahead and made 'the necessary preliminary arrangements' for the teaching of the arts and science in Pretoria. In January 1908 the Council of the Transvaal University College finally gave its approval to the transfer of arts and science to Pretoria, on condition that 'the larger question' of a university for the Transvaal should 'not be considered as disposed of by the present proposed reorganisation'. The question of an agricultural school at Frankenwald was placed in abeyance at the Council's insistence and because of the refusal of the trustees of the Beit bequest to release funds for such a school.[47]

Repeatedly during the negotiations Smuts stressed that he was not 'actuated by any local considerations or predilections' or by 'ulterior motives of any kind', and that his sole concern was to further the best interests of higher education in the Transvaal, and particularly to prevent 'the large exodus from the Colony of students requiring literary and scientific education of a University character'.[48] He was perfectly correct that the arts and science courses of the Transvaal University College in Johannesburg had not proved at all successful in attracting students, and this was not merely because Afrikaners failed to attend them. Old habits die hard, and English-speaking as well as Afrikaner parents continued to send their children to the Cape for a university education. Furthermore, in 1907 certain high schools in the Transvaal had been authorized to provide post-matriculation courses, thereby robbing the Transvaal University College of prospective students. Despite the problems of the Transvaal University College in Johannesburg, and despite Smuts's protestations, it is none the less evident that he was hostile to Johannesburg as a university centre.

For Smuts this hostility was neither political nor cultural, though both played a part in the wider Afrikaner prejudice against Johannesburg, and he was certainly alive to the predicament of the Afrikaner threatened by British cultural hegemony. But Smuts himself had no lingering hostility to Johannesburg as a town of Uitlanders, Randlords, and Progressives, and he entertained no narrow Afrikaner objection to a university that might promote a genuine assimilation of Boer and Briton. Rather his hostility to Johannesburg as the seat of a university was academic and puritan. As a product of the Victoria College, Stellenbosch, and Cambridge University, he associated university education with relatively quiet provincial towns, and found incongruous the idea of locating a university in a bustling industrial and commercial centre. When that centre happened to be Johannesburg, he found the idea positively obnoxious. There was always a strong puritanical streak in

Smuts, and this had been exposed when, in his first public office as Attorney General in Kruger's government in 1898, he had taken the responsibility for tackling the problems of vice and prostitution in Johannesburg. It became his task to enforce Law 2 of 1897 – the 'Ontucht Wet' – against prostitution, and the experience convinced him that Johannesburg was incorrigibly corrupt and vice-ridden.[49] Thereafter he visited the town as infrequently as possible. Furthermore, in a period of acute rivalry between Pretoria and Johannesburg it is evident that Smuts was intent on promoting the standing of Pretoria. One effective means would be to concentrate university education in the capital.

In Johannesburg the *Star* dismissed Smuts's tripartite scheme as 'grotesque', and denounced the Colonial Secretary for 'his complicity in a peculiarly poisonous project'.[50] For the *Star* Smuts's scheme repudiated Milner's vision of a Transvaal dominated by the influences of a British Johannesburg, and in practice was a total rejection of the whole idea that higher education should provide a major channel for the anglicization of the Afrikaner. The paper concluded that the real meaning of the scheme was that Boer and Briton in the Transvaal would remain apart for the purposes of higher education, which was unforgivable, for in its opinion 'the root of all evil' in the Transvaal lay 'in the great gulf fixed between the different interests and origins of its people'. It was this that had troubled Smuts's own committee on the organization of higher education in the Transvaal. In its report on Smuts's proposal for a tripartite structure the committee, after observing that 'there can be no common corporate existence in which students of the three branches can participate', commented:

> This effect of the proposed organisation is to be profoundly regretted. The students will represent the future aristocracy of the professional, agricultural, and industrial sections of the inhabitants. From their ranks the leaders of social and political life will be recruited. But they will not meet during their most impressionable years. They will have no opportunity to develop mutual understanding, toleration, and respect through the discipline of common fields, common class-rooms, a common hall, and a common chapel. The organisation proposed will indeed fail in respect of one of the highest of university functions, namely, the cultivation of social magnanimity. The aggregate of the ablest and most cultivated members of the three fundamental sections of the inhabitants of the Colony will remain, for all that university education will do, a mixture of disparate elements, not a blend in which differences of vocation and of race are lost or at least exist but to strengthen the whole. This is the cardinal weakness of the scheme . . .[51]

From the strictly academic standpoint, the main criticism levelled against the Smuts scheme was that by unnecessarily fragmenting effort and resources, it would hamper educational advance in the Transvaal, producing a proliferation of weak institutions instead of a single strong one. Although Pretoria and Johannesburg were to constitute branches of a single university college, with a common Council, it was widely anticipated that they would develop into separate institutions. 'Once one decides on a scheme of separate colleges', R.W.S. Schumacher, a member of the Council of the Transvaal University College, warned Sir Julius Wernher, 'the mistake will have been made, and it will be irreparable, because local jealousies will prevent an amalgamation at a later date, and the result will be a number of weak, isolated units as there are in the Cape Colony, instead of one strong, central body.'[52]

Schumacher's prediction was soon proven right. By mid-1909 so great was the friction between the two branches that it was decided to provide entirely separate institutions in Pretoria and Johannesburg. In April 1910, during its last session, the Transvaal Parliament duly voted to incorporate the Transvaal University College at Pretoria and to establish the South African School of Mines and Technology at Johannesburg. The move was seen as a triumph for Smuts, and his determination to make Pretoria the centre of higher education in the Transvaal. 'I can sum up the whole position in these words', Sir Percy Fitzpatrick declared during the second reading debate in the Legislative Assembly, 'that the Colonial Secretary has got his way. He has stuck to his scheme for a long time, and has got his way.'[53]

Smuts's transfer of the Transvaal University College to Pretoria, and his refusal to consider the creation of a university institution at Frankenwald, and thereby utilize the Beit bequest, were crippling blows to the movement to establish a university in Johannesburg, and more or less ensured that Johannesburg would be bypassed when provision was made for teaching universities in the new Union of South Africa.

V

All in all, the life-span of the Transvaal University College in Johannesburg represented a set-back for the cause of higher education in Johannesburg, and the movement, led by the Council of Education, to provide the foundations for a university there. Not that the years 1906–10 were without achievement. In late 1908 the building on the eastern end of Plein Square, intended to be the first of a larger plan for the square, was completed, and was formally opened by Lord Selborne in March 1909. Again, these years were important for the

Transvaal University College building, Plein Square

development of the organizational framework of an institution of higher learning. This included the formation in 1908 of a Senate, with a membership of full professors and heads of departments, together with other teaching staff co-opted from time to time, and divided into two faculties: arts and science in Pretoria, and applied science in Johannesburg. A Students' Representative Council had existed in Johannesburg since 1905, and in 1909 a College Union was formed composed of members of the Council, staff, and past and present students. The College also became more of an institution of higher learning by shedding its elementary evening classes, which in 1908 were taken over by the Transvaal Education Department.

For the rest, the history of the Transvaal University College in Johannesburg hardly constituted a record of success and advance. The College finances were in a parlous condition; the number of full-time students for the mining and engineering courses, after initial rapid growth, declined alarmingly in 1907-9, giving rise to anxious debates on how to recruit more students. The failure of the classes in arts and science to attract more than a handful of students confirmed Johannesburg's reputation for philistinism, and not even the Transvaal government would recognize the College's matriculation examination, on the ground that it would be a mistake to establish a rival matriculation board to the University of the Cape of Good Hope. Worst of all, perhaps, the atmosphere in the Transvaal University College was not happy. Not only was there the rivalry and tension that developed between the Johannesburg and Pretoria branches, but within the Johannesburg branch acute cleavages and tensions became evident.

One explanation that was given for this tension was the absence of a Principal capable of giving the College firm leadership. In 1905 Hele-Shaw had served as Principal, but when his contract expired at the end of the year he had returned to England. His stay in Johannesburg had not been at all happy. Initially he had been brought out in 1904 at the instigation of E.B. Sargant, Milner's Director of Education. Almost immediately he had become involved in the rivalry between Fabian Ware and Sargant. Ware, supported by Professor Lawn and Dr G.S. Corstorphine on the Institute's Council, unsuccessfully sought to block Hele-Shaw's appointment as Principal for 1905 on the ground that his ideas and methods were outdated. The in-fighting apparently became so intense that Milner refused to involve himself in the Institute's affairs as they were 'so mixed up with odious personal differences and intrigues'.[54] Although Hele-Shaw proved a very energetic administrator, personality conflicts continued to hamper his work as Principal, and there was never any question that his contract would be renewed. When he left, a motion in the S.R.C. that a presentation be made to him failed to find a seconder.[55]

H.S. Hele-Shaw

Hele-Shaw was not replaced and John Robinson, as Registrar, took responsibility for the College's administration. He also presided over the Board of Studies, the forerunner of the Senate. As he lacked any academic standing, Robinson was an inadequate substitute for a Principal, and his relations with the professorial staff were generally uneasy. In the opinion of John Yates, Hele-Shaw's successor as Professor of Mining, Robinson's position was untenable, and the College required a Principal. Yates, in a letter to Smuts in November 1907, urged that the Board of Studies could not be entrusted with the control of academic work in Johannesburg: 'There is too much jealousy, too many overlapping and conflicting interests among the members of the Board to permit of smooth and harmonious working without a head.' In September 1908 the report of a Council commission likewise recommended the appointment of a Principal, and suggested that he should be 'a Mining man of standing, strength and character and of tact'.[56]

The newly-formed Senate, however, perceived in the proposal to appoint a Principal a threat to its powers, and firmly opposed the idea. As it advised the Council:

> The appointment of a Principal would seem to be undesirable in view of the past history of the College. This aspect of the question it is difficult for us to discuss quite objectively, but it will be admitted that only those who have experienced from within the utter demoralisation occasioned by previous disastrous experiments, can fully appreciate the dangers which attend this new proposal.

The Senate added that it was 'anomalous' to think of attaching the principalship to the chair of mining, particularly when it was remembered that the Transvaal University College included a Faculty of Arts: 'The permanent appointment to the Principalship of the Professor of Mining in Johannesburg, must, inevitably, we believe, by lowering the status of the Arts Faculty, react disastrously upon the development of the Transvaal University College in Pretoria.' What the Senate wanted was for its chairman, elected on an annual basis, to 'discharge the functions associated with the office commonly known as Principal'.[57]

The advice of Senate was duly ignored, and in the middle of 1909 J.G. Lawn was appointed Professor of Mining and Principal. It was not an appointment that assisted the College in any real way, and in the next year Lawn took up the post of consulting engineer with the Johannesburg Consolidated Investment Company.

The fundamental cause of the tensions among the College's teaching staff, particularly in Johannesburg, lay not in the absence or presence of a Principal, but in a lack of finance and insufficient full-time students, which generated a sense of insecurity.

In the optimistic days of 1905, when Lance and Robinson had urged the case for a university and had predicted a rapid rise in student numbers, appointments had been made freely, but for 1908 three professors were retrenched and, at the insistence of the teaching staff, cuts were also made in the administration. The chief victim on the administrative side was Robinson, whose large salary, apart from anything else, made him an obvious target for retrenchment. The teaching staff considered that three administrative officers, that is an accountant and two typing clerks, one each for Johannesburg and Pretoria, were perfectly adequate for the administration of the College, rather than the existing complement of six officers, including Mr Robinson:

> This gentleman has since the College was founded, received over five thousand pounds from it . . . The sum he has received would have secured the services of any other person of his qualifications, such as the Registrar of one of the other Colleges in South Africa, for at least eight or ten years. We are therefore of the opinion that no injustice will be done by his immediate retrenchment, with compensation on the scale set forth in the draft Civil Service Bill of the Transvaal Government.
>
> We would point out that the Council has not hestitated to retrench three of their most distinguished professors, who were admittedly not overpaid, and whose work reflected great credit on the College.[58]

The letter was written on 14 May 1908. The Council simultaneously reached the decision that it should use the opportunity provided by the transfer of the elementary evening classes to the Transvaal Education Department, and Robinson's appointment to manage them, to dispense with Robinson's services to the Transvaal University College. Those services had not been inconsiderable. Robinson, who had previously acted as secretary to the Council of Education, had played an active role in the founding of the Transvaal Technical Institute and its elevation to the status of the Transvaal University College, and had been in office ever since the inception of the Institute. He was given a gratuity of five months' salary and a hearty vote of thanks.[59]

Despite the almost inevitable clash between teachers and administration in a period of retrenchment, it was among the teachers themselves that the tensions were most acute, notably the confrontation of 1907-8 between John Yates, the Professor of Mining, and John Orr, the Professor of Engineering. It is impossible to do justice to the personality conflicts of those early days, but it is evident that there was a substantial divergence of principle and interest between Yates and Orr. Yates saw the salvation of the College as lying in the extension of evening classes, whereas Orr was the foremost champion of the so-called 'sandwich system' for engineering students to help counter the decline in the number of full-time students. Under this system students would first apprentice themselves, and then divide their time equally between the College and 'the works' or mine, spending six months at each. Its adoption was urged on the grounds that the system worked 'at Home', and that students who would otherwise be unable to afford to attend the College for day classes would now 'manage to earn enough during six months to keep them through the remainder'.[60] The system was approved by Senate against the opposition of Yate's, who saw it as a threat to the evening classes.[61]

Yates lost more than his fight against the 'sandwich system'; he also lost his post. His conflict with Orr had done much to poison the atmosphere at the College. Certainly, he had made an implacable enemy of Orr having had the temerity to denounce the Professor of Engineering as a 'blithering idiot' in 'the presence of the College Porter'.[62] In the course of 1908 Yates also fell out with his day students, suspending two of them from attendance at lectures, and complaints were subsequently registered against him by some students. At the request of the Senate the Council appointed a commission to inquire into these complaints, which concluded that 'although Professor Yates was not incompetent, yet, judging from the evidence that had been laid before them, the interests of the College would be best served by appointing a more capable, and, if possible, an outstanding man, for the teaching of Mining'.[63]

Yates was firmly convinced that he had been 'got at' by some of his colleagues, who 'influenced' his students to produce an 'atrocious concoction' against him, and this despite his 'brilliant record' both prior to and after joining the College. It did not escape his notice that the decision to dismiss him was linked to the decision to appoint a Principal who would also be the Professor of Mining.[64]

Yates saw his predicament as rooted ultimately in the problems of the College, notably the lack of discipline among students, their poor attendance at lectures, the decline in student numbers, and poor examination results. It is evident that attendance at lectures by third- and fourth-year students was extremely erratic and, given the small numbers involved, this clearly had a demoralizing effect on certain lecturers, not excepting Yates. But the main problem was the relative lack of full-time students; for 1908 the total enrolment for the day courses in Johannesburg was a mere forty-five students shared among eight professors. It was, again, among third- and fourth-year students that the slump in numbers was most evident, and this was attributed by the Senate to a variety of factors, the deep economic depression since 1906, the general lack of financial assistance for students in the form of bursaries and scholarships, and the readiness of the mines to hire engineers after their second year of study, rather than insisting on the full diploma. The Senate none the less felt sure that: 'As regards the future . . . the introduction of the Sandwich System, if approved by the Council, is certain to effect a radical improvement in the number of students attending the College.'[65]

Clearly, many of the problems that confronted the Transvaal University College in Johannesburg were to be expected of any pioneer institution in a colonial society, particularly in a period of economic depression. The main set-back to the Johannesburg College as an embryo university derived not from its teething problems, but from the political intervention of Smuts transferring arts and pure science studies to Pretoria. Paradoxically while Smuts's next step in helping to negotiate the diversion of the Beit bequest to Cape Town put an end to any hope that Johannesburg or Frankenwald would provide the site for one of the Union's first universities, ultimately it served to regenerate the movement to found a university on the Rand, and for the first time gave that movement a genuinely popular base. When the University of the Witwatersrand, Johannesburg, was finally established, it was to be the product not of the munificence of an individual benefactor but of a civic movement.

Notes

1. *R.D.M.*, 19 Jan. 1903.
2. *Cape Hansard*, 3rd Session of the 8th Parliament, 1891, 64.
3. Quoted in the *African World*, 21 Jan. 1911.
4. *Cape Hansard*, 1st Session of the 9th Parliament, 1894, 300.
5. 'Paul Daniel Hahn', *South African Journal of Science*, April 1918.
6. M. Boucher, *Spes in Ardus: A History of the University of South Africa* (Pretoria, 1973), 87–8.
7. *Cape Hansard*, 1st Session of the 9th Parliament, 1894, 300–3.
8. *S.A.M.J.*, 26 Aug. 1893 and 1 Sept. 1894.
9. E.A. Walker, *The South African College and the University of Cape Town 1829–1929* (Cape Town, 1929), 55.
10. Annexure to the *Report of the Transvaal Technical Education Commission*, July 1903.
11. E. Rosenthal, 'History of the University of the Witwatersrand' (unpublished MSS., University Archives), 51.
12. Ibid., 57.
13. Annexure to the *Report of the Transvaal Technical Education Commission*, July 1903.
14. For the social background of students at the Kimberley School see the attendance register kept by Orr, University Archives.
15. See C. Headlam, *The Milner Papers* (London, 2 vols, 1931–3), II, 319–23.
16. See John Maud, *City Government: The Johannesburg Experience* (Oxford, 1938), chap. 3; G.A. Leyds, *A History of Johannesburg* (Cape Town, 1964), chap. 13; Charles van Onselen, 'The World the Mineowners Made', *Review*, 3, 2 (Fall 1979), 289–302.
17. D. Denoon, *A Grand Illusion* (London, 1973), esp. pp. 35–40 for Milner's population estimates.
18. Headlam, *Milner Papers*, II, 367.
19. J.W. Horton, *The First Seventy Years 1895–1965: Council of Education, Witwatersrand* (Johannesburg, 1968), chap. 1.
20. Denoon, *Grand Illusion*, 77.
21. Horton, *Council of Education*, 36.
22. *Report of the Transvaal Technical Education Committee*, 6–10.
23. Minority Report by Dr C. Porter, Ibid., 11–12.
24. *R.D.M.*, 21 May 1903; *Star*, 30 July 1903.

25. *S.A.M.J.,* 9 Dec. 1905 & 27 April 1907.
26. Minutes of the T.T.I. Council, 25 Sept. 1903; Lawley to Milner, 3 Oct. 1903, MS. Milner 1207.
27. Fitzpatrick to J. Wernher, 7 March 1902, in A.H. Duminy and W.R. Guest (eds), *Fitzpatrick: The South African Politician, Selected Papers 1888–1906* (Johannesburg, 1976), 305.
28. *R.D.M.,* 14 May 1903.
29. Clause 14 of the Will of Alfred Beit, Eckstein & Co. Record Dept.
30. Solomon to Selborne, 2 April 1906, Papers of the Lieutenant-Governor of the Transvaal Colony (L.T.G.), vol. 140, 114/96.
31. M. Boucher, 'The Transformation of the University of the Cape of Good Hope, 1910–1918', *South African Historical Journal,* 3 (Nov. 1971), 67–8.
32. 'Report to His Excellency the Acting Lieutenant Governor re Permanent Institute in Johannesburg and Permanent Colonial Institute', Dec. 1906, and minutes of the T.T.I. Council, 9 Feb. 1906.
33. Ibid., 16 Feb. 1906. The expression 'tinpot university' was used by Justice Wessels in a speech in Pretoria in August 1906. See the *Star,* 27 Aug. 1906.
34. Memorandum on 'Provision for University Education in South Africa', Dec. 1906, T.T.I. Documents 1903–7.
35. For correspondence on the conference see L.T.G., vol. 140, 114/96.
36. Merriman to Smuts, 17 Feb. 1907, MS. Smuts V.
37. W. Ritchie, *The History of the South African College 1829–1918* (Cape Town, 2 vols, 1918), II, 529–30.
38. Boucher, 'Transformation of the University of the Cape of Good Hope', 68.
39. Selborne to Lyttelton, 11 Dec. 1905, L.T.G., vol. 139, 114/52.
40. Horton, *Council of Education,* 43.
41. H.M. Robertson, 'The University of Cape Town 1918–1968' (unpublished draft), 9.
42. *The Transvaal: Legislative Assembly Debates,* 1st Session of the 1st Parliament, 1907, 1981–3.
43. R.W.S. Schumacher to J.W. Wernher, 2 Dec. 1907, Eckstein & Co. Record Dept.
44. *The Transvaal: Legislative Assembly Debates,* 1st Session of the 1st Parliament, 1907, 1981–3.
45. Minutes of the T.U.C. Council, 1 Nov. 1907.
46. Report of the Committee appointed by the Colonial Secretary to consider the question of the organization of Higher Education in the Transvaal, *Correspondence Relating to the Organisation of Higher Education in the Transvaal,* T.G. 24 of 1908.
47. Acting Assistant Colonial Secretary to Registrar, Transvaal University College, 24 Jan. 1908, Ibid.
48. Acting Assistant Colonial Secretary to Registrar, Transvaal University College, 3 Dec. 1907 & 24 Jan. 1908, Ibid.
49. For the puritan in Smuts see W.K. Hancock, *Smuts: The Sanguine Years 1870–1919* (Cambridge, 1962), esp. chap. 1. For Smuts and 'ontucht' see C. van Onselen, 'Prostitutes and Proletariats', *Studies in the Social and Economic History of the Witwatersrand, 1886–1914* (London, 2 vols, 1982), I, *New Babylon,* 103–62.
50. *Star,* 28 Nov. 1907.
51. *Correspondence Relating to the Organisation of Higher Education in the Transvaal.*
52. Schumacher to Wernher, 2 Dec. 1907, Eckstein & Co. Record Dept.
53. *The Transvaal: Debates of Both Houses of Parliament,* Extraordinary Session of the 1st Parliament, 1910, 217.
54. Denoon, *Grand Illusion,* 201; and the correspondence of Hennen Jennings, July 1904, Eckstein & Co. Record Dept, vol. 281.
55. S.R.C. minutes, 23 Oct. 1905.
56. Copy of letter of Yates to Smuts, Nov. 1907, T.T.I. Documents 1903–7; T.U.C. Council minutes, 5 Oct. 1908.
57. Letters to the Council, 16 April and 17 Oct. 1908, T.U.C. Documents 1908–9.
58. Letter to the Council, 14 May 1908, Ibid.
59. T.U.C. Council minutes, 21 May & 25 June 1908.

60. Report of the sub-committee on the training of engineering students by the sandwich system, Sept. 1908, T.U.C. Documents 1908–9.
61. Minutes of joint Senate & Council committee on the sandwich system, 12 Nov. 1908, Ibid.
62. John Orr to Dr Breyer, chairman of the Senate, 8 Sept. 1908, Ibid.
63. T.U.C. Council minutes, 5 Oct. 1908.
64. Yates to W.F. Lance, chairman of the Council, 26 & 31 Aug. & 4 Sept. 1908, T.U.C. Documents 1908–9.
65. T.U.C. Senate minutes, 17 Oct. 1908, Ibid.

2
FROM SCHOOL OF MINES TO UNIVERSITY

I

WHEN MOVING the School of Mines Bill in the Transvaal Parliament in 1910, Smuts emphasized that what was being established was not merely a Transvaal institution, but a South African School of Mines and Technology, which would attract students from all parts of South Africa, and which would possess the potential to become 'one of the best mining schools in the world'.¹ The School of Mines accepted this view of itself and its role. With the making of Union, it came to favour the creation of a national teaching university, in Cape Town, with itself serving as the technological faculty for such a university. The School was even prepared to acquiesce in the diversion of the Beit bequest for the purposes of such a university, which would fulfil the old ideal of Rhodes, bringing together Boer and Briton to produce the future leadership of the new nation. The Botha government's diversion in 1916 of the Beit bequest for the founding of a University of Cape Town, mainly for English-speaking students from the Cape, was seen on the Witwatersrand as a denial of this ideal, and as an act of larceny by Cape interests. 'Crafty Capetown: Juggling with the Beit Bequest', protested a headline in the *Sunday Times,* and the article complained about the 'greedy spirit which the Cape has displayed'.² The protest on the Witwatersrand against this diversion of the Beit bequest produced the impetus which six years later led to the founding of the University of the Witwatersrand, Johannesburg.

II

Between 1910 and the outbreak of World War I in August 1914, the South African School of Mines and Technology made impressive progress, particularly when compared with the disappointing record of the Transvaal University College in Johannesburg before 1910. With the recovery from the depression of 1906-9, and the implementation of the sandwich system, student numbers began to increase, and for 1913 some 139 day students registered at the school. The permanent teaching staff also expanded, and by 1913 numbered 21 professors and lecturers. Of the original appointments in 1904, Orr, Robertson, Wilkinson, and Young were still on the staff, while H.G. Breijer, the Professor of Mathematics, G.H. Stanley, the Professor of Metallurgy, and R.A. Lehfeldt, the Professor of Natural Philosophy and Physics, also traced their appointments back to the old Transvaal Technical Institute. New appointees included G.S. Corstorphine, the Principal; J.S. Cellier, the Professor of Mining; R.H. Charters, the first Professor of Civil Engineering; W. Buchanan, the Professor of Electrotechnics; and H. Le May, the lecturer in applied mathematics. In law J. Colin Murray had served as part-time lecturer since 1906.

Students at the School were drawn predominantly from Johannesburg (50 per cent) and the rest of the Transvaal (20 per cent), with a fair sprinkling from the Cape, but only a handful from Natal, the Free State, and elsewhere. The advance of secondary education in the Transvaal was reflected in the distinctly higher proportion of students who had received their schooling there, rather than the Cape, than had been the case in the days of the Transvaal Technical Institute. They did not, however, constitute a majority of the student body before the outbreak of World War I. King Edward VII and Jeppe Boys' High Schools, with St John's and the Marist Brothers' Colleges, were the main feeder schools in the Transvaal to the School of Mines. The day students at the School were drawn overwhelmingly from the middle classes; they were mainly the sons of professional and business men, farmers and small entrepreneurs. Relatively few were sons of clerks, and fewer still came from what might be described as a working-class background.[3] The large majority of third- and fourth-year students were in mining.

The evening classes broadened considerably in scope between 1910 and 1914 with the introduction, in response to the demands of professional bodies, of courses in architecture, accountancy, and pharmacy. Evening classes in technical and scientific subjects continued to be held at Plein Square and along the Reef, though in 1913 and 1914 they were severely disrupted by the mineworkers' strikes. These classes were attended mainly by apprentices, but also by mine officials and others who wished to qualify for the various government certificates for mine managers, surveyors, overseers, mechanical engineers, and engine drivers.

The pre-war years at the School of Mines were notable for defining the relationship between Council and Senate and for attempts to create a sense of identity in the student body. Senate's long-standing demand for representation on the Council was partially met by the inclusion of the Principal on the Council, and the Council began to curb its inclination to act on important matters without reference to the Senate. The students, for their part, while seeking to establish more of a corporate identity for the School and themselves, reacted strongly against attempts to intensify institutional discipline.

In material terms, conditions and provisions for students at the School of Mines represented a distinct improvement over those that had prevailed under the Transvaal University College. Some improvements, notably more adequate provision for scholarships, had been made in the last year of the Transvaal University College in Johannesburg. In 1909-10, partly in response to the poor enrolment of the previous years, a number of major scholarships were established, notably the Chamber of Mines research scholarship for post-diploma work, the Hennen Jennings, Barnato, and Neumann scholarships awarded on the results of the first-year mining engineering examination, and the Rand Mines, Consolidated Goldfields, and E.R.P.M. scholarships to 'enable selected students from the evening classes' to take day courses. Other improvements were introduced by the School of Mines, including the acquisition in 1911 of 'Sunnyside', Milner's former residence in Parktown, as a student hostel which replaced Highfield Terrace, a row of houses in Doornfontein that had previously served that purpose.

For those concerned with the quality of student life, the School's main defect was that it lacked corporate sense. The student *Magazine* complained the School was like 'a roly-poly without the jam'.[4] A major concern of the Council, Senate, and student leaders was consequently to promote a sense of common identity at the School or, as the *Magazine* put it, to 'infuse more momentum into our corporate life'. The first appearance of the *Magazine* in 1914 was part of this endeavour, as was the School's adoption, two years earlier, of a crest, depicting a kudu's head, and a coat of arms. In 1914 the S.R.C. and student body agreed to adopt a green, maroon, and blue-striped blazer, with a kudu's head on the pocket. A blue blazer was reserved for those given 'colours' for sport.[5]

It was chiefly through sports that both the students and the School authorities sought to encourage a 'healthy' corporate spirit. In 1911 the Council acceded to the request of the S.R.C. to levy a compulsory sports fee of £1 on all students. The main difficulty confronting student sports was the fact that the School did not possess any playing fields of its own. Only the rugby club, which utilized the fields at the Wanderers, adjacent to Park

Station, was able to participate in regular leagues, and consequently rugby was established as the major sport at the School. Three teams were entered into leagues, and in 1913 the School of Mines was admitted to the first league. The tennis club, for its part, staged an annual tournament at the End Street courts.

Perhaps inevitably in an institution that was still very much in a formative phase, the question of student discipline loomed large. This was particularly true of discipline in the student residence, or College House. Given that the School of Mines saw itself as serving all South Africa, and given the long standing doubts as to the moral suitability of Johannesburg as the centre for a residential university, the management and disciplining of College House gave rise to considerable concern. In the days of the Transvaal Technical Institute, student behaviour at Highfield Terrace had caused genuine alarm, and the first dean, Professor Wilkinson, had soon resigned. The students of the School of Mines were handed down 'great and scandalous tales' of the way their predecessors had behaved at Highfield Terrace.[6] During Professor Dobson's tenure as dean, from mid-1905 to the end of 1909, matters evidently improved, for when Professor Robertson took over as dean in 1910, he maintained that although the tone of residence life was 'common and inclined to vulgarity', it was nevertheless basically free of scandal. This absence of scandal he attributed to 'the fact that the African student is a more orderly person than the Home student'. Nevertheless, Robertson was disturbed by the opportunities that existed for 'a clever student to beat rules regarding staying out overnight and the like', and recommended that College House be fenced in and the appointment of 'a man to observe closely the intimate life of each student'. This person, to be appointed instead of the matron, was to be called the 'College House Steward'. Robertson's idea was that the steward could, without detracting from the diginity of the College House, 'penetrate into the rooms of the students during sickness, cleansing of rooms, disturbance of the peace etc.' and report back to the dean. The Council evidently thought the proposal had merit, for in 1911 the matron was replaced by a steward. The steward, however, did not restrict his brief to observing the students; he also observed the dean, and in December 1912 reported to the secretary of Council 'regarding the lax manner in which the Dean had carried out his duties, especially during the latter half of the year'.[7] For 1913 a new dean was appointed, Professor R.B. Young.

At Plein Square the main disciplinary problem concerned attendance at lectures, at which notes were often dictated. The School's rules laid down that attendance at lectures was essential. One device to which Senate had resorted in order to encourage attendance was to provide for a system whereby lecture notes might be called in for inspection. In mid-1912 the Principal and

Professor of Mining, Professor G.R. Thompson, decided to invoke this provision, and called upon the third-year mining class to submit their mining lecture notes for his inspection.

Appointed in 1911 as Lawn's successor, Thompson, previously Professor of Mining at Leeds University, though a specialist in coal mining, had little understanding of gold mining on the Reef. From the outset he had experienced great difficulty in maintaining any sort of discipline over his classes. Students who attended his lectures apparently spent more of their time munching sandwiches than taking notes. When he asked the twenty students in the third-year mining class to hand in their notes they refused, maintaining their united front even when those who were bursary holders and dependent on favourable reports from the Principal for the renewal of their bursaries, were singled out for interviews with the Principal. At the beginning of August the class was suspended by the Senate for their failure to comply 'with the regulations regarding lecture notes'. The suspension provoked the first major student protest at Plein Square. Nearly all the day students struck in sympathy with the suspended students, effectively bringing the work of the School of Mines to a standstill.

The deadlock was finally broken on 7 August when Professor Thompson and the suspended students came to terms, the latter agreeing to submit their notes. But the question of future practice remained to be settled. In October the S.R.C. submitted to the Council a petition signed by 87 students asking the Council to receive a student deputation 'on the subject of handing in Lecture Note-books, as they were dissatisfied with the Senate's Resolution, and they wished to obtain a definite ruling from the Council'. On 9 October a special Council meeting received J.B. Te Winter, the chairman, and W.C. Lindemann, the honorary secretary, of the S.R.C.

The deputation argued that lecture notes should never be used for assessment purposes, and asked Council to rule on an ambiguous Senate resolution that 'while the membership of the Senate as a whole have no intention of giving marks for Lecture Notes, they hold that a professor has a right, after reasonable notice, to inspect students' Lecture Notes, and give a specified number of marks for them'. Although the S.R.C. representatives gave the Council a perfectly adequate explanation why it was preposterous even to consider assessment based on lecture notes, Council came to the conclusion that the students 'had not made out a particularly strong case'. Council none the less referred the matter to a sub-committee, and its recommendations, which were conveyed to the Senate, evidently helped to defuse the whole issue.[8] Professor Thompson resigned at the end of the year, and was virtually never heard of again.

After Thompson's confrontation with the students, Council at last realized that even though they were running a School of Mines, the Professor of Mining was not necessarily best suited to act as Principal. Council selected as successor to Thompson as Principal Dr George Steuart Corstorphine, one of their own number, and indeed chairman during 1912. He was appointed to the chair of economic geology. As Professor of Mining the Council appointed J.S. Cellier, a product of the Kimberley School of Mines.

G.S. Corstorphine

Corstorphine was the first Principal to serve for any length of time, remaining in office until his death in January 1919. A Scot, he was educated at the University of Edinburgh, and in 1895 came to South Africa as the first Professor of Geology and Mineralogy at the South African College. He had been appointed specifically to organize the College's mining course, and directed it until he left the College in 1902. In that year he moved to Johannesburg to take up the post of consulting geologist to Consolidated Goldfields, and from 1908 maintained his own private practice. By all accounts he was humane, understanding, and industrious. His principalship was most significant for broadening the School of Mines into an aspirant university, and for launching the campaign that led ultimately to the establishment of a university in Johannesburg.

III

Under the terms of the Act of Union, the responsibility for higher education was handed to the Union government, and for secondary and elementary education to the provincial governments. In 1916, after two false starts, a commission of inquiry, and much negotiation, F.S. Malan, the Union's first Minister of Education, carried the legislation that established the basic structure for a system of university education in South Africa.⁹ The legislation of 1916 provided for teaching universities at Cape Town and Stellenbosch and for a federal university of South Africa, with its headquarters in Pretoria. The South African School of Mines and Technology was to be a constituent college of the latter, together with the Transvaal University College in Pretoria, Natal University College in Pietermaritzburg, Rhodes University College in Grahamstown, Grey University College in Bloemfontein, and Huguenot College in Wellington. The Beit bequest of £200 000, together with another £325 000 given by Sir Julius Wernher, Otto Beit, and De Beers for the founding of a national University of South Africa at Groote Schuur, was awarded to the University of Cape Town.

The initial diversion of the Beit bequest, and the provision of another £300 000 by Sir Julius Wernher and Otto Beit, was negotiated by Smuts in 1910 for the declared purpose of establishing 'a South African University on the Groote Schuur Estate'. In 1909 Smuts had met Otto Beit in London, when he had again raised the possibility of using the Beit bequest to establish an agricultural college at Frankenwald. Otto Beit, as always anxious to ensure that money bequeathed by his brother was put to proper use, again rejected the proposal as his brother had specifically stipulated that the bequest was for the founding of a university, and not an agricultural college. Then, according to the account of their meeting provided by Wilfred Murray, the first Registrar of the University of Cape Town:

> Otto Beit brought forward the suggestion that the bequest might go a long way towards achieving Cecil Rhodes' old dream of a great National University on his Groote Schuur Estate which was now the property of the nation, and expressed the opinion that it might be materially added to were it devoted to such an object. Smuts hailed this suggestion with much satisfaction and indicated later in a letter written in July, 1910 — shortly after the date of Union — that a sum of half a million pounds might suffice for such a purpose.[10]

With Union, Otto Beit and Wernher were captivated by the idea of a national university with Cape Town, as the mother city, the appropriate site. Smuts also greatly favoured Cape Town. 'The only objection I see', Wernher wrote to Lionel Phillips about situating a national university in Cape Town, 'is that the people are such a sleepy and lazy lot, no doubt owing to the climate.'[11]

Wernher duly agreed to give £250 000 and Otto Beit £50 000 in addition to the original Beit bequest, with the provisions that the new university must be a 'Residential Teaching University', and afford 'equal opportunities to all' requiring university education. When Smuts requested clarification of this latter provision they indicated that they meant 'All Whites', adding that the university must give them 'the very best instruction'. 'We have no wish to create difficulties, but we would put it to you that to obtain this result bi-lingualism must stand back; then only will you succeed to draw from this country men who will be able to establish a standing for the new University equal to that of the Home Institutions.'[12]

For the first Union government of Louis Botha and his South African party, the abandonment of bilingualism in any truly national university was too tall an order to be met. As Lionel Phillips, an M.P. of the British-oriented Unionist Party and with L.S. Jameson trustee of the Wernher bequest after Wernher's death in May 1912, recalled of the first Union Parliament: 'There were members of the House to whom language was an obsession and who would have sacrificed higher education at the shrine of the *taal* fetish.'[13] In his first university bill of 1911, which provided for a postgraduate university at Groote Schuur, Malan sought to protect the principle of bilingualism. But the bill ran into such extensive criticism on other grounds that it was never submitted to Parliament. As the University Commission of 1914 reported: 'It was felt that while such an institution might serve some useful purposes, and stimulate some branches of research, it would not constitute a residential and teaching University in the broad sense contemplated by Sir Julius Wernher and Mr. Beit.'[14]

Malan's second bill, that of 1913, provided for a university that would take students after they had passed the intermediate examination for a degree, or its equivalent, thereby leaving the existing colleges responsible for work up to the intermediate stage. The bill made no provision for bilingualism, which provoked a storm of protest in Afrikaner circles. Old President Steyn of the Free State reflected this anger when he said that Afrikaners dared not sell their children for half a million pounds.[15] As it was impossible to proceed with the bill, Malan, on the recommendation of a parliamentary select committee, referred the whole question of university reform, and the use of the Beit and Wernher bequests, to a commission headed by Sir Perceval Laurence, the recently retired Judge President.

In response to Malan's proposals of 1911 and 1913, and in evidence given to the Laurence Commission, the Council of the South African School of Mines and Technology and the Witwatersrand Council of Education adopted a clear and consistent line of policy. They were prepared to relinquish the ideal of a university in or near Johannesburg, and to acquiesce in the diversion of the Beit bequest, for the sake of a national teaching university at Groote Schuur, which would replace the present University of the Cape of Good Hope and the existing colleges. The School of Mines would constitute the technological faculty of the university, thereby obviating the need for an engineering faculty at Cape Town.[16]

As Theodore Reunert sought to impress on the Laurence Commission, Johannesburg would 'gladly abandon any local ambitions' in order to secure the establishment of one central residential teaching university. Both the School of Mines and the Council of Education urged that the true interests of higher education in South Africa required the foundation of a national university to replace the existing colleges. There were eight university colleges in the country, including the School of Mines, with no more than 1 300 students between them. The colleges were too small and weak, offering in the main instruction that more properly belonged to a high school than a university. A national teaching university, by concentrating resources, would make possible higher standards and specialization by professors, it would end the 'cursed' system of constant cramming for a multitude of external examinations, and would bring about a 'union between the students belonging to the two leading white races in the Country'. But in its memorandum to the Laurence Commission, the Council of Education did enter the caveat, 'In the event of the ideal of one national University for South Africa being unattainable the Council of Education will return to its original scheme of a Johannesburg University.'[17]

The submissions of the School of Mines and the Council of Education to the Commission were, as Laurence himself described them, 'exceptional', but they were not as disinterested as they pretended to be. They were designed to protect the position and autonomy of the School of Mines in the reorganization of higher education in South Africa, to undercut Pretoria as a rival educational centre to Johannesburg, and to promote the elusive goal of the assimilation of the Afrikaner in 'British' institutions of higher learning. The *Burger*, the mouthpiece of the newly-founded National Party, contended the only reason why Johannesburg was prepared to forfeit the Beit bequest was because it lived in the hope of rooting out racialism, which translated meant, crushing the Victoria College at Stellenbosch to death and founding at the foot of the Rhodes Monument a single national English university for the whole Union.[18] The submissions also reflected an awareness that Johannesburg, and the educational infrastructure in the Transvaal, had never made the progress envisaged by Milner and Alfred Beit when they had contemplated a university on the Rand. Johannesburg's white population had simply not met Milner's estimate, and the Transvaal's matriculants continued to lag far behind the Cape.[19] Finally, the Senate of the School of Mines was determined that the School should continue to develop along largely scientific and technological lines. Professor G.S. Corstorphine, in his capacity as Principal, expressed this overtly to the Commission: 'One thing I think many members of the senate feel particularly is that they would not like to see a chance of scientific and technological work being swamped by a senate in which the literary element was very much in the majority.'[20]

The distinct impression that the representatives of the School of Mines got in giving evidence to the Laurence Commission was that the Commission was 'not there to listen to their evidence and to obtain their views, but rather – amid a mass of irrelevant discussion — to give expression to their own opinions and to urge upon them the establishing of a second university in the North as a solution to the difficulty'.[21] For the Commission, because of South Africa's scattered population, the idea of a single national university was not a practical possibility. It recommended instead two federal universities, one southern the other northern, with the School of Mines serving as the faculty of technology for both. As the Beit bequest had originally been intended for the Transvaal, the Commission recommended that £125 000 should be awarded to the Transvaal – £50 000 for the central seat of the northern university at Pretoria, £50 000 for the School of Mines, and £25 000 for the Council of Education. The balance would go to the central seat of the southern university at Groote Schuur, which would also receive £150 000 from the Wernher bequest.[22]

The Laurence Commission submitted its report to the government on 15 July 1914, the eve of the outbreak of World War I, which was to bring new turmoil to South Africa, including an armed Afrikaner rebellion in October. At first it seemed that the university question would be shelved until after the war. Not only did South Africa's active participation in the war have a divisive impact on society, but no one had been pleased with the recommendations of the Laurence Commission. Otto Beit and the trustees of the Wernher bequest were adamantly opposed to dispersing the funds among a number of institutions. The School of Mines, as a consequence of the experiment in college federation between Johannesburg and Pretoria in 1908-9, now opposed a federal scheme as unworkable. The South African College continued to maintain fundamental antagonism to federalism. In these circumstances, the Witwatersrand Council of Education, which since a friendly court action in 1909 had been in receipt of the interest on the Beit bequest, considered approaching Otto Beit and Sir Lionel Phillips with a scheme to extend university education on the Witwatersrand, but rejected the notion until conclusion of the war. According to Theodore Reunert, the former chairman of the Council and a member of its syndic: 'We, at all events, felt that our hands were tied by our loyalty and that to introduce such a contentious question would be a disloyal act towards General Botha and his Government . . .'[23]

What was to infuriate the leaders of the university movement on the Witwatersrand, and to give rise to allegations of bad faith, was that the South African College had no hesitation in approaching Beit, Phillips, and Jameson during 1915 and getting their approval to donate the Wernher-Beit bequests to a proposed new University of Cape Town. In June 1915 the South African College submitted to F.S. Malan, and to Beit, Phillips, and Jameson in England, a memorandum rejecting the Laurence Commission's report, and proposing instead to incorporate the South African College as a university, with new buildings and residences at Groote Schuur to be financed by the Wernher-Beit bequests. On 17 August Thomas Maitland Park, the editor of the *Cape Times* and a member of the Council of the South African College, met Beit, Phillips, and Jameson in London, and secured their approval for the South African College scheme. All parties to the London meeting believed that the University of Cape Town would then become the only teaching university in South Africa.[24]

That the destination of the Wernher-Beit bequests was settled behind closed doors, without anyone else knowing, and with no one to represent the other interested parties, particularly Johannesburg, for which the Beit bequest had originally been intended, caused great resentment on the Rand. John O'Hara, the Mayor of Johannesburg, complained in a letter to Phillips, 'the Capetown institution has gone behind our backs and stolen our heritage'.[25] The government, for its complicity in assisting the South African College, was also charged with bad faith. In the general election of October 1915, which deprived the Botha government of its independent majority and forced it to rely on the support of the Unionists, the university question had not been an issue. It was universally acknowledged as a question that had been shelved until after the war. Yet as soon as the general election was over, the government announced in the press that in the next session of Parliament legislation would be introduced granting to the South African College a charter of incorporation as a university, and that the Wernher-Beit bequests would be given to it.

The government's full scheme for university education in South Africa, unfolding during the course of November, involved the creation of three new universities, teaching universities at Groote Schuur and Stellenbosch, and a federal University of South Africa composed of the remaining colleges. The Wernher-Beit bequests were to go to the proposed new University of Cape Town at Groote Schuur.

These arrangements were made possible by two developments. The South

African College had successfully persuaded Otto Beit and the trustees of the Wernher bequest that a University of Cape Town was the next best thing to the unattainable national university at Groote Schuur, while the death of J.H. Marais of Coetzenburg in May 1915, and his bequest of £100 000 to the Victoria College, provided the financial basis for the conversion of the college into an Afrikaner university. The Marais bequest, unknown to Beit, Phillips, and Jameson when they gave their approval to the proposal for a University of Cape Town, was of the greatest importance to F.S. Malan and the Botha government in deciding the university question. The government could now satisfy both major language groups among white South Africans that it was catering for them even-handedly. But one potential major aggrieved interest remained: the Witwatersrand.

The government's first announcement on 10 November that the Wernher-Beit bequests were to go to a proposed University of Cape Town caused an immediate flutter at the School of Mines and in the Council of Education. A telegram, intercepted by the wartime censorship department, was sent to London to find out whether Otto Beit and Lionel Phillips approved. The syndic of the Council of Education sought to enlist the support of Rand M.P.s against the scheme; and at the end of December it prepared a pamphlet, *The Witwatersrand and the University Problem,* which argued that as the proposed Cape University would not be a national university, it did not justify Johannesburg losing the Beit bequest, and that Johannesburg should therefore again seek its own university.

In London, Otto Beit and Lionel Phillips were indeed very unhappy at the turn of events. Beit later informed Carruthers Beattie, the first Principal of the University of Cape Town, that:

> In advising the donors to agree to part with the money, Sir Lionel Phillips and Sir Starr Jameson were prompted by the belief that there was to be no competing concern and we were horribly upset when the Bill to be laid before Parliament was received here and we found that you were only one of three Universities all dealt with under the same Act. We, the donors, however, at that time felt that it might be looked upon as going back on our word if we were again to refuse to part with the money and thus our consent was allowed to stand.[26]

Beit added that he possibly regretted the decision, as the result was the creation of three universities all exercising 'equal pressure upon the Government for large funds'. Even so this was not an attitude at all helpful to the Witwatersrand. The desire of the Witwatersrand was to add to the pressure by creating a fourth university in Johannesburg.

Mayor O'Hara   Theodore Reunert

On the Witwatersrand, John O'Hara, Johannesburg's mayor, and a handful of individuals closely associated with the School of Mines, led the fight against the government's proposals. Samuel Evans, the chairman of the School's Council and also chairman and managing director of Crown Mines; Professor G.S. Corstorphine, the Principal of the School of Mines; Theodore Reunert, a partner in the mining engineering firm of Reunert and Lenz and a longstanding member of both the syndic of the Council of Education and the Council of the School of Mines; and Henry John Hofmeyr, a Johannesburg attorney, likewise a member of both the Council syndic and the School Council, were, with O'Hara, the key figures in organizing the agitation on the Witwatersrand. It had been Samuel Evans's initiative to give the aggressive Mayor O'Hara an organizing role in the agitation. At a special meeting of the School's Council on 30 December 1915, he suggested that it would probably be wise for the School of Mines to effect a political alliance with the Rand mayors through the agency of the Mayor of Johannesburg. In the event, O'Hara was to play a crucial role in engineering a popular protest on the Rand.

In preparing the battle lines against the government's proposed legislation, the Council of the School of Mines as a body took a curiously inactive role. At its special meeting of 30 December to consider the government's proposals, the

Council showed itself to be more bemused and resigned than actively hostile. It was not to meet again until 3 March 1916, the day after the second reading debate in the House of Assembly had opened. The syndic of the Council of Education, by contrast, met on 27 January, and again on 15 February, following the publication of details of the government's bills in the *Government Gazette Extraordinary*. At this latter meeting the decision was taken to attempt to block the university bills, and towards the end of February a special Council meeting was held to ask the government to postpone the bills until after the war.

To its meetings the syndic of the Council of Education invited Mayor O'Hara, who immediately became active in mobilizing the Rand municipalities and preparing the ground for a major agitation. On 28 January, at the request of the syndic, O'Hara sent a telegram to Lionel Phillips, then in London, demanding on behalf of the white population of the Witwatersrand that he do his best to prevent the diversion of the Beit bequest, and advising that the Witwatersrand mayors would soon be meeting to consider the 'grave position'. Phillips cabled back that the Transvaal government had itself refused to utilize the Beit bequest, which was now due to revert to Otto Beit, and gave his opinion that the transfer of the South African College to Groote Schuur represented the nearest approach attainable to a national university. He added that he would soon be sailing from England on the S.S. *Kenilworth Castle* and that when he arrived in Cape Town he would be glad to discuss the interests of the Rand with its representatives.[27] O'Hara also cabled Otto Beit, who replied that he would accept whatever advice Phillips sent from South Africa.

When the Rand mayors met in early February the details of the government's bills, which confirmed the worst fears for the Witwatersrand, had been published. As the Council of the School of Mines concluded at its meeting of 3 March, the bills suggested that it was 'the intention of the Government to settle the whole question of the higher education of the Union as if no such place as Johannesburg existed'. It was this sense that the interests of Johannesburg and the Witwatersrand had been entirely ignored, as well as outrage at Cape Town's 'theft' of the Beit bequest, that underlay the storm of protest on the Rand against the university bills. The loss of the Beit bequest might have been accepted if something had been done to compensate the Witwatersrand, but instead Johannesburg and the Witwatersrand were apparently discriminated against on every issue, including even the headquarters for the new federal university, which was to be Pretoria. For a community whose development and growth had been considerably speeded up by the impact of war; which had acquired a new sense of permanence and stability, symbolized by the opening of Johannesburg's fine new Town Hall;

and which was proudly conscious of its size and its importance in the nation's economy, the university legislation was an insult. In their protest published in the *Star* on 9 February the Witwatersrand mayors demanded to know: 'Is the Rand, with its enormous and growing European population, to be indefinitely deprived of facilities for giving higher education to its sons?' The Witwatersrand's white population of a quarter of a million was more than twice that of the rest of the Transvaal, and the Rand contributed 60 per cent of the revenue of the Union government, 'Yet it is provided with worse higher educational facilities than districts which are contributing less than 1 per cent'.

In Parliament, regional considerations dominated the debate over the university bills. Although the Witwatersrand had been a Unionist stronghold in the general election of October 1915, the Unionist Party failed to turn the government's university proposals into a national issue, and to attack them along national lines. The party was simply not prepared to treat the university question as one of confidence in the government, nor are the reasons for this hard to seek. Their pledge to keep the government in office so long as it continued to prosecute the war against Germany rendered them 'an opposition party unable to oppose'.[28] In response to the university bills, moreover, the party divided along regional lines. Unionist M.P.s never united in denouncing the government's 'racial' approach to university education, and its niggardly and short-sighted attitude to Johannesburg, but pursued the interests of their own regions. Unionist M.P.s from the Witwatersrand were generally critical of the bills; Cape Unionists, showing scant regard for the interests of Johannesburg, positively welcomed the proposal to establish a university at Groote Schuur.

In the House of Assembly a concerted attempt was made to form a Witwatersrand bloc on the university issue. Before the second reading debate opened on 2 March, Rand M.P.s of all parties 'from Randfontein to Springs' had been thoroughly canvassed by O'Hara and the three representatives of the School of Mines, Corstorphine, Evans, and H.J. Hofmeyr, who had travelled to Cape Town for the purpose. Three meetings were held with the Rand M.P.s, who formed themselves into a Committee of Rand Members of Parliament on the University Bills, chaired by Patrick Duncan, the Unionist member for Fordsburg and a former member of Milner's 'kindergarten'.[29]

The School of Mines representatives and the Rand M.P.s also met F.S. Malan to request that the government introduce a bill giving Johannesburg its own university, with courses in the arts, pure science, and medicine. Malan responded that he could not at present agree to arts and science courses in Johannesburg as that 'would mean a row with Pretoria, which the

Government were not prepared to face'. He further made it quite clear that 'the Government could not possibly make any increased grants under present conditions'.[30] O'Hara and representatives of the School of Mines also descended on Lionel Phillips as soon as he reached Cape Town — apparently they hired a tug to get to him before he actually docked — but they failed to convince him that the time was opportune to found a university, financed by the Beit bequest, in Johannesburg.[31]

According to Patrick Duncan's contemporary account, the Rand M.P.s were 'strongly against' any attempt to wreck the University of Cape Town Bill, including the award to Cape Town of the Beit bequest. The 'general opinion' was that the first step, even though Malan had made it clear that the government could not finance new courses, was to persuade the government to remove the restriction on the teaching of arts and pure science at Johannesburg. Duncan explained in a letter to J. Hartog on 3 April:

> It was quite clear to me, and, as I thought, to all of us, that if our request for permission to start university courses was to involve a demand for an immediate increase in the grant, the Minister had an unanswerable argument against us in the present financial situation. If, therefore, we were to carry our point, we had to go as far as to say that, even if he could not give us any money at present, we still wanted the Government to give permission at once to start courses in Arts &c if we could do so, and, when we had shewn what the demand was, we could come to him for a grant when the times were more opportune.[32]

In the second reading debate the government's university bills were criticized and attacked by Witwatersrand M.P.s of all parties. Two of the South African Party's Johannesburg members, Harry Graumann (Commissioner Street) and H.B. Papenfus (Hospital), strongly criticized the government for its negligent attitude towards Johannesburg and the Rand, while the Labour M.P.s for the Witwatersrand, W.B. Madeley (Benoni) and H.W. Sampson (Siemert), attacked the government for its failure to consult the electorate on the university question, and declared that the time was inopportune for considering university education. The Rand members of the Unionist Party were virtually unanimous in denouncing the government for ignoring the interests and aspirations of the Witwatersrand. The positive proposal put forward by Duncan was that the School of Mines should be freed of the restrictions imposed on its teaching by the Transvaal statute of 1910, and that, provided it could raise the necessary finance, it should be empowered to teach whatever courses it wished. He asked: 'Would the Minister give them permission to erect a University on the Rand without Government money?'.

At the beginning of the second day's debate on the University of South Africa Bill Malan announced that the government had given its approval to an amendment that would allow the School of Mines to extend its work, though no additional grants could be given it at present. He declared he perceived a change in Johannesburg's attitude to higher education. Previously Johannesburg had shown little interest in developing its own institutions, even for secondary education. Now the people of Johannesburg had decided to support their local institutions, and the government would not stand in their way.[33]

With that concession, Duncan believed that the Rand M.P.s had achieved all that was then possible, and that 'nothing was to be gained by pursuing the question of the bequests'.[34] This belief, however, was not shared in Johannesburg. 'The problem of finance', the *Star* commented, 'still remains unsolved.'[35] When O'Hara, Evans, and H.J. Hofmeyr returned to Johannesburg they determined that the best means of attempting to resolve the problem was by staging a last-ditch effort to recover the Beit bequest during the committee stage of the university bills.

The celebrated protest meeting held at Johannesburg's new Town Hall on 17 March served two fundamental purposes. First, to bring pressure on the Rand M.P.s to make a fight for the Beit bequest; and, second, to launch a fund-raising campaign to establish a university in Johannesburg. O'Hara, who summoned the meeting attended by 2 500 'ladies and gentlemen', rose from his sick-bed to denounce the proposed diversion of the Beit bequest as a 'shameless attempt to legalise piracy', and dismissed the Minister of Education as 'nothing more nor less than a wolf in sheep's clothing'. Though not in a position to commit the municipal council, he also announced that it was probable the council would offer Milner Park as the site for a university in Johannesburg. The meeting, which was cleverly stage-managed, was then addressed by Reunert and H.J. Hofmeyr on behalf of the Council of Education, followed by a series of spokesmen supposedly representing the major groups and classes in Witwatersrand white society. During the course of the meeting resolutions were passed condemning the government's proposed university legislation, and calling for the creation in Johannesburg of 'a fully-fledged University College financed by the State' with the right to evolve into 'a State-supported Teaching University'. Another resolution established a committee to campaign for a university in Johannesburg and to raise 'such endowment and guarantees as may be obtainable towards developing the College and University referred to'. A final resolution called for copies of the previous resolutions to be sent to the Prime Minister, the Minister of Education, and the parliamentary representatives of the Witwatersrand. The meeting closed with the national anthem played by Alfred Hollins, described in the programme as 'the Blind Organist'.[36]

Cartoon in the *Rand Daily Mail*, 3 March 1916

The immediate effect of the meeting of Friday 17 March was to widen the cleavage that had been developing between the leaders of the Johannesburg agitation and Duncan together with some of the Unionist M.P.s from the Witwatersrand. Before the meeting O'Hara had sent two telegrams to Duncan, as chairman of the Committee of Rand Members on the University Bills, demanding that the Rand M.P.s press for the removal of all references to the Wernher-Beit bequests in the University of Cape Town Bill. Duncan had refused, cabling back that the Rand M.P.s believed that any attempt to deprive Cape Town of the Wernher-Beit bequests would serve no good purpose. After the meeting of 17 March O'Hara was able to cable on behalf of the 'two thousand five hundred citizens present including representatives from Reef towns', that the Rand M.P.s 'should fight this matter out to a finish'. On 21 and 22 March he bombarded Duncan with more telegrams: 'We cannot understand hesitancy and reluctance our members in pressing Rand's claim for its due share Wernher Beit bequests.'[37] To intensify the pressure on Duncan, O'Hara also attempted to stage a meeting in Duncan's own constituency of Fordsburg, supposedly with a view to 'strengthening' Duncan's hand in dealing with the university question, and to win over Lionel Phillips.[38]

Duncan was clearly chagrined by the 'peremptory telegrams which have been hurled at our heads', and he stubbornly refused to abandon the stance he had adopted on the Beit bequest. He and those Rand M.P.s who supported him were 'not prepared to make fools of ourselves at the order of Hofmeyr, Reunert and Sam Evans'.[39] The result was a split among Rand M.P.s during the committee stage of the university bills, which got under way on Monday 27 March. Led by H.B. Papenfus, the South African Party member for Hospital, J.W. Quinn, the Unionist member for Troyeville, and Dewdney Drew, the Unionist member for Germiston, more than half the Rand M.P.s challenged the diversion of the Beit bequest. Duncan, supported by Hugh Wyndham (Turffontein), R. Raine (Ophirton), and Richard Feetham (Parktown), who was later to serve as Chancellor of the University of the Witwatersrand, would go no further than move an amendment to the University of South Africa Bill which provided that the constituent colleges had the right to promote legislation to incorporate themselves as universities. The amendment was accepted by Malan, though he pointed out it was really quite unnecessary 'as a private Bill would meet the position'.[40]

It was during the committee stage that the main rhetorical attacks were launched in Parliament against the transfer of the Beit bequest to the University of Cape Town. In moving an amendment to delete the relevant clause in the University of Cape Town Bill, Quinn declared that Johannesburg had been 'filched' and denounced the Minister of Education for having 'secretly and stealthfully perpetrated this illegality'. Papenfus emphasized that Johannesburg itself had never refused the bequest. W. Rockey (U., Langlaagte) complained rather mutely that 'the money had been diverted from its original purpose by some rather dishonourable intrigue', but Dewdney Drew stated bluntly that Cape Town had 'got away with the swag': 'The Cape Town College Council was the operating gang in the transaction and the Government were accomplices after the fact.'[41]

This sound and fury effected nothing, and in early April the university bills were finally passed. However, to a meeting of the Council of Education on 14 April, Reunert could claim with justice that 'although we have failed to get any portion of the £200,000 we certainly have got more facilities than we should have if this agitation had not been'.[42] The School of Mines had been given the legal authority to expand its work, and even offer courses in the arts and pure science. The Minister of Education had agreed that Frankenwald should go to the School of Mines, and the Johannesburg Town Council had indicated its willingness to grant land at Milner Park for a university. Even more important, the idea of establishing a university in Johannesburg had been popularized, and a definite campaign launched to create and finance the university. At the protest meeting of 17 March a Witwatersrand University Committee had been appointed of all those who had addressed the meeting, with power to add to their number. They immediately co-opted the mayors of all the Rand municipalities, Professor Corstorphine, and Colonel William Dalrymple, the chairman of the Witwatersrand Council of Education, managing director of the Anglo-French Exploration Company, and vice-president of the Transvaal Chamber of Mines. This committee would seek to raise the funds for a university of the Witwatersrand in Johannesburg.

Patrick Duncan and Lionel Phillips were never quite forgiven for the role they played in 1916. It was rumoured that Duncan had in fact helped to influence Otto Beit to divert his brother's bequest to Cape Town. Lionel Phillips was simply dismissed as a disappointment as a supposed friend of Johannesburg and higher education there.[43]

IV

Five years after the passage of Malan's university legislation of 1916, Parliament approved the private Act for the establishment of the University of the Witwatersrand, Johannesburg. In the intervening period the School of Mines expanded very rapidly, in student numbers and the range and number of courses offered. The Witwatersrand University Committee, for its part, mounted a major propaganda and fund-raising campaign to create a university that would be at once practical and democratic in its service of the community.

Although the 1916 legislation gave the School of Mines the option to remain independent, it was decided that the School should become a constituent college of the University of South Africa, primarily because this would enable its students to gain degrees and not merely diplomas. The new federal university began operation on 2 April 1918, with the Transvaal University

College in Pretoria as its largest constituent college, followed by the South African School of Mines and Technology, with 191 full-time students.

In all but name, the School of Mines became again a university college following Malan's decision to allow Johannesburg the opportunity to show what it might achieve of its own accord. In 1917, in addition to its traditional diploma courses in engineering and law, and the diploma courses in commerce and accountancy started in 1915, the School launched courses in the arts and pure science, the latter intended to lead to degree work in medicine as well as science. For 1917 eight arts departments were created: English, Logic and Philosophy as a single department, History, Economics, Education and Psychology, Geography, Classics, Dutch, and French. Two new science departments were created, Botany and Zoology, which together with the established departments in Chemistry and Physics provided the preliminary science subjects for first-year medical students. By 1920 the School possessed 31 departments, compared with 12 in 1916. Student numbers increased considerably, particularly after the conclusion of World War I in November 1918. From a war-time low of 77 day students in 1916, numbers jumped to 173 in 1917, 301 in 1919, and 635 in 1920. The classroom accommodation for these new departments and students was provided mainly by the Tin Temple, the former municipal offices on Plein Square that had been vacated by the municipality following the completion of the new Town Hall.

In recognition of this dramatic development the School began to call itself the University College, Johannesburg, in 1919, and in the next year was formally given that title by Act of Parliament. In 1921 the University College enrolled 812 students.

The phenomenal development of Johannesburg as a centre of higher education between 1916 and 1921 requires explanation. For those who had long championed the idea of a university in Johannesburg the explanation was quite simple. When the restrictions Smuts had placed on Johannesburg were removed, the town revealed its hitherto frustrated interest in creating a genuinely civic university. According to this view, until 1916, technical education apart, massive misconception and prejudice had deprived Johannesburg of the opportunity to reveal and develop its interest in higher education. As the Johannesburg press complained, the town was still widely regarded as a mere temporary stopping place for a transient 'Uitlander' population, whose interests were entirely materialistic. It was depicted as a place of incitement and turbulence quite unsuited for parents to send their 'impressionable progeny' for a higher education. These misconceptions and prejudices were as prevalent after 1916 as before, but from that date Johannesburg seized the opportunity to 'prove our case' for a university. As

The Tin Temple, Plein Square

Colonel Dalrymple put it to the annual general meeting of the Council of Education on 29 July 1919: 'Despite the restricted place so long assigned to it, and notwithstanding the attitude so long displayed by the Government towards its ambitions, the Johannesburg University College had emerged from its trials with amazing vigour . . . It was the third largest university centre in South Africa, and a reluctant Government had been forced to acknowledge that the Rand needed a university college, and knew how to use it.'[44]

This was a viewpoint that contained a strong element of truth. It had been the intervention of government, partly inspired by prejudice against Johannesburg, that had gone far to prevent the gradual evolution of a university college on the Witwatersrand. The new departments established after 1916 served to fill a vacuum that need never have existed. Unquestionably, the loss of the Beit bequest, coupled with the apparent unfairness of government policy towards Johannesburg, served as the trigger for a sustained campaign to establish a university in the town, and provided the main emotional impetus behind the campaign. None the less, it is evident that there had been a great change between 1906, when the first abortive experiment in providing classes in the arts and science in Johannesburg had been made, and 1916, when the active campaign to create a university in Johannesburg began. In the intervening decade the Witwatersrand had grown enormously, its system of secondary education had made significant advances, and its economy had greatly diversified. Considerably aided by the war, the Witwatersrand generally, and Johannesburg in particular, was emerging as a major commercial and industrial centre supplementing and complementing its importance in mining. Johannesburg's town centre had developed into the largest retail outlet in South Africa; the town, focus of all major railroads in South Africa, housed the headquarters of the Union's railway administration, and served as the distributive centre for goods for most of Africa south of the Zambezi. Its accountancy firms, which had been founded to cater for the mining houses, led the nation in their field, while small manufacturing industries, notably in clothing, furniture, glassware, pottery, and engineering, were beginning to appear.

Johannesburg's emergence after 1916 as a centre for higher education was in part a product of this growth and diversification. The development of Johannesburg had encouraged a sense of civic pride, and self-consciousness. That Johannesburg had no university was regarded as a slight to her standing and significance. 'In the United States, Canada and Australasia', advocates of a university emphasized, 'there is not a single town with a population approaching 100,000 Europeans in which no provision has been made for university education.' The development on the Witwatersrand of secondary industries during the war years, and the role that the war had played in Britain in bringing the universities directly into the service of industry, also served to encourage the idea of establishing a university in Johannesburg. Although the leaders of the university movement were closely associated with the mining industry, their sense of the possibilities in prospect extended far beyond the immediate requirements of their own industry. They believed in the future of Johannesburg and the Witwatersrand. The university they envisaged would help sustain the Witwatersrand's growth, its economic expansion and diversification.[45] As Colonel Dalrymple urged in his chairman's address to the annual general meeting of the Council of Education on 26 February 1920:

> These days see new needs rapidly arising because the war has widened our horizon. The modern university must be alert, and ready to lead. She must apply science to industry; provide teachers for our ever widening system of education; train doctors and conduct medical research to save the nation's man power; provide well equipped men and women for our municipal and national services, as well as for commerce and industry; and she must 'tap new and rich lodes in our national brain power'.[46]

The campaign to raise finance stressed the utilitarian value that a university would have for the Witwatersrand. As J.D. Rheinhallt Jones, who was appointed secretary to the Council of Education in 1919, urged in one of a series of articles on 'Our University' in the *Star* in 1921: 'The Great War has served to drive home the fact that the Universities are of far greater direct usefulness than was ever imagined before, and has also shown how much more serviceable they may become, not alone in the realm of pure knowledge, but also in the development of industry and commerce.'[47] Much of the propaganda was directly designed to counter the notion that universities should properly be situated in secluded places and committed to the pursuit of knowledge for its own sake. Instead it was stressed that the modern university belonged in the midst of the modern city, and existed to benefit the community materially. E.P. Stibbe, the new Professor of Anatomy, stated in his contribution to 'Our University': 'The university is now no longer the retreat of the classical scholar; it is the office and workshop of the man of action. University life and training do not now make recluses; they turn out men who come into touch with, and in a measure control, the whole life of the community.'[48]

The appeal for funds, and the local campaign for a university charter, were chiefly waged by the Witwatersrand University Committee. Given the strategy was to associate as many local interests as possible with the Committee, it necessarily developed into a rather large and unwieldy body, but the executive and finance committees were controlled by those who had for long dominated the university movement on the Rand: Colonel Dalrymple, Samuel Evans, H.J. Hofmeyr, Theodore Reunert, and, until his death in 1919, Principal Corstorphine.

At the outset, largely as a consequence of O'Hara's influence, the propaganda campaign waged by the Witwatersrand University Committee was strongly populist. A truly 'democratic' university was proposed, offering a ladder upwards to the sons of the poor. As was urged in a memorandum that O'Hara sent to the Chamber of Mines in November 1916, the contention that South Africa could not afford a university specifically for the Witwatersrand, and that the people there could send their children to Cape Town or Pretoria for a university education, represented 'the attitude adopted in all countries by reactionary politicians who oppose the extension of university education to the people and who wish to keep the university door closed to the poor classes and opened only to the sons and daughters of the well-to-do section of the community, the parents who can afford to send their children away from their homes for higher education'. A university in Johannesburg would offer a university education to many thousands of young men and women who would otherwise be unable to afford it.[49]

Some members of the Witwatersrand University Committee were concerned that this democratic appeal was strongly laced with racism. O'Hara's letters and the Committee's pamphlets regularly stressed that 'The fact that every year hundreds of parents on the Witwatersrand are obliged to send their sons out into the world insufficiently educated is felt by the Committee to be a scandal which should be remedied without a moment's delay, particularly when it is remembered that the European in South Africa has to face the competition of an overwhelming coloured population.' When in June 1917 the Committee published its programme, it did so under the title *Education of Europeans in the Witwatersrand Area*. It proposed not only a university but an integrated scheme for the overhaul of the entire system of white education on the Witwatersrand, with a view to preserving 'European' ascendancy:

> The presence of natives in such overwhelming numbers in our midst renders the thorough education and training of European children on the Witwatersrand a matter of supreme importance. It is absolutely necessary for us to do everything possible to stop the manufacture of incompetent workers, poor whites and unemployables, which is undoubtedly taking place on a large scale at the present time. To accomplish that we must discourage in every possible way the employment of boys and girls in occupations which leave them with no useful training when they grow up: we must establish an educational system that will give every child an outfit for life, a system that will develop the body, preserve the health, train the mind, and form the character, so that our children enter upon their life's work adequately equipped.

There was a sensitive perception of the problems facing the poor whites, who had been gravitating in increasing numbers to the towns, and of the disastrous consequences for many white youth of a system which allowed them to leave school after standard 5 for engagement in 'work which involves them being thrown out of employment as soon as they ask for an adult's wage'. In marked contrast, the attitude to blacks was basically hostile, which perturbed Walter Webber, a Johannesburg attorney and member of the Committee. 'I consider it our duty and our interest', he told O'Hara, 'to devote earnest attention to the education of the natives, and to avoid any possibility of suspicion that it is our policy to keep the natives uneducated in order to prevent them from competing with the European. Such a policy is a dangerous one, and in so far as it is carried out will have a more detrimental effect on the European than on the native.'[50]

The Witwatersrand University Committee envisaged their university as serving the new educational system the Transvaal required by providing university education for teachers in training, as well as for the general needs of the Witwatersrand through faculties of engineering, law, commerce, architecture, agriculture, and medicine, and a veterinary college. The

Committee's vision encompassed 'The encouragement of Research work of all kinds by the creation of special Research Professorships, Fellowships, Scholarships, Grants, etc., and the provision of the necessary equipment with a view to the full performance of the University's obligation in respect of the advancement of knowledge.'[51]

The importance of research, particularly for industry, was stressed throughout the campaign for a Johannesburg university. John Orr, the Professor of Mechanical Engineering, contended in his presidential address to the annual congress of the South African Association for the Advancement of Science on 2 July 1917, 'perhaps the greatest lesson of the war had been the realisation of the necessity of greater scientific methods in relation to industry'.[52] G.H. Stanley, the Professor of Metallurgy and Assaying, similarly urged that science was the 'helpmeet' of industry in his contribution to 'Our University': 'Already the college has been of material assistance to industry, and it is to be anticipated that perhaps the most important result of the grant of a charter will be the stimulus afforded to scientific research, which in turn will inevitably react to the benefit of the whole community.'[53]

Even before the war, the importance of local research, whether conducted within a university or by university-trained people, had been gaining increasing recognition, particularly in the mining industry. It was no accident that the first major scholarship given by the Chamber of Mines to the School of Mines had been for research, and the School of Mines had early on drawn up provisions regulating contract research.[54] In the campaign for a university it was emphasized that industries other than mining would benefit from local research.

It is almost impossible to escape the conclusion that, in the effort to persuade local industry and commerce to support a university for the Witwatersrand, virtually everyone who spoke or wrote in favour of a university had been instructed to emphasize the utilitarian value of such an institution for the community. What is quite certain is that the Johannesburg daily press, which had been actively recruited to canvass the virtues of a local university, pursued such a strategy. The articles in the *Star* on 'Our University' consistently stressed the practical and material advantages that a university of the Witwatersrand would provide, and the *Rand Daily Mail,* which had been suspect during the crisis of early 1916, likewise followed a strongly utilitarian line. An editorial of 1 December 1919 on the 'Rand University Movement', described the leaders of the movement as men of 'vision' with confidence in the commercial and industrial destiny of South Africa. In commerce, what the country required of a university was 'men who have been trained in economics and finance, men who are acquainted with foreign languages and commercial law, men who are able to collect and collate information as to markets, and men who understand the principles of international trade.' In support of the proposal to establish a department of Bantu Studies at the Johannesburg college the *Mail* even ran an editorial on the administrative advantages of 'Studying the Natives Scientifically'.[55]

In the main, the leaders of the university movement wanted a university that would prove its 'usefulness' to the community, and promote the material development of the Witwatersrand. But they also wanted a university that would make some claim to academic distinction. This last was an important consideration when the Council of the School of Mines appointed its former Classics professor, Jan Hendrik Hofmeyr, successor as Principal to Corstorphine. Then but 24 years of age, Hofmeyr's scholastic record, at the South African College and Oxford, was exceptionally brilliant. He was seen as the man who could transform the School of Mines into a truly great university. He possessed another advantage. He was an Afrikaner. This would help the new university establish the 'non-racial' image that the leaders of the university movement on the Witwatersrand had always sought.[56] For these reasons Council decided in March 1919 to appoint Hofmeyr as Principal rather than James Ogg, the Professor of Physics, who had served as Acting Principal after Corstorphine's death.[57]

V

The progress of the School of Mines to university status between 1916 and 1922, although reasonably rapid, was not without obstacles. The government remained sceptical, even hostile in its attitude towards Johannesburg's ambitions, while fund-raising proved very difficult in time of war and later, of economic depression.

The Witwatersrand University Committee launched two major financial appeals, in 1917 and in 1919. The first was designed to raise current funds required to support the new work undertaken by the School of Mines. The second was intended to raise a capital sum for the proposed new university. Colonel Dalrymple and Theodore Reunert, later assisted by Rheinallt Jones, were the key organizers in these campaigns.

The Committee's main financial support came from the Johannesburg Town Council and the other Rand municipalities; the Council of Education; the Chamber of Mines, which donated £25 000 to current expenses and another £25 000 to the capital fund; the Central Mining and Investment Corporation; De Beers; Johannesburg Consolidated Investment; and the two major banks,

National and Standard. Large personal donations came from Otto Beit, who gave £8 000, Sir Abe Bailey, G.F. Jooste, D.A. McCubbin, and Herbert Ainsworth. Dalrymple proved particularly skilful as a fund-raiser, as when he played on the rivalry between National and Standard ultimately to extract £20 000 from each. By May 1921 the Committee had raised £171 000 for the building and endowment fund.

Overall, Dalrymple was most disappointed at the sums donated. In particular he thought commercial concerns, property owners, and individuals should have been more generous. £171 000 had been contributed by only 184 subscribers, which in his view clearly demonstrated that 'the community as a whole, has not yet risen to the significance of this movement'.[58]

Although, after the conclusion of World War I, the Union government did come forward to give financial assistance to the School of Mines in its new ventures, F.S. Malan continued to apply a brake to Johannesburg's ambitions. Long convinced that a university in Johannesburg would prove a very expensive proposition for the government, he believed that Johannesburg's proposals showed scant regard for the demands of economy, or for the interests of other centres. He consequently refused the School of Mines permission to establish either an agricultural faculty or a veterinary college, and compounded resentment in Johannesburg by providing for a veterinary college at Onderstepoort near Pretoria. In early 1919 he sought to block the foundation of a medical school in Johannesburg by refusing, under the terms of the Anatomy Act of 1911, to permit the dissection of the human body in the Witwatersrand area. He soon gave way on the issue, but his actions confirmed his reputation as an enemy of higher education in Johannesburg, or as J.H. Hofmeyr put it, 'the cruel step-mother to our Cinderella'.[59]

In his parting shot as Minister of Education, prior to the general election of February 1921, Malan indicated that he would not give his approval to the application Johannesburg had made in late 1920 for a university charter. He intimated that the secession of Johannesburg from the University of South Africa would bring about a major disruption of the federal university. In his opinion the time was not yet ripe for either the college at Johannesburg or Pretoria to withdraw. Following the merging of the Unionist with the South African Party, and the general election of February 1921, Malan was replaced as Minister of Education by Patrick Duncan. With his blessing the private bill, granting Johannesburg a university charter, introduced by Richard Feetham was carried. Johannesburg at last possessed a university.

To many outside Johannesburg, the idea of the town serving as the home of a university still seemed absurd. In August 1921 Sir George Cory, of Rhodes

University College and a well-known historian of South Africa, wrote to W.M. Macmillan, the new Professor of History in Johannesburg:

> Yes, we noted that you want to become a university on your own. I don't see why you shouldn't — your aims and objects seem to be so different from the rest of us — of course I don't know the details, but are you not really a big (very big) Technical Institute where the hard-up and struggling workingman wants to get some sort of diploma by attending evening classes? Is it true that compulsory subjects for your B.A. are banking, bootlace-making, painting and house-decorating? With Yiddish as the medium? I should think that whitewashing would be a very useful M.A. subject in a country such as this.[60]

Cory's letter spoke volumes for the prejudices that had hampered Johannesburg's efforts to establish its own university.

Notes

1. *The Transvaal: Debates of Both Houses of Parliament,* Extraordinary Session of the 1st Parliament, 1910, 209.
2. *Sunday Times,* 26 March 1916.
3. T.T.I. Register.
4. *Magazine: S.A. School of Mines and Technology,* No. 1 (Oct. 1914), 6.
5. Ibid., 32.
6. Ibid., 6.
7. 'The administration of College House', Dec. 1910, S.A.S.M.T. Documents 1910–12; S.A.S.M.T. Council minutes, 20 Dec. 1910 & 5 Dec. 1912.
8. Ibid., 2 Aug., 2 & 9 Oct. & 12 Dec. 1912.
9. See Boucher, 'Transformation of the University of the Cape of Good Hope'.
10. Quoted in Robertson, 'The University of Cape Town 1918–1968', 8.
11. Wernher to Phillips, 20 July 1910, Eckstein & Co. Record Dept., HE 145.
12. *Correspondence in Regard to a National University,* H. of A. No. 2 of 1913, 30–33.
13. Lionel Phillips, *Some Reminiscences* (London, 1920), 207–8.
14. *Report of the University Commission,* U.G. 42 of 1914, para. 226.
15. Boucher, 'Transformation of the University of the Cape of Good Hope', 73.
16. S.A.S.M.T. Council minutes, 25 Jan. 1911; and *University Commission,* appendix X.
17. Ibid., appendix X & XI.
18. *De Burger,* 26 March 1916.
19. *University Commission,* appendix III, for matriculation statistics; minutes of evidence, 6093, for Milner's 'very optimistic estimate of the white population Johannesburg will be able to maintain'.
20. Ibid., 5320.
21. S.A.S.M.T. Council minutes, 30 March 1914.
22. *University Commission,* paras 255–61.

23. Reunert at the Johannesburg Town Hall, 17 March 1916, quoted in Witwatersrand University Committee, *Correspondence between His Worship the Mayor of Johannesburg and Sir Lionel Phillips* (Johannesburg, 1916).
24. Ritchie, *South African College,* II, 634–8; Boucher, *Spes in Ardus,* 134.
25. O'Hara to Phillips, 28 March 1916, *Correspondence.*
26. Beit to Beattie, 11 Nov. 1918, Beattie Collection BC 215 20.9 in the University of Cape Town Libraries.
27. Quoted in *South African Universities: Witwatersrand Mayor's Protest* (Johannesburg, Feb. 1916).
28. See N.G. Garson, 'South Africa and World War I', *Journal of Imperial and Commonwealth History,* 3, 1 (Oct. 1979).
29. Minutes of the syndic of the Council of Education, 1 March 1916, MS. Council of Education A. 4.1.
30. Duncan to Hartog, 3 April 1916, MS. Duncan B.C. 294 A 32.51.
31. For the incident of the tug see E. Rosenthal, 'History of the University of the Witwatersrand' (unpublished MSS., University Archives), 254.
32. Duncan to Hartog, 3 April 1916.
33. For financial reasons Hansard was not published during the war years. For the above debates see the *Cape Times,* 3 & 7 March 1916.
34. Duncan to Hartog, 3 April 1916.
35. *Star,* 8 March 1916.
36. See *The University Question: Report of the Speeches delivered at a Public Meeting of Citizens in the Town Hall Johannesburg* (Johannesburg, March 1916).
37. Telegrams reprinted in *Correspondence between His Worship the Mayor of Johannesburg and Sir Lionel Phillips.*
38. Ibid.; J. Tyndall to Duncan, 24 March 1916, MS. Duncan B.C. 294 A 32.47; O'Hara to Phillips, 18, 20 & 28 March 1916, in *Correspondence.*
39. Duncan to Hartog, 3 April 1916.
40. *Cape Times,* 28 March 1916.
41. Ibid., 2 & 4 April 1916.
42. Minutes of the Council of Education, 14 April 1916, MS. Council of Education Ab. 3.1.
43. For Duncan see Alan Paton, *Hofmeyr* (London, 1964), 87.
44. *R.D.M.,* 30 July 1919.
45. R. Christie, '"Slim Jannie" and the Forces of Production: South African Industrialization, 1915–1925', *I.C.S. Collected Seminar Papers,* No. 22 (1977).
46. *Star,* 26 Feb. 1920.
47. Ibid., 18 Feb. 1921.
48. Ibid., 17 Feb. 1921.
49. O'Hara to E.A. Wallers, 22 Nov. 1916, Transvaal Chamber of Mines O.I. 5.
50. Extracts from letters received from committee members regarding the draft programme, Witwatersrand University Committee minutes, etc., 1917–18.
51. Witwatersrand University Committee, 'Appeal for Funds', May 1919.
52. *R.D.M.,* 3 July 1917.
53. *Star,* 16 Feb. 1921.
54. S.A.S.M.T. Council minutes, 3 Nov. 1911.
55. *R.D.M.,* 8 Dec. 1919.
56. Paton, *Hofmeyr,* 78; Evans to Malan, 6 March 1919, MS. F.S. Malan, ACC. 583, vol. 14.
57. S.A.S.M.T. Council minutes, 4 March 1919.
58. Witwatersrand University Committee, 'Proceedings at Annual General Meeting held on 20th. May, 1921'.
59. Ibid.
60. W.M. Macmillan, *My South African Years* (Cape Town, 1975), 148.

PART II
The New University

3
A TURBULENT BEGINNING

I

WEDNESDAY 1 March 1922 was designated as 'the appointed day' for the inauguration of the University of the Witwatersrand, Johannesburg. No ceremony marked the occasion. Indeed, for the general public nothing had happened but a change in name. There was no move of headquarters from Plein Square, for the building programme at Milner Park was still in its very early stages, and few new departments were established.

Some attempts had been made to plan an inauguration ceremony, but on 7 February the Council decided that 'circumstances' required its postponement. 'Circumstances' were indeed most uncomfortable both within and without the new University. A major storm was brewing over the enforced resignation of the Professor of Anatomy, and hardly had the University opened for its first session when classes had to be cancelled as Johannesburg and the Witwatersrand were engulfed by civil war. On 10 March General Smuts, the Prime Minister, proclaimed martial law, and came to Johannesburg to direct operations personally against the striking white mine workers. With the strikers entrenched in Fordsburg, and along the Brixton ridge, to the west of Milner Park, Smuts used the Biology block nearing completion at the University's Milner Park site to survey the scene and plan the attack on Cottesloe school and the ridge. The fighting along the Rand lasted for four days, and 153 people were killed before the strikers were finally subdued. The University's own sympathies in the conflict were never in question. The strikers, though they were battling to preserve the colour bar in the mining industry, were seen as 'Bolsheviks'. Staff and students alike, many of them veterans of the Great War and intensely loyal to Smuts, rallied to the defence of law and order. Those who did not enlist volunteered as special constables to patrol the streets and suburbs. R.W. Taylor, a commerce student, and L.F. Gregorowski, an assistant lecturer in law and son of the judge, made 'the

First graduation ceremony, 4 October 1922
Standing: Professor J.H. Hofmeyr (Principal); Sir William Dalrymple (Chairman of Council); H.J. Hofmeyr (President of Convocation)
Seated: General Smuts; Prince Arthur of Connaught (Chancellor); Sir Robert Kotze (Vice-Chancellor); Theodore Reunert

supreme sacrifice' in responding 'to the call of duty in connection with the revolutionary outbreak'.[1]

The inauguration ceremony, and the University's first graduation, were finally held on the morning of 4 October at the Town Hall. They were presided over by Prince Arthur of Connaught, Governor-General of the Union of South Africa and Chancellor of the new University. Despite his earlier opposition to a university in Johannesburg, Smuts was awarded the University's first honorary degree. The other recipient of an honorary degree was Theodore Reunert, in recognition of his valuable services to education on the Witwatersrand. In the afternoon, Prince Arthur laid the foundation stone of the central block then under construction at Milner Park.

II

The form of government of the new university was provided for in the private Act establishing the University of the Witwatersrand, and in the statutes drafted in accordance with the Act by a joint committee of Council and Senate of the University College, Johannesburg, and approved by Parliament.

The Act and the statutes recognized seven constituent elements in the government of the University. The University was to possess a Chancellor who as its head conferred all degrees. A Vice-Chancellor, elected by the Council from its own members, was to act for the Chancellor when necessary and was *ex officio* a member of the Senate. These were largely ceremonial posts. The effective head of the University was to be the Principal, appointed by the Council to exercise 'general supervision' subject 'to such regulations as may be framed by the Council'. The Principal was *ex officio* a member of the Council, and chairman and chief executive officer of the Senate. He was also eligible for the office of Vice-Chancellor. The governing and executive authority in the University was vested in the Council, consisting of the Principal, eight appointees of the Governor-General, three appointees of the Witwatersrand Council of Education, the Mayor of Johannesburg, three representatives of Senate, two persons elected by Convocation, and two persons elected by past students and major donors. The Senate, composed of the Principal, Vice-Chancellor, two additional members of Council, and the professors and heads of departments of the University, was to regulate 'the discipline and instruction of the several departments, lectures, and classes' of the University. The University was to include several faculties, and boards of these faculties, under a dean, were to serve as committees of the Senate for the purposes of recommending syllabi, courses of study, and examinations within each faculty. Finally, there was to be a Convocation, consisting of the graduates and academic staff of the University. It was empowered to elect the Chancellor, as well as two members of Council, and to discuss and state its opinion on any matters relating to the University. Convocation was to meet annually, and when specially summoned.

Under the statutes Senate was allocated rights of initiative in purely academic matters, and rights of consultation in academic appointments. In consultation with the Senate, Council was to appoint the professors, lecturers, and other teachers of the University, and no head of department was to be dismissed by Council except after consultation with the Senate. Senate was given no direct voice, other than through its representatives on Council, in the appointment of the Principal, or in the control of the University's finance. These were reserved entirely for the Council.

This system of government was derived from those new civic universities that had emerged in Britain since 1870. It was a diarchy, with the great mass of power vested in the Council, in which the lay members were in a strong majority, while power over strictly academic matters was vested in the academic Senate. In British university charters in the nineteenth century the trend had been to assert the powers of Council while limiting Senate to an advisory role in purely academic matters. The charter of the University of Birmingham in 1900, as a classic instance, had contained a veritable 'litany' of the overriding powers of Council, conferring on that body the general power 'to review and control or disallow any act of the Senate and give directions to be obeyed by the Senate'.[2] Subsequently the tendency then had been for charters to give greater weight to the role of Senate, providing for its participation in appointments and in general legislation as well as for its effective control in purely academic matters.

Power was vested in Councils in the nineteenth century because they undertook financial responsibility for the new civic universities. Lacking the endowments of the older universities, and until very late in the century without significant state support, the new universities were almost entirely dependent on fees and the fund-raising activities of their Councils. Given the parochial nature of these universities, their Councils tended to be dominated by local notables, and the funds they solicited came very largely from local businessmen.[3]

The University of the Witwatersrand, founded as a state-supported university, received from the state a liberal subsidy. The state, in turn, had a large representation on the University Council. In the relations between the University and the state, the main constitutional checks imposed on the autonomy of the University related to the dismissal of academic staff, its use of public funds, and amendments to its constitution. To protect members of the academic staff against unfair dismissal it was laid down that no professor, lecturer, or other teacher might be dismissed from his office without the consent of the Minister of Education. To protect the funds given by the state to the University, it was laid down that while the University was free to establish such new departments as it might deem fit, no money granted to the University from public funds might be applied to these departments, except with the consent of the Governor-General. Amendments to the University's statutes and regulations were required to be submitted to the Minister of Education and tabled in both Houses of Parliament for approval.

The severest checks on the University's autonomy concerned the use of public funds. Save in rare instances, as when the Native Recruiting Corporation and the Witwatersrand Native Labour Association provided the funding for a Department of Bantu Studies on a temporary basis, the University was initially dependent on government approval for major new developments. In 1922, the University's Council in effect exercised no real discretion as to how it might utilize grants given by the state. The regulations framed under the Higher Education Additional Provision Act 1917 determined that government grants were given in aid of specific items of expenditure. The government grant towards salaries amounted to three-quarters of the approved salaries of all officers whose posts had received government recognition; the grant towards maintenance and general expenses represented one-half of the expenditure incurred by the University in the previous year; and the grant towards the debt charges on government loans amounted to three-quarters of the charge. As the report of the Adamson Committee on university subsidies in 1933 commented, 'No doubt the policy of directing the flow of government assistance along specific channels was deliberate and was adopted in order to retain a considerable measure of control over the new experiment in higher education.'[4]

In 1923/4, following the recommendations of a departmental committee, a new formula for university grants was adopted to allow universities more freedom in allocating the resources at their disposal. The previously separate and specific grants for operating expenses were merged in a single general purposes grant, and Council, when applying it to the general expenses of the University, was permitted to use its discretion. As the Adamson Committee put it, 'The centre of gravity of control, we might say, shifted from the government to the institutions.'

Relaxation of government control meant that the University now enjoyed substantial autonomy. This is not to imply that henceforth relations between state and University were to be smooth. But further controversy lay in the future. Of immediate importance was the question dramatically raised during the University's first year of existence, namely that of how its constitution was to work in practice, and in particular the relative status of Council and Senate in the running of the University.

III

1922 was by far the most turbulent year in the University's history. The Milner Park campus has never since been used as a base for domestic military operations, and while the University has since been involved in many a *cause célèbre*, none has rivalled in its bitter intensity the altercation over the resignation of Professor E.P. Stibbe, the Head of the Department of Anatomy and former Dean of the Faculty of Medicine of the University of South Africa. The affair, which started under the University College, put to an early test the new University constitution, and provided both Council and Senate with an unfortunate start to their relations as the governing bodies of the University.

The three representatives of Senate apart, the Council of the new University was virtually self-chosen. Excluding its statutory component, its members were drawn almost entirely from mining and professional groups. The membership of the new Council was settled by the Council of the University College in December 1921. At its meeting on 6 December a list was drawn up of eight persons who were duly nominated to serve as the Governor-General's nominees on the Council of the University. Seven were members of the old Council: Alexander Aiken, a leading Johannesburg accountant; John Emrys Evans, vice-chairman of the National Bank of South Africa and a director of Johannesburg Consolidated Investment, one of the major mining groups; Sir Robert Kotze, the government mining engineer; Robert Niven, partner in a local firm of construction engineers and contractors; Bernard Price, chief engineer of the Victoria Falls and Transvaal Power Company; Senator W.K. Tucker, the government land surveyor; and Mr Justice Charles Ward of the Transvaal Provincial Division of the Supreme Court. The one newcomer was Sir Julius Jeppe, chairman and managing director of the South African Townships, Mining, and Finance Corporation and also chairman of the Johannesburg Hospital Board. As Jan Hofmeyr, the Principal, had informed the Secretary for Education in Pretoria, Jeppe was needed on the Council to assist with the development of the medical school. Three stalwarts of the old Council, Samuel Evans, Theodore Reunert, and the chairman William Dalrymple, who had been given a baronetcy in 1920, were appointed to the new Council by the Witwatersrand Council of Education. It was further arranged that two other stalwarts, Henry John Hofmeyr and Professor J.G. Lawn, now joint managing director as well as consulting engineer of Johannesburg Consolidated Investment, would serve as the nominees of Convocation. As it was delicately phrased in the Council minutes of 6 December, it was 'understood that Professor Lawn and Mr H.J. Hofmeyr would be nominated as representatives of the Convocation'. In a complaint later entered by Professor R.A. Lehfeldt, one of the Senate's representatives on Council, it was alleged that Lawn and Hofmeyr were returned by highly irregular means. Though required by the University's interim statutes, the notice advising members of Convocation of their right to submit nominations was never sent. Consequently, Lawn and Hofmeyr were returned unchallenged.[5]

The two *ex officio* members of the Council were the Mayor of Johannesburg and the Principal, and in December 1921 it was determined that Jan Hendrik Hofmeyr would be the University's first Principal. In November Council had unanimously requested Hofmeyr to accept appointment as Principal for another three years, beginning in March 1922, when the new University would come into being. Hofmeyr indicated his willingness, provided Senate agreed. At the Council of 6 December Professor R.B. Young, a Senate representative on Council, reported that Senate concurred in Hofmeyr's re-appointment, and Hofmeyr accepted.

Two mining men, both graduates of the Kimberley School of Mines, were elected to represent past students on the Council: E.C.J. Meyer, general manager of the East Rand Proprietary Mines, and W.H. Visser, chief surveyor for Johannesburg Consolidated Investment. Senate's representatives on the new Council were elected on 1 March 1922, at the first meeting of the Senate of the University of the Witwatersrand. Professor Young, Head of the Department of Geology and secretary of the Senate, was re-elected, and was joined by Professors R.A. Lehfeldt, Head of the Department of Economics, and C.E. Moss, Head of the Department of Botany. The two newcomers were highly critical of Hofmeyr, and particularly his actions and those of the old Council which led to the resignation of Professor Stibbe.

Prior to the Stibbe affair, although never loved, Hofmeyr had generally been respected by the academic staff of the University College. They recognized him to be a virtual genius, and it was felt that his prodigious achievements as a student brought credit to the College of which he was Principal. He had matriculated at the age of twelve, and graduated from the University of the Cape of Good Hope with first-class honours at fifteen. He completed a second bachelors degree at sixteen, and his masters in classics at seventeen. He wrote a biography of his uncle Onze Jan Hofmeyr the following year, and then went up to Balliol College, Oxford, as a Rhodes scholar, where he was awarded a double first. In 1917 he had been appointed Professor of Classics at the School of Mines, and in 1919, Principal. As Principal he established a formidable reputation as an administrator, displaying great efficiency and an amazing grasp of detail. He forgot nothing. He was also a skilled diplomatist, able to settle differences between conflicting parties with both firmness and justice. None the less, by the time of his resignation he had alienated most of his colleagues, and had precipitated a serious crisis of management.

In part, what Hofmeyr lacked was physical presence and style. G.E. Pearse, the University's first Professor of Architecture, has recalled: 'He was an amazing man, shabbily dressed but he had control of everything.' He captured people's attention by his command of words, not by his appearance. Appearance did not concern him. He wore ill-fitting, crumpled suits, and cycled each day to Plein Square, invariably emerging at his office with bicycle pump in hand. Legend has it that when Stibbe first arrived at Park Station, and was met by Hofmeyr, he supposed the Principal to be the college handyman, and gave him his heaviest bag to carry.

As Principal Hofmeyr was generally admired by the students. He was flexible in dealing with them, and knew them all by name. He was none the less felt to be remote, by staff as well as students. Few on the staff regarded him as a colleague, and fewer still as a friend. Even his old Balliol friend, John Macmurray, who came to Johannesburg as Professor of Philosophy, found him cold, and the friendship was never really renewed. He was seen as too much the authoritarian, and his attempts to 'clean up' the University College, and thereby ensure its moral standing and decorum, caused particular resentment among staff. Those who suffered through his interventions in their private affairs, and apparently they were many, resented the authority Hofmeyr chose to exercise. In the quarrel over Stibbe this resentment found full expression.[6]

Hofmeyr was thus, in some ways, an unfortunate choice as Principal. His academic and administrative capacity was exceptional, and his understanding of what a South African university could be was, in many ways, ahead of the times. But he was handicapped by his youth and inexperience, his rigid interpretation of sexual mores, and a reluctance to contain his mother's meddling in University College business. In the Stibbe affair, moreover, he displayed a regrettable inability to accept that he might have made a mistake.

Mrs Hofmeyr was a powerful influence in her son's life when he was appointed Principal of the School of Mines, and continued to be so when three

Jan Hofmeyr and mother

years later, at the age of 27, he became Principal of Wits University. She was a very formidable woman. Even Smuts, who was afraid of no man, was reputedly afraid of Mrs Hofmeyr. She was overwhelmingly possessive and protective towards Hofmeyr, and accompanied him virtually everywhere he went. A standard College joke was that Mr Hofmeyr and the Principal had been seen together at Milner Park. The part of the College's life which concerned her most was its moral welfare, and her moral code was evidently simple in content, and severely applied. When the women's residence was opened at Milner Park alongside College House, the men's residence in which the Principal and his mother were installed pending the construction of a Principal's house, Mrs Hofmeyr apparently took it upon herself to spy on the girls through field-glasses to ascertain whether they kept their curtains closed when dressing. After one year at Milner Park the women were moved to Sunnyside in Parktown, and both campus residences were reserved for men. The move served a double purpose: it rescued the girls of Roedean School from the prying eyes of men students at Sunnyside, and the girls of Wits from the prying eyes of College House. Mrs Hofmeyr's interest and censure in these matters extended to the behaviour of staff. They were expected to set an example of unblemished moral probity to the youth in their charge.

Hofmeyr apparently shared his mother's puritan values. The two together were ferociously frugal. At Oxford, Hofmeyr had managed to save a large portion of his Rhodes scholarship, and boasted of it. As dean at Milner Park he sought to contain hostel costs by such expedients as regulating the supply of hot water, and even reducing the amount of water in the cisterns in the women's residence. On sexual matters Hofmeyr was strongly puritan and to all appearances not interested in women. Probably the closest he ever came to sharing a bed with a woman was when the students at College House placed a female anatomical model in his bed, a prank that could have done nothing to encourage him to look favourably on either the Anatomy Department, or its head.[7]

Mrs Hofmeyr, by all accounts, was an irrepressible scandalmonger. The University folklore is clear that it was she who persuaded her son to take action against Professor Stibbe, for his unconventional relationship with a College typist.

Stibbe is reputed to have been loved by his students and both appreciated and liked by his colleagues. He was an accepted authority on his subject, had contributed to *Gray's Anatomy,* and was a fine teacher. 'As a dissector', Dr Lawrie Adler has recalled, 'he had no equal, as a teacher he had few peers, as a man he was unique.' In late December 1921, when most of the academic staff had already left town for the summer vacation, Stibbe resigned under duress, as a consequence of action initiated by the Principal.

Sir William Dalrymple

E.P. Stibbe

Some time during 1921, Stibbe's wife and children had gone to the coast for a holiday, Mrs Stibbe having arranged for her husband to stay in a boarding-house run by the mother of the head College typist, Miss Frances Roy. Stibbe took Miss Roy to the cinema on several occasions, and soon discovered that the lady was better company than his wife. The liaison continued after the return of Mrs Stibbe. This relationship was so overt that the Principal felt constrained to speak to Professor Stibbe, who advised Hofmeyr that it was none of his business. On 16 November Stibbe was informed in writing by Hofmeyr that his liaison should end. Two and a half weeks later Stibbe received another letter, this time advising him that he should end his connection with the University College. This letter, dated 2 December, quoted the resolution by the Council that day: 'That the Council is of opinion that Dr Stibbe's connection with the College should be severed; that he be informed of this, and that, if it is his desire to do so, he may bring the matter to the notice of the Senate.'[8]

Council's resolution was in response to Hofmeyr's demand that Stibbe leave the College. Council shared Hofmeyr's view that members of the academic staff were not simply teachers, but should offer a moral example to their students, and it was no doubt anxious to counter the notion that Johannesburg was not morally suited to be a university centre. But at no stage did Council dismiss Stibbe. Council's resolution, though it gave the impression of dismissal, did not serve notice on Stibbe. Rather it advised him that it was its opinion that he should go. The process of dismissal itself was a veritable quagmire, and the Council was neither sure of its rights nor of the procedure to be followed. The Act of the Transvaal Parliament which established the School of Mines, and applied to the University College, empowered Council to 'terminate' engagements of both teaching and administrative staff. However, the Act which established the University of the Witwatersrand required the consent of the Minister of Education before Council might dismiss a member of the academic staff, and the University's statutes stated that Council might dismiss a head of department only after consultation with the Senate. Council's resolution had intimated that Stibbe might refer to the Senate, but made no mention of the minister. At its next meeting on 6 December, which was rather better attended, Council decided the question of Stibbe's removal required full investigation. Consequently a four-man committee headed by Mr Justice Ward was appointed to examine the procedure and principles to be adopted on questions of dismissal or termination of contract.

This committee reported back on 13 December. The report, which has not survived, was adopted, and the subsequent action of Council provides a fairly clear guide to its contents. Council was warned of the problems involved in a confrontation with Senate, and possible appeal to the minister, that an action for dismissal would entail, and was advised the wiser course would be to persuade Stibbe to resign. A three-man committee, consisting of Mr Justice Ward, H.J. Hofmeyr, and Professor Young, was instructed to approach Stibbe. On 23 December Young reported to Council that Stibbe 'had requested him to hand in his resignation from the Chair of Anatomy, to take effect from 1st July, 1922'. Council agreed to accept the resignation and to thank Stibbe for his services to the University.

It is likely that it was at this meeting that Council took the highly irregular decision to destroy the original minutes of the meeting of 2 December, and to substitute revised minutes which did not mention the resolution against Stibbe. The official minutes would then contain no evidence that Council, after only a single meeting and in breach of the rules of natural justice, had decided against Stibbe before his resignation. Hofmeyr was evidently not happy about this move. At the meeting of 6 December he had declared that Council must choose between Stibbe and himself. To protect his own position for the future, in the absence of an official minute, he required the chairman of Council to prepare and sign the following statement:

That the Council is of opinion that Dr Stibbe's conduct has been such as to render desirable the severance of his connection with the College. Endorsed at meeting of 23rd Dec. 1921.

W. Dalrymple
Chairman[9]

Stibbe afterwards claimed he was obliged to resign under duress. Of the three men who had interviewed him, Ward and Hofmeyr claimed that he was never threatened with dismissal, but Young believed he was told he would be dismissed if he refused to resign.[10] The official stance adopted by Council was that the committee had never been instructed to present Stibbe with the alternatives of dismissal or resignation, and that Stibbe's resignation represented a voluntary agreement with the committee.[11]

When news of Stibbe's resignation, and the circumstances leading to it, filtered out, the academic staff who knew him were outraged, and animosity to Hofmeyr and his meddling mother flared into the open.

As Patrick Duncan, the Minister of Education, explained in a letter to Lady Selborne in England, the central issue in the Stibbe affair was whether a man's personal conduct should affect his status as a professor:

> ... the Senate of the University – about 30 professors and lecturers – are in a state of rebellion over the compulsory retirement of one of their number because of some domestic complications. The professors took the view that if one of them discovered too late that he preferred another lady to his wife and thereby caused domestic trouble and public scandal he was none the worse a professor for that. The council on the other hand being respectable bourgeois took quite a different view and he resigned.[12]

But there was more to it than that. Apart from the issue of whether or not Stibbe had been forced to resign by unfair means, there was the substantive principle of who should sit in judgement on the honour or competence of a member of the professorial staff. Senate claimed the right of judicature at first instance, and that for Council to have proceeded against Stibbe without reference to it was unconstitutional. What was ultimately at stake for Senate was its role, and relationship to Council, in the government of the University.

The Senate at Plein Square had long been noted for its assertiveness, particularly concerning its own status or in matters affecting the rights of the academic staff. The professionalism displayed by the Johannesburg professors at the meetings of the Senate of the University of South Africa had certainly impressed the other members of that body, who considered themselves babes-in-the-wood in comparison. When the School of Mines officially became the

University College, Johannesburg, in 1921 the local Senate had finally secured one of its long-standing aims in gaining representation on Council. The next year, when the University was established, Senate's representation on Council was increased from two to three.

Senate took up the cudgels on behalf of Stibbe, with both conviction and determination, at an extraordinary meeting on 27 February 1922, passing by twenty-two votes to one a resolution condemning Council's action. The sole dissentient, Professor W.M. Macmillan, the Head of the Department of History and a friend of the Hofmeyrs, saw the resolution as essentially a vote of no confidence in the Principal. 'Rightly or wrongly', he has recalled in his autobiography, 'I felt I must stand by Hofmeyr, since it seemed to me that the senate of sophisticated academics was being unduly harsh towards a young and inexperienced principal.'[13] But, in the battle of wills that followed between the 'sophisticated academics' of the Senate and the resolute lawyers and businessmen of the Council, it was the former who were to be outmanoeuvred and bested.

For the Senate meeting on 27 February Stibbe had prepared a statement which charged that he had been 'forced out of his position for insufficient reasons and by unfair means'.[14] The men who had encouraged him to make the statement, and to attempt to get the Council to reinstate him, were John Macmurray, who destroyed his friendship with Hofmeyr by assisting Stibbe, J.P. Dalton, the Professor of Mathematics and a very powerful personality, and C.M. Drennan, the Professor of English. Their concern was twofold: to rescue Stibbe's career, and to establish the rights of Senate in disciplinary matters concerning academic staff. At the meeting of 27 February, Senate duly established a committee to examine the University statutes as they pertained to the whole question of conditions of service for academic staff.

The meeting at the end of February proved perhaps the most bitter and stormy of all. For Hofmeyr, who as Principal was chairman of the Senate, it must have been an intolerable experience. Senate meetings, with their comparatively small membership, were necessarily claustrophobic affairs. Hofmeyr could not avoid a very personal confrontation with his critics, and the nervous twitching of his face made his acute discomfort apparent.

Hofmeyr first sought to silence Stibbe by ruling him out of order, and conveying Council's instruction 'that Prof. Stibbe had resigned, that his resignation had been accepted, and that on no account could the case be reopened'. Senate promptly overruled the Principal, and Stibbe was allowed to present his statement, though Hofmeyr advised at a later meeting that Mr Justice Ward had upheld the validity of the ruling from the chair and consequently, 'any resolution passed in contravention thereof could not, if challenged, be maintained as a resolution binding the Senate'. Stibbe, like Hofmeyr, was extremely tense when he presented his statement. He was also very angry, and this led him to make a personal attack on the Principal's mother, whom he denounced as the cause of all his troubles. That brought Hofmeyr to his feet, declaring that the discussion could not continue unless Mrs Hofmeyr's name was left out. Stibbe, overcome by the whole business, then sat down. At a later meeting he indicated that he was prepared to withdraw the remarks he had made about Mrs Hofmeyr.

This stormy meeting was the last of the Senate of the University College, and the first meetings in March of both the Council and Senate of the new University were concerned with formal and procedural matters, including the election of Sir Robert Kotzé as Vice-Chancellor. At one stage it had been intended that Hofmeyr should be made Vice-Chancellor, but Council decided to give the post to Kotzé instead.

At the end of March Senate returned to the Stibbe affair, and successfully requested the reception of a deputation to place 'the Senate's position clearly before the Council'. There followed a prolonged fencing match between Senate and Council, with Council generally managing to counter the lunges made by Senate. It simply rejected Senate's contention that Stibbe had been forced to resign by being presented with the alternative of dismissal and should therefore be given the chance to reconsider his resignation. At the crucial meeting of 4 April, Council turned down Professor Young's motion proposing a compromise settlement that would allow Stibbe to keep his chair. Instead, Professor Lawn's motion refusing to consider Stibbe's resignation as null and void was accepted. In part this motion stated:

> The Council had arrived at no decision in regards to the merits of the Case when the suggestion was made for the appointment of a Committee to confer with Professor Stibbe. It gave no instructions to the Committee to present him with such alternative [resignation as an alternative to dismissal]. Of the three Members of the Committee two have definitely informed the Council that no such alternative was presented. The third now merely states that Professor Stibbe was told there was a probability of dismissal if he did not resign. The Council therefore regards the arrangement come to with Professor Stibbe as an honourable agreement. It regrets that he should have sought to go back on it.

It added that to satisfy Senate of its 'desire to do justice at all costs' Council was prepared, should Senate so desire, to ask the minister to appoint an investigator into 'the question of whether or not any injustice has been done to Professor Stibbe'. Should the minister's verdict go against Council it promised to 'take appropriate action to redress the wrong'.

This offer of what was in effect an arbitration between itself and Professor Stibbe was the best made by Council; beyond that it would not go. It was an offer Senate treated with deep suspicion. In its reply to Council on 10 April, Senate implied that Council had misrepresented the facts in its claim that, when a committee was appointed in mid-December to confer with Stibbe, no decision on the merits of the case had been taken. The letter to Stibbe dated 2 December proved Council had already made up its mind. Senate then pointed out that, as it had not been informed of the charge or charges made against Professor Stibbe, it would find it difficult to decide what terms of reference would provide a satisfactory basis for arbitration proceedings. More damaging, Senate desired to know how a satisfactory investigation and arbitration would be possible 'if, as has been officially stated, the records have been destroyed'. Senate concluded by appealing for an internal settlement by mutual agreement between itself and Council, but intimated that, failing such a settlement, it would accept arbitration.

For almost two months Council, Senate, and Stibbe continued to haggle over the arbitration offer. Senate firmly advised Stibbe not to accept the terms of arbitration offered by Council, as these placed the onus on Stibbe to maintain his charge that he was forced out of his position for insufficient reasons and by unfair means. Instead Senate urged a full inquiry within the University into the events leading to Stibbe's resignation. Council refused to be moved, advising Senate at the end of May that as its offer had not been acceded to, proceedings should be initiated to appoint Stibbe's successor. Thereupon Stibbe and the Senate gave way. On 2 June Colonel Stallard, K.C., was appointed arbitrator.

Senate later came to the conclusion that the choice of Stallard as arbitrator was unfortunate. Like Hofmeyr, he was a bachelor and a puritan. The text of his award has not survived, but he found that Stibbe had resigned voluntarily, and that there was, therefore, no case for his reinstatement.[15] The award was read by Hofmeyr to Council at its meeting on 24 July, and to Senate at its meeting the next day. He appealed to Senate to accept the award, and consider the matter closed. The appeal was met by a frigid silence.

Hofmeyr was hoping for the impossible if he supposed that matters would now rest. Feelings had run too high for that. Professor Eustace Cluver, Stibbe's partner at the medical school and a boyhood friend of Hofmeyr, has recalled, the Principal had no conception of the contempt and anger most members of the Senate had for the award. They believed they had been outmanoeuvred, and were determined on retribution. Nor were members of the Council inclined to be magnanimous in their victory. They had been outraged by Senate's insubordinate behaviour in questioning and challenging the actions of Council, and some members of Council were most anxious to see Senate put firmly in its place. 'As for the Senate', Alexander Aiken wrote to Hofmeyr, 'they will have to be dealt firmly with, but the better sort amongst them must surely realise how far astray they have gone.'[16]

One of the most unpleasant months in the history of the University, and according to Paton's biography the most desperate in Hofmeyr's life, followed the handing down of the Stallard award. Senate moved into full-scale rebellion, and showed itself quite prepared to destroy the Principal. When Macmurray led a deputation to the Principal, and Hofmeyr asked, 'What shall I do?', Macmurray replied, 'You must resign, the whole staff is against you.'[17]

At a series of Senate meetings at the end of July and the beginning of August, the two-man committee of Professors J.P. Dalton and J.M. Watt appointed to watch the arbitration proceedings reported back. To Hofmeyr's acute discomfort Dalton focused particularly on the evidence given by the Principal in the arbitration, and the nature of the charges he had made against Stibbe. At the meeting of 4 August, at the request of the Senate, Hofmeyr was forced to make a statement about his evidence. Then, according to the minutes:

> In answer to a request by Prof. Drennan, the Principal then made the following statements:-
> That he had nothing to say against the moral character of Professor Stibbe.
> That he considered Professor Dalton to be a man of the highest moral character.
> That certain points which had been referred to in evidence at the arbitration case should now, in his opinion, be dropped and forgotten.

On 9 August Theo Haarhoff, the Professor of Classics and another of Hofmeyr's old friends who had broken with him, proposed the motion:

> Having the full evidence of the arbitration case before it, this Senate considers that the conduct of Professor Stibbe has not been such as to make it necessary that he should sever his connection with the University.

It was withdrawn the next day after discussion.

What saved the Senate from proceeding along a path that could end only in the destruction of the Principal, and that diverted its energies into more constructive channels, was the intervention of the Minister of Education, Patrick Duncan. At the meeting of 4 August it was announced that the minister had read the award of the arbitrator, and that he requested to be allowed to attend a meeting of the Senate at which the matter could be discussed. A week later the minister arrived to address the Senate.

Hofmeyr bitterly resented Duncan's intervention, but it was designed to rescue the Principal. Duncan saw himself as coming to Johannesburg 'to beard the Senate' in the effort to make peace. He wrote to Lady Selborne of the affair that had prompted his mission:

> Professors and schoolmasters and parsons are most unreasonable people. They magnify specks of dust into rocks of offence and are always for the letter of the law as against the endless adjustments and compromises by which life goes on. They set up idols for themselves — we all do that — but they take theirs desperately seriously.[18]

Duncan met the Senate in two special sessions; on 11 August, when the meeting lasted from 2.15 to 4.45 pm, and on 16 August, from 2 to 5.35 pm. On both occasions Professor James Findlay, the Head of the Department of Accounting, presided in the absence of Hofmeyr. No official record was kept of what was said, but it seems that Duncan encouraged the Senate to accept that there was nothing further to be gained from attacking the Principal and Council, and that it should concentrate rather on helping to ensure that there would be no repetition of the recent unhappy events, and on adjusting the University's constitution so as to make it more workable. Afterwards the minister was thanked for his attendance by acclamation.

At the end of August Duncan called together a joint meeting of Council and Senate to discuss the working of the University's constitution. Subsequently, committees of both Council and Senate were established 'to confer together and report to their respective bodies in regard to the future working of the constitution of the University, so as to obtain that harmony and confidence between the Council, the Principal and the Senate, which is necessary in the best interests of the University'. The Council committee was composed of H.J. Hofmeyr, Niven, Price, Visser, and Sir Robert Kotzé. Professors Lehfeldt (convener), Dalton, Haarhoff, Macmurray, and Moss, all by now bitter critics of Hofmeyr, were elected to the Senate committee, which styled itself the reconstruction committee.

Hofmeyr himself was thoroughly alarmed by the whole development, and became even more alarmed when Council agreed to discuss the demand of Senate for direct advisory functions in the general management of the University. As he saw it, Senate had now launched a direct attack on his powers as Principal. What Senate was after, he told Duncan when the minister attended the University's inauguration ceremony on 4 October, was to 'reduce the Principal's position to that of a mere mouthpiece of the Senate'. Duncan tried to reassure him that the creation of new machinery whereby Senate might express its opinion on certain matters normally handled by the Principal did not *ipso facto* deprive the Principal of all authority and initiative, and that while it was often a trial to one's temper to have to try to carry one's colleagues instead of acting autocratically one gained by it in the end. Hofmeyr refused to be reassured. The Senate he saw as a body intent only on humbling him, and depriving him of his powers. He held the minister partly responsible for his predicament. As he wrote to Duncan:

> If you will pardon an entirely frank expression of opinion, as I know you will, I cannot help feeling that the speech made by you at the joint meeting of Senate and Council was an unfortunate one. It was in effect a rebuke to the Council, an indication that it had been wrong in its attitudes, without any corresponding rebuke to the Senate. In any case, followed up as it was by Macmurray's unrebuked impertinences which almost seemed to follow naturally on it, it had the unfortunate effect of leaving the extremist section of the Senate cock-a-hoop. They proceeded to pack the Senate side of the Committee with men of their way of thinking, declaring at the same time that the Minister had given them the chance of a lifetime, leaving them in fact free to change statutes or anything else that might be in the way of their wishes. The burden of any subsequent statements has been 'when we meet the Council's representatives, *and have the support of the Minister,* we shall do so and so'.

For Hofmeyr the immediate issue was simple, 'Either the Principal must retire, or in some way our extremist friends must be humiliated and in consequence lose their prestige with the Senate, thus enabling the Principal to recover his.'[19]

Hofmeyr did not resign, neither were the 'extremists' in the Senate humiliated. During 1923 there emerged from the deliberations of the reconstruction committee, and negotiations between Senate and Council on a variety of issues, a series of compromises that allowed Senate a greater role in the management of the University without depriving the Council and Principal of their ultimate control in non-academic matters, and a statement of conditions of appointment which more clearly defined the position and rights of academic staff. It had been Stibbe's misfortune to have run foul of the Principal and Council before the conditions of appointment in the new University had been drawn up; it was the experience of the Stibbe affair that led to the inclusion in those conditions of more precise provisions than might otherwise have been on dismissal and suspension.

The reconstruction committee of Senate certainly adopted a wide brief. But although it managed to secure concessions in a number of directions, these were all in the nature of compromises and never amounted to the surrender by Council that Hofmeyr had dreaded. This was evident from the report presented by the reconstruction committee in late April 1923. By then it had succeeded in establishing two joint committees of Senate and Council to assist the Principal. The first, a direct consequence of the Stibbe affair, was a committee of discipline to deal with complaints made against the conduct of members of the teaching staff. The second was a committee on hostels, to advise on the general control of the student residences. According to the reconstruction committee, effective control was still left in the hands of the Principal, and it complained bitterly of Council's 'grudging attitude' in allowing Senate any role in regard to the hostels. In another direction Council agreed to give Senate the right to allocate the annual departmental grants, while retaining full control over the global budget for the University, and in the view of the committee failed to meet the 'general criticisms' levied against its financial management. On one other issue, the composition of Council, the reconstruction committee at first drew a complete blank. It contended that Council did not adequately represent the community of the Witwatersrand, and urged that when the terms of appointment of Aiken and Jeppe expired in early 1923, the Governor-General should appoint in their stead the Bishop of Johannesburg and Advocate F.A.W. Lucas. This did not happen. Both Aiken, who had become chairman of the all-important finance committee of Council, and Jeppe had been firm supporters of Hofmeyr over the Stibbe affair, and the Principal strongly advised Duncan to see that they were retained on Council despite any contrary proposal from Senate. Aiken, he told the minister, was very keen and virtually indispensable, particularly on financial matters, and Jeppe was likewise a useful member of Council. Duncan listened to Hofmeyr rather than the Senate, and both Aiken and Jeppe were renominated for 1923. It was only later in the year, following the death of Mr Justice Ward, that a place was found on Council for the Bishop.[20]

After its report of 26 April 1923 the reconstruction committee seems to have faded away; there are no further references to it or its activities in the minutes of Senate. Its brief had not included conditions of appointment in the University, and these were settled by Council in direct consultation with the Senate. The initial regulations governing conditions of appointment were adopted by Council in November 1922, but a number of important additions were made during 1923, including provisions relating to suspension from duty.

On the crucial question of dismissal or termination of contract, the conditions adopted by Council in November provided essentially for the procedure to give effect to the relevant provisions in the Act and the statutes. Any member of the teaching or administrative staff had a right of appeal to the minister before dismissal. Intimation of the intention to appeal had to be given to both Council and the minister within fourteen days of the receipt of notice from the Council. The proposal of Senate that the conditions of appointment should go somewhat beyond the Act and the statutes, and that they should require Senate be consulted before any member of the teaching staff was dismissed or discharged, was turned down by Council.[21]

From Council's standpoint, the main oversight in the regulations adopted in November was that they made no provision for summary action against a member of staff, and this gap was filled during 1923 when Council devised a scheme for suspension from duty. The main negotiation with Senate was over questions of procedure. Senate proposed that notice of suspension should be given in writing to the person concerned within one month of the alleged act held to justify suspension, together with an explicit statement as to 'the nature and the time and place of occurrence of such act'. Council responded that, because of the difficulty in obtaining precise details, in many instances such a procedure would prove impractical, and proposed instead that suspension should take place within seven days after *prima facie* proof of any complaint or charge against a staff member had come into the hands of Council or the Principal. The person suspended should be informed in writing 'in such detail as may be possible' of the charges against him. This was the formula finally adopted, with the addition, at Senate's request, that the person to be suspended should, wherever possible, be given the opportunity to make a statement on the charge against him before notice was served.[22]

By late 1923, with procedures for dismissal and suspension agreed, a repetition of the Stibbe affair was rendered virtually impossible. Council continued strongly to disapprove of indulgence by members of staff in unconventional relationships, and there would still be instances of staff being harassed over their private conduct. But the cavalier treatment meted out to Stibbe could not be repeated.

In the wake of the Stibbe affair, the real problem facing the University was not so much in making readjustments in the system by which it was to run its affairs, but in repairing the damage that had been done to human relationships within the University and in restoring confidence between Council and Principal on the one hand, and Senate on the other. Hofmeyr, for the rest of his tenure as Principal, was never to regain the confidence of Senate. Never thereafter fully trusted, it was as well both for him and the University that Smuts offered him the post of Administrator of the Transvaal in February 1924. Half the Senate was prepared to sign a petition asking him to decline the offer and to remain as Principal; the other half was evidently relieved to see him go.

Nor were relations between Council and Senate quick to recover. From the standpoint of members of the Senate, Council had earned a reputation for 'bullying' that would take more than a handful of 'grudging' concessions to alter. A major improvement in relations seemed imminent when Council consulted Senate over Hofmeyr's successor, but the goodwill then created was soon dissipated by the wrangle that developed between the two bodies when the principalship again became vacant in 1927. The majority on Council refused to accept Senate's nominee as Principal, R.F.A. Hoernlé, largely because he had criticized the way in which Stibbe had been treated.

As for Stibbe, his career ultimately recovered from the devastating blow it had received. He married the university head typist, Miss Roy, who, throughout the whole affair, had continued to do Hofmeyr's typing. After first setting up practice in Johannesburg, Stibbe returned to England in 1925, and worked in the anatomy departments of Durham, Liverpool, and University College, London, before becoming Professor of Anatomy at King's College, London. He died in 1943, aged 58. In 1975 the University named one of its anatomy laboratories after him.

Notes

1. Senate minutes, II, 20 March 1922.
2. G.C. Moodie and R. Eustace, *Power and Authority in British Universities* (London, 1974), 34.
3. Michael Sanderson, *The Universities and British Industry 1850–1970* (London, 1972), 61–3.
4. *Report of the Committee of Enquiry into Subsidies to Universities, University Colleges, and Technical Colleges*, U.G.8 of 1934, 5.
5. Lehfeldt to Duncan, 22 November 1922, U.O.D. E33/12, vol. 2.
6. Paton, *Hofmeyr*, chaps 8–10.
7. The material on Hofmeyr is gleaned from Paton's biography, and taped interviews with Professors E.H. Cluver, O.G. Backeberg, and I.D. MacCrone, and Dr L. Adler.
8. Paton, *Hofmeyr*, 10; Senate minutes, II, 10 April 1922.
9. MS. Hofmeyr, Aa.
10. Council minutes, I, 3 April 1922.
11. Ibid., 4 April 1922.
12. Duncan to Lady Selborne, 15 Aug. 1922, MS. Duncan.
13. Macmillan, *My South African Years*, 151.
14. Report of Joint Committee of Council and Senate, 1 May 1922, Council Miscellaneous, I.
15. Macmillan, *My South African Years*, 151; Cluver interview.
16. Aiken to Hofmeyr, 22 July 1922, MS. Hofmeyr, Aa.
17. Paton, *Hofmeyr*, 108.
18. Duncan to Lady Selborne, 15 Aug. 1922, MS. Duncan.
19. Duncan to Hofmeyr, 7 Oct. 1922, and draft of Hofmeyr's reply, MS. Hofmeyr, Aa.
20. Report of reconstruction committee, 26 April 1923, Council Misc., I; Hofmeyr to Duncan, 1 Dec. 1922, U.O.D. E33/12, vol. 2.
21. Council minutes, I, 22 Nov. 1922.
22. Ibid., 4 May, 8 June & 10 Aug. 1923.

4

ADMINISTRATION, FINANCE, AND BUILDINGS

I

During its first six years the University of the Witwatersrand was served by two Principals. Jan Hofmeyr resigned in early 1924, and was succeeded by Sir William Thomson, who held the office until the beginning of 1928. Although their terms of office were short, their principalships were of the first importance for the development of the new University. Hofmeyr certainly left a distinct impression on the University.

Under its private Act the University was empowered to establish Faculties or Departments of Arts, Science, Commerce, Law, Medicine, Engineering, Education, Music, and Veterinary Science. In 1922 the first six were established as faculties, the last three as departments. At the beginning of 1922 there were 37 departments, and 73 members of the academic staff, including 33 professors, 12 senior lecturers, 7 lecturers, 9 junior lecturers, 3 demonstrators, 3 instructors, and 6 part-time lecturers in law, banking, medicine, and surgery. Six years later, when Humphrey Raikes took over from Sir William Thomson as Principal, the number of departments had risen to 48, and the academic staff to 191, of whom a third were officially classified as part-time. Over the same period the total number of students rose from 1 030 to 1 476. The Faculty of Arts by 1928 was firmly established as the largest single faculty with 13 departments and 571 students.

In any small university, and particularly a new university, the quality of its teaching departments depends very heavily on the calibre of its departmental heads. Whether by luck, or good judgement or some combination of both, the new University of the Witwatersrand succeeded in assembling, by the standards of the time, an excellent professoriate. With the assistance of a London committee, most had been recruited from overseas, a fairly high proportion being Scots, but even at this early stage there were several South Africans. A feature of the professorial team assembled under Hofmeyr and

Thomson was the long service many of its members were to give the University. It was essentially the team that was to lead the University into, and through, the thirties.

The principalships of Hofmeyr and Thomson also saw the campus at Milner Park assume its basic shape. By 1928 the University had completed its move from Plein Square to Milner Park, and in the instance of the medical school, to Hospital Hill. One of Hofmeyr's main achievements was to gain the government's agreement to provide £500 000 in loans for the University's building programme at Milner Park and the medical school.

II

To the great advantage of the University of the Witwatersrand its first Principal, Jan Hofmeyr, not only possessed a clear conception of what a university should be, but was able to direct its formative stages. His conception of a university, which was in advance of his times, at least for South Africa, was very different from the essentially practical and utilitarian view that had dominated the movement to establish the University. He saw and fully appreciated that the University should provide a sound practical and professional training for those who wanted it, but he was equally determined that it should be very much more than merely a school for professional training.

The criticism is sometimes made of South African universities that they are basically 'vocation-oriented'; that, regardless of where they supposedly stand ideologically, they all have served the cause of white supremacy in South Africa, producing the professionally skilled graduates who bolster the system of white supremacy in its economic, technical, and professional aspects.[1] In the years before World War II, it is certain that the professional faculties of the University of the Witwatersrand serviced rather than challenged the system of white supremacy in South Africa. A Coloured doctor, and an Indian lawyer apart, the graduates of the University's professional faculties were all whites.[2]

It was Hofmeyr's ideal for the University of the Witwatersrand that it should possess a Faculty of Arts of standing as a counterpoise to the professional faculties. More, he believed the professional faculties themselves should be open to liberal influences. In the educational sense, his conception of a university was distinctly liberal. As Principal he managed to impose something of his conception on the University of the Witwatersrand, which would probably have taken a very different shape had it not been for the influence of Hofmeyr. But on certain fundamental issues he was defeated. The university that emerged in the 1920s did not altogether fit his ideals. Certainly more professional in bias, it was perhaps rather less open in its admissions, than Hofmeyr desired.

Hofmeyr first put forward his conception of a university at the inauguration of the University College, Johannesburg, on 1 August 1919. In his speech he stressed that a university should provide very much more than a professional training: 'The primary concern of the old School of Mines was to give its students certain necessary knowledge for the practice of their profession . . . The primary concern of the University of Johannesburg would be to fit its students, not for a particular profession, but for life in general and for citizenship.' The fundamental task of a university was to provide its students with a liberal education: 'The usefulness of the knowledge which the university imparted was not the criterion of its success. People had come to regard education as a means to increase their wage-earning capacities instead of regarding the wage or salary as a means to a far higher end. People who argued that the classics would not bring in bigger dividends were blind to the fact that the value and importance of a study for educational purposes did not depend on its usefulness in that sense. The aim of a university in its propagation of knowledge was the cultivation of the intellect, and the cultivation of the intellect lay in fitting it to apprehend and contemplate truth. It would be the function of the university to see that its students did not end up merely as doctors or engineers, but also as educated men with high ideals of citizenship and service.'

The second great duty of a university, Hofmeyr continued, was 'in respect of the discovery and publication of truth'. Universities did not merely teach, they carried out research: 'Studies of all kinds lost their vitality and their educational value if they were not continually being expanded, continually securing new points of view, new correlations, new meaning.' As he stressed in some later speeches, the functions of a university with regard both to research and instruction could only be performed in a context of academic freedom, and he strongly advocated the need for diversity within a university.

The third duty of a university, Hofmeyr stated, was to the community. It should be open to all groups in the community, knowing 'no distinctions of class or wealth, race or creed', and it should provide the community with leadership, assisting it to resolve the most fundamental of its problems:

> We have still to learn much in South Africa as to the duty of the university to the State and to the community. Our colleges have in the past certainly played their part in the moulding of great men. In this respect neither of the two older colleges has reason to be ashamed of its

service to South Africa, but they have not yet produced great movements; they have not been the home of lost or any other causes. They have not, to any great extent, applied themselves to the solution of our South African problems nor to the co-ordination and direction of the thoughts of those who, scattered up and down the country, have sought to grapple with these problems. It will, I hope, be the boast of the University of Johannesburg that it is truly South African in respect of the service rendered by it to South Africa, as well as of the healthy national spirit prevailing within its walls.

He wished to see the future 'University of Johannesburg' provide South Africa with leadership to resolve 'the racial problem', by which he meant English/Afrikaans relations in the white community, to tackle the economic or 'poor White' problem, and in facing 'the native problem', the 'most difficult and yet most specially South African of them all'. The essence of this last, he stated, was 'the eternal problem of the reconciliation of justice and apparent expediency'. He added that it was a problem on which South Africa's university colleges had 'hitherto been almost entirely silent'.[3]

In several respects the University of the Witwatersrand was to serve the community along the lines suggested by Hofmeyr. In the 1920s and 1930s Afrikaners formed a significant proportion of the student population. However, only a handful of blacks attended the University prior to World War II. At no stage did the University become a training ground for national statesmen, but in the 1920s and 1930s it certainly emerged as the foremost centre for the liberal critique of South African society. In his Phelps-Stokes lectures to the Institute of Race Relations in 1933, Edgar Brookes was able to state: 'The centre of gravity of South African liberalism has shifted from Cape Town to Johannesburg . . . the most effective institutional witness for liberalism in South Africa is that of the University of the Witwatersrand.'[4]

Within the University, Hofmeyr advanced his ideal of a liberal education by building up a Faculty of Arts of considerable distinction. In the number of departments, as well as in the number of students, the Faculty of Arts was also by far the largest from the inception of the University in 1922. Where perhaps Hofmeyr failed was in not altogether fusing the professional faculties together with the liberal arts and pure sciences in a truly integrated university community. His biggest defeat in this regard was over the medical school. He believed very strongly that the medical students should receive at least their pre-clinical education and training on the Milner Park campus, where they would be exposed to the influences of the wider university community. The first medical professors at the University, and the medical profession in Johannesburg, felt otherwise, and insisted on the primacy of the professional training to be given the University's medical students. They desired that the full medical training be provided at a medical school located on Hospital Hill, about 1,5 kilometres to the east of Milner Park, but where the town's major medical facilities and amenities were situated. They won the day, and the full medical school was established on Hospital Hill.[5]

On 1 March 1924, at exceptionally short notice, Hofmeyr resigned from the University to become Administrator of the Transvaal at the invitation of Smuts, the Prime Minister. Smuts had clearly been impressed by the way in which Hofmeyr had handled the University's negotiations with the government, particularly over finance, and by his work on government commissions dealing with provincial finances and educational administration. 'He is of course wanting in administrative experience', Smuts told a critical C. Louis Leipoldt, editor of *De Volkstem*, 'but I hope he will overcome that difficulty, and none of the men [you] mentioned have had bigger administrative experience than he has for the last four years in the running of a new concern like the Rand University.'[6]

Hofmeyr continued during March to carry out the duties of Principal, and after he had moved to Pretoria in April he travelled to Johannesburg for the next few months once or twice a week to assist the University. In 1926 he returned to the University Council as a nominee of the Governor-General, and was promptly elected Vice-Chancellor in succession to Sir Robert Kotzé. He served two terms as Vice-Chancellor, until 1929, when he was elected to Parliament. In 1939 he was made Chancellor of the University, which position he held until his death in December 1948.

While Council conducted its search in 1924 for a successor to Hofmeyr, Professor L.F. Maingard, the Head of the Department of French, served as Acting Principal. Council wanted as Principal another classicist, Professor A.C. Paterson, formerly of the Transvaal University College. When he declined the post, Council appointed as the University's second Principal Sir William Thomson, who took office in October 1924. Drawn out of retirement to assume the post, Thomson was intended as a caretaker Principal until the University could find the right candidate for the long term. Though his appointment was initially for one year only, Sir William served the University as Principal for a little over three years.

A Scot, educated at Edinburgh University, Thomson was aged 67 and had retired for nearly two years when he agreed to assist the University by becoming its Principal. He had first come to South Africa in 1883 to take up an appointment as Professor of Mathematics at the Victoria College, Stellenbosch, where he taught among others Smuts, J.B.M. Hertzog, and F.S. and D.F. Malan. In 1895 he had forsaken the academic side of university work for the administrative to become Registrar of the University of the Cape of Good Hope. In 1918, when the University of South Africa replaced the University of the Cape of Good Hope, he had moved to Pretoria as Registrar, where he remained until his retirement in 1922. He had then returned to Scotland, where he was knighted for his services to higher education in South Africa.

Thomson, recognizing that he was a caretaker Principal, did not seek to give a strong lead. Hating controversy of any sort, he sought to run the University with as gentle a hand as possible. The croquet played at the Principal's house over week-ends epitomized his pace in dealing with the University's affairs. Nevertheless, during his tenure the University continued to grow satisfactorily and some notable milestones were attained. During his principalship the dental school was founded, the medical school embarked on postgraduate diploma work, the chair of law was established, and the Faculty of Engineering embarked on a new era with the appointment of three new professors. It was also during Thomson's principalship that the University admitted its first black student, a Coloured in the medical school.

III

By today's standards, the administration in 1922 was exceptionally small. In the University's first year the administrative staff after the Principal consisted of the Registrar, H.W.J. van der Brugge, the Accountant, W.H. Jones, a clerk, three typists, and three caretakers. When Principal Hofmeyr left in 1924, a junior clerk was appointed to act as Registrar's clerk.

The duties of the Registrar were quite formidable: responsibility for the general correspondence of the University; attendance at all meetings of Council, Senate, and the faculties and committees of the University; preparing the minutes of Council, Senate, and their committees; the conduct of examinations, publication of results, and arrangements for graduation. He supervised the maintenance of buildings, hostels, and sports grounds, and the supply of water, light, electricity, and gas; undertook most interviews with staff on internal matters, and handled complaints and inquiries from students, parents, and the general public. Together with the Principal he was responsible for general staff matters, the control of building operations and the provision of equipment, the preparation of University publications such as the *Calendar,* and the allocation of bursaries and scholarships. As Van der Brugge complained in a memorandum of February 1925, the post of Registrar was impossible: 'I need hardly mention that, as far as my own person is concerned,

Sir William Thomson

H.W.J. van der Brugge

the strain has been very great, and I am the only member of the staff who has been unable to take as much as a week of my annual leave. As a matter of fact, it is quite obvious that the present position of affairs leaves no room at all for the annual leave of Principal and Registrar, and, besides, threatens chaos in case of illness of either.'

Van der Brugge had been appointed Registrar at the beginning of 1922, the first Registrar of the University of the Witwatersrand. His predecessors, styled Secretary of Council, were D.P. Suttie, who served from 1918 to 1921, and W.E. Cursons, who had first been appointed Secretary of Council in 1906 and had become head of the administrative office following the departure of John Robinson in 1908, when the old T.U.C. had abolished its post of Registrar. Van der Brugge likewise gave long service, remaining as Registrar until his retirement in 1935, at the age of sixty.

A Hollander, Van der Brugge had come to South Africa towards the end of 1896 to serve as a civil servant in the South African Republic. The Kruger administration was well stocked with Hollanders, and Van der Brugge joined the telegraph department. After the Anglo-Boer War he worked as a translator, and in 1914 entered the Transvaal Education Department as a teacher, having secured a B.A. in classics from the University of the Cape of Good Hope in 1910. When he joined Wits as Registrar he also possessed the degrees of M.A. in philosophy and Bachelor of Laws of the University of South Africa. A cultured shrewd man, with a sharp mind, he proved an efficient Registrar, and also contributed to the University by writing the words of its *Alma Mater*. Throughout his tenure as Registrar he persistently complained that he was overworked. It is true that he attended an enormous number of meetings, as Council and Senate met very much more frequently then than now, but it was observed that somehow he always managed to look busy even when he was not. In 1925 his pleas for more assistance were successful, and he was given a chief clerk in the Registrar's office, O.G. Backeberg, later Professor of Chemistry.

The University's first Accountant, W.H. Jones, who had joined the staff of the old School of Mines in 1912, was to continue in charge of the accounts office until 1937. A self-trained man, he was no mere cypher, controlling the University's accounts with a strong hand. Noted for his outspokenness, he was able to put professors in their place when the occasion warranted. He was, however, always most considerate in his dealings with junior staff. In 1925 he was likewise given more assistance, and acquired a bookkeeper, D.A. Dodds.

In those days no professor or department had secretarial help. The University considered that it employed the absolute minimum administration, and that its cost effectiveness was superior to any other university in the country.

For students, the administrative officers of the University were necessarily remote. Students came more into contact with the residence deans and matrons, the groundsmen, and some of the technical and maintenance staff. In the early years of the University the residence deans and matrons tended to change over regularly, in part because of the rule that persons who married were barred from office. However, the reason why the first dean of Dalrymple House, Margaret Hodgson, lasted for so short a time was that she simply could not tolerate the interference of Hofmeyr and his mother. Her successor, Miss M. Swansbourne, was to serve for 14 years.

The University's first groundsman, C.W. Hubbard, had been appointed in 1920 when Milner Park was being laid out, and he remained in charge of the playing fields until his retirement in 1953. He was known and loved by all students who played sport, and became noted for his grass cricket wickets. On the maintenance side the best known figure was the carpenter, F. Pugsley, whose appointment went back to 1906, and who remained in the University's service until his retirement at the end of 1940. Pugsley, a truly delightful person, was a cabinet-maker in the old tradition. In an explosion in 1908 at the old Transvaal University College he had lost an eye, but his 'eye' for assessing levels in woodwork never deserted him. Two future directors of maintenance at the University, John Reekie and Alec Fergusson, received their basic training from him.

The African staff at the University was employed under the heads of buildings, grounds, and hostels. The staff was overwhelmingly male, and most were housed at the University. 'Native quarters' were constructed at both Milner Park and at the medical school, and the African staff in the student hostels were accommodated at the hostels. Facilities for the African staff at the University appear to have been no better than anywhere else. In 1925 the Hostels' Committee recommended that the cook at College House be given some sort of private room as he objected to sharing a room 'with six or seven ordinary house boys', and that 'some facilities for washing be given to the native boys'. The committee reported to Council, 'At present, when they do wash, they can only do so by taking a tin of water into their lavatory or standing in the kitchen courtyard.'[7]

IV

Today the University's Milner Park site strikes some observers as being grossly overbuilt; for them it has become the proverbial concrete jungle. During the principalships of Hofmeyr and Thomson, there was a considerable programme of construction, and a stately series of buildings appeared along the top of the ridge. But what struck the visitor then was the newness of the buildings, and the rawness of their surroundings. Some attempt was made to lay out the grounds, but there were few paved areas, and the ground was either muddy when it rained or exceptionally dusty when dry. The campus did not have the conventional atmosphere of a university. Herman Charles Bosman, who attended the University in the 1920s and later gained fame as a novelist, found himself thoroughly alienated by the buildings. In the late 1940s he wrote: 'I was a student at the Witwatersrand University in the early days, when there was still the smell of wet paint and drying concrete about the buildings at Milner Park, and there was something in my eighteen year old soul that revolted at all this newness — and when I went there recently, to attend a play in the Main Hall, I was still appalled at the feeling that Wits had not acquired any of the external characteristics of poise and suavity. The girl who sold me a programme was gauche.' He still hoped that one day Wits would acquire what he supposed to be the right atmosphere for a university: 'There must be tall old trees through whose branches the sunshine falls dappled on the walls. There must be winding lanes and unexpected vistas and sequestered nooks. There must be mildew and ruin and dilapidated facades.

There must be aged and crooked corridors and aged and crooked professors. All these advantages — or disadvantages — will no doubt accrue to the Witwatersrand University in time.'[8] The University has been built and maintained to a rather different design.

The diversion of the Beit bequest to Cape Town ensured that the university in Johannesburg would be located near to the town centre, rather than at Frankenwald. Even though the estate was given to the University of the Witwatersrand, the funds for developing access to it as a university site no longer existed. Had the University been situated at Frankenwald, by now it would undoubtedly have come to possess much of that atmosphere that Bosman valued, but it could never have served the Witwatersrand as the more accessible site at Milner Park has permitted. For those who conceived of the University as a 'democratic', if for whites only, institution, Milner Park fitted their conception far better than Frankenwald.

After the loss of the Beit bequest in 1916, Mayor O'Hara held out the prospect of the municipal ground at Milner Park as the site for a university. But there were some who preferred the Wanderers Club grounds, alongside Park Station and very near to the headquarters of the School of Mines at Plein Square. The Wanderers would have provided a central site, accessible by rail to the entire Witwatersrand, but the Witwatersrand University Committee concluded that to ask for the ground would be impolitic. 'Some members', W.E. Curson, secretary to the Witwatersrand University Committee, reported to Lionel Phillips in late June 1916, 'put forward a proposal that the Wanderers' Ground might be obtained, but the antagonism which would very likely be raised, if such a proposal were made public, was sufficient to decide all but one member to vote in favour of the Milner Park scheme, though no doubt the central position of the Wanderers' is a strong point in its favour.'[9] The Site and Buildings Sub-Committee of the Witwatersrand University Committee subsequently made a formal application to the Johannesburg Town Council for a grant of some 80 acres of land in Milner Park for a university site. On 31 August 1916 the Town Council unanimously agreed that the ground should be 'reserved for the purpose of establishing a University and all that may pertain to the efficient conduct of such an institution'.[10] Sixteen additional acres from the farm 'Braamfontein' were donated by the Transvaal Consolidated Lands and Exploration Company, the land company of the Wernher-Beit mining group. The Witwatersrand University Committee, acting in conjunction with the Johannesburg Hospital Board and the South African Institute for Medical Research, also managed to persuade the government to reserve the ground on Hospital Hill immediately adjoining and north of the Institute for a medical school.

The hillside site known as Milner Park, at the western end of the commanding Hospital Hill ridge, lay about 1,5 kilometres to the north west of the town centre, and could be reached by tram from town. It had become municipal property in 1903 when, at the instigation of Lord Milner, the Transvaal government handed it over as a free gift to Johannesburg, as the town was virtually without any public lands for parks and other open spaces. Prior to the Anglo-Boer War the site had served variously as farmland, a quarry, a rubbish tip, and a tollgate. The road to Auckland Park had cut diagonally across the site, and when tolls were imposed on wagons by the Kruger regime in 1891 a tollgate was built at the Ameshoff Street end, under the control of Commandant de Meillon.[11] In 1906 the western half of Milner Park was given to the Witwatersrand Agricultural Society on an 80-year lease for a show ground.

Hofmeyr considered Milner Park an ideal location. In his contribution to the special supplement on the University in the *Rand Daily Mail* of 1 November 1923, he stated, 'Barely a mile from the town's centre and easily accessible from every part of it, yet isolated from the noisy bustle of its life, looking on the one side over the most beautiful portion of Johannesburg away to the dreamy distances of the Magaliesberg, and on the other over the industrial activity to which it owes its being, this University set upon a hill is indeed admirably placed for the linking together of the idealistic and the practical, which is not least among its tasks.' As neighbours to the west the University had the Witwatersrand Agricultural Society, to the east, the Lion Brewery and the white working-class suburb of Braamfontein.

Initially, as the paymaster, the Witwatersrand University Committee was responsible for the development of the Milner Park site. In 1918, a competition was staged for the lay-out of Milner Park. Twenty designs were received, with the first premium going to Messrs Lyon and Fallon of Cape Town. Their proposals were accepted for situating the main buildings on the crown of the ridge at the southern end of the projected campus, with the student residences and the Principal's house towards the northern end and the playing fields below.

Given the total absence of hostel and sporting facilities at Plein Square, and the very limited hostel facilities available at Sunnyside, the first developments authorized at Milner Park were for sports fields and the construction of student residences. In 1919 a start was made to preparing a football field and tennis courts at the northern or bottom end of Milner Park, and a competition was held for the design of the student residences and the Principal's house. The assessor was E.H. Waugh, the municipal building surveyor and architectural adviser to the Witwatersrand University Committee. The winner was John

Perry of Cape Town. Limited funds meant that the Principal's house was delayed, but building the student residences began in 1920. The men's residence, College House, was first occupied in March 1921, while the building was still incomplete, and in 1922 the women's residence, Dalrymple House, received its first students.

At first, conditions in the residences were very primitive, not only because they were incomplete but also as a consequence of the spartan ideas of Principal Hofmeyr, who until the Principal's residence was completed, served as the dean of College House. An article in the *University College Magazine* for June 1921, entitled 'How to Grin and Bear It', described the conditions that prevailed at College House in its first year:

> Many former residents of Sunnyside on their arrival were delighted to find several Spartan innovations imported direct from Oxford. The use of hard benches in place of comfortable chairs with backs has proved a blessing: it is fortunate Oxford never introduced the practice of using hot shaving water on cold mornings or of partaking of breakfast in bed on the morning after the night before.
>
> As may be guessed, inmates of College House have been put to a series of inconveniences (said to be good for them), ranging from inadequate and inhospitable common room accommodation to the trouble of using paraffin oil lamps in the place of electric light that took a long time to be installed. As it was, serious efforts did not appear to be made with regard to the latter until an alarming consumption of oil brought to light the fact that certain people, overcome by worry and hard work, had developed suicidal tendencies and were applying it to the hair. The sigh of satisfaction that went up when the current was at length switched on caused an earth tremor sufficiently powerful to make at least one workman realise that he had been laying more than the regulation three hundred bricks a day.
>
> Turning from contemplation of the building itself to the ground on which it stands, various drains, trenches and holes, all cunningly hidden by building material, at once commend the traveller to wariness. The position of these obstructions is continually changing, with the result that, while endeavouring to dodge the wire that tore one's trousers the previous evening, an unsuspected and apparently inanimate pile of bricks somehow deals one a blow on the face. People arriving here in future are advised to acquire extensive mountaineering experience, to pass an examination in first aid, and to develop the faculty of seeing in the dark.

The influence of Hofmeyr and his mother was even more evident in the construction of the Principal's house. Some members of the Council had been anxious that the Principal should occupy a prestigious residence, but Hofmeyr and his mother insisted that finance did not allow for extravagance, and that a modest bungalow was all that was required. A modest bungalow was constructed.

In late 1920 the Witwatersrand University Committee decided to hand over the control of the building operations at Milner Park to the Council of the University College. By then a competition had already been staged for the design of the main teaching buildings. The assessors, E.H. Waugh, W.H. Stucke, and Principal Hofmeyr, awarded the first premium to Mr Frank Emley of Johannesburg, the second to Messrs Cowin and Powers, and the third to Messrs Hawke and McKinley. When Messrs Cowin and Powers entered an objection to the assessment, they were appointed joint architects with Mr Frank Emley. G.E. Pearse, who in 1921 became Professor of Architecture, later described this arrangement as 'a most unfortunate decision'.[12] On the advice of the Witwatersrand University Committee, Council appointed John Barrow as the contractor for the buildings. He was to be paid a percentage of the estimated cost, with incentives for savings and speed.[13]

The lay-out adopted for the teaching buildings at Milner Park provided for a main line of three buildings, flanked in front by a building at each end. The first to be constructed was the Botany and Zoology block, to the north east of the planned main line of buildings. It housed the Departments of Geology and Applied Mathematics as well as those of Botany and Zoology, all of which had been most uncomfortably accommodated in the Tin Temple at Plein Square. They occupied their new quarters for the 1923 session, but only after a major battle had been waged between Professors Fantham of zoology and Moss of botany over the lighting for the two small museums in the building. Fantham insisted on top light, Moss on south light. Ultimately Hofmeyr called in Professor Pearse to arbitrate. Pearse has recalled: 'I tried to reason with Professor Fantham by pointing out that a top lighted museum was a thing of the past and by using windows high up and between the cases on three sides one could get better results. He refused to discuss the matter with one so ignorant and eventually got his own way and the unfinished block was the result. Professor Moss refused to use another room for his purpose because it faced north with the result that most of his specimens were kept locked up in packing cases and deteriorated badly.'[14]

The three buildings placed on the crown of the University ridge were intended as the showpieces of the new campus: the Chemistry and Physics block to the east, the central block for arts departments, administrative offices, a circular library and a great assembly hall, and an Engineering block to the west. In the original design the central block, with its great portico and

The original design for the new buildings at Milner Park

The opening
of the central block
by the Prince of Wales,
23 June 1925

An aerial view of Milner Park, 1930

columns, was to be crowned by a massive dome in the Renaissance style, but on the advice of Mr F. Williamson, a graduate of Liverpool University who was brought out by Mr Emley to assist with the design of the three main buildings, this was abandoned as costly and useless. On Williamson's recommendation the buildings were faced with pre-cast concrete blocks.[15] An earlier suggestion to build in stone had been rejected by Council on the ground of cost.

The Chemistry and Physics block was the first finished of the three, and was occupied in the middle of 1924. The central block followed. Its foundation stones had been laid by His Royal Highness Prince Arthur of Connaught, on the University's inauguration day, 4 October 1922. The stones of warm-toned granite, quarried from Baviaan Kop some 25 kilometres north of Johannesburg, were inscribed respectively in English and Dutch. For lack of funds, the north front only of the central block was built. It was officially opened by His Royal Highness the Prince of Wales in June 1925. The first Engineering block was completed at the end of 1925, and was occupied at the beginning of 1926.

The design for the first teaching buildings at Milner Park was completed with the construction of the North West Engineering block between 1926–8. The building, which housed the engineering laboratories and workshops for the Departments of Electrical and Mechanical Engineering and Mining, was officially opened by the Prime Minister, General J.B.M. Hertzog, on 25 August 1928. Hertzog, like his predecessor as Prime Minister, Smuts, was given an honorary doctorate by the University.

One of the conditions imposed on the University for the grant of the Milner Park site was that at least until 1924, the road that ran diagonally across it be retained for use by carts 'conveying refuse from Parktown and the Northern suburbs'. Another road was constructed on the site, running immediately in front of the main line of buildings from Jan Smuts Avenue to the showgrounds. At the Jan Smuts entrance to it the main gates of the University were erected. The road remained a feature of the campus until 1964. It provided parking, directed students to their main meeting ground, the steps leading up to the central block, and also served to create a sense that the University constituted part of the town. Another condition imposed on the University for the grant of Milner Park was 'That the University grounds, except that portion in the immediate vicinity of the hostels, shall at all times be open to the public and be subject to the same By-laws which apply to the Council's parks at the present time.'[16]

On Hospital Hill, the foundation stone for the medical school was laid by Lord Buxton, the Governor-General, on 28 January 1920. By the middle of

The medical school

the next year two storeys of the south and west wings of the medical school building, and one room of the third storey at each end of the building, had been erected, although not completed. J.W. Watt, the Professor of Pharmacology, later recalled: 'When I arrived in May 1921, I found myself making arrangements for my first classes on the unfinished floor of a room at present occupied by Dr Bernstein. There were no doors or windows in this room and I had to use bricks and pieces of stone as paperweights while I was arranging my notes and illustrative material for my first lectures.' He added: 'I may say that the best cricket pitch in Johannesburg at that time, was in the anatomy dissecting hall.'[17] Because of financial constraints, further construction ceased in 1921, and all the medical departments were obliged to share the incomplete building. It was not until 1924 that the construction of the east wing was undertaken, and until 1928 that the north wing was built.

Raymond Dart has vividly described what conditions were like at the medical school when he arrived at the end of 1922:

> The Medical School was a two-storeyed, L-shaped building, screened behind 10-ft. brick walls that had originally formed a garrison area below a fort of President Kruger's time. No gardens had been laid out and, to add to the general air of dereliction, high grass and Mexican marigold

weeds filled the space between the ancient brick wall and the doors of
the school. Few townspeople even knew of the school's existence.

The Department of Anatomy consisted of a dissecting hall with three
side rooms and opened on to a lecture theatre. This was separated from my
private office by the students' cloakroom. The architect had overlooked
the necessity for planning water taps, electric plugs, gas or compressed
air for student laboratories. My permanent staff consisted of one simple-
minded preparator of material in the mortuary basement underground.

The walls of the vast, high-roofed dissecting hall above this mortuary
were besplattered with marks that emphasized its customary use by the
students for practising football and tennis. The zinc-covered, trestle-
type dissecting tables supported dried-up portions of corpses whose only
covering were hessian sheets.

Our first inspection of these conditions left my wife, whom I had
taken from her medical studies at Cincinnati, in tears — a woman's
prerogative I rather envied at that moment.[18]

For all that, the occupation of the medical school building during 1921 had represented a considerable improvement for medical students, who had previously spent much of their time scurrying between classes at Plein Square and the wood and iron lean-to building in the grounds of the Institute for Medical Research where Stibbe had begun his teaching in anatomy.

As the University's building at Milner Park and Hospital Hill progressed so there was a gradual winding down of Plein Square as a centre for the University's work. Plein Square was sold to the Railways and Harbours Administration for £100 000, and in terms of the agreement the old T.U.C. building was handed over to the railways at the end of 1924. At the beginning of the next year the administrative offices of the University were transferred to the central block at Milner Park. Apart from evening classes, only classes in engineering and architecture continued to be taught in the Tin Temple at Plein Square, pending the completion of the Engineering blocks at Milner Park.

It was often said at the time that the University's buildings at Milner Park were imposing without but cheap within.[19] There was nothing imposing about the exterior of the Botany and Zoology block, and it looked rather out of place in front of the impressive line of main buildings. Inside, all the new buildings were indeed stark, particularly with their bare concrete floors. In the winter they were impossibly cold. In an investigation undertaken in the Faculty of Science after the winter of 1924, all departments complained that the cold working conditions had caused ill health among both staff and students, and interfered with their work. The Department of Botany reported:

'Students complained of cold and rheumatism and shivered, and could not do practical work, such as cutting sections properly. One senior student could not take the June class examination on account of rheumatic hand. Two members of staff decided to stay in Johannesburg during July vacation to do research but suffered from rheumatism due to the cold rooms, and so could not pursue their researches.'[20] In 1925, at great expense, the University installed a hot-water heating system both in the Milner Park buildings and the medical school, while the concrete floors were covered with cork linoleum.

As only the north front of the central block had been constructed, the University had no assembly hall. Consequently the Town Hall was used for large formal gatherings of the University, notably graduation ceremonies. For large meetings on campus, the main lecture theatre in the Chemistry and Physics block first served as the venue, and after 1928 the drawing hall of the North West Engineering block was used. But if the University had no assembly hall, it did possess an observatory following the agreement in 1925 between Yale University and Wits to erect the Yale Observatory Southern Station at Milner Park. The observatory remained in operation until 1945.

IV

In the 1920s Milner Park seemed to offer almost limitless scope for the future development of the University. E.H. Waugh, the University's honorary advisory architect for the initial building programme, predicted that one day facilities for housing as many as 3 000 students might exist at Milner Park.[21] The obvious barrier to such massive development was insufficient finance.

In the debates on the University of the Witwatersrand Bill in the House of Assembly, the point had been made that the proposed university would be inadequately endowed. By comparison with universities in the United States, Canada, and Australia, as well as the University of Cape Town, Wits was without question very poorly endowed. By the close of the University's first year of operation, the Witwatersrand University Committee had succeeded in raising £172 364 for a building and endowment fund. Additionally the University had negotiated the sale of Plein Square to the Railways and Harbours Administration for £100 000, the equivalent today of approximately R2 million. U.C.T., for its part, possessed £834 500 on investment in 1922.

To finance the University's building programme the Council relied heavily on loan finance, primarily from the government but also from the Witwatersrand University Committee. In the early 1920s the terms for government loans were very generous for Wits, and the northern universities and colleges generally. The government was responsible for three-quarters of the interest and redemption payments for buildings for tuitional purposes at Wits, paying £3 for every pound by the University, as compared with a rate of £2 to £1 for universities in the Cape Province. The differential rate was justified on the basis that building costs were higher outside the Cape. For private loans, approved by the Treasury, the government contributed towards interest not exceeding 6 per cent in the same ratio as it did for loans given by the government.[22] Private loans not authorized by the Treasury were the University's entire responsibility.

In 1920 the Council of the University College believed that it had pulled off something of a coup in arranging the sale of Plein Square. The railways had been anxious to secure the square, and they were given it at a bargain price, for it was worth very much more than £100 000. No charge was made for the land, which had originally been granted by the Transvaal government to the Transvaal Technical Institute, and the £100 000 was intended to represent the money put into the building by the Witwatersrand Council of Education. The bargain for the University College was the Smuts government's undertaking to provide loans for the erection at Milner Park of buildings for the arts and pure science departments of the College, and for buildings 'adequately providing for the work which, but for the transfer of the property, would continue to be conducted at Plein Square, that is, accommodation for the Engineering Departments of the College, Library, and Hall'.[23] Before Hofmeyr left the University as Principal, the government had come to accept that this meant it was committed to providing Wits with £500 000 in building loans.

Initially, however, the bargain ran into severe difficulties. Government officials regarded the immediate demands made by Wits as excessive, but the main problem was a fall in the price of gold, which threw the country into depression and caused the government acute financial embarrassment. For the 1920/21 financial year, the government had granted a loan of £50 000, including £25 000 for the medical school, and had authorized a private loan of £35 000. For 1921/22 Principal Hofmeyr advised the Secretary for Education, George Hofmeyr, that the University College would require £230 000 in building loans. A flabbergasted Secretary for Education commented in the margin, '£230 000 for *one* centre – compare with £200 000 for all centres during current year'. Not only was Principal Hofmeyr's request rebuffed, but the government stalled on the purchase of Plein Square, creating legal complications concerning the transfer. According to the original Crown grant, the square was to be used exclusively for the purposes of education, and the point was raised that the railways did not quite fit the description of an educational institution.[24]

For the fiscal year ending in March 1922, although the Council considered £170 000 the minimum required for building operations, the loan allocated by government was £35 000; £20 000 for the medical school and £15 000 for hostels. The government also authorized the raising of a private loan of £35 000 for the science buildings, and stood surety for the National Bank for an overdraft of £15 000. Consequently the University College had to raise another £85 000 independent of government assistance, giving a total of £120 000 to be raised by private loans. Though £70 000 was provided in loans by the Witwatersrand University Committee and the Witwatersrand Council of Education, this still left £50 000 to be found privately.[25] On a visit to London, Principal Hofmeyr succeeded in negotiating a loan for this amount from the Guardian Assurance Company. As the loan was subject to a government guarantee which was not forthcoming, it fell through.[26] Eventually the government found itself obliged to give the University College an additional loan of £35 000 for 1920/21 to finance the work on the science buildings.[27] It was this that allowed a start to be made to the Chemistry and Physics block.

By March 1922, when the University opened, the government had given £120 000 in building loans, and the Witwatersrand University Committee had loaned an equal amount towards the building programme. By the end of April these sums had been virtually exhausted, and Hofmeyr advised the Council the University's building programme would have to come to a complete halt unless additional funds were raised immediately. The Witwatersrand University Committee had very little in reserve, and it would be months before Parliament would sanction the government's estimates for 1922/23. There remained two options; either to borrow from banks and insurance companies on the security of the insecure agreement with the Railways and Harbours Administration for the payment of £100 000 by July 1923 for Plein Square, or special assistance from the government. The latter option was chosen, with limited success. In May 1922 the Secretary for Finance advised that as the Treasury objected neither to providing £45 000 for the science buildings in 1922/23, nor £20 000 for hostels, it also had no objection to monthly issues of £6 000 for these buildings pending the passage of the main Appropriation Act for 1922. The medical school, however, could expect no further funds for its construction:

> *Medical Building Extensions.* In 1921–22, it was stated that the total cost of these buildings was to be £45,000 of which £25,000 was issued in 1920-21 and £20,000 in 1921-22, thus completing the commitment.

It is now stated that the total cost of these buildings is to be £70,000 and that a further £25,000 is required in 1922–23. The Treasury has not approved of the additional loan and regrets that it is unable to provide any further funds in 1922–23 for this service.[28]

In the event, the government did allow £5 000 for the medical school in 1922/23, in addition to the £65 000 granted for buildings at Milner Park.

Thereafter Principal Hofmeyr found it rather easier to raise funds for capital purposes. For 1923/24 the University was granted £90 000 in government loans for the construction of the east wing of the medical school, to complete the Chemistry and Physics block, and the initial stage of the central block. For the next financial year, £85 000 was awarded in government loans for the first Engineering building and the central block. As the University's private loan of £35 000 authorized by the Treasury had been converted into a government loan, this brought to exactly £400 000 the loans that Hofmeyr had secured from the government. In addition the University acquired a significant capital investment fund of its own with the payment during 1923 and 1924 of the purchase money of £100 000 for Plein Square, and the receipt of a special grant of £25 000 from the Johannesburg Town Council. The Witwatersrand University Committee, for its part, had accumulated a capital sum of £186 000 by the end of 1925, of which £108 000 was held by the University in the form of loans for buildings, mainly student residences and also the Principal's house.

Before his departure as Principal, Hofmeyr informed the Secretary for Education that, in the foreseeable future, the University would be seeking another £200 000 in government building loans, but he was very firmly advised that the Treasury was not prepared to agree to a total commitment to the University in excess of £500 000, of which £400 000 had already been provided.[29] With Hofmeyr's departure and the formation of the Hertzog Pact government in June 1924, it again became difficult for the University to secure government loans for building purposes, and there was some question whether the new government would even grant Wits the additional £100 000 to which it believed itself entitled. There was a distinct feeling among the Hertzog government's Nationalist supporters that Wits had been exceptionally favourably treated, and beyond that the government was determined to curb expenditure on universities. For 1926/27 the government granted the University a loan strictly limited to £50 000 for the second Engineering block, and in August 1927 the Secretary for Education advised all universities that their general purposes grant might not be increased in 1928, and that no additional building loans would be placed on the 1928/29 loan estimates. On behalf of Wits, Sir William Thomson reminded the Secretary for Education that the Treasury was committed to a loan to the University of £500 000 for buildings, and that the University required the balance of £50 000 in 1928/29.[30] In the event, the University was given a government loan of £50 000 for 1928/29 to construct the northern wing of the medical school, and add another floor to the Biology block, but the terms of the loan were far less favourable than those given previously. The formula applied for government loans awarded after April 1925 put the government's contribution to the interest and redemption payments on a pound for pound basis, compared with the previous ratio of £3 to £1 for northern universities.

When Sir William Thomson retired as Principal at the beginning of 1928, the University's indebtedness on loan account stood at £552 000, while the cost of property at Milner Park and the medical school amounted to £576 000. The £500 000 negotiated in government building loans, with £50 000 yet to be paid over, had been allocated as follows:

	£
Hostels	60 000
Medical school	70 000
Science buildings	135 000
Central block	70 000
Engineering buildings	165 000

The University's expenditure in 1927 on interest and redemption payments totalled £31 000, and the government's grant towards these payments was £16 700, by far the largest paid to any university in the country.[31]

In 1927 the Hertzog government embarked on a systematic attempt to contain the growth of public expenditure on higher education. In that year a University Commission was appointed under the chairmanship of J.C.P. van der Horst. It was given a specific directive to consider 'the possibility and desirability, with a view to economy and to other needs in the field of education, of revising the basis of State-aid to Universities and Technical Colleges'.[32]

Since the fiscal year 1923/24 government aid towards the general expenditure of universities had been in the form of the general purposes grant, which was automatically increased by a maximum of 10 per cent each year in proportion to the increased revenue secured by a university from fee income and other independent revenue.[33] On average, the general purposes grant received by Wits amounted to about 40 per cent of the University's total income, and the Council was free to use its own discretion in applying the grant to the general expenses of the University. The system was generally approved within the University, for it encouraged growth and gave the University considerable autonomy in its use of public funds. Indeed, the idea of gearing the state subsidy to university income, rather than expenditure, as had previously been the case, had been actively canvassed by Principal Hofmeyr in the evidence he had given to the departmental committee on government grants in 1922.[34] He and the University's Council had fully appreciated the potential for growth of such a system. What annoyed them was the limit of 10 per cent placed on the annual increase in the grant, for it operated to deprive the University enjoying the full benefit of its growth in student numbers and increased fee income. For 1923 the Council complained that because of the 10 per cent limitation, the University's general purposes grant was £6 600 less than which the Council considered it was 'entitled to receive'.[35]

The general purposes grant awarded to the University for 1923/24 amounted to £45 930, and the grant for interest and redemption charges to £10 800, giving a total of £56 730 from government sources. The University's own financial year coincided with the calendar year, and for 1923 it received a total of £48 000 in government grants, almost half the total University income of £97 600. Other grants, including an annual grant of £10 000 from the Johannesburg municipality, amounted to £18 200. Fee income, which included fees for the evening classes and for examinations, totalled £29 000.[36] By current standards, the fees charged for full degree courses were remarkably low: £24 per annum for the B.A. and B.Sc., or £20 if the fees were paid within a month of the beginning of each term, rising to £40 per annum for medical students from their third year onwards, or £35 if the fees were paid at the beginning of the term.

For the remainder of the 1920s the government subsidy to the University, including the grant for interest and redemption payments, usually amounted to slightly more than half the University's income and expenditure. For 1924/25, after a deputation from the University had seen the Minister of Education on the subject, the 10 per cent rule for the general purposes grant was not enforced, and the University was given a general grant of £58 000, plus a grant of £14 500 for interest and redemption charges. By 1927/28 government grants to the University totalled £83 860, including £67 160 for general purposes. Government grants to the University of Cape Town for the same year totalled £85 280, including £76 680 for general purposes, and to the University of Stellenbosch they totalled £46 410, including £41 460 for general purposes.

According to government figures, on a cost per student basis the University of the Witwatersrand was very much more expensive to the government than the University of Cape Town or the University of Stellenbosch. For 1927 the government grant per student at Wits was £60.78, as against £47.05 at U.C.T. and £49.96 at Stellenbosch. The total cost per student was given as £116.96 at Wits, £95.59 at U.C.T., and £84.73 at Stellenbosch. The average cost per student for all universities and university colleges in 1927 was £90.95, and the average government grant per student was £52.34, or 58 per cent of the total.[37]

At the old School of Mines, the cost per student had traditionally been very much higher than in the other institutions of higher learning in the Union, because of the technical nature of the work undertaken. The Faculties of Engineering and Medicine in the new University helped to ensure that the average cost would remain high. In terms of the range of faculties and departments, student numbers, and over-all expenditure, Wits was strictly comparable only with U.C.T. and here the official government figures on cost per student were rather misleading as their calculations failed to distinguish between full and part-time students. With the incorporation in 1923 of the South African College of Music, U.C.T. possessed significantly more part-time students than Wits. For full-time students, Wits was only marginally more costly than U.C.T.

Where Wits and U.C.T. differed very markedly in the 1920s was in the way in which they spent their general purposes grant and other income. Essentially, Wits pushed ahead very much faster with its building programme at Milner Park than U.C.T. did at Groote Schuur, with the result that Wits allocated a much larger proportion of its budget to the equipment and maintenance of buildings and laboratories, whereas U.C.T.'s main initial investment was in full-time teaching staff. The accounts of the two universities are not readily comparable because different bookkeeping practices were employed, but it is evident that U.C.T. devoted a significantly larger proportion of its annual income to salaries. In 1925, when the annual expenditure of both universities was of the order of £130 000, U.C.T. spent £93 300 on salaries, wages, and pensions to maintain a teaching staff of 170 and an administrative staff of 18, whereas Wits spent £68 700 to maintain a teaching staff of 125 and an administrative staff of 13.[38]

It is also evident from the accounts that in the 1920s neither Wits nor U.C.T. spent more than a derisory sum upon their libraries. In 1927 Wits spent £1 859, Cape Town £2 563. Indeed, Wits did not even possess a proper central library. At Plein Square, the old School of Mines had housed the Seymour Memorial Library, a collection of mining and technological literature founded in memory of an American engineer killed during the Anglo-Boer War and intended 'for the free use of the inhabitants of Johannesburg'.[39] In 1927, after a long wrangle over whether the library should be moved to

Milner Park, the University agreed to transfer the custody of the Seymour Memorial Library to the Johannesburg Public Library, although the trust remained vested in the University Council. At Milner Park, the various departments all supposedly ran their own libraries, and in most instances these catered for the teaching and research interests of staff rather than the needs of students. In 1926 a start was made with the establishment of a central library at Milner Park with the creation of a reading room on the top floor of the central block and the formation of a Reading Room and Library Committee. During its first year of operation, books from the Departments of English, History, and Classics were housed in the reading room, but many heads of departments were reluctant to allow their books to be transferred to it. In October 1927 the Reading Room and Library Committee properly complained to Senate that, 'A University without a good library to which students are allowed access is in an anomalous position and greatly hampered in its work.'[40]

By 1926 the University had run into considerable difficulties with its annual expenditure. The University had pursued a policy of growth, but liabilities had accrued faster than income. At the end of 1926 the University's accumulated deficit amounted to nearly £6 000, a state of affairs the Council's annual report attributed 'largely to expenditure on equipment necessitated by the occupation of the new buildings, and which should be considerably reduced, if not entirely avoided, in future'. But the Council was alarmed by the size of the University's recurring expenditure, and in 1926 set up a special committee, consisting of Sir Robert Kotzé and P.M. Anderson, to 'recommend economies in the matter of staffing and equipment, compatible with continued efficiency'.[41]

In certain quarters both within and outside of the University it was believed that Wits had given too great a priority to growth, and the multiplication of departments, rather than concentrating upon the development of areas of particular strength. An editorial in the *South African Mining and Engineering Journal* of 28 August 1926 strongly argued that it had probably been a mistake to create in Johannesburg a university that aimed to be 'catholic and broad', instead of focusing on technical training and research in engineering and medicine, for which Johannesburg was ideally suited.

> Unfortunately there is evidence that in its very rapid growth, the local institution has far exceeded its justifiable development, and it would almost seem that the wider interests of education have been subordinated to the interests of the institution itself. Departments not peculiar to the genius of the place have been allowed to multiply, and those deserving of special encouragement are languishing, partly owing to the absorption of funds in bricks and mortar and concrete for housing the former, which

funds might have provided the necessary and extensive laboratory equipment required by the latter.

For this state of affairs the *Journal* blamed the 'academical section' of the University, which it alleged had 'stampeded' the Council.

An article in the *Rand Daily Mail* in the same month echoed the view that the University had created a number of departments which hardly justified the expenditure lavished upon them, and which absorbed funds required for the development of important or 'key' departments. As examples of new departments that served as a drain on the University's finances, while attracting only a handful of students, the *Mail* cited the Department of Architecture in the Faculty of Engineering, and the Departments of Music and Bantu Studies in the Faculty of Arts. The *Mail* also pointed out that the Department of Mining and Metallurgy, which had helped give birth to the University, was no longer earning its keep: 'Fewer than 20 students enjoy the services of a professor of mining, a professor of metallurgy, and a lecturer in metallurgy.' By contrast several departments in the Faculty of Arts and Science had exceptionally large student enrolments, and few staff. In this regard the *Mail* cited History and Philosophy; Geography with 150 students and a lone professor to carry on all the work; and English with 370 students taught by a staff of two, a professor and a lecturer. 'Friendly critics of the University administration', the *Mail* concluded, 'while appreciating the fact that an institution of this character should not be too narrow in the choice of subjects in which it is proposed to afford instruction, are of the opinion that if financial stress necessitates economies, they should be practised in these departments which would least affect its value as a teaching centre.'[42]

As perceived by S.F.N. Gie, who succeeded George Hofmeyr as Secretary for Education in 1927, Wits and the other South African universities and university colleges had grown too rapidly, proliferating departments, while sacrificing certain essential facilities, notably libraries, in order to finance new posts. He blamed the system of state subsidy, which he contended encouraged quantitative competition among universities rather than qualitative development. In arguing the case in his report for 1928 for stabilizing the general purposes grants to universities, Gie asserted:

> It will probably be found possible to promote the real interests of university education if the annual grants are no longer automatically increased and, if generally speaking and with due regard to special needs and circumstances, the State expenditure on this type of education were to a large extent stabilized. This would enable the institutions concerned to recover from a period of growth which has not in all respects been healthy. Under the existing system of financial subsidy a premium is set

on increased enrolment and extensions of work for this purpose, and evidences of keen inter-institutional competition for students have not been lacking. It would benefit university education if improving the quality of their work became the main objective of all our university institutions, and if with this end in view they gave primary consideration to the needs of such departments of study as their resources warrant.[43]

Within Wits, in response to the University's financial difficulties, Senate urged a public appeal for funds rather than curtail the University's growth. On 3 May 1926 Senate unanimously adopted the resolution proposed by Professors Fantham of zoology and Dart of anatomy: 'The Senate begs to point out to Council that the continued state of financial stringency, with its attendant anxieties, tends to promote dissatisfaction and unrest, and to hamper the natural development of the University; that, in its opinion, the best solution is an appeal for funds, and that this appeal, already long-delayed, should take place at an early date.' A joint committee of Council and Senate was subsequently formed to investigate the prospects for a fund-raising campaign, but sadly concluded that 'there would be but a poor response if a campaign for funds were to be organised in Johannesburg at the present time'.[44]

With experience of the Witwatersrand University Committee's fund-raising campaigns, the chairman of Council, Sir William Dalrymple, was very sceptical of the chance for success of another campaign. Ideally, what he wanted was some sort of enforced levy on the local community to assist the University in its early stages of development. A suggestion that had been canvassed in 1916, when the campaign for a university was launched, was that a special tax should be levied on the mining industry for higher education in Johannesburg. The suggestion had been quickly squashed by the mining industry.[45] Dalrymple's new proposal was for the imposition of a municipal rate for higher education, but his idea went no further than the Town Council.[46]

One option remained if the University was to balance its books; to introduce economies. In its report of August 1926 Council's special committee on the University's finances recommended that economies should be effected, chiefly in staffing, that would amount to approximately £5 000. In the event, little by way of economy was effected in 1927. Indeed, the University's expenditure on revenue account rose by £20 000 to £162 300, which was £1 800 in excess of its revenue for the year. The University's accumulated deficit at the end of 1927 was consequently in the order of £7 600, and a year later it had risen to over £9 000. In the six years between 1922 and 1928, the University's expenditure had almost doubled to £179 000.[47]

In 1929 the Hertzog government finally took direct action to contain the growth in state expenditure on higher education. In its report in 1928 the Van der Horst Commission on universities, technical colleges, and their finances, recommended that the government grants to universities be stabilized for a period of years, though they should not be reduced: 'The prevalent feeling that State expenditure for universities has increased, is increasing to an alarming extent and that it must be diminished is not justified, and a recommendation to change the present system of State subsidy would be an unwise expedient'.[48] In the next year the government duly reduced the maximum annual increase in the general purposes grant from 10 to 5 per cent, and in 1930 the grants to universities were stabilized. In 1930 the University's state subsidy was £98 000 out of a total income of £187 500.[49] That represented a peak in state subsidy. Thereafter the great depression took its toll, and Wits and the other universities of South Africa were to find their grants drastically reduced.

It was, in short, the good fortune of Hofmeyr and Thomson to preside over the University at a time when growth was not only the accepted order for universities and university colleges in South Africa, but also when the system of state subsidy was designed to encourage growth. When H.R. Raikes became Principal in 1928, the philosophy of sheer growth was already under challenge in government circles, and it was to be his misfortune to have to contend with the financial consequences of a major economic depression.

The growth of the years 1922 to 1928 was not necessarily as expensive to the University as might be supposed. The extensive use of honorary and part-time staff represented a vast saving for the University. Engineering apart, the professional faculties relied heavily on such staff. Most of the full-time lecturing staff in the new University were members of the Faculties of Arts and Science. Their salary scales ranged from £300 to £350 for a junior lecturer, £400 to £500 for a lecturer, £450 to £650 for a senior lecturer, and £800 to £1 100 for a professor. Women lecturers were paid on a lower scale. To compensate for the high cost of living in Johannesburg, members of the permanent staff were also entitled to a local allowance based on that paid by the Public Service of the Union in Johannesburg.

Notes

1. James Moulder, 'University Neutrality: Some Puzzling Reflections in a South African Mirror' in H.W. van der Merwe and David Welsh (eds), *The Future of the University in South Africa* (Cape Town, 1977), 245–59.

2. See chap. 9.
3. *Star,* 1 Aug. 1919; *R.D.M.,* 2 Aug. 1919.
4. E. Brookes, *The Colour Problems of South Africa* (Lovedale, 1934), 84.
5. Interview with Professor E. Cluver.
6. J. van der Poel, *Selections From the Smuts Papers,* V (Cambridge, 1973), 218.
7. Council minutes, I, 16 Feb. 1925.
8. H.C. Bosman, *A Cask of Jerepigo* (ed. by Lionel Abrahams, Cape Town, 1978), 112–13.
9. W.E. Curson to Lionel Phillips, 21 June 1916, U.O.D. E33/3.
10. Mayor John O'Hara to the S.A.S.M.T. Council, 1 Sept. 1916, Ibid.
11. John Maud, *City Government: The Johannesburg Experience,* 148; Charles van Onselen, 'The Main Reef Road into the Working Class', *Studies in the Social and Economic History of the Witwatersrand, 1886–1914, II, New Nineveh,* 111–70; G.E. Pearse, 'Notes on the Site and Buildings of the University of the Witwatersrand', University Archives.
12. Ibid.
13. Council minutes, I, 12 Oct. 1920.
14. Pearse, 'Notes on the Site and Buildings of the University'.
15. Ibid.
16. Johannesburg Municipality, Council minutes, 22 Oct. 1920.
17. J.M. Watt, 'The History of the Medical School of the University of the Witwatersrand', *Leech,* 25, 4 (1955).
18. R.A. Dart, *Adventures with the Missing Link* (London, 1959), 32–3.
19. Paton, *Hofmeyr,* 82.
20. Council minutes, II, 20 March 1925.
21. *R.D.M.,* 19 March 1923.
22. For the system of loans to universities see *Report of the University Commission,* U.G. 33 of 1928, Appendix IV.
23. E.H. Farrer, Secretary for Finance, to Sir William Hoy, South African Railways and Harbours, 27 Nov. 1920, U.O.D. E33/18.
24. J.H. Hofmeyr to the Secretary for Education, 9 Nov. 1920, U.O.D. E33/13, Vol. I; Secretary for Lands to Secretary for Justice, 26 April 1922, and reply from Secretary for Justice, 27 April 1922, U.O.D. E33/18.
25. Secretary for Education to Minister of Education, 29 July 1921, U.O.D. E33/13.
26. Secretary for Finance to Secretary for Education, 26 Aug. 1921, Ibid.
27. Secretary for Finance to Secretary for Education, 20 Sept. 1921, Ibid.
28. Secretary for Education to Principal Hofmeyr, 11 May 1922, Ibid.
29. Secretary for Finance to Secretary for Education, 2 Feb. 1924, U.O.D. E33/18.
30. Thomson to Secretary for Education, 22 Dec. 1924, U.O.D. E33/13.
31. *Annual Report of the Department of Education for the year ending December 1927,* U.G. 49 of 1928, 14 and 38.
32. *Report of the University Commission,* U.G. 33 of 1928, 4.
33. See chap. 3.
34. Council minutes, I, 7 Feb. 1922.
35. *Annual Departmental Reports 1923/4,* Department of Education, U.G. 15 of 1925, 9.
36. 'Statement of Revenue and Expenditure for the Year Ending 31st December 1923', Finance Committee, I.
37. *Annual Report of the Department of Education for the year ending December 1927,* U.G. 49 of 1928, 38–9.
38. *Annual Departmental Reports 1925/6,* U.G. 6 of 1927, 277.
39. For a full account of the Seymour Memorial Library see R.F. Kennedy, *The Heart of a City: A History of the Johannesburg Public Library* (Johannesburg, 1970), chap. 12.
40. Senate Misc./169/27.
41. Council Misc./64/26.
42. *R.D.M.,* 23 Aug. 1926.
43. *Annual Report of the Department of Education for the year ending December 1928,* U.G. 51 of 1929, 7.
44. Council Misc./67/26.

45. Lionel Phillips to E. A. Wallers, 30 Nov. 1916, MS. Central Mining.
46. Witwatersrand University Committee, executive minutes, 23 April 1923.
47. *Annual Report of the Department of Education for the year ending December 1928,* U.G. 51 of 1929, 47.
48. *Report of the University Commission,* U.G. 33 of 1928, 29.
49. *University of the Witwatersrand, Johannesburg, Annual Report 1930.*

5
ARTS AND SCIENCE

I

Perhaps surprisingly, in 1922 Arts was by far the biggest faculty. In the year of the University's foundation, twelve departments, all of which had been established since 1917, were located in that faculty. The Department of Bantu Studies was added in 1923. One-third of the University's full-time students were in the Faculty of Arts. What was quite remarkable for a university that was regarded by many as essentially a technical institute, was the calibre of the professors, and indeed some of the students, in Arts.

Although it possessed nine departments, the Faculty of Science was, in terms of students registered, one of the smallest of the faculties. Law alone of the original faculties had fewer students, 49 in 1922 as against 113 in science. Five of the Faculty of Science's ten departments, mathematics, applied mathematics, physics, chemistry, and geology had been established before the post-1916 expansion. Their pre-war heads all entered the service of the University, although Lehfeldt had moved from physics to economics.

II

The Faculty of Arts was staffed primarily by men recruited from overseas, particularly Britain. For the most part, those who were to gain prominence, and establish enduring reputations, did so by interesting themselves in their new society. For some this interest was political, for others scholarly, and yet others, a combination of both. But by one means or another they made themselves directly relevant to their new society. As a consequence, Wits soon established a reputation for itself as a home of 'liberalism' in South Africa, and as a major centre for the scholarly study of the peoples and cultures of South Africa. This reputation was not dependent on the activities of members of the

Faculty of Arts alone. The lawyers, notably O.D. Schreiner and W.H. Ramsbottom, certainly enhanced the reputation of Wits as a centre of liberalism, and Raymond Dart of the Department of Anatomy virtually created the University's international reputation for the study of the peoples of South Africa, with his discovery of the first Australopithecine skull, the Taung skull. None the less, because of the nature of their disciplines, it was from among members of the Faculty of Arts that the University produced most of its critical and scholarly students of South African society and its peoples.

In his first address as Principal in August 1919 Hofmeyr had commented that South African universities and colleges had so far done little to apply themselves 'to the solution of our South African problems'. More than a decade later, Edgar Brookes, Professor of Native Law and Administration at the Transvaal University College in Pretoria in the 1920s, likewise commented that when the Union's university system was established during the World War, there had been 'no sign that the South African Universities were specially interested in the great problems of life just outside their own doors'. By the beginning of the 1930s the situation had changed dramatically. Brookes observed in 1933 that four of the country's five universities had established departments of Bantu studies, that several other university departments had moved towards 'a realistic study of South African life, which inevitably means the inclusion of the Native in the picture', and that students were displaying a new interest in the 'Native Problem', notably through the National Union of South African Students and Bantu Studies Circles at the various universities. For the development of liberal thought and a liberal critique of South African society, Brookes considered that the University of the Witwatersrand had assumed the lead not only among universities, but in the country as a whole. As he saw it, Cape liberalism had faded into the background and had virtually been replaced by 'the Johannesburg school of liberalism, with its greater reliance on economic facts in the place of sentiment and tradition'.[1]

The emergence of a 'Johannesburg school of liberalism' at the end of World War I was a response to the development of secondary industry on the Witwatersrand during the war years, and to the acute African unrest on the Rand in the period 1917-20, when the 'black Bolsheviks of Johannesburg' with their 'Socialist method of pitting black against white' appeared to run amok, not only to whites but also to some black activists like Sol Plaatje in Kimberley.[2] The advance of secondary industry on the Witwatersrand during World War I convinced economists such as R.A. Lehfeldt, who had become Professor of Economics at the School of Mines in 1917, that urban whites would in future have to accept a permanent black population in their midst. As he pointed out in *The National Resources of South Africa*, published in 1922, migratory labour was not suited to manufacturing: 'It is not quite satisfactory even on the gold mines to employ for the roughest work natives who return to their kraals after a short engagement, and have no home life where they work, but it would be impossible in factories; for factories need some training even on the part of their least skilled hands, and that means permanence of employment.'[3] What alarmed whites at the end of World War I was not only the militancy of black urban and migrant workers on the Witwatersrand, especially Johannesburg, but also the apparent radicalization of some members of the embryonic black middle class. It was this that inspired efforts at co-option and reform, including the formation of the Joint Councils of Europeans and Natives in 1921. As Selope Thema, a 'moderate' African leader, recalled, the meeting that established the Johannesburg Joint Council, was held at a time of extreme tension, when white and black South Africans seemed to be at the parting of the ways. The meeting proved 'an eye-opener to African leaders who never thought that there were white men and women in South Africa with human hearts. For the first time they met with Europeans, not as masters and servants, sellers and buyers, officials and members of a subject race, but as human beings and fellow-citizens.'[4]

The role played by the School of Mines and then the University of the Witwatersrand at the end of World War I and during the early 1920s was to bring together those men and women who were to provide the 'Johannesburg school of liberalism' with its intellectual leadership. W.M. Macmillan moved from Grahamstown to Johannesburg in 1917 to become Professor of History. In 1922 Margaret Hodgson, later Mrs Ballinger, joined his department. J.D. Rheinallt Jones came to Johannesburg in 1919 as secretary of the Witwatersrand Council of Education and organizing secretary of the Witwatersrand University Committee, and in 1923 R.F.A. Hoernlé arrived from Britain to occupy the chair of philosophy at Wits. His wife, Winifred, was made lecturer in the Department of Bantu Studies. In 1924 I.D. MacCrone was appointed lecturer in psychology in the Department of Philosophy.

Following the formation in 1924 of General J.B.M. Hertzog's first government, based on a pact between Nationalist and Labour parties, the segregationist policy of government provided the main focus for liberal attention. In 1926 Hertzog proposed three 'Native Bills'. The Native Lands Further Release and Acquisition Bill was supposed to make more land available for the reserves; the Union Native Council Bill aimed to create an advisory Council of fifty Africans, thirty-five of them to be elected; and the Representation of Natives in Parliament Bill sought to remove the African voters from the common roll in the Cape and to provide instead for seven white M.P.s to represent Africans from all provinces. The latter bill was central to Hertzog's segregationist policy, and required a two-thirds majority in Parliament as it revoked one of the entrenched clauses of the South Africa Act. It was not until 1936, following the formation of the Hertzog/Smuts Fusion government, that Hertzog was able to secure the necessary two-thirds majority. His 'Native Bills', in revised form, were then all enacted.

Hertzog's ten-year campaign for the 'Native Bills', and their final enactment, divided liberal opinion. Some, like the Non Racial Franchise Association in the Cape and the Johannesburg Joint Council, remained uncompromising in their defence of the Cape franchise; others were more pragmatic in approach and wished to attain the best possible arrangement for blacks in return for the loss of the Cape franchise. Yet others again were alarmed by the overtly political action taken by some of the Joint Councils in opposing the Hertzog Bills, and pressed instead for the formation of a non-political, fact-finding body that would seek to educate public opinion and combat racial prejudice through the publication of its researches. In 1929 the Institute of Race Relations was founded as such a body, with its offices, provided rent-free, at the University of the Witwatersrand.

At Wits, Macmillan and Hoernlé provided the main intellectual thrusts behind the University's emergence as South Africa's leading centre of liberal thought. The two men adopted very different approaches. Macmillan was the more radical, certainly the more polemical and political; Hoernlé was the more articulate, the more closely attuned to the 'scientific' study of African culture and racial attitudes offered by the new social anthropology and psychology. Macmillan maintained that history taught 'that South Africa was suffering from bad government and bad administration' and that 'the remedy was political, to substitute good laws for bad'. In his opinion, 'political action to force reform of vicious legislation was to be urged rather than palliatives and amelioration'. Other liberals at the University saw things differently: 'These others . . . were inspired particularly by anthropology and by American sociologists, who had begun to think in terms of a quasi-philosophical or psychological "race conflict" which must be studied before any remedies could be proposed. Among them was my friend Rheinallt Jones, and probably also Professor and Mrs Hoernlé.' Macmillan contended that while their approach might produce much worthwhile research, it promoted too little by way of political action. The approach Macmillan censured came to be enshrined in the Institute of Race Relations, which did much useful work 'recording for the world and posterity the iniquities of the South African system' but which 'has had no effect on politics'.[5]

W.M. Macmillan   R.F.A. Hoernlé

Macmillan considered himself a social democrat, and his ideas and associations sometimes alarmed more 'moderate' liberals. Soon after his arrival in Johannesburg in 1917, Macmillan established links with the white trade union movement in Johannesburg, and the Workers Educational Association. In 1922 he saw some of the leaders of the Rand mine-workers' strike as 'high minded socialists'.[6] After the strike he came more into contact with blacks, involving himself in the Joint Councils of Europeans and Natives, and meeting black workers through the Industrial and Commercial Workers Union when it moved its headquarters to Johannesburg in 1925. When Edgar Brookes complained in 1933 of those who spoke 'the language of Johannesburg with the accent of Moscow', he had Macmillan and some of his students in mind.[7] Macmillan regularly contributed articles on South Africa to the *New Statesman*.

Born in Aberdeen in 1885, Macmillan had come to South Africa at the age of six. He was educated at the Victoria College, Stellenbosch, and Merton College, Oxford, which he attended as one of the first Rhodes scholars. In 1911 he was appointed lecturer in history and economics at Rhodes University College, Grahamstown, where he began his investigation of social and economic questions in South Africa, beginning with the poor white problem. After moving to Johannesburg he secured the papers of Dr John Philip, the famous (to many at the time, infamous) missionary to the Cape in the first half of the nineteenth century. This opened a decade of sustained research that was to produce what he called 'a revised version of South African history'. Between 1927 and 1930 he published his famous trilogy — *The Cape Colour Question; Bantu, Boer, and Briton: The Making of the South African Native Problem,* and *Complex South Africa* – which established the basis for a liberal and economic interpretation of South African history. The first two books dealt with the Cape colony, chiefly in the first half of the nineteenth century; the last was mainly an investigation of social and economic conditions in South Africa in the 1920s.

With Eric Walker at Cape Town, Macmillan became the first of the professional English-language historians of South Africa. In his work he reacted strongly against the pro-colonist, anti-missionary interpretation of Cape history established by G.M. Theal and Sir George Cory, who despite never having been trained as historians pioneered the writing of South African history. Utilizing his missionary sources, Macmillan sought to rehabilitate 'missionary policy' at the Cape, particularly as it concerned the coloured population, while countering the approach that 'treats South African history as the story of the fortunes only of its European pioneers'. In contact with such people as R.H. Tawney, J.L. Hammond, and Sidney and Beatrice Webb in England, he also saw himself as bringing to South African political history something of their socio-economic approach. His work was both polemical and historical, and conveyed the fundamental message that the fortunes of white and black in South Africa were inseparably linked. Problems among whites in the twenties, notably the 'poor white' problem, for him were directly related to black poverty. 'The lesson stands out clear for him who runs to read', he wrote, 'that the root of most South African ills to-day is to be traced directly to disregard in the past of the place of the Natives in the community.' His basic message was clear: 'The plain but difficult lesson for all to learn is that in the long run what is best for the Native is best for the European, as well as *vice versa*.'[8]

Generally rather shy and reserved, Macmillan had nevertheless a strong combative streak in him, sometimes revealed in Senate, but which was expressed chiefly in his writings and public addresses. In the 1920s he wrote a series of aggressive articles on worsening conditions in the reserves, which Hertzog in Parliament denounced as 'political'. After Macmillan's return from overseas leave in 1931, he sought to rally the Johannesburg Joint Council, of which he was chairman, in opposition to Hertzog's segregation policy. This brought him into direct conflict with Oswald Pirow, the Minister of Justice, and E.G. Jansen, the Minister of Native Affairs. In his autobiography,

Macmillan gives the impression that his altercation was with Pirow alone, but after a major brush with the Minister of Justice in September 1932 he then confronted the Minister of Native Affairs over the 'Native Bills'. Their exchange reached its climax on 10 November 1932 when, in defiance of the minister, Macmillan published their correspondence in the *Rand Daily Mail*.[9] The same day an agitated Principal Raikes wrote to Macmillan to rebuke him for his public attack on the minister, that might prejudice the University's future relations with the government:

> I feel very strongly that the University should not muzzle members of its staff. But this naturally implies that members of the staff will not take such action as may jeopardise the relation between the University and the Government without being authorised so to do by the Council.
>
> I am not prepared to say that the action you have taken in this instance has jeopardised our relations with government, but I feel that it may well have serious repercussions in that direction.
>
> Under the circumstances I feel bound to say, both as a private citizen who is keenly interested in the development of the Native, and as Principal, that the publication of the letter can do no good and may do very great harm, both to the development of the Native and the position of the University.

Macmillan was convinced that the government had put pressure on Raikes and that, because of the economic depression, the University was particularly vulnerable to such pressure. Before the next Council meeting, Macmillan was summoned 'urgently' by Raikes. According to Macmillan's own account, he offered to resign, but Raikes was determined to avoid that as he did not 'want to make the University notorious by victimising me'.[10] Macmillan did not then resign, but took the overseas leave that had already been granted him for 1933. He was never to return to Wits as a member of staff. On 13 September 1933, he cabled his resignation to Raikes.

Although his lectures were not carefully structured, Macmillan was an especially inspiring teacher, greatly loved and admired by most of his students. Among these students, several were to establish international reputations as historians, notably Lucy Sutherland and C.W. de Kiewiet. Other historians of South Africa, including J.S. Marais, who later occupied the chair of history at Wits, also owed much to the inspiration of Macmillan. In the seventies his work was rediscovered by historians of South Africa, and again served to inspire creative effort.

Hoernlé, for his part, produced beautifully structured, polished lectures, and he was undoubtedly one of the most stimulating lecturers at Wits in its early years. Together with Dalton, he was one of the charismatic giants in the early history of the University. His classes were enormously popular, although, unlike Macmillan, in his years at Wits he did not produce any professional scholars in his own field. He possessed a clear, systematic mind, and both as public speaker and teacher his great strength, and the secret of much of his appeal to audiences and students alike, was his marvellous lucidity. I.D. MacCrone, Hoernlé's colleague and later Principal of the University, has recalled what tremendous gifts of exposition Hoernlé possessed, his capacity to explain clearly without having to over-simplify, and also his ability to inspire. He spoke English and Afrikaans with a soft German accent, and moved people in a way Hofmeyr could not. His chief contribution to liberal thought in South Africa between the world wars was that he made it both systematic and inspiring.

R.F. Alfred Hoernlé succeeded John Macmurray as Professor of Philosophy in 1923. He already possessed an international reputation as a philosopher when he came to Wits at the age of 43. Born in Germany, he had spent his early years with his missionary parents in India and received his schooling in Germany before going up to Balliol. After Oxford he lectured in philosophy at St Andrew's University in Scotland, the South African College in Cape Town, Armstrong College in the University of Durham in England, and at Harvard University in the United States, where he was departmental chairman for two years. In 1920 he returned to Armstrong College as Professor of Philosophy. In 1913 he married Agnes Winifred Tucker, who was the daughter of Senator W.K. Tucker, and who studied social anthropology at Cambridge. Because of his wife's ill-health he returned to South Africa in 1923 to the chair of philosophy at the University of the Witwatersrand. He was to remain at Wits until his sudden death in July 1943.

A disciple of the late nineteenth-century British philosopher, Bernard Bosanquet, Hoernlé belonged to the Idealist school of philosophy, and in particular the branch known as Absolute Idealism, which made him the exponent of the synoptic approach, or 'seeing things together' in all their multifarious relationships. He was the author of a number of major philosophical works: *Studies in Contemporary Metaphysics* (1920), *Matter, Life, Mind and God* (1923), *Idealism as a Philosophy* (1924), and *Studies in Philosophy*, collected essays published posthumously in 1952. In the judgement of John Passmore in *A Hundred Years of Philosophy*: 'His talent was devoted rather to the skilful and sympathetic interpretation of philosophy than to the working out of fresh philosophical ideas.'[11] None the less some firmly believed that Hoernlé, had he remained overseas, could have developed into a philosopher of the first rank.

After taking the chair at Wits, increasingly Hoernlé's creative energies were directed away from philosophy. Though he produced a number of philosophical essays during his twenty years at Wits, they were few and far between, and he had perhaps come to accept that the school to which he belonged was no longer at the cutting edge of philosophy. Apart from which he possessed considerable administrative and executive abilities, and in his early years at Wits he became greatly involved in University affairs. He was Dean of the Faculty of Arts in 1925 and became a dominant figure in Senate. In December 1926, when it was announced that Sir William Thomson would retire the next year after his brief tenure as Principal, Senate, at the instigation of Dalton, nominated Hoernlé for the principalship. But Council would not appoint him, the opposition within Council being led by Jan Hofmeyr, now Vice-Chancellor. Hofmeyr had studied under Hoernlé at the South African College, and had greatly admired him, but would not forgive him for his criticism of the way the Stibbe affair was handled. When he arrived from England, Hoernlé declared that Hofmeyr had been both stupid and un-Christian in his harsh dealing with the unfortunate Stibbe, and had compounded the offence in 1924 by successfully opposing the proposal to award an honorary degree to Hofmeyr. Council appointed H.R. Raikes as Principal. Ten years later Hoernlé stood for the principalship at Cape Town, but was again passed over.

Following his failure to secure the principalship at Wits, and inspired by his wife, who was lecturer in social anthropology in the University's Department of Bantu Studies, Hoernlé became increasingly preoccupied with public issues, notably the racial problem. In the newly founded Institute of Race Relations, he rapidly emerged as a leading figure. In 1934 he became chairman of both the executive committee and the council of the Institute, retaining both positions until his death. During his last ten years he became the leading spokesman for white liberal opinion in South Africa, and is today generally regarded as the most systematic of South Africa's liberal theorists between the world wars.

In his memoir of Hoernlé, MacCrone claimed that Hoernlé's politics directly reflected his philosophy. 'Again and again', he wrote, 'we find Hoernlé . . . protesting against one-sidedness, exclusiveness, narrowness of thought and feeling as compared with the liberal ideals of comprehensiveness and universality, tolerance and fair-mindedness in political relations, which he derived from his synoptic philosophy.'[12] Some liberals, like Edgar Brookes, made defence of the rule of law against the inroads of the state the essence of their liberalism, but Hoernlé's liberalism was rooted in a sense that the whites were doing an injustice to the black population in South Africa. In his essays and speeches of the thirties, many of them a response to the segregationist legislation proposed by Hertzog, Hoernlé accurately dissected the anatomy of white domination in South Africa, political, economic, educational, social, and even sexual. His fundamental protest against the system of white domination was that it was generally employed to promote 'the welfare of the White group at the expense of that of the non-European groups'.

As represented by Hoernlé, the primary mechanism of white domination was the policy of segregation. He maintained that a genuine separation of races in South Africa was impracticable, and that segregationism was therefore essentially dishonest:

> For, you cannot really 'segregate' people whom you need, on whom you are dependent for labour, and without whom the whole structure of White civilization in South Africa would collapse. You cannot segregate them in any way which will – fairly and squarely – set them free from your grip so as to work out their own independent, or parallel, development. And, if you segregate them whilst still holding them tight in your economic system, you are in fact introducing a caste system, a system of disguised helotry and serfdom, which is in bitter conflict with the whole Christian and humanitarian tradition of European civilization, and makes a grim mockery of the missionary efforts of the Christian churches.

He perceived that the role of the reserves was to provide the South African economy with a supply of cheap black labour, while enabling white South Africa to justify the exclusion of blacks from full rights of citizenship. In 1936, in a lecture to the council of the Institute of Race Relations, he pointed out that segregationists wanted 'territorial segregation, in order to have easily accessible reservoirs of Native labour, where at the same time the Native labourer can have his own home and keep his family, so that he need not be paid for his labour in the White areas a wage sufficient to maintain his family, while, on the other hand, the fact that the Native has his own society in the Native reserves makes it easier to treat him in the White areas as a stranger and an outsider.'[13]

Hoernlé also consistently emphasized that it was idle to talk of the Africans 'developing along their own lines'. His own firm conviction was that 'the Bantu are destined to become civilized according to our, i.e., the Western, pattern of civilization'. It was their historical destiny to assimilate Western civilization, no doubt with nuances of their own. Consequently it was the historical duty of whites 'as their civilized fellow-citizens, not to withhold from them any opportunity for development which they are able to use, nor to put any permanent or insuperable obstacles in their path'.[14] Hoernlé did not, however, argue the case for a full integration of peoples in South Africa. So long as there was no caste structure, limiting opportunity of development, he believed that in order to minimize friction and tension 'we should not reject a type of social structure within which these different racial groups, living alongside each other, maintain each for itself, a high degree of group cohesion and identity'. In particular, he defended the maintenance of a sex-barrier between white and black: 'It is not only compatible with, but the condition of, our Western civilization doing its work for our Native fellow South Africans, communicating to them those things which we most value ourselves, which they most desire to share, and which we have no right to withhold.'[15]

In 1939, in his Phelps-Stokes lectures in Cape Town, Hoernlé caused a furore in liberal circles by indicating his preference for a total separation of the various peoples of South Africa. He posed the question whether a 'liberal native policy' was possible in South Africa. His contention was that assimilation did not represent the only policy for South Africa consistent with liberal principles, but that policies of parallel development without territorial segregation, or of total separation could also be regarded as legitimate applications of sound liberal ideals. He stated that complete assimilation, a thorough-going parallelism, and total separation were all three unrealizable, but that liberals had nevertheless to answer the question in which direction they wished to encourage developments. He answered in favour of the last: 'For the Native peoples of the Union, at any rate, it should be clear that there is no *escape from White domination by way of Parallelism or Assimilation, but only by way of Total Separation.*'[16]

During the thirties the handful of radicals at the University and in the white community regarded Hoernlé as something of a fence-sitter. In his Phelps-Stokes lectures he was seen to come down on the wrong side of the fence. In the final resort, he was anxious that liberals should not become men without influence in South Africa, and the conclusion he had reached was that the only influence open to them was to attempt to humanize, and so far as possible exploit for the benefit of blacks, the entrenched system of segregation. 'At any rate', he declared, 'if the liberal choice among the three schemes were for Total Separation, there would be, at once, created a more favourable psychological atmosphere for co-operation with all those who are keen on the development and enlargement of the Native Reserves; who do not in principle oppose Native progress along the lines of European culture; and who contemplate, and would welcome, the growth of a vigorous and self-reliant national spirit among the Native peoples.'

Until 1936 when it became a separate department, psychology was taught as a two-year course in Hoernlé's Department of Philosophy. This, together with his wife's position as lecturer in social anthropology in the Department of Bantu Studies, meant that Hoernlé was closely attuned to the anthropological and psychological approaches to race problems and attitudes. For some, like J.D. Rheinallt Jones, the first director of the Institute of Race Relations, the 'scientific' basis of these disciplines provided a far more promising approach to South Africa's race problems than did a study of the country's history.

J.D. Rheinallt Jones

In his presidential address of 8 July 1926 to Section E of the South African Association for the Advancement of Science on 'The Need of a Scientific Basis for South African Native Policy', Rheinallt Jones stated: 'Political experience and historical knowledge have not given us the panacea for our racial difficulties, but have led us instead into a wilderness where the road is lost in the thick undergrowth of racial pride, passion and prejudice.' He looked instead to the 'scientific study' of 'the Native' by anthropologists and psychologists to provide a more constructive understanding of the country's race problems. The country's universities, he asserted, were now organizing departments to 'undertake the study of Native life'. 'A definite responsibility', he declared, 'rests upon scientific workers in the fields of anthropological and psychological research to collect the data from which general principles may be deduced to guide the country in the adoption of a sound policy in race relationships.' His own expectation concerning these principles was apparent:

> If the civilisation of a people or an individual can be measured by the degree of emancipation from the power of animistic beliefs, and of social organisations based upon these beliefs, and if we accept the conclusion that the Bantu people are capable, at whatever rate of progress, of assimilating our rationalised civilisation, any Native policy which seeks to drive the Native back into the Bantu Culture, is setting the Native's face

in the wrong direction – not towards liberty, but into thraldom. Rather should it aim at surrounding and permeating Native life with all these civilising agencies which enrich our own life – such as educational and religious teaching, economic development, hygienic organisations and governmental control. To give every encouragement to those who show signs of adopting civilised ways would be logical.[17]

Cape Town University in 1918 established the first department of African studies in South Africa when it set up a Department of African Life and Languages with government financial support. The Smuts government refused to finance a second such department in Johannesburg, consequently delaying its foundation until 1923, when it was established with financial assistance from the Witwatersrand Council of Education, and the mining industry through the Native Recruiting Corporation and the Witwatersrand Native Labour Association. As Rheinallt Jones, representing the Witwatersrand Council of Education, urged upon the Chamber of Mines, 'the Industry would benefit by the increased expert knowledge of native questions' which would follow the creation of such a department at Wits, though he conceded 'that there would be little direct material advantage to the mining industry'.[18]

It was with the express aim of assisting whites to 'know the Native' so that they might deal more successfully with 'the Native Problem', and secure the goodwill of blacks through a sympathetic understanding of their culture, that the Department of Bantu Studies was established at Wits. As Clement Doke, appointed as a lecturer in the department, urged in the *Rand Daily Mail* in November 1923, the Witwatersrand, with its vast black population, representing so many 'Bantu tribes' with as many languages, made Johannesburg the obvious centre for the study of 'the Native' with a view to getting 'at the back of the black man's mind'. 'The administrator in native territories', he wrote, 'whether magistrate or native commissioner, the missionary, the public official who deals directly or indirectly with natives, the municipal superintendents of native affairs, according to the provisions of the new Urban Areas Act, all of these need training in native history, native traditions and folk-lore, native indigenous law, in the social customs and religion of the native people, among whom or for whom they are to work.' Hofmeyr, in a statement in the *Mail* on what he believed to be the special contributions Wits would make to South Africa, claimed that its medical school would provide the base for the conquest of disease in Africa, its engineering faculty would furnish the men and ideas for building up the country's industrial future, and its Department of Bantu Studies would make valuable contributions 'to the unravelling of that problem which is most fundamental in South African politics, and should be most prominent in South African scientific investigation'.[19]

Rheinallt Jones, the secretary of the Witwatersrand Council of Education, one of the founders of the Johannesburg Joint Council, and an enduring liberal, was the key figure in helping to set up the Department of Bantu Studies at Wits. A Welshman by birth, he had already served the University by acting as organizing secretary of the Witwatersrand University Committee, and in 1921 he had established the journal *Bantu Studies* to promote 'the scientific study of Bantu, Hottentot and Bushman'. At his request the journal was published by the Witwatersrand Council of Education, and in 1923 the Witwatersrand University Press was founded to publish the journal and other manuscripts approved by the Council of Education, which provided the funds, and the University Senate, which gave the academic stamp of approval.[20] Rheinallt Jones remained an editor of *Bantu Studies,* re-named in 1942 *African Studies,* until the end of World War II. For a short period, from 1927 to 1929, he was Assistant Registrar in the University, and he also lectured in a part-time capacity in Native Law and Administration. In 1930 he became adviser on race relations to the Institute of Race Relations, and his post was later changed to director. From 1937 to 1942 he was a Senator representing Africans of the Transvaal and Orange Free State. He subsequently became adviser on 'Native Affairs' to the Anglo-American Corporation.[21]

Originally, the Department of Bantu Studies was under the headship of Max Drennan, the Professor of English. The first two full-time appointments in the department were C.M. Doke, lecturer in Bantu philology, and Winifred Hoernlé, lecturer in ethnology. They were assisted by Edgar Brookes, who came over from Pretoria to lecture on Native Law and Administration, and the Revd A.T. Bryant, who had previously been appointed as a research fellow in Zulu ethnology.

The department was composite, the lecturers in different subjects working independently of each other. Doke was a first-rate linguist. The son of a Baptist minister, he came to South Africa in 1903, when aged 10, and as a young man had made contact with African societies and languages through his involvement in Baptist missionary work. In 1919 he was awarded the M.A. of the University of South Africa for his grammar of the Lamba language, and in 1921–2, with the help of a loan from the Witwatersrand Council of Education, he attended the School of Oriental and African Studies at London University, and obtained the diploma in Comparative Bantu. On taking up his appointment at Wits, Doke worked particularly on the Zulu language, and pioneered an analytical and descriptive model for Bantu grammar, so as to provide 'a Bantu grammar for Bantu languages'. In 1924 he was awarded the

D.Litt. by Wits for his thesis on the phonetics of the Zulu language, which was published in a special number of *Bantu Studies,* and in 1927 he produced his *Text Book of Zulu Grammar.* In 1931 he was appointed Professor of Bantu Languages and Head of the Department of Bantu Studies, retaining these positions until he retired in 1953. His greatest achievement was in 1948, when the Witwatersrand University Press published the *Zulu-English Dictionary* he had prepared with Dr B.W. Vilakazi, the Zulu poet and prose writer who was appointed to the department in 1935. Ten years later the W.U.P. published the *English-Zulu Dictionary* prepared by Doke and D. McK. Malcolm of Natal University and J.M.A. Sikakana of Wits. The dictionaries remain among the most comprehensive and scholarly yet produced for any Bantu language.

Doke was never simply a linguist. Believing that a knowledge of Bantu languages was essential as the means to understand African customs and traditions, he undertook wider social studies, publishing in 1931 *The Lambas of Northern Rhodesia.* The department's social anthropologist, A. Winifred Hoernlé, was to make a significant contribution to social anthropology in South Africa as a teacher and as a director of research. In A.R. Radcliffe-Brown U.C.T. possessed one of the doyens of social anthropology, but he proved more a disruptive than a creative influence in their Department of African Life and Languages, whereas at Wits Winifred Hoernlé was to lay very solid foundations for the study and teaching of social anthropology. A follower of Durkheim, she espoused an essentially sociological concept of anthropology, and together with Radcliffe-Brown pursued a functionalist approach, which examined social facts in terms of their function within a culture, and disregarded their historical evolution. This approach insisted on the importance of intensive field-work, and Mrs Hoernlé conveyed to her students the sense that field-work was the *sine qua non* of social anthropology. Before coming to Wits in 1924 she had undertaken research into the social structure of the Khoi people of Namaqualand and South West Africa, and this provided the basis for several pioneering descriptive papers on the Nama Hottentots. While at Wits she produced a number of important papers, but her major role was as a teacher and a director of the work of others. Though not a particularly good lecturer, she kept fully abreast of all new developments in social anthropology. She insisted on high standards of scholarship, and from the outset oriented her students towards research. She combined a fine mind with a gentle manner, and was generally enormously helpful to students, her chief legacy. They included Max Gluckman, one of the most brilliant products of Wits prior to World War II, a pioneer of conflict theory, and later Professor of Social Anthropology at Manchester University; Ellen Hellmann, who pioneered the study of urban African workers; Eileen (Jensen) Krige and her husband J.D. Krige, who together published in 1943 *The Realm of a Rain-Queen* based on extensive field-work among the Lovedu of the Transvaal Lowveld, and both of whom were to hold the chair of social anthropology at the University of Natal, Durban; and Hilda (Beemer) Kuper, who was to publish several major works on the Swazi and to become Professor of Anthropology at the University of California, Los Angeles.

Winifred Hoernlé lectured at Wits for thirteen years. In 1934 she was made senior lecturer, retiring three years later. In 1949, in recognition of her services to the community in social welfare and race relations as well as her work in social anthropology, the University awarded her an honorary doctorate.

Much of the work of the social anthropologists in the twenties and thirties was designed to counter race prejudice among whites by explaining 'the Native' to white society, and by indicating that Africans were capable of assimilating Western civilization. For the study and understanding of the nature of race prejudice among South African whites, the pioneering work was undertaken by I.D. MacCrone, the first full-time lecturer in psychology appointed at Wits.

Born at Wellington in the Cape in 1898, MacCrone graduated from U.C.T. in 1917, then served as a gunner in the South African Heavy Artillery in France in the last year of World War I. He returned to U.C.T. for his M.A., and then proceeded to New College, Oxford, to read Politics, Philosophy and Economics. After Oxford he went to Columbia University in New York, where he began his study of race attitudes. In 1924 he was appointed lecturer in psychology in the Department of Philosophy at Wits. Previously psychology had been offered by W. Reith Macgregor, the Professor of Education, but it had soon become evident he knew no psychology. MacCrone's special interest in psychology was psycho-analysis, and his approach was strongly academic; he had little interest in the application of psychology. Although not a particularly inspiring lecturer, his classes were large, in part because psychology was required for students studying for a teachers' certificate. When Wits established a separate Department of Psychology in 1937, MacCrone was elected professor. He continued as head of department until 1963, when he was appointed Vice-Chancellor and Principal of the University. He retired at the end of 1968, and died in 1981, aged 83. In liberal circles he is best remembered for his active role in the 1950s to protect Wits and U.C.T. as 'open' universities, and for his work for the Institute of Race Relations.

With Hoernlé's encouragement, MacCrone applied his American experience to the investigation of race attitudes in South Africa, publishing several articles. In 1935 he was awarded the Ph.D. by Wits, and two years later his thesis was published by the Oxford University Press as *Race Attitudes in South Africa: Historical, Experimental and Psychological Studies*. This was a major landmark, for it represented the first full and systematic attempt to analyse race attitudes, chiefly among whites, in South Africa. The book was divided into three sections. In the historical section, MacCrone contended that the eighteenth century was the formative period for white race attitudes in South Africa, and more particularly that it was the 'frontier' experience in the Cape that radicalized and intensified the race attitudes which the first Europeans brought with them to the Cape. On the frontier the trekboers found themselves isolated from civilized society, physically dispersed, and in conflict with other groups. To preserve their own identity and group cohesion in this hostile environment, and to avert their 're-barbarization', they stressed the two things about themselves that most distinguished them from the 'barbarians': their religion and their race. 'Under such circumstance', MacCrone contended, 'the intense and exclusive group consciousness of the frontier found expression in a consciousness of race and social supremacy which coincided almost uniformly with the distinctions based upon creed and colour.'[22] In the experimental section of the book MacCrone sought to measure and describe the social distance between various groups in contemporary South Africa, and in the psychological section he employed Freudian analysis to examine the principles and forces underlying race prejudice.

MacCrone's emphasis of the importance of the eighteenth century and the frontier for the shaping of race attitudes among whites in South Africa, reflected important contemporary trends in South African historiography, and also American historiography with the impact of F.J. Turner's 'frontier thesis'. Today different perspectives prevail, and Marxist historians particularly emphasize the crucial significance of the impact of mining capitalism at the end of the nineteenth century and the beginning of the twentieth for the development of a fully-fledged ideology of race in South Africa.[23] None the less, for several decades MacCrone's book was recognized as a major contribution towards the understanding of race attitudes in South Africa, and was accepted as a standard text on the subject. For liberals, it was intended to convey a sense of optimism rather than pessimism; to encourage a sense of pragmatism rather than inflexible adherence to principle. In his preface, MacCrone stated: 'But if we can succeed in avoiding the wish which quite evidently fathers the pessimists' thinking, we may find ample evidence in support of the view that, while a doctrinaire adhesion to principle has no future in South Africa, there is a very good chance that some solution will be found in terms of a more realistic and progressive application of those principles which are professed by all enlightened men.' There was little, however, in the book that was positively encouraging to liberals, and possibly it contributed to the pessimistic tone struck by Hoernlé in his Phelps-Stokes lectures in 1939. MacCrone's fundamental message was that race attitudes among whites in South Africa 'are a very important element in the total situation, and that they cannot simply be ignored or brushed aside by dismissing them as a form of race or colour prejudice'.[24]

Although Macmillan had left the University by the time MacCrone's book appeared, it was no doubt one of those extensive studies of 'minds' that exasperated him as likely to produce a 'paralyzing conservatism'. More congenial to Macmillan were the economists at Wits, R.A. Lehfeldt and after him S. Herbert Frankel, with their basic message that economic development rendered whites and blacks increasingly interdependent. In his presidential address to Section F of the South African Association for the Advancement of Science in July 1920, Lehfeldt declared that segregation as a policy for South Africa was quite impossible as: 'The natives are so thoroughly incorporated in the industry of South Africa that to exclude them and require them to live in certain districts, while the Europeans lived in others, would revolutionise the country.' He predicted that the races were destined to live side by side indefinitely, and that 'racial mixture is . . . inevitable'. He concluded: 'Remembering the immediate problem of how the white and black races are to attain satisfactory economic relations with one another, I would venture to close with an aphorism – that a country will in the end belong to the people who do its work.'[25] Lehfeldt's student, and successor in the chair of economics, S. Herbert Frankel, was to emerge as one of the foremost liberal economists of South Africa.

Lehfeldt, who headed both the Department of Economics and Economic History and the Department of Statistics, had first come to Johannesburg as Professor of Physics in 1906. He had graduated from St John's College, Cambridge, with a B.A. in 1890, and had also secured a D.Sc. at London University before taking up the chair of physics at the Transvaal University College. From 1915 he gave courses in economics to all fourth-year students at the School of Mines, and when a Department of Economics was set up in 1917 he decided to abandon physics for economics. According to Frankel, he was a quite brilliant mathematician and statistician, and what interested him particularly was the application of mathematical methods to economic and sociological problems. In 1916 he published a little book on *Economics in the Light of War,* and thereafter followed a number of works on currency questions and on the distinctive features of the South African economy: *Gold Prices and the Witwatersrand* (1919), *The National Resources of South Africa* (1922), *Restoration of the World's Currencies* (1923), and *Controlling the*

Output of Gold (1926). *The National Resources of South Africa* was a particular landmark as it incorporated the first estimate of South Africa's national income, and represented the first attempt at a comprehensive analysis of the country's economic activities. Lehfeldt also published textbooks on *Money,* and *Descriptive Economics.* As a teacher he was noted for his conscientiousness, professionalism, and his use of seminars when teaching senior students. Though shy by disposition, when moved, as over the Stibbe affair, he could become quite assertive. His death in 1927 was mysterious and bizarre. He was found dead on some pillows next to his bathtub, with his arms in chains, and a wristwatch attached to one of his feet, which had been placed against an activated electric radiator. Some thought it was murder, most thought it was suicide, and at the inquest Professor Dalton claimed it was an experiment that had gone wrong. The magistrate recorded an open verdict: 'Found electrocuted'.

Interest in things African and South African at the new University was not confined to those committed to attempting to resolve South Africa's racial problems or those professionally trained in African studies. Professor Raymond Dart, in the Department of Anatomy, established an international reputation as a physical anthropologist with his work on fossil man-apes in southern Africa. In the Faculty of Arts, P.R. Kirby, the first Professor of Music, and L.F. Maingard, the Professor of French and Romance, likewise responded to the challenge of South Africa by developing a strong interest in the culture of its indigenous peoples.

Kirby, a Scot and the son of a musician, was trained in music at the Royal College of Music, London, where he obtained the A.R.C.M. diploma in composition. He also graduated in philosophy and biology from Aberdeen. In 1914, at the age of 27, he came to South Africa as organizing inspector of music to the Natal Education Department. While in Natal he first began his studies of African music. In 1921 he was seconded to the University College, Johannesburg, as Acting Professor of Music, and was subsequently appointed to the chair of music at Wits, where he remained until his retirement in 1952.

Kirby was a vivid personality; an extrovert, of great energy and cheerfulness, and violent enthusiasms, he enjoyed the ability to become passionately interested in things well outside his own academic field. He responded to what he described as 'the call of South African history' by editing the diary of the explorer Dr Andrew Smith for the Van Riebeeck Society and by seeking to unravel the mysteries surrounding the sinking of the 'Grosvenor' treasure ship off the Wild Coast. A compulsive talker, his conversation and lectures were replete with anecdotes told in his distinctive Scots accent. What brought him prominently before the public eye, and helped to make the

C.M. Doke

I. D. MacCrone

R.A. Lehfeldt

P.R. Kirby

University an important part of the cultural life of Johannesburg, was his enthusiasm for staging what he called 'musico-dramatic' productions, sometimes with the musical score written by himself, and unusual operatic works. He helped in the design of the Great Hall, and after its opening in 1940 he put on an annual stage performance. He founded the University Orchestra, which participated in these performances, and also gave an annual concert in the Great Hall, thereby providing students with valuable experience in performance.

Under Kirby the Department of Music, which was never large, became noted more for music history and musicology than for practical training. It was as an ethnomusicologist that Kirby established his main reputation. Encouraged by Doke and Raymond Dart, Kirby pursued his interest in African music, and between 1930 and 1934 carried out a major series of ethnographical expeditions, notably in the northern Transvaal, to survey the musical practices of the African peoples in South Africa. The outcome was his book, *The Musical Instruments of the Native Races of South Africa,* published by Oxford University Press in 1934, the first systematic study of African musical instruments, and as such a landmark in the study of African music. Kirby's interest was in the instruments and how they were played, rather than music they produced. His magnificent collection of African musical instruments is today housed in the Africana Museum, Johannesburg. Kirby's real tragedy was that he did not follow up on his seminal study of 1934, but wandered into other fields. As a composer he was fairly active, and he wrote the music for *Alma Mater,* the academic song of the University.[26] His lecturers were Cornelius Duggan, one of the Rand's leading teachers of pianoforte, and W.P. Paff, who served the University until his retirement at the end of 1956.

On some of his expeditions Kirby was accompanied by L.F. Maingard, appointed in 1921 Professor of French in succession to Morgan Watkin, the first incumbent of that chair. Soon after assuming the professorship, which he retained until his retirement in 1947, Maingard introduced the teaching of Italian and Portuguese, and the department was renamed the Department of French and Romance. On occasion, Maingard served as Acting Principal of the University, notably between Hofmeyr's resignation in March 1924 and the appointment of Sir William Thomson in 1925. A rather difficult, pugnacious man, Maingard had a general interest in philology, which led him to study the languages of the Korana and Bushman peoples. His work, published mainly in *Bantu Studies,* was of a pioneer nature, but of limited value to later generations of scholars.

A department of immediate relevance to South Africa that Wits lacked at its inception was Afrikaans, although it did possess a Department of Dutch. In 1918 Grey College, Bloemfontein, and in 1919 Stellenbosch University became the first institutions of higher learning to make appointments for the teaching of Afrikaans. It was not until 1928 that Wits named its first junior lecturers in Afrikaans and Nederlands, Abel Coetzee, a specialist in Afrikaans language and folklore, and J.J. le Roux. In 1929 a Department of Afrikaans replaced that of Dutch, though it continued under the headship of the Professor of German, J.D.A. Krige.

Prior to the appointment of Coetzee and Le Roux, some Afrikaans had been taught in the Department of Dutch, under Krige's aegis. Krige, a member of the well-known Afrikaans family of that name, was born in 1888 at Richmond in the Cape. He had gone to Germany at the age of 10, and then studied at the University of Ghent, before returning to South Africa in 1914. In 1917 he was appointed Head of the Departments of German and Dutch at the School of Mines, and he continued as Professor of German and Head of the Department of German until his retirement in 1950. It was never a particularly large department during his tenure. As a person Krige was very shy, exquisitely polite, and unassuming. In 1972, when the University offered him an honorary degree as part of its golden jubilee celebrations, he declined on the ground that his achievements were 'not really sufficient to merit an honorary degree'.

At Wits in its early years, the great champion of the Afrikaans language was Theo Haarhoff, the Professor of Classics. Haarhoff came to Wits from U.C.T. in 1922 as the successor to H.J.W. Tillyard, who had accepted the chair of Russian at Birmingham University after serving as joint Professor of Classics with Hofmeyr. Haarhoff was to remain Professor of Classics until 1957, although he would have preferred it otherwise. For the venturesome and the ambitious, serving in the same position at the same institution for 35 years can prove soul destroying. In 1930 the opportunity to go to U.C.T. as Professor of Nederlands and Afrikaans, had for domestic reasons to be declined. In 1944, political opposition from the Broederbond and other Nationalist groups forced him to refuse the rectorship of the University College of the Orange Free State. Haarhoff was a Smuts man, and because of the passions aroused by South Africa's participation in the war against Germany, Nationalists in the Free State vehemently opposed his appointment, making it impossible for him to accept the rectorship. 'My coming', he wrote bitterly in his letter of refusal, 'would be the signal for strife to flame up anew and the fires will be continuously fed. The intrusion in the academic field of bodies that are at once unscrupulous and implacable, complicated the issue enormously. It really shocked me to find what a hold these bodies have on past and present students. The mere fact that an academic post could be made a political issue shows how far people are from understanding what a university should be.'[27] His kindliness and sense of humanity never deserted him, but he was thereafter a disappointed man.

Although a fervent supporter of the Afrikaans language, Haarhoff was never acceptable to the Nationalist Afrikaner establishment. In the broadest sense, a liberal and a humanist, he believed very deeply in the virtues of tolerance and co-operation, and throughout his life he sought to promote harmony between Afrikaans- and English-speaking whites in South Africa. In *Stranger at the Gate,* published in 1938, he instanced the Roman Empire as a model of 'racial co-operation'. After the formation of the Nationalist government in 1948, he emerged as a critic of enforced *apartheid* between whites and blacks.

As a classicist Haarhoff established a certain eminence. Like his boyhood friend, Hofmeyr, he had been a Rhodes scholar, and before coming to Wits Oxford University Press had published his Oxford B. Litt. thesis, *Schools of Gaul.* At Wits he became more interested in literary subjects, and in 1931 received a D.Litt. from the University of Amsterdam for a dissertation on 'Vergil in the Experience of South Africa'. It was published as *Vergil the Universal.* Vergilian studies continued as one of his major interests, his annual 'Vergil lecture' becoming something of a feature at Wits. He wrote voluminously on classical antiquity, and a range of other subjects, and he is undoubtedly best remembered for his book *Life and Thought in the Greek and Roman World,* which he wrote with M. Cary, the Professor of Ancient History at London University. Haarhoff wrote his own poetry in Afrikaans, but his main contribution to that language was his translations of several of the classics into Afrikaans. By these translations he sought to prove the range and flexibility of Afrikaans, a language he did much to publicize overseas. Within South Africa, he was ever anxious to encourage an appreciative awareness of Afrikaans among English-speaking whites.[28]

T.J. Haarhoff

The Department of Classics offered courses in Latin, Greek, Ancient History and, after 1927, Classical Life and Thought. Miss M.V. Williams, A.I. Wagner, and G.J. Acheson served Haarhoff for many years as lecturers.

The Department of English in 1922 was headed by an accomplished mediaevalist, Professor C.M. Drennan, who was assisted by J.G. Lawrie. Drennan, a graduate of the Universities of London and Cambridge, was one of the original Arts appointments in 1917, serving as Professor of English until he retired in 1931. During his career he edited several Chaucerian texts and one of Langland, and he also wrote a short textbook on modern literary criticism. A contributor to *Punch,* he was noted for his vivid sense of humour, and was particularly popular as a lecturer. He had a gift for conveying the zest as well as the learning of his subject. An important contribution he made to the University was in establishing links with the local community, mainly through his columns in the *Rand Daily Mail* and *Sunday Times.* Lawrie, an ebullient personality, was to remain on the academic staff until 1941.

The remaining two departments in the Faculty of Arts, Hebrew and Education, were both run by part-time staff. In 1919 the Chief Rabbi J.L. Landau, a distinguished scholar of modern Hebrew letters and an ardent Zionist, was appointed Professor of Hebrew, and he continued to lecture on a part-time basis until 1940. During this period the Department of Hebrew remained very small, and it perturbed Landau that non-Jewish students displayed no interest in Hebrew. The Department of Education was under the aegis of Professor Reith Macgregor, a dour Scot and Principal of the Johannesburg Training College for Teachers. When he retired in 1935 the department went into temporary abeyance. It had offered a one-year course towards the B.A. and B.Sc. and a two-year programme for the B.Ed. The University did not offer professional training for school teachers.

III

In addition to a full range of degrees in arts, music and education, the Faculty of Arts offered a series of diplomas in languages, and a higher and a lower diploma in Bantu Studies. A major aim of the Department of Bantu Studies was to attract to it public servants who dealt with 'the Native', and its diplomas were specifically designed for civil servants. The lower diploma was also intended to be useful to missionaries.

The regulations for the B.A. degree required candidates to complete eleven qualifying courses, including at least one course in either English or Dutch, and to major in two subjects. The three-year majors, in addition to English and Dutch, were French, German, Italian, Bantu, Latin, Greek, Hebrew,

History, Music, Pure Mathematics, and Geography. The two-year majors were Logic, Ethics, and Psychology in the Department of Philosophy, Economics, Social Anthropology, and Roman Law. English, Latin, and History proved the most popular of the three-year majors, while Ethics and Psychology were overwhelmingly the favourites of the two-year majors. None of the diplomas, including Bantu Studies, attracted more than a handful of students.

As early as the twenties, there was a slight majority of women in the Faculty of Arts. At least a quarter of the Arts students were also students at the Johannesburg Training College for Teachers, previously known as 'the Normal College'. Teacher training was the responsibility of the provincial administrations, and what the Transvaal Education Department did was to allow students to undertake a full B.A. or B.Sc. course at the University while contemporaneously passing through the various stages of the second or professional part of the Teachers' Second Class Certificate programme at the Training College. The successful completion of five university courses, two at the second-year level, exempted students from part one of the certificate examination. The so-called T^2 certificate students divided into two groups. The first studied full-time for three years, secured their professional certificate and then went out to teach, often completing a degree through afternoon and evening classes at the University. These classes in the Faculty of Arts were designed primarily for teachers wishing to secure a degree. The second group studied full-time for four years, obtaining both a degree and a teachers' certificate. They would normally complete their majors at the University in their third year, and the fourth year would be devoted to the completion of their professional subjects and training. The courses in Ethics I, Psychology I, and the History of Education offered at the University counted as 'professional subjects', two of which were frequently taken by students in their last year both for their certificate and to complete their degree.[29]

Between 1922 and 1927, Thomson's last year as Principal, 309 students completed their B.A. degrees at Wits. Twenty-nine qualified for the B.A. in 1922, and seventy-six at the end of 1927. Two students qualified for the B.Mus. In the same period sixteen students were awarded their Master's degree, including C.W. de Kiewiet and Lucy Sutherland in history, and Herbert Frankel and Eileen Jensen in economics.

In the early years of the University, and indeed the whole period prior to World War II, relations between students and teaching staff in the Faculty of Arts were very different from those that pertained later. There was then a far wider gulf between students and staff than now. There was generally little real debate between students and staff, and students were normally expected to be deferential and uncritical. Almost without exception, the sole emphasis in teaching was on lectures, rather than tutorials, and lectures themselves were sometimes given at dictation speed.

An Arts student of those early days, who was later to gain notoriety for killing his step-brother, then fame as an author, Herman Charles Bosman, recalled that he had little respect for the staff at Wits: 'I could not reconcile myself to the idea that any really first-class man from Europe would bring himself to apply for so obscure and – as I then thought – Philistine – an appointment as a professorship in a South African mining town university where the reinforced concrete slabs were still wet inside.'[30] Bosman showed his contempt for the staff of the English department by entering in his own name one of Shelley's lesser known poems in a competition run by the University magazine, only revealing its true authorship after it had been awarded third prize. The incident caused a considerable public stir, and was raised in Parliament by the M.P. for East London North, appropriately named Brigadier-General Byron. In the debate on the education vote in the House of Assembly on 8 June 1925, Byron complained: 'It is a very serious matter that we should have in our universities professors who do not command the confidence of their pupils and who could make such a mistake.' Byron was appalled that Wits could employ professors so ignorant that they 'did not even know of the existence of this particular poem', but the Minister of Education declined to reprimand the University. Instead, he cited the case of one Charlie Chaplin who was awarded second prize in a small-town competition for the man who could best imitate Charlie Chaplin.[31]

In later years Bosman developed more of a respect for those who had taught him at Wits. 'I feel only a sense of humble gratitude', he confessed, 'towards those men from overseas who came to the Witwatersrand University when it was first started, bringing with them the vital breath of culture that includes the Near East and Alexandria and the Renaissance, that rich Old World of thought in whose inspiration alone the soul of man can find a place for its abiding.'[32]

A sense of what an able student might get out of the Faculty of Arts at Wits in its early years is provided by the recollections of Max Gluckman. From I. Schapera, who spent a year lecturing in social anthropology at Wits, Mrs Hoernlé, W.M. Macmillan, Herbert Frankel, and I.D. MacCrone, he learnt that African society could not be studied in isolation, but that its interactions with white society were critical to its understanding.[33] This awareness was fundamental to the development of his ideas on conflict theory.

IV

The Faculty of Science, like Arts, was staffed mainly by full-time professors and lecturers. Together, the two faculties possessed the greater part of the

University's full-time staff. Far fewer students were registered in the Faculty of Science than in Arts, but it provided service courses for students in engineering and medicine, and it developed an enviable record in producing research students. By the end of 1927 some seventeen students had qualified for the M.Sc., including O.G. Backeberg in chemistry, Edna Janisch and Edgar Mendelssohn in geology, and Eddie Roux in botany.

The two longest-serving members of staff in the Faculty of Science in 1922 were R.B. Young, Professor of Geology, and J.A. Wilkinson, Professor of Chemistry. Both had been members of the original staff of the Transvaal Technical Institute.

Like the heads of the geology departments at U.C.T. and Stellenbosch, Young was a Scot, a graduate of Edinburgh and Glasgow Universities. His initial appointment to the Transvaal Technical Institute had been somewhat fortuitous. He was offered the chair in geology during a visit to the Rand, having spent a short spell at the South African College in Cape Town, deputizing for his brother. He held the chair until his retirement in 1934. He was an able teacher, research worker, and administrator. Whereas H.S. Shand at Stellenbosch achieved international eminence as a petrologist, Young established his department as the main centre in South Africa for geology in general, giving more emphasis than Shand to practical aspects such as field-work and economic mineral deposits. In Johannesburg, mining geology was necessarily of the first importance. Young's personal research interest was the sediments of the Witwatersrand system, especially the gold-bearing banket, and in 1917 he published *The Banket: A Study of the Auriferous Conglomerates of the Witwatersrand, and Associated Rocks*. His was an important pioneer achievement, and though much new information has since been added, the book still serves as a standard work of reference. Young's later researches centred upon the Transvaal dolomite. He also did a considerable amount of private consulting work, especially during the development of the East Rand mines. An excellent organizer, in his capacity

R.B. Young

J.A. Wilkinson H. Stephen

first as chairman of the Advisory Board of Industry and Science and then as chairman of the Research Grant Board, he did much to promote scientific research. He also served for many years as secretary of Senate. Two of his students, Edna (Janisch) Plumstead, later to gain international eminence as a palaeobotanist, and Edgar Mendelssohn, who became a specialist in mining geology, joined his staff as lecturers. Both provided the University with distinguished service.[34]

The Professor of Chemistry, J.A. Wilkinson, affectionately known as 'Loots', was a Cambridge graduand. He was noted for his friendliness, his interest in students, and his ability to bring things to life in his lectures. He was more of a teacher than an academic, and was sometimes criticized for not keeping up to date in his field. He retired in 1933. His life at Wits from 1926 was complicated particularly by Henry Stephen, who in that year was made Professor of Organic Chemistry, and who later succeeded Wilkinson as Professor of Chemistry.

Stephen was a product of Manchester University's Department of Chemistry during the Dixon-Perkin-Rutherford era. A brilliant organic chemist, he had already established a major reputation before coming to Wits. During World War I he had been seconded as research assistant to Dr Chaim Weizmann in the Ministry of Munitions, where he worked upon a revolutionary method for the production of mustard gas, for which he was awarded the O.B.E. In World War II Stephen, Colonel W. Bleloch, and Dr Taverner were to be invited by General Smuts to plan the local manufacture of mustard gas, and at Klipfontein, for the first time in South Africa, they produced small quantities of the gas.

Stephen was a tremendous personality as well as an outstanding chemist. Vital and vigorous, with an incredibly bright and alert mind, he was to exercise a major influence on Raikes, who was likewise a chemist. He was not, however, a team man. He was exceptionally ambitious, preferring to go his own way, and gained a reputation as an arch intriguer. His impact on some of his colleagues was frankly demoralizing. The man who suffered most at his hands was Wilkinson, who came to regret ever securing a second chair in chemistry.

With Wilkinson's retirement, the Departments of Chemistry and Organic Chemistry were merged under Stephen, who thereafter resisted any attempt to separate them. Stephen's retirement in 1954 was not much lamented by his colleagues, though none would deny that he had put organic chemistry at Wits on the map. Chemical engineering, which was the responsibility of the Department of Chemistry, also made enormous advances after Stephen had taken over from Wilkinson. In the twenties chemical engineering was the 'Cinderella' of the engineering courses; in the thirties it came much more into its own.

Two lecturers in chemistry in the twenties who were to give the University long service were J.B. Robertson, a dour Scot and orthodox chemist, and O.G. Backeberg, who was appointed lecturer in organic chemistry in 1927. The first Rhodes scholar produced by the South African School of Mines and Technology, Backeberg was to become Professor of Organic Chemistry when the chair was re-established after Stephen's retirement.

The mathematics professors in the new University, J.P. Dalton and Herbert Le May, had both served on the staff of the School of Mines, joining at about the same time. Dalton became Professor of Mathematics in 1914, and Le May had been appointed lecturer and Head of the Department of Applied Mathematics the previous year. In the early history of Wits Dalton, a man of very considerable intellectual ability, was one of the truly powerful characters. An Irishman, he had received his university education in Scotland, and soon established himself as an extremely versatile academic. Before joining the School of Mines as Professor of Mathematics, he spent two years as a researcher in thermodynamics at Leiden University, Holland, three years as a lecturer in physics at University College, Dundee, and another year as lecturer in physics and applied mathematics at the Victoria College, Stellenbosch.

J.P. Dalton   H. Le May

When the University College, Johannesburg, established a Department of Actuarial Science, he gave the lectures. Because of his wide range of interests Dalton did not concentrate on developing pure mathematics as a discipline. What he taught was sound, if a little old-fashioned compared with what was happening elsewhere in the world. As a lecturer Dalton was compelling; even engineering students listened to him in silence. He produced a number of important papers, and one major book, *Symbolic Operators,* published by the Witwatersrand University Press in 1954.

Dalton did not subscribe to the idea of the university as an ivory tower, and played an active role in developing links between Wits and the wider community. He would on occasion give special lectures designed to acquaint the Johannesburg public with developments in the sciences, and in 1921 gave a celebrated series on Einstein and the theory of relativity, later published as *The Rudiments of Relativity*. With Macmurray and Macmillan he was involved in the Transvaal Workers' Educational Association. The lectures he gave to the association in late 1933 on social insurance were published the following year by the Witwatersrand University Press. Probably his most memorable public lecture was in the series offered by the University in June 1932, entitled 'Our Changing World View', on recent thinking in the fields of science, economics, education, literature, and philosophy. General Smuts gave the first lecture on

'Some recent scientific advances in their bearing on Philosophy', and expounded his holistic philosophy. Dalton delivered the second lecture on 'The material world – yesterday and to-day', and proceeded to reject Smuts's notion of 'a semi-mystical union of mind and matter'. He concluded: 'Instead, therefore, of a Union of Matter and Mind, I see in the New Physics a deliberate attempt to compel Mind to perform its proper function as an interpreter of the observed facts, and to prohibit it from attempting any longer to squeeze Nature into a mould of its own contriving.'[35]

The lecture was typical of the man. He was nothing if not forthright and combative. Some saw him as ruthless and unsympathetic, though his integrity was never questioned. He never feared making enemies, nor hesitated to oppose any cause he thought bad. He made no attempt to hide his low opinion of some of his colleagues, particularly those in the medical school. It was in the Senate that the full power of his personality was felt. He possessed a biting, sarcastic tongue, and his forays on the side of justice were feared by all who fell foul of justice, or him. Hofmeyr knew well what it meant to be opposed by Dalton. He served the University until 1946. Nearly twenty years later, in October 1965, he died at St Winifred's on the Natal south coast in poverty. He had taken his pension in a lump sum and invested it unwisely.

Among Dalton's lecturers in the Department of Mathematics in its early days were C.J.M. Constancon, a colourful personality who had joined the staff in 1917 and served until his retirement in 1945, and C.W. Kops, who lectured in actuarial science. John Kerrich, appointed as a junior lecturer in 1925 and later to become Professor of Statistics, and Frank Young, appointed in 1927 and destined to serve in the University for 45 years, were both pupils of Dalton.

Compared with Dalton, Le May was a rather unremarkable person. A Scot, and a graduate of Glasgow University, he had no higher degree and was consequently regarded by some of his colleagues as under-qualified. His promotion to professor in 1923 caused something of a stir in Senate. While he established a tradition for competent teaching in applied mathematics, later continued by Arthur Bleksley, he was apparently a bit of a schoolmaster in his attitude towards students and junior staff, and showed little interest in research. His strength was as an administrator, serving on Council from 1931 until his retirement from the University in 1951, and in 1949 acting as Principal.

When Professor Ogg moved to Cape Town at the end of 1919, his successor in the chair of physics was a 39-year old Welshman, H.H. Paine, who had served with distinction in the war, being awarded the Military Cross. Paine was a graduate of the University College of Wales, Aberystwyth, and

Cambridge. He held the chair of physics until his retirement in 1946. Paine was a very kindly person, but also very sensitive, being particularly shy with students. His senior lecturer, another Welshman, G.T.R. Evans, succeeded Paine in the chair of physics in 1947. Together they taught physics to science, engineering, and medical students with a devotion that has become legendary. Despite his heavy teaching burden Paine maintained an interest in research, working primarily on the physical properties of colloidal solutions. After his retirement, the University appointed him honorary research professorial fellow, and in 1972 he was awarded an honorary LL.D. He remained a familiar figure on campus until his death in 1980.

H.H. Paine

When the Departments of Botany and Zoology were established in 1917 they attracted to Johannesburg C.E. Moss and H.B. Fantham, both Cambridge graduates. Moss was to serve as Professor of Botany until his sudden death in 1930, and Fantham as Professor of Zoology until the end of 1932, when he became Strathcona Professor of Zoology at McGill University, Montreal. Both men were outstanding scholars in their fields, and both undertook important research at the University.

Though he was regarded as a difficult person by his colleagues, intellectually Moss was one of the leading lights at the new University. An aggressive little man with a shock of white hair that stood up from his forehead, he 'not infrequently caused an uncomfortable liveliness at meetings'.[36] His initial research interest in England was ecology, and he contributed important sections to the volume on *Types of British Vegetation,* edited by A.G. Tansley, and published in 1911. Thereafter, as curator of the herbarium at Cambridge, he turned more to taxonomy for his research, and was responsible for the first three volumes of the *Cambridge British Flora*. At Wits, Moss worked tirelessly to classify the plants of South Africa, identifying and filing over 20 000 specimens. The herbarium he established at Wits stands as his finest monument, and is generally recognized as among the best in the

C.E. Moss

H.B. Fantham

world. In 1922 Moss, after having been warned by Hofmeyr to stop seeing her, married his senior lecturer, Margaret Heatley, a graduate of Wellesly College. She continued lecturing at the University until 1950, and carried a heavy teaching burden. Moss produced several postgraduate students at Wits, mostly notably Eddie Roux, later to become Professor of Botany at the University.

Moss shared, with Professor Fantham, the first of the teaching buildings to be constructed at Milner Park, the Botany and Zoology block. Like Moss, Fantham was also a difficult person, but nevertheless succeeded in building up a department noted for its scholarship and research. Fantham's wife, Dr Annie Porter, was also an academic, and a first-rate zoologist. She was attached to the South African Institute for Medical Research, and lectured to Wits students on parasitology.

As a researcher, Fantham specialized on the protozoa. Before coming to Wits, he had written the sections on protozoa in *Animal Parasites of Man* by Fantham, Stephens, and Theobald, and with his wife a popular book, *Some Minute Animal Parasites*. At Wits he made a survey of the parasitic protozoa and soil protozoa of South Africa, publishing numerous research papers. He also interested himself in questions of human heredity and 'race admixture', warning against a mixing of the peoples in South Africa. Unquestionably, his became the leading research department in the faculty in terms of the number of research students produced. Three of his M.Sc. students, Nellie Paterson, Clara Weinbrenn, and Joanna Schuurman, joined his staff. Nellie Paterson went on to Cambridge for a Ph.D., and later became senior lecturer in zoology at Wits. Fantham's most famous student was Botha de Meillon, who became an international expert on malaria after completing his D.Sc. at Wits on 'South African Insects of Medical Importance'.

Fantham was an able administrator, and for four years served as the second Dean of the Faculty of Science. In 1921 he was president of Section D of the South African Association for the Advancement of Science, and in 1927 grand president of that Association. But he was not an easy person to get on with. He was something of a paranoiac, and drove two of his senior lecturers out of the department. G. Evelyn Hutchinson, who was senior lecturer in 1927-8, and who subsequently went to Yale University, where he became a world authority in his field of freshwater ecology, has recalled:

> Once in Johannesburg I discovered that my duties were to run the elementary lab and to give a course on contemporary problems in biology. This sounded nice enough. I also learned that there were three junior lecturers in the department, all women, one Afrikaner, one English, and one Jewish, which again sounded reasonable. When I got to know these ladies better, I discovered that they were essentially readers, in the medieval sense of the word. They read lectures prepared by the professor. The departmental library, which constituted the entire collection of zoological books and periodicals in the university, was kept in the professor's room, which did not make for easy access. My course at first was not good, but it would have been better if it had not been attended by the professor. I gradually came to realize that I was not wanted, and during my second year this was made clear by my being suspended from all teaching duties. Unlike my predecessor, I was not physically thrown out.[37]

During his brief tenure at Wits, Hutchinson made a significant contribution to the freshwater ecology of the Transvaal.

In 1922, as today, the Department of Geography had its home in the Faculty of Science, though it took many of its students from the Faculty of Arts. The first lecturer in geography at the School of Mines, James Hutcheon, died in 1920, and in the next year John Wellington was appointed senior lecturer and Head of the Department of Geography at the age of 29. In 1923 he was made professor, a position he retained until his retirement at the end of 1957. A graduate of London and Cambridge, he was an excellent teacher of undergraduates, and an especially keen researcher. His particular interests were physical geography and geomorphology, and he undertook a thorough study of the South African landscape, making a major contribution to the understanding of the physical geography of southern Africa. Shortly before his retirement Cambridge University Press published in two volumes his *Southern Africa: A Geographical Study*. The work ranks as one of the best of its kind for any continent, and for it Cambridge University awarded him a Sc.D. He was the first geographer to be given the degree by that University. Wellington was both earnest and very religious, and a man of great integrity. This sometimes led him to make stands in Senate when most of his colleagues were prepared to be more accommodating, and among his critics he gained a reputation as a great fighter of lost causes. Prior to World War II, he did not produce many postgraduate students, but one of them, Stanley Jackson, was to succeed him in the chair of geography.

J.H. Wellington

V

The Faculty of Science offered three degrees, Bachelor (including Honours), Master and Doctor of Science, and no diplomas. Candidates for the B.Sc. were required to complete nine courses, including two majors and one Arts course. The three-year majors were pure mathematics, applied mathematics, physics, chemistry, botany, zoology, geology and mineralogy, and geography. Anatomy, physiology, and psychology constituted the two-year majors available to B.Sc. students.

Between 1922 and 1927 the Faculty of Science produced 95 B.Sc. graduates, 53 men and 42 women. It was a very stable faculty in terms of the number of graduates produced each year; 13 at the end of

1922, rising to 17 at the end of 1927. For students thinking of proceeding to medicine, anatomy and physiology proved a popular combination of majors; otherwise chemistry was the only consistently popular major. Geography attracted far fewer majors for the B.Sc. than the B.A., and applied maths and physics attracted few majors. Before World War II there were few professional openings for physicists in South Africa outside teaching, and this served to restrict the number of students wishing to major in physics.

Notes

1. Brookes, *Colour Problems*, 79–84.
2. Brian Willen, 'Sol Plaatje, De Beers and an Old Tram Shed: Class Relations and Social Control in a South African Town', *Journal of Southern African Studies*, 4 (1978), 195–215.
3. Lehfeldt, *The National Resources of South Africa* (Johannesburg, 1922), 34.
4. E.H. Brookes, *R.J.: John David Rheinallt Jones* (Johannesburg, 1953), 4. See also J.W. Horton, 'South Africa's Joint Councils: Black-White Co-operation between the Two World Wars', *South African Historical Journal*, 4 (1978), 29–44.
5. Macmillan, *My South African Years*, 214–6.
6. Ibid., 154–7.
7. Brookes, *Colour Problems*, 110–11.
8. Macmillan, *Complex South Africa* (London, 1930), 18.
9. Ibid., 213–30; *Star*, 7 Sept. & 2 Nov. 1932; *R.D.M.*, 5 & 10 Nov. 1932.
10. Macmillan, *My South African Years*, 228–30; Macmillan to Mona Tweedie, 10 Nov. 1932, MS. Macmillan.
11. John Passmore, *A Hundred Years of Philosophy* (London, 1957), 89–90.
12. Hoernlé, *Race and Reason* (ed. by I.D. MacCrone, Johannesburg, 1945), vii–xxxvi.
13. Ibid., 98–9.
14. Ibid., 73–4.
15. Ibid., 42 & 74.
16. Hoernlé, *South African Native Policy and the Liberal Spirit* (Cape Town, 1939), 182–3. See also M. Legassick, 'Race, Industrialization and Social Change in South Africa: The Case of R.F.A. Hoernlé', *African Affairs*, 75 (1976), 224–39.
17. J.D. Rheinallt Jones, 'The Need of a Scientific Basis for South African Native Policy', *South African Journal of Science*, 23 (1926), 79–91. See also P. Rich, 'The South African Institute of Race Relations and the Debate on Race Relations, 1929–1958', *African Studies*, 40 (1981), 13–22.
18. Minutes of meeting in Chamber of Mines, 17 Oct. 1922, WNLA 65/30.
19. *R.D.M.*, 1 Nov. 1923.
20. Minutes of the Syndic of the Council of Education, 25 Feb. & 20 May 1922.
21. Brookes, *R.J.*; and Brookes, 'J.D. and Edith Rheinallt Jones' in R.M. de Villiers(ed.), *Better Than They Knew* (Cape Town, 1972), 136–61.
22. I.D. MacCrone, *Race Attitudes in South Africa* (London, 1937), 130.
23. See M. Legassick, 'The Frontier Tradition in South African Historiography' in S. Marks and A. Atmore (eds.), *Economy and Society in Pre-Industrial South Africa* (London, 1980).
24. MacCrone, *Race Attitudes*, v.
25. R.A. Lehfeldt, 'Labour Conditions in South Africa', *South African Journal of Science*, 17(1920/21), 85–95.
26. For more on Kirby see his autobiography, *Wits End* (Cape Town, 1967).

27. Haarhoff to Franklin, 28 June 1944, Haarhoff file, Staffing Registry.
28. For a full list of Haarhoff's publications see the bibliography compiled by C.S. McCleery, University of the Witwatersrand Library, 1968.
29. 'Memorandum on the relationship between the Johannesburg Training College for Teachers and the Witwatersrand University', May 1925, Senate Misc.
30. Bosman, *Jerepigo*, 112–3.
31. *House of Assembly Debates,* IV, 4176–4221.
32. Bosman, *Jerepigo,* 112–3.
33. Max Gluckman, 'Anthropology and Apartheid: The Work of the South African Anthropologists' in Meyer Fortes and Sheila Patterson (eds), *Studies in African Social Anthropology* (London, 1975).
34. For more information on Young see the *Dictionary of South African Biography* (Pretoria, 1968), I, 892–3.
35. *Our Changing World View* (Johannesburg, 1932), 15.
36. Obituary by J. Ramsbottom, *Journal of Botany,* Jan. 1931.
37. G. Evelyn Hutchinson, *The Kindly Fruits of the Earth* (New Haven, Conn., 1979), 195.

6

THE PROFESSIONAL FACULTIES

I

At its inception the University possessed four faculties preparing students for the professions: engineering, which included architecture; medicine, which came to include dentistry; law; and commerce. In 1929 dentistry became an independent faculty, thereby completing the prewar list of faculties within the University.

The twenties was generally a difficult decade for the professions, giving rise to alarmist talk of an over-supply of university graduates. It was simultaneously an important decade for defining and protecting access to the professions in South Africa. During the decade Parliament enacted legislation to supplement or supersede pre-Union laws regulating admission to several of the professions. It passed the Admission of Advocates Act (1921), which amended the pre-Union laws on the admission of advocates; the Chartered Accountants Designation Act (1927), which conferred upon the members of the four provincial societies of accountants the use of the designation Chartered Accountant (South Africa); the Architects and Quantity Surveyors Act (1927), which established the Institute of South African Architects as a national statutory body and restricted the right to practise to registered architects and quantity surveyors; and the Medical, Dental, and Pharmacy Act (1928), which established the South African Medical Council and the South African Pharmacy Board as statutory bodies. This last Act had first been proposed in 1923, but had been held up by the contentious clause 34, which provided penalties for practising by unregistered persons.[1] Although the idea of securing statutory recognition and protection for professional engineers was also mooted, no proposals were submitted to Parliament.[2]

Much of this legislation was strenuously opposed by practitioners threatened with exclusion. In the case of the chartered accountants a complicated compromise had to be devised. Under the so-called 'Pearce

Agreement' special provision was made for admission to the provincial societies of established public accountants who had not previously belonged. The purpose of the legislation was to provide status and protection for recognized practitioners, while assuring the general public of their credentials. The legislation was welcomed by the universities as it afforded protection to their graduates. As the *South African Architectural Record* commented on the Architects and Quantity Surveyors Act: 'The chief benefits of the Bill are that the public will not so much in this generation but certainly in the next be assured that when they employ an Architect or Quantity Surveyor they will be employing a fully qualified well trained and skilled professional man, while from the students' point of view they will feel that after putting in some five years of technical training and devoting their time to study and passing their examinations they will be protected from competition from the unqualified.'[3]

A major concern at Wits, as in university circles generally in the early twenties, was the apparent danger of an over-supply of professionals in the country. On 29 October 1923, Professor Lehfeldt proposed in Senate that 'While it is a good thing that as many citizens as have the necessary capacity should go through a university curriculum in Arts or Pure Science, the number of students at the South African Universities and Colleges in professional curricula is becoming larger than the country is able to find employment for.' The motion was withdrawn after lengthy discussion, and it did not thereafter become policy at Wits to discourage students from embarking on professional curricula. On the contrary, the University became distinctly alarmed when the number of students in mining engineering diminished in response to the apparent lack of professional opportunity. It was in the late twenties, and more particularly the thirties, that a sense of great opportunity in the professions returned, notably in engineering and medicine, and that the University's professional faculties truly came into their own.

II

The early twenties were especially difficult years for the engineering faculty. Although the University had grown out of a school of mines and technology, it was engineering, and particularly mining, that languished at the inception of Wits. Between 1922 and 1927 the University produced the grand total of 110 B.Sc. graduates in engineering, 42 in the combination of mechanical and electrical engineering, 47 in civil engineering, 12 in chemical engineering, and 9 only in the combination of mining and metallurgy.

Mining and metallurgy caused most concern. Many supposed the paucity of graduates in these fields was explained by the contraction of employment and promotion possibilities in the gold mining industry, with the decline in the number of producing mines from 46 in 1920 to 36 by 1926. Within the engineering faculty at Wits, however, the tendency was to blame the industry's appointment practices, particularly its alleged preference for overseas graduates to fill senior managerial posts, and its readiness to give top appointments to men who had risen from the ranks, qualifying 'simply by experience'. These practices served to discourage young men from embarking on a long and expensive professional course at the Witwatersrand's own university. The industry, for its part, claimed that it appointed trained personnel from abroad precisely because the local university did not provide sufficient graduates. What is evident is that by 1927 the Chamber of Mines had become distinctly alarmed at the dearth of mining graduates from Wits. The Gold Producers' Committee of the Chamber undertook a thorough investigation of the problem. The technical advisory committee concluded that, 'so far as mining and metallurgy were concerned the University had been disappointing, and had not proved a satisfactory successor to the South African School of Mines and Technology'.[4]

The Chamber of Mines maintained two constant themes in its expressions of concern. First, that the Witwatersrand, among the world's greatest mining centres, should possess one of the world's major mining schools, which clearly it did not. Second, that the Chamber was simply not receiving a satisfactory return upon its massive investment in the University. Since 1917 the Chamber had given £47 000 in direct grants to the University and its predecessors. Nine mining and metallurgy graduates in five years was 'clearly a very poor return for the support which the University had obtained from the mining industry'.[5] The contention of those in the mining industry was that the mining course at Wits was too academic in content, and not sufficiently cognizant of the practical needs of mining, and that standards were too high, thereby discouraging students from embarking on the course.[6]

As a result of the concern expressed by the Chamber of Mines, a joint committee was set up representing the mining industry and the University, which reported in 1928. The committee stated that the mining industry was anxious to employ many more technically educated South Africans than it had been possible to obtain in recent years. It desired that the graduation of young men 'of the right class and of a desirable type should be made somewhat easier', and consequently recommended changes in the courses for mining students, particularly the simplification and streamlining of those in mathematics and applied mathematics. It also investigated ways of bringing the academic and practical training of mining engineers into closer contact. The 'sandwich' system, so favoured by John Orr, had been abandoned for logistical reasons in 1917, but since 1924 the University had sought to provide mining students with extensive practical training by arranging for them to be employed on the mines during their fourth and final year, while attending lectures on Friday afternoons and Saturday mornings. The committee pronounced this system to be a success, but recommended that students on the mines be released to attend lectures during the whole of Friday.[7]

The recommendations of the joint committee were acted upon, and thereafter the number of mining and metallurgy students at the University rose considerably. In 1926 there were 12 students of mining and metallurgy, 3 in their final year; by 1931 the number had risen to 87, 11 in their final year, and by 1936 to 192, 30 in their final year.[8] The improved prospects of the industry, especially in the boom following South Africa's abandonment of the gold standard in 1932, was the decisive influence in this expansion. But important also was a decline in the fear of miners' phthisis. As Principal Raikes explained to the Secretary for Education in June 1934: 'In the early days of the University the department of Mining was not very strong. But as early as 1928 the new scheme for Mining Education undertaken in conjunction with the Chamber, began to take effect, and with the overcoming of the fear of phthisis and the idea that the life of the industry was short, the numbers rapidly increased.'[9]

The first De Beers Professor of Mining and Surveying at the new University was G.A. Watermeyer, who had been appointed in 1921. Of the original chairs of the Transvaal Technical Institute, mining had known far more incumbents than any other, but Watermeyer's appointment afforded some continuity. He served as Professor of Mining until 1934, and continued as Professor of Surveying until 1939. A graduate of the old University of the Cape of Good Hope, and fully qualified as a government land surveyor, before his appointment to the University he had worked with mining groups, notably the Albu group. Surveying was his main strength and interest. He was later to develop a full degree course in it. Watermeyer always maintained close contact with the Chamber of Mines and the mine managers along the Reef, and in 1932 he together with his senior lecturer, S.N. Hoffenberg, published a comprehensive study of *Witwatersrand Mining Practice*. Watermeyer was a truly delightful person, most highly regarded by both his students and colleagues. The pride of his life was his fine beard, but it once landed him in trouble. On a field trip with his students in the Eastern Transvaal he was mistaken by a Nelspruit policeman for Beauty Bell, a notorious criminal who sported a very similar beard and who had escaped gaol. Watermeyer soon

G.A. Watermeyer

G.H. Stanley

established his identity, but his embarrassment caused great amusement to his students.

G.H. Stanley, the Professor of Metallurgy and Assaying in the new University, was one of Hele-Shaw's appointments. He was to hold the chair until his retirement in 1939. A product of the Royal School of Mines in London, Stanley was a fine teacher, very much liked by his students, and he was also active in industry and research. He was something of a pioneer of the local iron industry, and during World War I designed the first two blast furnaces at Vereeniging. In 1935 he established and became the first director of the Minerals Research Laboratory, the forerunner of the National Institute for Metallurgy. His lecturer in the twenties, who was to remain in the department until his retirement in 1955, was D. Millin, brother of Mr Justice Millin and brother-in-law of Sarah Gertrude Millin.

Outside mining, engineering at the new University was dominated by 'Jock' Orr, the Professor of Mechanical Engineering, and one of the best known figures at Wits in its first years. Together with J.G. Lawn, on the Council, he provided a living link between the new University and the old Kimberley School of Mines. His chair, along with the chair of mining, was endowed, appropriately enough, by De Beers, and he was officially styled the De Beers Professor of Mechanical Engineering. At the request of De Beers after Orr's death in 1954, it was renamed the John Orr chair.

Orr was what was known as a 'colourful' figure. Like so many of the staff of the original Technical Institute in Johannesburg, he was from Scotland, and he always took great care to emphasize his Scottishness; he had a marked Scots accent, was a long serving member of the local Caledonian Society, and he had an enviable capacity for the Scots brand of whisky. He was a very large man, full of energy and enormously industrious. A pen portrait in the student magazine noted: 'Whether he is tearing along the Main Reef Road after delinquent continuation school pupils, or is "fixing" a student in practical work on the mines, or is helping some lame dog over a stile, the Professor of Engineering travels at top speed.' Though very popular among the students, he was not without enemies. He was inclined to be overbearing, determined to get his own way, and a hard taskmaster.

As the first professor of engineering in South Africa, Orr laid the foundations for the professional training of mechanical and electrical engineers on the Witwatersrand. He was not himself a great engineer, and was not particularly theoretically minded, but he was an excellent organizer, and provided his students with a sound practical background. In his own career Orr had served a regular apprenticeship, and worked as a journeyman, in addition to graduating from Glasgow University with a B.Sc. in mechanical and electrical engineering. He was always thereafter a strong advocate of extensive practical training for engineering graduates. By the time the University of the Witwatersrand was established this particular emphasis on the practical was being questioned by those who stressed the managerial function of the professional engineer. Orr perhaps was not the man best suited to ensure that mechanical engineering in the new University would reflect newer trends in the profession. By 1922 he was already in his twenty-fifth year as a professor of engineering in South Africa, and fairly set in his ways. Orr seems to have recognized this, and used the opportunity provided by the transfer of engineering from Plein Square to Milner Park in 1925–6 to break from the University. The technical evening classes for artisans were now separated from the University, and Plein Square became the headquarters of the Witwatersrand Technical Institute, later the Witwatersrand Technical College, with Orr as its first director.

As Dean of the Faculty of Engineering until his departure from the University, and because all engineering students were required to take courses in mechanical engineering, Orr exercised a considerable control over the other engineering departments, and tended to treat the non-mining departments as mere appendages of mechanical engineering. His initial colleagues in the chairs of civil engineering and electrotechnics were his fellow Scots, R.H. Charters, appointed, in 1916 as the first Professor of Civil Engineering at the School of Mines, and H.J.S. Heather, since 1914 Professor of Electrotechnics. Chemical technology, the predecessor of chemical engineering, was the responsibility of the Department of Chemistry and Chemical Technology under Professor J. A. Wilkinson. Neither Charters nor Heather were university graduates, and apparently neither made much impact on their professions. Where Charters did stand up to Orr was in opposing the 'sandwich' system. In 1916 he secured its abolition for civil engineers, and soon thereafter it was abandoned entirely on the ground that the diversification of the School of Mines made it impossible to arrange special terms and classes simply to suit engineering students.

Both Heather and Charters left the University shortly before Orr; Heather retiring at the end of 1924, and Charters died suddenly in 1925. Consequently in 1926 a new trio assumed leadership of the non-mining engineering departments – Professor William John Walker, yet another Scot, succeeded Orr, and was to remain in the chair of mechanical engineering until 1952; Professor William G. Sutton succeeded Charters and held the chair of civil engineering until his appointment as Principal in 1954; and Professor Oswald Raymond Randall was appointed to the chair of electrical engineering, which he was to hold until 1948.

For engineering, 1926 was a far more important date than 1922. In 1926, the first engineering block at Milner Park was occupied, while the University appointed the professorial team that would reorganize the teaching of engineering, and give it much more academic tone. More or less simultaneously economic developments within South Africa greatly stimulated the demand for engineers of all descriptions, with the result that engineering at Wits moved out of its depression and into a boom period. The policy of the Hertzog Pact government, formed in 1924, was to promote the diversification of the national economy, and particularly to encourage local manufacturing industries. The introduction in 1925 of protective tariffs, and the formation of the Iron and Steel Corporation of South Africa (ISCOR) as a state enterprise in 1928, provided a new basis for manufacturing and engineering industries in South Africa. Previously, mechanical, electrical, and civil engineers had depended for employment largely on the mines and public services, such as the railways. Now a range of new opportunities began to open up, and this was reflected in student enrolment. Between 1926 and 1930 the number of engineering students at Wits virtually doubled from 193 to 371.

Although the new trio of engineering professors did not constitute a great team, at least in so far as Walker and Randall quarrelled endlessly, it is clear in retrospect that they launched engineering at Wits into a new era. Walker was recognized as the man with sparkle. Born in Abroath, Angus, Scotland, he had begun his career in engineering as an apprentice, and then took his B.Sc. at the

University College, Dundee, where he graduated with distinction in electrical engineering. From 1914 to 1921 he lectured in mechanical engineering at the Manchester College of Technology, and during the war years assisted with research into aero engines for Britain's infant air force. He then spent a spell as senior lecturer in engineering and machine design at Dundee, before taking up his appointment at Wits. He was to serve the University for 26 years, proving most effective both as an engineer and teacher. His skill and training ensured his effectiveness as an engineer; his powerful command of the English language greatly assisted his effectiveness as a teacher. An essential part of his achievement was to extend the horizons of mechanical engineering at Wits beyond practical mining. Active in research, he did much work in internal combustion engineering, heat regeneration, fluid friction, heat transmission, and aerodynamics, undertaking research on behalf of the S.A.A.F. during World War II. During his career, he contributed over 70 papers to the proceedings and journals of scientific and technical institutions and associations. Several of his papers won awards. Walker was also most concerned to promote the status of engineers in the community, and helped to found the Engineers Association of South Africa with a view to securing statutory recognition and registration of graduate engineers. As a person Walker was not always easy to get on with, and he was particularly determined to defend what he defined as his 'individuality'. In his later years it is evident that he developed something of a persecution complex, and convinced himself that the University had not truly appreciated his services.

Sutton was a local product. He was educated at King Edward VII School, Johannesburg, and in 1913 gained his B.A. with a distinction in physics through the South African College in Cape Town. After serving in German East Africa in World War I, he attended the University of Cape Town, and qualified for the B.Sc. in engineering in 1918. The next year he joined the Union Irrigation Department as an assistant engineer, and remained in government service until joining Wits.

Sutton, Professor of Civil Engineering for 28 years, was a very effective head of department. It was he who developed civil engineering at Wits as a strong department. When he took over the department he was the only member of staff, with a mere handful of students; when he left to become Principal in 1954 there were eight members of staff and some hundreds of students. As important as sheer growth was the fact that he gradually managed to assert the independence of civil engineering, freeing it from its domination by mechanical engineering. This domination was a legacy of Orr's. Throughout in the period prior to World War II, though, Sutton was hampered by the fact that his laboratory equipment was installed in the mechanical engineering laboratory. In 1941 civil engineering finally acquired its own laboratories with the opening of the Hillman building. Outside of his department, Sutton's main contribution to the University was as an administrator. From 1935 until 1954 he served continuously as a representative of Senate on Council, except for four years during World War II, when he was general manager of the Central Organization of Technical Training in the Department of Defence and later chief technical adviser in the Department of Commerce and Industries. Somewhat withdrawn and shy as a person, he remained a bachelor until he assumed the principalship.

The third of the new engineering professorial appointees in 1926, O.R. Randall, also served the University for more than 20 years. A graduate of the Universities of London and Birmingham, Randall lectured at Birmingham University before coming out to South Africa and Wits as Professor of Electrical Engineering. From the early 1930s he suffered from ill health, and this interfered seriously with his researches, which never really got off the ground. He was none the less an outstanding teacher, and devoted himself to building up his department. Like Sutton, he resented domination by mechanical engineering, which was grouped together with electrical engineering for the degree until 1931, and he consequently often clashed with Walker. Otherwise, as a person he was gentle, and rather shy. His students regarded him with great affection, and he was respected by the profession.

Prior to World War II, the Department of Architecture was also located in the Faculty of Engineering. Founded in 1921, it was the first university school of architecture in the country, and was associated with the engineering faculty as G.E. Pearse, the first Professor of Architecture at the University, believed that civil engineering and architecture were closely allied as professions.

Architecture had been taught long before 1921, but only in evening classes, which did not require matriculation for entry. The first evening classes in architecture had been provided by the Transvaal Technical Institute, in response to the building boom after the Anglo-Boer War. An integrated four-year course had been established by the School of Mines following the passage in 1909 of the Transvaal Architects (Private) Act, which provided for the registration of architects and the foundation of the Association of Transvaal Architects as a statutory body. Successful completion of the course, and four years of professional and practical experience as an assistant to an architect, qualified a person for registration.

When World War I ended the Association of Transvaal Architects took a further step to develop architecture as a profession in South Africa by requiring students entering architecture in the Transvaal to have matriculated. The obvious next step was to establish a degree in architecture. In 1920, in response to the request of the Association of Transvaal Architects and its promise of financial assistance, the Council of the University College agreed to establish a chair of architecture and offer a full degree course.

The choice of Geoffrey Eastcott Pearse as the first Professor of Architecture was something of a surprise, not least to himself, for he possessed no university experience, neither as a student nor as a teacher. In a very real sense, he was the local boy who made good. As a youngster, before the Anglo-Boer War, he had lived in Ameshoff Street, across the way from the stone quarry and farmlands which later became the site for the University of the Witwatersrand. Between the Anglo-Boer War and World War I he attended the evening classes in architecture offered by the Transvaal Technical Institute, went to Britain to qualify as an Associate of the Royal Institute of British Architects, and then worked in Herbert Baker's office on the design of the Union Buildings. After serving with the Royal Engineers in the war, he set up practice in Johannesburg and lectured to the evening classes at the School of Mines. On the basis mainly of the latter, he was appointed Professor of Architecture in March 1921.

Pearse was to continue as Professor of Architecture until his retirement in 1948, during which time the school of architecture at the University established a formidable reputation for itself. As an architect Pearse was fairly conservative, and as a man he was difficult, but he understood young people, and he was to have a major influence on the buildings at Wits and on architecture in South Africa generally. He was a superb draughtsman, and greatly interested in the Cape-Dutch heritage in South Africa. His talent and his interest were reflected in his two major published works, *Eighteenth Century Architecture in South Africa*, which appeared in 1933, and *Eighteenth Century Furniture in South Africa*, published in 1960.

From the outset Pearse was a powerful proponent of the case for a full degree training in architecture. He instituted a diploma course for part-time students, and although it proved popular, he consistently disparaged it, urging the necessity for students to undertake the five-year degree course. In a paper on architectural education delivered in 1928 to the Institute of South African Architects, he denounced the pupilage system as a scandal, the part-time diploma as unsatisfactory for 'it is only in one or two instances, where an architect's office is well equipped and his chief is sympathetic, that we have obtained satisfactory results', and the degree course he extolled as that required of a true profession. He also gave evidence to the select committee on the Architects and Quantity Surveyors Bill in favour of a full professional training for architects.[10] The problem before 1928 was that very few students were prepared to embark on the degree course, and only three B.Arch.

graduates were produced by Wits during the twenties, H.C. Tully, William McIntosh, and Rex Martienssen. After the passage of the Architects and Quantity Surveyors Act in 1927 there was a steady if unspectacular increase in the number of full-time students in architecture, but the diploma course continued to prove the more popular route to qualification.

Between 1925 and 1928 Pearse had as senior lecturer in his department A. Stanley Furner, an English architect and painter who did much to raise standards in the department and who exercised a considerable influence on its students. It was a major loss to the department when he decided to go into private practice in Johannesburg. By then the Wits school of architecture had obtained international standing in that its degree course was recognized by the Royal Institute of British Architects, which meant that Wits graduates qualified for election as associates of the Institute. Within South Africa, U.C.T. had also established a school of architecture, but it was rather isolated by comparison with the Wits school, favoured by 'its naturally strategic position in the vital centre of building activity in South Africa'.[11]

In 1928 the school of architecture also introduced a three-year diploma in quantity surveying, but by agreement with the University of Pretoria in 1931 it was decided that quantity surveying education in the Transvaal should be centralized at Pretoria, and architecture at Wits. For B.A. students at Wits, Pearse offered a course in the history of fine arts. As he had long been interested in heraldry, he also took responsibility for designing the University's coat of arms. He recommended that the arms should have an open book, representing a seat of learning, superimposed on a cog wheel, representing technology on a gold field, and a watershed, representing the Witwatersrand. The two rivers symbolized the Vaal and the Limpopo. He objected to retaining the kudu's head as a crest, but was overruled.

III

Without question, in 1922 medicine was the most controversial faculty in the University. The controversy that surrounded that faculty went well beyond the furore raised by Stibbe's enforced resignation. Indeed, the very establishment of a medical school in Johannesburg had been a major source of controversy, and F.S. Malan, as Minister of Education, had at one stage threatened to block its creation by refusing to proclaim the Anatomy Act. Given the general situation at the end of World War I, and with a medical school already established at U.C.T., Malan seems to have believed that there was no need for haste in creating a medical school in Johannesburg. In any event, he was convinced that the government did not have the funds to meet all Johannesburg's demands for higher education. The compromise he finally suggested in early 1919 was that as a *quid pro quo* for his agreement to establish a medical school in Johannesburg, the Council of the School of Mines should agree to abandon the idea of an agricultural school. The Council refused to entertain such a bargain. As Hofmeyr informed Malan, the government 'would always be at liberty to refuse any request that might be made' to finance an agricultural school on the Witwatersrand.[12] Malan duly backed down, and on 1 July 1919 the Anatomy Act was proclaimed for the area embracing the magisterial districts of Johannesburg, Krugersdorp, Germiston, and Boksburg. A week later the School of Mines announced the appointments of Dr E.P. Stibbe to the chair of anatomy, and Captain E.H. Cluver to the chair of physiology.

When the University of the Witwatersrand opened in 1922, many at the University, and in the medical profession, believed that Malan should have stuck to his guns and refused to authorize the proclamation of the Anatomy Act for the Johannesburg area. There was a strong sense that the students at the Wits medical school were being trained for a profession that had no need of them. During the World War, and in the influenza epidemic of 1918, doctors had been in very short supply, helping to fuel the demand for adequate facilities for the training of doctors in South Africa. But by 1922, following an upsurge in new registrations of doctors from overseas, large enrolments at the country's two medical schools, and the onset of economic depression, fears were aroused that the country would soon be overstocked with doctors. A South African doctor warned in the *British Medical Journal* of 13 August 1921, 'the number of students who are now coming forward threatens so to overcrowd the profession, that it will be intensely difficult for many to make even a living'. 'The total white inhabitants in all the Provinces and Rhodesia', he pointed out, 'only amount to a little over one million, for which there are more than sufficient doctors already available.' Even among the million or so whites, a good many could not afford the services of a doctor.

The apparent threat of an over-supply of doctors caused such concern that in September 1922 the *Students' Magazine* at Wits ran a special editorial, 'The Medical Profession in South Africa'. It cited the statement of a senior staff member at the Johannesburg General Hospital that the Wits medical school was 'a superfluous institution' and 'that South Africa will not have any room for its graduates'. The editorial warned 'That parents to-day are too prone to giving their sons and daughters over to the study of medicine simply because it is a "paying" profession; and that students who intend entering the medical profession should know exactly the nature of the "thorny" path they will have to tread.'

Dismissing these fears as groundless, the new medical school at Wits did not hesitate to canvass actively for students. Professor Dart, the new Professor of Anatomy, was foremost in publicizing the Wits medical school. The *Journal of the Medical Association of South Africa* pointedly observed in 1927, on the question of whether the medical profession was becoming overcrowded 'most people, always excepting some optimistically-minded Witwatersrand Professor given to thinking in terms of square mileage, would, three or four years ago, have answered this question with a very emphatic affirmative couched in a very despondent tone'. But by 1927, the *Journal* was no longer so convinced of a looming problem of medical unemployment, though it remained most concerned about the prospects for doctors' earnings.[13]

No one denied that Johannesburg provided an ideal location for a medical school. It was the industrial and commercial centre of South Africa, had the largest concentration of peoples, black and white, in the Union, and possessed the country's best clinical and research facilities. The Johannesburg General Hospital, founded in 1888–9, and in close proximity its branches, the Queen Victoria Maternity Hospital, the Fever Hospital, and the Transvaal Memorial Hospital for Children, provided the basic complex required for a teaching hospital. In 1925 the Non-European Hospital was added. Along the Reef, there were another forty or so hospitals, including the City Deep Central Native Hospital and the Crown Mines Central Native Hospital, both within the Johannesburg municipal boundaries. As important as these clinical facilities was the presence on Hospital Hill of the South African Institute for Medical Research, established in 1912 by agreement between the Union government and the Witwatersrand Native Labour Association, acting on behalf of the mining industry of the Transvaal, with a view to combating fatal diseases among the workforce on the Rand mines. From the first the Wits medical school established close links with the Institute for Medical Research, which undertook a considerable amount of teaching on behalf of the medical school.

It was at a meeting at the Institute for Medical Research in April 1916, at the height of the wartime agitation for the establishment of a university in Johannesburg, that the registered medical practitioners of the Transvaal first declared the time had arrived to create a medical school in the Transvaal. Next year, the School of Mines provided courses in chemistry, physics, botany, and zoology for the first year of the medical curriculum, but because the School was unable during wartime to recruit suitable staff in anatomy and physiology, the courses for the second year were not offered in 1918. At the end of 1918, with the conclusion of hostilities in Europe, another attempt was made to find professors of anatomy and physiology, but the combination of a poor initial response to the School's advertisements in Britain together with the government's obstructionism, delayed appointments until July 1919. Consequently the second year of the medical curriculum was not offered until 1920.

Following the arrival in mid-1919 of Stibbe and Cluver to fill the chairs of anatomy and physiology, the medical advisory committee of Senate, which included local medical men, proceeded to draw up its recommendations for the establishment of a complete course of medical education in Johannesburg. For the combined degrees of M.B. (Bachelor of Medicine), B.Ch. (Bachelor of Surgery), the committee recommended a six-year programme with a series of four professional examinations. At the end of the first year candidates were to take the first professional examination in the pre-medical sciences; at the end of the first term of the third year, complete the second professional examination in organic chemistry, anatomy, and physiology; at the end of the fourth year, complete the pre-clinical sciences by sitting the third professional examination in pathology and bacteriology, and pharmacology and materia medica; and at the end of the sixth year, to take the final professional examination in the clinical medical subjects. In addition to the full-time professors in anatomy and physiology, the committee recommended the appointment of a full-time professor to the chair of pharmacology, materia medica, and therapeutics, but for the remaining pre-clinical and clinical subjects it strongly recommended the appointment of part-time professors and teachers drawn from the Institute for Medical Research, and practising physicians and surgeons. The Institute for Medical Research was to be approached to provide for the teaching of pathology and bacteriology; part-time professorial appointments were to be made for the major advanced medical subjects, medicine, surgery, and obstetrics-gynaecology, and the remaining clinical subjects were to be taught by part-time lecturers and instructors drawn from the ranks of local specialists and practitioners. The idea of following the example of Cape Town, and appointing full-time professors of medicine, surgery, and midwifery, was deliberately rejected by the committee: 'After very careful consideration the Committee found itself not in favour of this method, both on the ground of teaching efficiency and because of local circumstances. It was felt that the teachers of the practical branches must be men who are in daily contact with the practice of their profession, as the chief aim of the Medical School is to train general practitioners and not specialists.'[14]

On 3 October 1919, on the advice of Senate, Council adopted these recommendations. Against the wishes of Principal Hofmeyr, it had also been decided that the medical school should be located on Hospital Hill rather than at Milner Park. The original design, in other words, was that the medical school should develop a practical rather than a theoretical bias, and that it should be rooted in the profession rather than the wider university. As the *South African Medical Record* had predicted in June 1919 of the country's two medical schools, 'If we may venture a peep into the future, we fancy that the two schools will develop on different lines, familiar to us from the experience of older countries, that of Capetown reflecting the type in which the University is the determining factor in all things, as in Edinburgh, that of Johannesburg the hospital type of school so familiar in London.'

In 1921 John Mitchell Watt arrived in Johannesburg to take up the chair of pharmacology, thereby completing the full-time professorial appointments in the new medical school. Watt was to retain the chair until his retirement at the end of 1957. His 38 years of service were interrupted only by his secondment for four years during World War II to manage medical supplies at Defence Headquarters in Pretoria. His colleague as Professor of Physiology, Eustace Cluver, was likewise long associated with the University, though his service was rather more broken. Stibbe's successor as Professor of Anatomy, Raymond Dart, served the University continuously from 1923 until his retirement at the end of 1958, a tenure of 36 years.

Given the significant number of Scots who accepted appointments to the staff of the new medical school, and the large number of Jewish students, the school was sometimes referred to as 'the Scottish mission to the Jews'. Though he was a South African by birth, Watt certainly counted himself among the Scots. Born in Port Elizabeth in 1892 of Scottish parents, Watt received much of his schooling in Scotland, graduating in medicine from the University of Edinburgh in 1916. After serving in the Royal Army Medical Corps for three and a half years, he joined Professor Arthur R. Cushny's Department of Materia Medica at Edinburgh University for the 1920/1 session, and then came to Johannesburg to take up the chair of pharmacology. He never thereafter forgot his Scottish background, and at functions was often to be seen in a kilt. As a person he was very pleasant, if a little pompous. As a teacher he was effective, although in the early days pharmacology was a very limited subject, and he took a keen interest in student affairs. He was also active in administration and research. After Stibbe's fate had been settled in 1922, Watt was elected as the first Dean of the Faculty of Medicine, and served in that capacity until March 1925. At the end of World War II he served as dean for another three years. From 1922 to 1927, and again from 1930 to 1938, he was a representative of Senate on the Council, and in 1928, when the South African Medical Council was founded, he became the University's first representative. In his research Watt worked extensively on South African plants and their medicinal value, and he was fascinated by traditional African medicine and its

J.M. Watt   E.H. Cluver

use of herbs. Altogether he published over 50 original papers, and in 1932 together with Dr Maria Breyer-Brandwyk produced the classic work on *The Medicinal and Poisonous Plants of Southern Africa*. This work, which established its authors' international reputations, was later expanded to include East Africa.

The appointment of Eustace Cluver as the first Professor of Physiology raised some eyebrows. He was at the age of only 24, and had no teaching experience. There was no question, however, that he was an exceptionally able young man. Born at Robertson in the Cape, he had received his early education at the Boys' High School and at the Victoria College, Stellenbosch, before proceeding to Oxford in 1914 as a Rhodes scholar. At Oxford he obtained a first class honours in the final school of physiology. In 1917 he was elected to a senior demyship at Magdalen College, and in 1918 went to King's College Hospital in London as Burney Yeo scholar. For the last months of the war he served as a captain in the South African Medical Corps in France. When he was appointed to the chair of physiology in Johannesburg in 1919 it was realized that he would be little older than many of his students, who would likewise be returning from the front, but this did not hamper Cluver in his teaching. He proved very popular with his classes, and as a keen sportsman, joined the students on the sportsfields, playing rugby for the first fifteen.

The young Cluver had no intention of remaining for the rest of his career as Professor of Physiology at Wits, and at the end of 1926 he relinquished the chair to join the Union Department of Health as Assistant Health Officer. He proved most successful as a state health officer and in 1938, when Sir Edward Thornton retired, he became Secretary for Health and Chief Health Officer of the Union at the age of 44. In 1934 he had re-established his connection with the University when the Union Department of Health took responsibility for teaching public health at the medical school, and in 1939 he was made honorary Professor and Head of the Department of Public Health. In the next year, Cluver became director of the South African Institute for Medical Research, and in 1941 assumed the position of part-time professor and Head of the Department of Preventive Medicine, which replaced public health. He retained the latter chair until his retirement from the Institute for Medical Research at the end of 1959. In January 1960 he was appointed the first full-time Dean of the Faculty of Medicine, and assumed what was effectively his third chair, the titular professorship of medical education. He served as dean for three years. During his career Cluver wrote extensively on public health, preventive medicine, and medical legislation in South Africa. Some 150 publications stand to his name, including several books that became standard in their field. His work *Public Health in South Africa* first appeared in 1934 and has since gone through six editions. In 1951 he edited a textbook on *Social Medicine,* and in 1955 he published his massive study *Medical and Health Legislation in the Union of South Africa.*

The man who put the medical school, and indeed the University, truly on the map was Raymond Dart. Yet it was almost entirely fortuitous that Dart came to Wits. To begin with, the University possessed a perfectly adequate Professor of Anatomy, until Stibbe was forced to resign over a non-academic issue. Then Dart was not the University's first choice as Stibbe's successor. The person Senate recommended was a Dr Thomson, but before he could be appointed by Council he withdrew his application. Senate then resolved on 9 October 1922 that the position be re-advertised, but Council insisted that an appointment had to be made immediately, and that Senate consequently 'make a recommendation on the applications now available'.[15] In the circumstances, Senate recommended the appointment of Dart. As for Dart, a young Australian then enjoying the bright lights and intellectual stimulation of the northern hemisphere, he had absolutely no desire to go to Wits, or any other institution in South Africa. He felt he had been inveigled into applying for the chair at Wits by Professor Grafton Elliot Smith, under whom Dart had served as senior demonstrator in anatomy at University College, London, and was absolutely appalled when he was given the post.

Born in Toowong, a suburb of Brisbane, Queensland, in February 1893,

Dart received his education in Australia. After graduating B.Sc.(Hons.) at Queensland University he proceeded to Sydney University to take up medicine, and was awarded the M.B.,Ch.M.(Hons.) in 1917. Ten years later he was to be awarded the M.D. of Sydney University. After serving in the Australian Army Medical Corps both at home and in England and France in 1918–19 he spent a year under Elliot Smith at University College, London, and then went to the United States for a year as one of the first foreign fellows of the Rockefeller Foundation. It was after he had returned to London from his trip to the United States that he was persuaded to apply for the chair of anatomy at Wits.

R.A. Dart

Dart arrived in Johannesburg in January 1923, and found the place to be even worse than he had feared. He was convinced that he had been dispatched to a primitive backwater, and the medical school itself seemed to be a shambles. The school building on Hospital Hill was a partially completed L-shaped structure, squalid in appearance and quite bereft of many of the ordinary facilities required for work in anatomy. Distracted for so long by the Stibbe affair, the Faculty of Medicine was disorganized, and not even the regulations for the curriculum had been properly worked out. Nor did it help matters that Dart sensed a degree of personal animosity towards him for having taken the place of the beloved Stibbe.

A man of considerable energy and resource, physical and intellectual, Dart accepted that his dreams of a research career in neurology had ended, and that the task ahead of him was that of a pioneer in helping to build up the Wits medical school virtually from scratch. He threw himself into the task. In his first year he agreed to serve as secretary of the Faculty of Medicine and in 1925 he took the office of dean. He was to remain dean until 1943, the longest term of service in that capacity in the history of the medical school. During his tenure the Wits medical school grew very considerably both in size and eminence, and this owed much to Dart's concern and drive, as well as the fame that he acquired for himself and the school over the Taung skull. What Dart perceived was that the medical school might easily become the 'Cinderella' of the University unless it pushed hard for itself, so he was determined to play a full role in University affairs, soon establishing himself as a powerful figure in Senate. He devoted a tremendous amount of energy to building up the facilities of the medical school, as in creating the medical school library.

Dart was undoubtedly one of the truly great and colourful characters in the history of Wits. He had an explosive nature, was full of verve and vigour and new ideas, and certainly given to histrionics. A showman, as well as very emotional, in his time he put on some dazzling performances in Senate. As the occasion demanded, he could be angry and sarcastic, earnest and emotional, or gentle and persuasive. His lectures, notably his first lecture to second-year students, were very often showpieces, and he became enormously popular among the students. He was a great believer in visual demonstrations, and was quite prepared to swing from the hot-water pipes in the lecture hall to illustrate the brachiating of Congo gorillas, crawl like a crocodile to illustrate the movements of reptiles, and lift weights in front of his students to demonstrate human muscles. As a physical fitness fanatic, he happened to possess some useful muscles.

Dart's mind was an incredibly fertile one, full of ideas and suggestions, and he was never afraid to voice them, and work for them. He did not necessarily seek controversy, but he certainly provoked it, for many of his ideas challenged established norms, as when he insisted on the advantages of teaching general anatomy in a single year instead of over two. Inevitably, he made a fair number of enemies. His enemies in South Africa liked to refer to him as 'that wild man from Australia'; those he made in the northern hemisphere dismissed him simply as 'the wild man from the South'. The people who really loved and appreciated Dart were his students, for he was not only stimulating but also deeply interested in them. With students he was generally warm, compassionate, understanding, and helpful, though sometimes also provocative and outspoken, and he devoted many long hours to assisting them with their problems.

Dart's international fame at the time, and his status today as one of the great scientists of this century, stemmed from his discovery and interpretation of the australopithecine man-ape. Like his appointment at Wits, the discovery was in many ways fortuitous. Dart was not by inclination or training a 'bones' man; his particular interest was the human nervous system. But he was intent on building up an anatomy museum at the medical school, and urged his students and assistants to look out for appropriate skeletons. Miss Josephine Salmons, a student demonstrator in the Department of Anatomy, duly secured a fossil baboon skull from the Northern Lime Company, which was quarrying limestone at a place then called Taungs, now Taung, in the northern Cape. R.B. Young, the Professor of Geology, soon thereafter undertook an expedition to the area, and Dart asked him to keep his eye open for more fossils. At Young's request the quarry manager at Taung railed two box-loads of fragments to Dart, including a fossilized skull that had served as a paperweight in the manager's office. After carefully extracting the skull, which had belonged to a primate approximately 5 years old, Dart recognized that it possessed features intermediate between those of man and ape. The forehead displayed human lineaments, the teeth were distinctly human, and the brain-cast, while very much smaller than that of a human child, was different from that of any known ape. Nothing like it had ever before been discovered, and Dart was convinced that he had come across a 'missing link' between man and the apes. In the article he published in *Nature* in February 1925 announcing his discovery, Dart declared 'It is manifest that we are in the presence here of a pre-human stock, neither chimpanzee nor gorilla, which possesses a series of differential characters not encountered hitherto in any anthropoid stock'. Dart named the creature *Australopithecus africanus,* or the southern ape of Africa:

> Unlike Pithecanthropus, it does not represent an ape-like man, a caricature of precocious hominid failure, but a creature well advanced beyond modern anthropoids in just those characters, facial and cerebral, which are to be anticipated in an extinct link between man and his simian ancestor. At the same time, it is equally evident that a creature with anthropoid brain capacity, and lacking the distinctive, localised temporal expansions which appear to be concomitant with and necessary to articulate man, is no true man. It is therefore logically regarded as a man like ape. I propose tentatively, then, that a new family of *Homo-simiadae* be created for the reception of the group of individuals which it represents, and that the first known species of the group be designated *Australopithecus africanus,* in commemoration, first, of the extreme southern and unexpected horizon of its discovery, and secondly, of the continent in which so many new and important discoveries connected with the early history of man have recently been made, thus vindicating the Darwinian claim that Africa would prove to be the cradle of mankind.

Dart's assessment of the Taung skull rested on some inspired and brilliant deductions, particularly his conclusion that the creature had walked upright. His claims evoked considerable public interest throughout the world, and they also provoked a good deal of controversy. Most leading physical anthropologists rejected his claims as extravagant or preposterous. Elliot Smith,

Dart's former mentor, was highly sceptical, while Sir Arthur Keith was entirely dismissive. As he wrote in *Nature,* 'The skull is that of a young anthropoid ape – one which was in its fourth year of growth, a child – and showing so many points of affinity with the two living African anthropoids, the gorilla and the chimpanzee, that there cannot be a moment's hesitation in placing the fossil form in this living group.'[16] Despite rejection by leading anthropological opinion, Dart clung to his views, and found a staunch supporter in Dr Robert Broom, the Scottish-born palaeontologist who had settled in South Africa at the turn of the century. It was Broom's later discoveries at Sterkfontein (1936) and Kromdraai (1938) that served to confirm Dart's original views, and began to swing anthropologists towards accepting *Australopithecus africanus* as a species of pre-man. Today the consensus seems to be that *Australopithecus* was indeed a genus on the threshold of humanity. Professor P.V. Tobias, Dart's successor in the chair of anatomy, has assessed the long-term significance of Dart's work: 'In retrospect, Dart's great contribution was that he forced the world of palaeoanthropology to the realization that there had been, at one time, small-brained members of the family of man. A small brain alone is not sufficient to disqualify one from membership of the Hominidae. It compelled scientists to another realization, namely that not all parts of the ancestral hominids' bodies had become hominized or man-like at the same rate or time. Thus, *Australopithecus africanus* had clearly begun to be hominized in its teeth, the poise of the skull on the spine, the form of the brain, the posture and gait, but it had not yet started the hominizing trend towards disproportionate aggrandizement of the brain. Such a pattern of development we call *mosaic evolution.*'[17]

Within the University Dart became a key figure in the promotion of African studies. Dart, Doke, Kirby, and Maingard formed something of a 'team' in the 1920s and 1930s, exploring the peoples and cultures of southern Africa. In 1936, together with Professor MacCrone, they undertook a famous expedition to the southern Kalahari to study the Khomani Bushmen. Their material was published in the next year by the Witwatersrand University Press as the *Bushmen of the Southern Kalahari.* In 1937 Dart also contributed the chapter on 'Racial Origins' to I. Schapera's classic volume, *The Bantu-speaking Tribes of South Africa.*

Apart from the three full-time professors in anatomy, physiology, and pharmacology, the medical school in its early years depended very heavily on part-time staff, and it was fortunate in securing the services of some distinguished local practitioners, specialists, and research officers. The Department of Pathology and Bacteriology was staffed entirely by members of the South African Institute for Medical Research. W. Watkins-Pitchford, the

Institute's director, served as honorary professor, J.G. Becker as senior lecturer in bacteriology, J.H. Harvey Pine as senior lecturer in pathology, and Annie Porter as senior lecturer in parasitology. The first clinical professors were O.K. Williamson in medicine, G. Ritchie Thomson in surgery, J. McGibbon in obstetrics, and W. Gordon Grant in gynaecology. When the course in forensic medicine was introduced in 1923, J.J. Levin was appointed to give the lectures, and in the next year J.T. Dunston was appointed as lecturer in psychiatry. Both men were later made professors, and were to give the medical school long service.

Ever optimistic, the University did not readily abandon its hopes of establishing a veterinary school, and in 1922 it appointed Professor R.W.M. Mettam as Head of the Department of Veterinary Anatomy in association with the medical school. In late 1924, the University finally conceded defeat, and accepted the concentration of all veterinary courses at Onderstepoort. Mettam was duly transferred to the Transvaal University College in Pretoria, and the Department of Veterinary Anatomy closed down.

Despite the fears expressed in the early twenties of overcrowding in the medical profession, enrolment at the medical school grew steadily throughout the decade, rising from 95 in 1922 to 241 by 1929. At first there was a distinct tendency for wealthier students to proceed overseas after completing their first year locally, but as laboratory and library facilities improved, and with Dart bringing a sense of international recognition to the medical school, this practice was on the decline by the end of the decade. Dart himself played a key role in developing library facilities at the medical school. He was instrumental in calling a meeting in March 1923 of representatives of the medical school, the Johannesburg Hospital Board, the South African Institute for Medical Research, and the *Medical Journal of South Africa* to discuss the formation of a joint library, and from this initiative arose the Witwatersrand Medical Library at the medical school. In July 1926, following the completion of the front wing of the medical school, Dart and two student honorary librarians, I. Goldblatt and J.W. Whyte, carried over from the General Hospital the books that provided the basis for the new library.[18]

At the end of 1924 the medical school at Wits produced its first four graduates, L. Klein, B. Kuny, G.F. Slade and G.C. Thompson. At a celebratory dinner at the Trocadero Restaurant in November they presented to the medical school a plaque fixed to a table to commemorate the occasion. In March of the next year they were duly capped M.B., B.Ch. at the University's graduation ceremony in the Town Hall. By the end of 1929 Wits had produced 96 medical graduates, and together with U.C.T. it provided in that year 42 per cent of the new doctors registered in South Africa.

In addition to undergraduate instruction, the medical school embarked on post-graduate instruction in 1926 with the introduction of a course for the diploma in public health. The course was provided at the instigation of Professor Cluver, who at the end of the year was to join the Union Department of Health. The Department of Health had been formed following the passage of the Public Health Act of 1919, and the medical school's new diploma was designed to help meet the increased demand for qualified public health officers. Dr Charles Porter, the Medical Officer of Health in Johannesburg and one of the early advocates of a university in Johannesburg, was appointed the lecturer in public health. In 1927 the medical school added diplomas in tropical medicine and hygiene, and in psychological medicine.

IV

In the main, the professional faculties and departments established in the new University were introduced either at the request or with the positive blessing of the respective professions themselves. Dentistry was something of an exception in that the foundation of a dental school at Wits was initially opposed by the South African Dental Association. In 1921 the University College had admitted several students to the pre-medical course on the assumption that they would be able to proceed to a degree in dental surgery in Johannesburg, but it was not until 1925 that a dental school at Wits was opened. The delay was caused by reservations and rivalries within the profession, and the lack of clinical facilities.

In 1921 the Witwatersrand University Committee announced that it had become one of its aims to establish a dental school in Johannesburg in association with the medical school. South Africa was then totally without facilities for the training of dentists, and the committee believed that Johannesburg provided an ideal site for such facilities as 'such training can only be provided alongside a Medical School'. It also contended that the creation of a dental school was in the immediate national interest: 'South Africa (more particularly the rural districts) is to-day sadly in need of well-trained dental practitioners, and it is right that such should be trained in South Africa.'[19]

Some members of the dental profession, which was still in the process of organizing and defining itself, saw matters rather differently, particularly when in the early twenties economic slump followed the post-war boom. Even more so than in the case of medicine, the dental profession became alarmed about the danger of over-supply in the profession. In April 1922 the South African

Dental Association was formed at a conference in Bloemfontein, and from the outset one of its concerns was that the supply of dentists was outstripping the demand for professional dental treatment. According to the first issue of the *South African Dental Journal*, a private publication which first appeared in 1927, the number of registered dentists in South Africa had gone up from 295 in 1910 to 678 by 1923, an increase of 130 per cent, whereas in the same time period the white population had gone up from 1,255 million to 1,599 million, an increase of only 27 per cent. As the *Dental Journal* saw it: 'The supply of dentists in South Africa has thus outstripped the demand very much, and there are more dentists here in proportion to the people than in any other country in the world. In Sweden for example, a most progressive country, with its six million people as against our million and a half [*sic*], there is the same number as here.' What concerned the *Dental Journal* was that 'the practical effect of this disproportion between the supply of dentists and the demand for their services has been to reduce the average income of the dentist throughout the country'.[20]

The Dental Association responded to the problem of declining incomes in a number of ways. One was to secure protection for registered dentists against the competition of 'dental mechanics', and this was finally achieved in 1928 with the passage of the Medical, Dental, and Pharmacy Act. Another was to attempt to increase the demand for professional dental treatment by educating the public as to the importance of dental hygiene. A third expedient was to attempt to contain the supply of new dentists. At first the Dental Association opposed the creation of a dental school at Wits, and when it had second thoughts and accepted the idea of a dental school, it pressed for a seven-year course which combined medicine and dentistry as against the five-year dental course implemented by Wits in 1925.

What Johannesburg lacked in 1921, when the University College first enrolled students with a view to training as dentists, was a dental hospital or clinic, and until at least a small clinic had been started it was impossible for the University to proceed with the full dental course. In March 1922 the Council empowered Principal Hofmeyr to approach the local dental association to help finance and administer a clinic in the Tin Temple, but in September Hofmeyr reported back that 'the Dental Association of Johannesburg had informed him that they were opposed to the establishment of a Dental Clinic in connection with the University and that this matter was, therefore, for the present in abeyance'.[21] Two main objections seemed to have been raised against the idea of starting a dental school in Johannesburg. The one was that such a school would flood the market with dentists, and the other was that its training could never compare with that provided by overseas institutions. That, at any rate, was the burden of the message given to Hofmeyr and Professor Watt, the Dean of the Faculty of Medicine, when in May 1923 they interviewed Dr B.M. Hunter, the honorary dental surgeon at the Johannesburg General Hospital, about the establishment of a dental school in Johannesburg. As Professor Watt reported Hunter's views to the Faculty of Medicine:

(a) The Union is being flooded with Dental practitioners and the establishment of a school locally would markedly increase the number wishing to practise in South Africa. At present the proportion of dentists to population is very high, much higher than is good for the maintenance of a high standard of life among dentists.

(b) The training which could be given here to Dental students cannot be good, on account of the fact that this University could not pay a sufficiently high salary to attract a really good Director. Further efficient lecturers in many of the specialised subjects, such as Dental Pathology, Dental Materia Medica, etc., could not be obtained locally: when Dr Hunter was asked whether there would not be local Dental practitioners public spirited enough to fit themselves for teaching these special subjects, he replied that he did not think so.

(c) The training of our graduates in Dentistry would be so poor that they would not be accepted in many places, probably not even in South Africa.

Hunter added that the Dental Association was opposed to the formation of a dental school, and he predicted that the school would be boycotted by local dentists.[22]

Hofmeyr's reaction was to call the Dental Association's bluff by advertising for honorary dental surgeons for the proposed clinic, but in the event the move proved unnecessary. In late June 1923 Hofmeyr was able to inform the Faculty of Medicine and the Council that the Johannesburg Dental Society, the local affiliate of the South African Dental Association, was now prepared to help found and support a dental clinic for teaching purposes, provided that the University agreed not to use it for such purposes for a period of two years.[23] A number of clinics had already made their appearance in Johannesburg, organized by rival groups to the Johannesburg Dental Society and for the purpose, it seems, of capturing business for themselves. One such clinic was the Johannesburg Dental Hospital founded by a Dr J.M. Coplans, who was later charged with using the hospital to divert patients to his own personal practice. In establishing the Johannesburg Dental Hospital, Coplans proposed that it should be used for the training of dental students, but as the status of the hospital was questionable, the University had not taken up the proposal. The decision reached by Council at the end of June was that the

Johannesburg Dental Society and the board of the Johannesburg Dental Hospital should be encouraged to co-operate in founding and supporting a dental clinic for teaching purposes, but that in case of disagreement the University should support the former.

With the establishment by the Johannesburg Dental Society of the Witwatersrand Dental Clinic in rooms secured by the University in the polyclinic in Bok Street, the University was invited to appoint representatives to its controlling board, as well as to the board of the Johannesburg Dental Hospital. In September 1923 Council agreed to appoint Hofmeyr and Professor Watt as the University's representatives on the boards of both clinics, 'but on the distinct understanding that this was only done for the purpose of effecting a reconciliation between the two sections'.[24] The attempt at reconciliation failed, and the conclusion reached by the Faculty of Medicine in early 1924 was that the University should withdraw its representation from both boards.

The meeting of the Board of the Faculty of Medicine on 23 April 1924 minuted that no good purpose was being served by the University's representation on the two boards, 'as in the case of one the Board does not function and in the other case the Board does not really control the Institution'. The minutes added 'Action seems likely to be taken against one of these Institutions on evidence pointing to unprofessional conduct on the part of the Dental members of their staff, which will bring discredit on the University's name if it is still connected with this Institution when such action materialises.' On 2 May Council agreed to withdraw the University's representation from the two boards.

When at the beginning of 1925 Council decided to proceed with a full degree course in dental surgery, it determined that the University should run its own dental clinic, and negotiated with the Johannesburg Dental Society for the transfer of its clinic. The clinic, which now became the Witwatersrand University Dental Clinic, was handed over virtually free of debt, and the equipment free of charge. But the saga of the clinic was by no means over. For instruction at the clinic an entirely honorary staff was appointed, and the eleven members dominated the University Dental Board set up by Council for the management of the clinic. What troubled Senate was that it had no proper representation on the Board, which reported directly to Council. Consequently, a joint committee of Council and Senate was appointed to investigate the constitution and functions of the Dental Board, and at the start of 1926, a year after clinical instruction was initiated, the Board was radically overhauled. Under the new constitution provision was made for equal representation of the Senate and the professional staff of the dental clinic, and in future the Board was to report to the Senate through the Faculty of Medicine. This was not a solution entirely acceptable to the professional staff, who recommended instead the foundation of a Faculty of Dentistry.[25] This recommendation was finally adopted in 1929.

The regulations and curricula for the degree of Bachelor of Dental Surgery had been framed by the Faculty of Medicine during 1924. Next year, Council gave the authority to institute the full course for the degree. The full course was to extend over five years, and not four as originally contemplated by the Faculty of Medicine, with the first two years given over to the general medical sciences and prosthetic dentistry. At the urging of the South African Dental Association, the Faculty of Medicine also declared itself in favour of a seven-year combined degree course in medicine and dentistry, with dentistry being regarded as a speciality of medicine.[26] The proposal, though earnestly discussed well into the 1930s, was never implemented.

As in the medical school, the clinical teaching staff in the new dental school was entirely part-time. The only full-time member of the teaching staff was J.C. Middleton Shaw, who was appointed lecturer in dental anatomy, physiology, and histology at the end of 1925. It was recognized that, while the dental students would take several of the same pre-clinical courses as the medical students, they would require specialist instruction in dental anatomy, and for that reason Shaw was appointed to the Department of Anatomy. In 1929 he was installed as the first director of the Oral and Dental Hospital, which replaced the old clinic, and in the same year he became the first Dean of the new Faculty of Dentistry. In 1931 he was made Professor of Dental Science, following the creation of the first chair in dentistry. He continued as director of the Oral and Dental Hospital, and as dean, until his retirement at the beginning of 1957, after 31 years of service.

An Irishman, and a graduate of Trinity College, Dublin, Middleton Shaw

J.C. Middleton Shaw

joined Raymond Dart's anatomy department at the age of 24. He immediately came under the influence of Dart, who was to have a tremendous impact on Shaw's research activities and his thinking about dentistry. In terms of research Dart put him to work in the anthropological field, and the outcome was to be Shaw's classic work on *The Teeth, the Bony Palate and the Mandible in Bantu Races of South Africa*. It was published in London in 1931, after having gained Shaw the D.D.S. of the University in the previous year. The young Shaw came to share Dart's view that a close relationship existed between dentistry and medicine, and he was consistently to stress the need for dental students to take the same basic science courses as the medical students. In 1933 he prepared an extensive memorandum for the Faculties of Medicine and Dentistry arguing the case for a conjoint degree in medicine and dentistry, and urging that dentistry was a speciality of medicine.

By today's standards Shaw's whole approach to dental education was very limited. He apparently had little understanding of the clinical side of dentistry and no real appreciation of the importance of clinical research. He is none the less the unquestioned father of dental education in South Africa, and the dental school at Wits was to bear his imprint until the day he left, and even after.

For the 26 years that Shaw served as director of the Oral and Dental Hospital and as Dean of the Faculty of Dentistry, he was virtually a dictator in the dental school. A man possessed of great strength and powers of leadership, he allowed nothing to stand in his way, and dominated all round him. Like his fellow Irishman, Dalton, he was fluent, persuasive, and combative, and provoked many a row in Senate. In the final analysis, he was tyrannical to those under him, and he was particularly unkind to students he did not like. To his equals he was at best an uncomfortable colleague, to his superiors he was often troublesome, as the hapless Principal Raikes discovered. Yet he was also warm-hearted, a good friend until his friendships suddenly snapped, and a man capable of giving the most superb advice. He was always revered by the dental profession in Johannesburg, and indeed in the country at large.

Middleton Shaw was never a purely University figure. He played an active and prominent role in dental affairs in the country, and was the founder of the Odontological Society of South Africa. In the years prior to World War II, when research in South Africa in any field, let alone dentistry, was rare, he established an exceptional reputation for himself as a researcher and a scientist.

For all his toughness and ability, Middleton Shaw ended his career a broken man. He resigned from the University in February 1957 as a consequence of personal problems, and committed suicide four years later.

Contrary to the pessimistic views expressed by Dr Hunter, the University experienced no difficulty in finding honorary part-time staff for its Bok Street clinic, and it was able to select from a wide range of candidates. Part-time staff at the original Witwatersrand University Dental Clinic included Dr Hunter himself in operative dental surgery, T.B. Berry in prosthetics, G. Friel in dental pathology, H.J. Foote in oral prosthetics, J.H. Breyer in dental therapeutics, and F. Hossack in dental radiology. Student numbers, however, were rather low during the twenties, and by the end of the decade the dental school had produced no more than six graduates.

V

Unlike the pattern in the other professional faculties, student enrolment in the Faculty of Law began with a flourish in the University's first few years, and thereafter diminished. The pre-World War II peak in student enrolment in the Faculty of Law was attained in 1923, with a total of 87. By 1927 the total was down to 47. The number of LL.B. graduates produced by the University in the pre-war period was always small, rarely into double figures each year. Between 1922 and 1927 some 23 students qualified for the LL.B. The majority of students in the 1920s sat the Law Certificate examination for attorneys.

Law classes in Johannesburg had first been given at the Transvaal Technical Institute in 1905, where students were prepared for the Law Certificate and the Civil Service Lower Law Examination of the Transvaal. Prior to this, law students in the Transvaal had depended entirely on private tuition. In 1909 the Transvaal University College added courses for the LL.B. examination of the University of the Cape of Good Hope, and also the Civil Service Higher Law Examination, and in 1916 the School of Mines introduced courses in commercial law for commerce students. By the time university status was achieved, the courses given by the Department of Law were all well established.

What law lacked in 1922 was a chair. The department was run entirely on a part-time basis, and ever since 1906 the part-time lecturer in law had been J. Colin Murray, a Johannesburg attorney and partner in the firm of Steytler, Grimmer, and Murray. Born in Scotland, where he had served his articles as a solicitor, Murray had come to South Africa in 1899 at the age of 23, and at the end of the Anglo-Boer War he had moved from Cape Town to Johannesburg. More or less from the moment he arrived in Johannesburg Murray combined active practice with teaching, and in effect what he did in 1906 was to take his students over to the Transvaal Technical Institute. He was to continue to teach formal law classes on a part-time basis for another 40 years. Although he possessed no degree, Murray made a fine attorney, and a fine lecturer, at least to begin with. He was also a very able administrator, and served as the first Dean of the University's Faculty of Law. During World War II he again served as Dean of Law, and for some time he was also Dean of the Faculty of Commerce.

For law at the University, 1926 was a major landmark. At Murray's instigation, a chair of law was finally established in that year, and a start made with full-time classes. The first occupant of the chair was R.G. McKerron, like Murray, a Scot. McKerron was to continue as Professor of Law until 1946, although he was absent as a member of the South African Army for the duration of World War II. Murray was appointed part-time Professor of Mercantile Law.

R.G. McKerron

McKerron was aged 26 when he first came to Wits; as old as the century, as he liked to put it. He already had an outstanding record as a student, first at Aberdeen University and then at Oriel College, Oxford, where he gained a first class in the honour school of jurisprudence and in the B.C.L., and achieved the high distinction of being elected Vinerian scholar. At Wits he became particularly interested in South African private law, notably contract and delict, and wrote a textbook on the law of delict. His first handwritten draft was destroyed in the fire of 1931, along with most of the law library. Undeterred he immediately rewrote the book, which was published in 1933 as *The Law of Delict*. Although many of McKerron's views have since come to be questioned, the book made a very considerable impact, and went through seven editions before his death in 1973.

As a lecturer McKerron was generally appreciated by his students, particularly the more able. Handsome and athletic, he was rather highly strung. According to the folklore of the law school he once made the mistake of arranging to give two lectures on two entirely different subjects in two adjoining but different rooms at the same time. Not wanting to disappoint either group of students, he spent the lecture period darting between the two classes and two sets of lecture notes. While he lectured to one class for a few minutes, the other got on with writing up their notes. In 1946 McKerron left the University to enter private practice. Some attributed his departure to the unsettling impact of his experiences during World War II, including a long and trying spell as a prisoner of war after the fall of Tobruk. Others believed that Wits had simply ceased to interest him. When he returned to the academic world in 1955 it was as Professor of Law at Rhodes University.

McKerron was the only full-time appointment in the Department of Law until 1935, when a second full-time chair was created. Part-time staff who assisted Murray and McKerron in the twenties included Oliver Schreiner and W.H. Ramsbottom, both of whom were to become judges of the Appellate Division, N.E. Coaker and Walter Pollak, both later Q.C.s, and H. Rissik.

VI

As with law, the Faculty of Commerce initially catered mainly for part-time students, though from the inception of the University it did possess a full-time chair of accountancy. This chair had been established at the School of Mines in 1915 at the instigation, and with the financial support, of the Transvaal Society of Accountants. Its first occupant was James Findlay, a chartered accountant from Edinburgh, and he continued as Professor of Accounting until his resignation in 1930.

Already by 1915, accountancy on the Witwatersrand was fairly well developed as a profession, catering mainly for the mining houses. The Transvaal Society of Accountants, founded in 1904, had a membership of 500, and prided itself on the standard of its final examination which granted admission to the society, and the right to practise in the Transvaal. Under the arrangement reached with the School of Mines, the School was in future to conduct examinations for the society. A diploma of commerce was granted to students who passed all the examinations, and those who obtained a good pass in accountancy, and satisfied the conditions as regards practical experience, became eligible for admission as members of the Transvaal Society of Accountants. When the School of Mines became a constituent college of the University of South Africa, a degree in commerce was introduced.

Shortly before the foundation of the University of the Witwatersrand, the General Examining Board was formed to ensure a common standard of examination entrance into the provincial societies of accountants in South Africa, and it took control of the intermediate and final examinations for entry into the profession. But this did not exclude the University from examining for the profession, and its accounting, auditing, and law courses for the B.Com. continued to be geared to qualifying students for membership of the Transvaal Society of Accountants. Under the arrangement reached in 1921, Wits, the University of South Africa, and the General Examining Board conducted joint examinations in these subjects. The papers and external examiners were identical. The advantage of the system for university students was that they could simultaneously meet requirements for both the B.Com. and entry into the profession. This system operated until the end of 1926, when the General Examining Body withdrew as it 'felt that it was losing the control of the qualifying tests of students coming into the profession through the Faculties of Commerce', and that the examination machinery was becoming 'complicated and cumbersome'. Students who enrolled thereafter, and wished to obtain both the B.Com. and the professional qualification, had to sit separate university and Board examinations.[27] From 1932 onwards the University was to offer special classes for candidates for the Board examinations.

Two undergraduate degrees were offered by the Faculty of Commerce in the 1920s; the B.Com. and the B.Econ. The former was a part-time degree, except for the first year, which could be taken full-time and which was designed to 'broaden the general educational foundation of the youth'. The latter degree was designed mainly for prospective economists and public servants. It was abolished in 1929, and a B.A. (Social Sciences) created in its stead.

The first Professor of Accounting and Dean of the Faculty of Commerce, James Findlay, was apparently not a particularly inspiring lecturer. Short, stout, and cheerful, as a man he was popular enough, but apparently he was not exactly abreast with what was happening in the profession in South Africa. He was a rather conservative Scot, a product of the 'old school', who made little attempt to adjust to the practices that governed accountancy in South Africa. For financial reasons he resigned in 1930, and went into private practice. He died in 1936, aged 56.

As his part-time lecturer in accounting Findlay possessed a very competent man in the person of Francis Dix. Locally trained, he was fully alert to local conditions, and was entrusted with the second- and third-year courses in accounting. For the rest, B.Com. students benefited most from the courses they received from professors and lecturers in other faculties, notably Dalton in actuarial science, Lehfeldt in statistics, and members of the Faculty of Law.

Student numbers in the Faculty of Commerce rose steadily from 133 in 1922 to 187 in 1927, but the number of B.Com. graduates was very small; 33 by the end of 1927. None had yet qualified for the B.Econ.

Notes

1. E.H. Cluver, *Medical and Health Legislation in the Union of South Africa* (Johannesburg, 1949), 3–4.
2. J.R. Draper, *The Engineer's Contribution: A History of the South African Institution of Mechanical Engineers 1892–1967* (Johannesburg, 1967), 242–3.
3. *South African Architectural Record,* March 1927, 27.
4. Minutes of meeting of the Technical Advisory Committee, 26 Aug. 1927, Chamber of Mines 95/1927.
5. Memorandum by the Gold Producers' Committee of the Transvaal Chamber of Mines, 10 Sept. 1927, Ibid.
6. *R.D.M.,* 22 Dec. 1927.
7. Report of sub-committee appointed by the conference between a joint committee of the Council and Senate of the University and representatives of the Gold Producers' Committee, 25 May 1928, University Archives File 565.
8. 'Statistics: Medicine, Engineering, General', University Archives 211.
9. Raikes to Secretary for Education, 26 June 1934, U.O.D. E6/66/17, vol. 1.
10. *South African Architectural Record,* Dec. 1929, 154–60; *Report of the Select Committee on Architects and Quantity Surveyors Bill,* S.C. 10 of 1926, 16–33.
11. G. Herbert, *Martienssen and the International Style: The Modern Movement in South African Architecture* (Cape Town, 1975); Monte Bryer, *The Faculty of Architecture of the University of the Witwatersrand, Johannesburg, and Its Role in the Community* (Johannesburg, 1977); G.E. Pearse, 'Reminiscences' (unpublished typescript).
12. Council minutes, I, 2 May 1919.
13. *Journal of the Medical Association of South Africa,* 22 Jan. 1927.
14. *The Medical Journal of South Africa,* Dec. 1919.
15. Senate minutes, II, 9 & 16 Oct. 1922.
16. Quoted in Dart, *Adventures,* 45–6.
17. P.V. Tobias, 'From Linné to Leakey: Six Signposts in Human Evolution' in Lars-könig Königsson (ed.), *Current Argument On Early Man* (Oxford, 1980), 1–12. See also Tobias, 'Homage to Emeritus Professor Raymond Dart on his 75th Birthday', *South African Journal of Science,* 62 (1968), 42–50.
18. F. Daubenton, 'Recommendations and a Report on the Witwatersrand Medical Library', July 1971, 11.
19. Report of the executive committee of the Witwatersrand University Committee for the year 1920–1921.
20. *South African Dental Journal,* I, 3–8.
21. Council minutes, I, 1 Sept. 1922.
22. Faculty of Medicine minutes, I, 23 May 1923.
23. Ibid., 20 June 1923; Council minutes, I, 29 June 1923.
24. Ibid., 10 Sept. 1923.
25. Ibid., II, 13 Nov. 1925 & 26 Feb. 1926.
26. Faculty of Medicine minutes, I, 23 April 1924 & 25 Aug. 1925.
27. See the *Report of the Accountancy Profession Commission (1934),* U.G. 49 of 1935; G.E. Noyce, 'The History of the Profession in South Africa', *South African Accountant,* 1 (1954), 3–12; Faculty of Commerce Misc./67/27 & 71/29.

PART III
Raikes: The First Decade

7

DEPRESSION AND RECOVERY

I

In January 1928 Humphrey Rivaz Raikes became the University's third Principal, an office he was to retain for 26 years, finally retiring because of ill health in February 1954. No other Principal of the University has served for more than one decade, let alone two. Under him the University grew very considerably. On his arrival as Principal, the University possessed 1 476 students; when he departed student enrolment had reached 4 277. His style of leadership was generally relaxed and humane, rather than assertive and dynamic.

Raikes's first decade as Principal was undoubtedly his most difficult. His initial appointment had been hotly contested by Senate, which would have preferred Hoernlé for the post. Council waited for a long time before giving him their full confidence, only confirming Raikes as Principal in July 1932. Soon after he assumed office the great depression disrupted the South African economy, forcing the government to make major cuts in its grants to universities. Politically, he had an awkward initial passage with Hertzog's Nationalist government, formed after the general election of 1929. It was only after Fusion in 1933 that he began to negotiate more confidently with government.

Although hostility among the academic staff to Raikes's appointment as Principal soon evaporated, it took a considerable time for him to establish his true stature within the University. General admiration for him as a man and as a leader dates from his efforts at the close of World War II to ensure that Wits would provide ample opportunities and facilities for returning soldiers. Before the war, though generally regarded as kindly and well-meaning, he was seen as lacking drive and initiative, and as rather ineffectual when dealing with the more assertive members of the academic staff.

According to the University's folklore, Raikes's initial appointment as

Principal was in the nature of an accident. In 1927 the University Council set up an overseas committee, which included Philip Kerr and Lionel Curtis, both former members of the Milner Kindergarten, and William Cullen. Their task was to find suitable candidates for the principalship. The story is told that the committee visited Exeter College, Oxford, to interview a favoured candidate, but found that he was away at the time. While looking for their man, they happened to bump into the Sub-Rector at Exeter, Humphrey Raikes, who so impressed them that they promptly nominated him for the principalship at Wits.

Whether the story is apocryphal or not, it is quite evident that the majority on Council was determined to appoint an overseas man and thus avoid having to appoint R.F.A. Hoernlé, the internal candidate favoured by the Senate. On 10 December 1926 Sir William Thomson, with the permission of the chairman of Council, had informed a special meeting of Senate that he would not continue as Principal beyond 1927, and that Council had begun to seek his successor. The Senate had then gone into committee, and after prolonged discussion resolved by 20 votes to 7 to recommend the appointment of Hoernlé as Principal. Hoernlé was the candidate of Dalton, then a Senate member of Council, but the majority on Council was determined not to have Hoernlé foisted upon them. Jan Hofmeyr, now Vice-Chancellor, led the opposition to Hoernlé in Council. He had neither forgotten nor forgiven both Hoernlé's criticism of his handling of the Stibbe affair, and his leading role in blocking the award of an honorary degree to him. That Hoernlé was Dalton's candidate for the principalship sealed the issue for Hofmeyr. He later wrote to Hoernlé acknowledging that he had opposed his appointment as Principal, but he strenuously denied that his opposition was based 'on some personal grudge or grievance'.[1]

In immediate response to Senate's nomination of Hoernlé, Council enlarged its special committee dealing with the appointment of a new Principal, and it in turn set up an overseas committee 'to find a suitable candidate overseas'. In June 1927 the overseas committee reported 'definitely recommending one name', that of Raikes. Thereafter followed a prolonged wrangle in Council, with Alexander Aiken, chairman of the special committee, urging the appointment of Raikes while Dalton strongly advocated the appointment of Hoernlé. It was not until mid-August that a decision was reached, and even then the vote was closely contested. At the meeting of 12 August the motion to appoint Raikes rather than Hoernlé was carried by 9 votes to 6. The mining and business contingent on Council, the Mayor of Johannesburg, and H.J. Hofmeyr and the Hon. J.H. Hofmeyr, voted for Raikes. The minority consisted of the three Senate members of Council, Professors Dalton, Findlay, and Young, Bishop Karney, Advocate Lucas, K.C., and the Revd J. Mullineux.

At the request of Sir William Dalrymple, the decision of Council was communicated to Senate at a special meeting on Monday 15 August. At the meeting Sir William Thomson announced that Council had decided to appoint as Principal Mr Humphrey Rivaz Raikes, age 36, unmarried, Sub-Rector of Exeter College, Oxford. Sir William made it clear that the appointment was on the recommendation of a distinguished overseas committee which had considered the claims of between 30 and 40 persons. Six criteria had been used to assess candidates for the principalship: '(1) academic qualifications, (2) administrative ability, (3) capacity to ensure happy relations with students and colleagues, (4) personal appearance, (5) facility in public speaking, and, generally, ability to make the University stand for learning, research, public spirit, and moral and intellectual character in the community which it serves.' After 'exhaustive' inquiries and discussions, the committee had interviewed four persons and had unanimously decided to recommend the appointment of Raikes. The committee considered his academic record 'excellent'. A product of Balliol College, Oxford, he had obtained a first class in the honour school of natural science in chemistry in 1914, was admitted to the M.A. degree in 1919 and that same year elected a fellow of Exeter College. He had served as a demonstrator in physical chemistry in the Balliol and Trinity College laboratories from 1920, and was made Sub-Rector of Exeter College in 1924. He had published three papers in the *Journal* of the Chemical Society, London. He also possessed a distinguished war record, serving with the First Battalion, the Buffs, and then with the Royal Flying Corps in the World War. In all:

> The Committee considered Mr. Raikes to be a man of energy, with a good appearance, and an excellent academic record, and one likely to be popular anywhere, his outstanding qualities being goodness, courage, idealism, and his personal influence with others; further, that he would undoubtedly be loved and respected by his students and liked by his colleagues, and that he had in him the makings of a first rate Principal.

Senate was not greatly impressed. After considerable discussion it went into committee, and on resumption in full meeting adopted by 21 votes to 9 the resolution: 'Senate pledges itself to support Mr. Raikes loyally if he decides to accept office, but suggests that in fairness to Mr. Raikes the Council should inform him that a considerable body of opinion in Senate is unfavourable to his appointment.'

Council duly cabled Raikes informing him of Senate's reservations. News of the differences concerning the offer of the principalship to Raikes was leaked to the press. On 24 August the *Rand Daily Mail* reported, though ten days had elapsed since the principalship had been offered him, no reply had been received from Mr Raikes. For the next ordinary meeting of Council on 9 September Raikes cabled his acceptance, and to the same meeting Dalton submitted his resignation as a Senate member on Council. After confirming Raikes's appointment, Council unanimously adopted the motion: 'The Council, in informing Senate of the acceptance by Mr. Raikes of the Principalship takes the opportunity to express its regret that it was unable to accept the Senate's recommendation. In the circumstances the Council more fully appreciates the Senate's declaration that it will give Mr. Raikes its loyal support. The Council looks forward with confidence to the continued co-operation of the Senate in the interests of the University.'

Raikes is the only Principal of the University who possessed no previous experience of South Africa. Indeed, he and Sir William Thomson are the only non-South Africans to have become Principals of the University. Their successors have all been appointed from within the University. A 'colonial mentality' among the majority on Council, and in particular a deference to the supposed merits of Oxford and Cambridge, helps to explain why Raikes should have been appointed in 1927. But the major reason was a determination to avoid having to make an internal appointment. Council itself was badly divided between Raikes's and Hoernlé's claims to the principalship, and it was the faction that had been associated with the removal of Stibbe that insisted on the appointment of Raikes, and the consequent rejection of Hoernlé. The shadow of the Stibbe affair still lay heavily over the University.

Ironically, those who led the opposition to Raikes's appointment were soon to become his main allies and friends, while several of those Council members who had stoutly urged his appointment emerged as his chief critics. Both Dalton and Hoernlé became good friends of Raikes, whereas Aiken dismissed him as ineffective and unsuitable. Jan Hofmeyr was similarly critical. Hofmeyr and Raikes were sometimes to clash when Hofmeyr served as Minister of Education, first from 1933 to 1938 and then from 1939 to 1948, and Raikes always felt that Hofmeyr was somehow undermining him.

Raikes's main attribute, his 'goodness', as the overseas selection committee had described it, made it impossible for Senate to mount a vendetta against him. When he arrived at Wits he was still relatively young, administratively inexperienced, and most unsure of himself. Indeed, he was downright nervous when presiding over Senate and when dealing with Council, which humiliated him in late 1930 by re-appointing him for another two years instead of on a permanent basis. If few people could actively dislike him, his critics on Council and Senate found him lacking in stature and drive. His earnest dedication to the University was patent, he was generally approachable, to students as well as staff, he tried hard to be fair-minded, and sought to run the University along humane lines. His interest in the welfare of the University's staff, and the activities of students, was genuine.

A tall, gangling man, Raikes did not cut an impressive figure. He was clumsy and ungainly, and achieved notoriety for his habit of falling asleep at public meetings. He would wake with a start at the end of the meeting, and then give a perfectly lucid and appropriate vote of thanks, as though he had heard everything that had been said. He suffered from narcolepsy, the physical effects of which made him a major butt of student humour. Nor was Raikes at all impressive as a speaker, lacking the capacity to express himself with conviction, and giving the impression of someone both shy and inarticulate. On one notorious occasion, when General Hertzog received an honorary degree from the University, Raikes attempted a few words in Afrikaans, which ended as gibberish. The poor man did not have the assurance to switch back to English. Hertzog was heard to ask: 'What sort of Principal has this University?' The incident was indicative of Raikes's sincerity, but also his lack of a sure touch.

H.R. Raikes

The son of an English country clergyman, Raikes was very English in his manner, devoutly Anglican in his religion, a man of undoubted integrity in dealing with others, if somewhat prim and strait-laced in his personal moral code. As Hofmeyr before him, he believed that members of staff in the conduct of their private lives should set an example to their students. Raikes took strong exception to those colleagues who breached the accepted mores of society. There was no repetition of the Stibbe affair, but from time to time members of staff encountered official disapproval of their respective liaisons. Raikes was married twice. His first marriage in 1931 to Joan Mullaly was soon annulled. In 1936 he returned to England to marry Alice Joan

Hardy, later headmistress of Roedean in Johannesburg. They had no children.

A distinctive feature of Raikes's principalship was his personal interest in almost everything that happened at the University. He personally signed on all new members of staff, thereby ensuring that he met everyone who joined the University staff. Wherever possible he would visit staff who had been taken ill; and he attended all student functions and sports meetings. A keen plumber, he would often himself repair leaks in the University's plumbing system, and personally tested the plumbing installed for the new dental building at Milner Park. His was a style of leadership, with its emphasis on personal contact and involvement, that was well suited to a University that was still relatively small, where students and staff were all known to one another.

The war, Raikes's personal commitment to the war effort, and his own efforts on behalf of ex-servicemen, served to give Raikes far more stature within the University and the wider community than had previously been the case. Prior to the war, Raikes had tried desperately to identify with South Africa, but his very Englishness, a touch of social aloofness, and his insensitivity to South African protocol, rendered such identification difficult. The war made him very much more 'relevant' in a South African context. It forced him to face up to certain things about South Africa, including the admission of blacks to the full medical training at Wits, as they could now no longer pursue their studies overseas, as well as virulent Nationalist attacks on himself and the University for their identification with the war effort, the admission of blacks, and alleged discrimination against Afrikaner students. At the end of the war Raikes's plans to make special provision for ex-servicemen at Wits gave him a cause that fully identified him with South Africa.

For the period prior to the war it is difficult to pin-point Raikes's particular impact on the University. He did not control the Senate at all firmly, and on occasion it would run away with him; he certainly did not have the ability to restrain such powerful and assertive personalities as Dalton, Dart, and Middleton Shaw. Probably his main contribution during these years was to help give to the University a more academic tone. He did not often speak in any depth or detail of how he conceived a university in general, or of his particular vision for Wits, but he did seek to educate the public and students as to the nature of a university education, and to indicate what Wits required if it was to make proper provision for such an education. As he stated in his graduation address of March 1935: 'Many people think that the University is nothing more than a glorified high school. But this is not the case. At school the underlying motive is the imparting of knowledge; at the University it is possible to cultivate the power to think.' University education, he frequently asserted, fell into three main divisions; the contact between teacher and student, that between student and student, and finally the self-education of the student. Of the first, he stressed the need for contact between teacher and student not only in formal lectures but in small discussion groups. Of the second he emphasized the crucial importance of a students' union for the proper development of a non-residential university. As to the third he emphasized the need to develop library facilities at Wits.[2] It was during the early years of his principalship that the University acquired a proper library, and it was under him that attempts were initiated to promote research within the University. The University, in short, ceased to be merely a forum for lectures.

As Principal, Raikes did not abandon his own academic and research interests. He frequently assisted with the teaching of chemistry, and in 1932 became President of the South African Chemical Institute. In 1947 he was made President of the Associated Scientific and Technical Societies of South Africa, and delivered his presidential address in November 1948 on 'Liquid Fuel from Coal'. In that year it had been decided to locate the first scheme for the manufacture of liquid fuel and oil from coal in the Vredefort district of the Orange Free State, and in his paper Raikes urged the case for developing the Eastern Transvaal as a second region for the production of liquid fuel from coal. He contended that 'we shall not achieve complete success in the Union till we have found a suitable area for large scale development outside the Vaal Basin and have established a Government laboratory for liquid fuel from coal research'.[3]

Raikes worked very hard at administration, and always got to his desk by about 7.30 in the morning, but he was not a good organizer and planner. Consequently, he was heavily dependent on the administrative staff under him, notably the Registrar. For the first eight years of his principalship Van der Brugge continued as Registrar, and Raikes was considerably influenced by him. In 1936 Ieuan Glyn Thomas became Registrar, and he was to serve in that position for the remainder of Raikes's principalship.

A Welshman by birth, Glyn Thomas was a scholar as well as an able administrator. A product of Merton College, Oxford, where he read history, he possessed a lucid, incisive, and agile mind, and was wide-ranging in his interests. He first came to South Africa in 1927, for health reasons. For a year he taught at the Ridge Preparatory School, but in 1928 he joined the administrative staff at Wits as the records and examinations clerk. He later wryly observed that Raikes rather liked the idea of having a clerk with an Oxford degree on his staff. In 1929, aged 23, he was made senior clerk, and in 1930 Assistant Registrar. Before he was appointed as the University's second Registrar, he was required to learn Afrikaans, which he did by spending six months at Stellenbosch University and the University College of the Orange Free State.

When Thomas took over as Registrar he was assisted by a chief clerk, two ordinary clerks, and several typists, and on the finance side by the accountant, W.H. Jones, and the bookkeeper, D.A. Dodds. He found himself overwhelmed by the mass of work he had to contend with, and soon appealed to Raikes for additional assistance:

> I think you should know that since the beginning of this year I have worked every Saturday afternoon and evening, and every Sunday, morning, afternoon and evening. I never start work later than 8:30 a.m. and rarely finish before 6:30 in the office. I have put in two or three hours after supper practically every evening, though sometimes there has been one evening in a week free of University work. For the last week I have had to start work at 7 or 7:30 in the morning, which means having to start walking from Parkview at 6:0 a.m. ±, there being no means of transport. I do not complain of all this, particularly as you say you work harder, but it is difficult to keep up the pace.[4]

A junior clerk was duly added to the administrative staff.

Without question, Thomas possessed almost all the attributes of a successful Registrar. He was amazingly efficient, with a grasp of the University's government and regulations that has become legendary; he never had to consult a regulation for he knew them all. Possessed of a clear, analytical mind, with definite ideas about most things, he was a master at producing succinct, polished memoranda. With his softly cadenced Welsh voice, he was a very fluent and persuasive speaker, whether on the public platform or in the committee room. In committee he was usually quiet and unobtrusive, never proffering an opinion unless called upon, but his observations were always pertinent and consequently sought after. Apparently, he was particularly effective in putting the University's case to government officials in a convincing, unambiguous, yet gentle and unassertive manner. He was also a man of great personal charm, sympathetic to individuals, particularly students, and a good listener. Many of the staff sought his help and advice. He was himself an asthmatic, with several of the nervous traits that accompany that condition, and this, together with his political activities, served to introduce an element of irritation into the working relationship that developed between him and Raikes.

Raikes desired Thomas to serve as his right-hand man, a position Thomas initially filled to perfection. Raikes became enormously dependent on Thomas, and he consequently got irritated when he found that Thomas was unreliable, that he was prone to severe attacks of asthma that would keep him away from the office for weeks, even months, at a time. He never turned against Thomas, but his sense of being let down by him was exacerbated by his belief that Thomas's wide range of extramural activities, including left-wing politics, interfered with his commitment to the University. This irritation was most marked during and immediately after World War II. In 1954, when W.G. Sutton succeeded Raikes as Principal, Thomas was made Vice-Principal on the understanding 'that appointment as Vice-Principal confers on the Vice-Principal no special right to be considered for appointment to the office of Principal, when it falls vacant'.[5] A. de V. Herholdt, who had joined the administration as a clerk in 1936, and who had undertaken most of Thomas's routine work when he was away ill, succeeded Thomas as Registrar.

I.G. Thomas

As Principal, Raikes had to suffer a greater degree of supervision from Council than his successors. The Councils Raikes had to contend with in the thirties continued, at least until 1936, to be largely dominated by persons connected with the mining industry. In 1936 the University's Act was amended so as to reconstitute the Council to give increased representation on it to Senate and municipal bodies. The size of Council was increased from 20 to 23, with the addition of a fourth member from Senate and two appointees of the Johannesburg City Council.

For the duration of the thirties Sir William Dalrymple continued as chairman of Council. A public-spirited gentleman, and a noted social personality, he was more a figurehead in the thirties than a positive leader of Council. Other founder members of the University Council who continued to serve in the thirties included Alexander Aiken, who was extremely powerful as chairman of the finance committee; Bernard Price, then general manager of the Victoria Falls and Transvaal Power Company and an exceptionally well-informed, probing member of Council; Samuel Evans, H.J. Hofmeyr,

H.J. Hofmeyr

R.N. Kotzé

R. Feetham

A. Aiken

Sir Robert Kotzé, and Robert Niven. Able, influential and long-serving members of the Council in the thirties also included P.M. Anderson, a product of the Kimberley School of Mines and general manager of the Union Corporation as well as a former president of the Chamber of Mines; Herbert R. Hill, also of the Union Corporation; John Hungerford, assistant general manager of African Explosives and Industries; A.H. Krynauw, general manager of E.R.P.M.; W. Grant McKenzie, an engineering graduate of the University and chairman of the finance committee after 1939; and Wolf Hillman and Pete Suzman, the first truly commercial figures on Council. A strong conservative influence on Council in the early thirties was Dr Hans Pirow, the first mining student at Wits to have secured a D.Sc. and brother of Oswald Pirow, Hertzog's Minister of Justice. The appointment in 1938 by the Governor-General of Mr Justice Richard Feetham and Mr Justice Oliver Schreiner greatly added to the liberal influence on Council. Professors Le May and Watt, and later Professor Sutton, regularly sat as Senate members on Council.

Until his death in September 1938 Prince Arthur of Connaught, the University's first Chancellor, continued in that office. He was succeeded by Jan Hofmeyr, the University's first Principal who remained Chancellor until his death in 1948. The Vice-Chancellor for most of the thirties was Henry John Hofmeyr, who served from 1930 to 1937. He was succeeded in turn by Sir Robert Kotzé (1937–1938) and Richard Feetham (1938–1947). It was only in 1948 that Raikes was elected Vice-Chancellor. Thereafter it became the convention to combine the offices of Principal and Vice-Chancellor, and in 1959 an amendment to the University's Act laid it down that the two offices must be held by the same person.

II

It was Raikes's misfortune to have to contend for much of his principalship with severe constraints on the University's finances, first as a consequence of the great depression and then as a result of the restrictions imposed by World War II. He suffered under these constraints in so far as he was anxious to see Wits acquire the basic facilities required of a university, and was generally more interested in promoting new developments than in looking for ways and means of saving money. At times he differed sharply from Alexander Aiken, chairman of the finance committee, and Jan Hofmeyr, the Minister of Education, over financial policy for the University. They tended to regard him as extravagant, and would press the case for consolidation whenever they thought he was getting too ambitious. His relations with Hofmeyr were at their worst after 1939 when Hofmeyr served as Minister of Finance as well as Minister of Education in the Smuts government. But for all their disagreements over policy, Hofmeyr and the officials of the Department of Education always had the greatest respect for the professional and forthright manner in which Raikes and his administration conducted the affairs of the University and dealt with the government.

Soon after becoming Principal, Raikes had to contend with the impact of the great depression upon the University's finances. The beginning of the world economic depression of the thirties is traditionally dated from the Wall Street crash of October 1929. From Wall Street the crisis spread to the rest of the American economy, and from the United States to the rest of the world. In 1931 the depression deepened as a consequence of the 'crisis within the crisis', the European monetary crisis which led to Britain's abandonment of the international gold standard in September 1931. South Africa's display of independence in remaining attached to the gold standard served to accentuate the decline in her exports caused by the depression. In December 1932 South Africa finally went off the gold standard, and this promptly resulted in a remarkable economic upswing in the country. Devaluation produced a rise in the price of gold from 85*s*. to 120*s*. an ounce, and in 1934 the price was fixed at $35 an ounce following America's abandonment of the gold standard. The new prices ensured the prosperity of the gold mining industry for the remainder of the thirties, and provided the foreign exchange to help finance South Africa's secondary industrialization.

For Wits, like the other universities and university colleges in South Africa, the country's depression was not simply a short, passing phenomenon that temporarily disrupted its finances. There was a fundamental restructuring of the system by which universities were financed. Government grants, quick to be cut, were slow to be restored, so that universities became more dependent on income from fees; new government controls were imposed on universities, and the way in which they spent their money; and loan financing for new university buildings was abandoned in favour of a scheme of outright government grants on a £ for £ basis. The Minister of Education primarily responsible for restructuring university finance was Jan Hofmeyr, who took office with the formation of the Hertzog/Smuts Fusion government in March 1933.

Hofmeyr's predecessor as Minister of Education, Dr D.F. Malan, was responsible for effecting the major cuts in state grants to universities in response to the depression. In 1930 he had stabilized the general purposes grants, and in 1931 and 1932 he imposed drastic reductions in government grants. The University of the Witwatersrand's state subsidy was reduced by a quarter. In 1930 the University's subsidy amounted to £98 000, including £16 000 towards interest and redemption payments; for 1932 the subsidy was reduced to £73 000. Malan, furthermore, also sought to curb university autonomy. In 1931 he submitted to Parliament a Higher Education Control Bill which went so far as to give the Minister of Education a veto power over university appointments. The notion that the state, as the chief paymaster of the universities, should have a voice in university appointments had already been canvassed by Dr Gie, the Secretary for Education, and the point Malan was intent on establishing was that universities when making appointments should no longer be free to disregard whether candidates were competent in both the country's official languages.[6] Malan later withdrew the bill. The Higher Education Financial Provision Act passed in 1931 was specifically directed to imposing restrictions on the financial freedom of universities. The Act validated the reductions made in university grants, required universities to submit their budget estimates for ministerial approval, and likewise to submit their plans for new developments for ministerial approval.

As a member of the Opposition, Hofmeyr had opposed the passage of the Higher Education Financial Provision Act, and had also criticized the methods employed in reducing university grants, particularly the way in which they discriminated against the University of the Witwatersrand, which still had to meet its exceptionally large interest and redemption charges.[7] On becoming Minister of Education Hofmeyr promptly moved to restore some stability to university financing, and set up a departmental committee, chaired by Sir John Adamson, the former Director of Education for the Transvaal and former Principal of Rhodes University College, to inquire into 'the provision of state subsidies to universities, university colleges, and technical colleges with a view to devising, if possible, a system of subsidy under which, while state control of public expenditure would be duly safeguarded, such institutions might count on a greater degree of stability and continuity in the development of their educational policy over a number of years'.

The recommendations of the Adamson Committee, with some later modifications introduced by Hofmeyr, laid the basis of the system of state subsidy to universities for the remainder of the pre-war period. Under the formula devised by the Adamson Committee, the state subsidies to universities were entirely linked to their independent revenue, rather than expenditure. For the three financial years 1934/5 to 1936/7, the committee recommended a stabilization of the main subsidy for each university on the formula:

(a) Fee Income: £1 for £1;
(b) Interest on Endowment: £1 for £1 up to a maximum of £15,000;
(c) Other Normal Recurrent Revenue: £2 for £1 on the first £5,000 and thereafter £1 for £1 up to a maximum of £15,000;
(d) Other Non-recurrent Revenue: £1 for £1 up to a maximum of £10,000 provided that a single gift of £500 or more must be regarded as an endowment on which only the interest would count for subsidy as in (b).

On the basis of the 1933 figures, the committee calculated this formula would give Wits a stabilization subsidy of £90 000 for the next three years, somewhat less than its peak subsidy of £98 000 in 1930, but substantially more than the 1933 subsidy of £73 000. Of all the universities, in fact, Wits would receive the greatest increase over 1933: 'The increase proposed is greatest, both actually and relatively, in the case of the Witwatersrand University which was hardest hit.' The committee recommended that the stabilization subsidy should be reviewed at the end of 1936.[8]

A major implication of the Adamson Committee's recommendations was that the state would cease to provide special grants in aid of loan charges; universities would have to meet their interest and redemption charges out of their general purposes grants. Although the committee was perturbed by 'the crippling load of debt charges' carried by several of the country's universities and university colleges, it did not recommend a reduction in the rates of interest charged 'as these were moderate at the time the loans were made'. For future building projects the committee made 'a somewhat revolutionary proposal': 'We recommend that the state should make a free contribution equal to half the cost of a building if and when a council sees a way, obviously the way of a special gift or of a sustained effort on the part of those interested, of meeting the other half; provided of course the Department of Education is prepared to recommend it on the ground that it will meet a real need.'[9] The scheme would serve as a check on over-ambitious building projects, and would reverse the process whereby universities had accumulated 'crippling' loan charges.

The formulae recommended by the Adamson Committee for state subsidies to universities and for £ for £ grants for the financing of new buildings were duly adopted by Hofmeyr. For Wits this meant that its government grant was fixed at £90 000 for the years 1934–6. When the situation was reviewed after the initial stabilization Hofmeyr revised the formula to benefit smaller institutions at the expense of the larger universities, and placed a £100 000 limit on the state subsidy to any one university. Because of Hofmeyr's modifications in the subsidy formula, Wits attained the limit of £100 000 only in 1939.

For Wits, the formulae adopted after 1933 for state subsidies meant that its subsidy had effectively been stabilized, rising by only 10 per cent from £90 000 in 1934 to the fixed limit of £100 000 in 1939. In 1930 the University's subsidy had been £98 000. In other words, for an entire decade, there had been virtually no growth in the University's state subsidy, and for three years the University had been subjected to massive reductions. Because the state subsidy was not increased, this forced the University to rely to a very much greater extent than before on fee income for its revenue.

The nature of the financial transformation was made clear in the Council's annual report for 1938. According to the figures presented by Council, the government grant for 1938 was £97 500, as against the maximum grant of £98 500 received in 1930. Fee income in 1938 was £115 200, as against £72 600 in 1934 and £49 200 in 1929. The proportion of revenue contributed by fee income had risen from 27 per cent in 1929 to 44,5 per cent in 1938, while the proportion derived from government grant had declined from 53 per cent in 1929 to 38 per cent in 1938. The average amount paid by a student in fees had been raised from £32 in 1929 to £48 in 1938, while the amount of government grant per student had fallen from £63 in 1929 to £41 in 1938.

What saved the University financially in the 1930s was the substantial increase in student enrolment, from 1 609 in 1930 to 2 544 in 1939, and the new scale of fees instituted in 1935, which considerably increased the fees for the first year of study. The new composite fee for the first year of the B.A. was £60, virtually doubling the charges, while the composite fee for the second and third years was £30 each, representing little change. Fee income promptly rose from £72 600 for 1887 students in 1934 to £97 500 for 2 040 students in 1935.[10]

By 1939 the University's total income was £277 600, and its expenditure for the year was £278 000. In 1930 the University's total income had been £186 800, and expenditure £187 500. For total income, the University's worst two years in the thirties had been 1932 and 1933, when income had declined to roughly £175 000, forcing major cut-backs in expenditure. A sense of the need to economize never left the University for the remainder of the thirties, and the squeeze became particularly acute again at the end of the decade as a consequence of the virtual stagnation in the state subsidy to the University.[11]

In 1931, the first year in which the state subsidy was cut, the University had been free to determine its own reductions in expenditure. Thereafter, following the passage of the Higher Education Financial Control Act, the University ceased to be a free agent, and was required to submit its estimates to the Minister of Education for his approval. The minister, D.F. Malan, insisted on reductions in certain areas, notably salaries. Although Council was reluctant to reduce salaries, which were already low, never having been increased since the University's foundation, Malan insisted that for 1932 the University produce a scheme of retrenchment and temporary reduction of salaries. The first scheme produced by the University's Council the minister deemed inadequate. At the end of 1931 it was finally agreed to impose the following percentage reductions from the next year:

for the Principal	9%
for Professors	7%
for Senior Lecturers	6%
for Lecturers and Junior Lecturers	5%

Four members of the permanent staff were retrenched. The other major reductions were made in the costs of administration, laboratories and libraries, equipment and furniture, grounds and improvements, and 'native wages'. Nor did government allow any relief to the University in meeting its interest and redemption charges, which in 1932 amounted to £34 000.[12]

In 1932 the University's deficit was approximately £1 400, but with the restoration of salaries the following year this increased to £5 000, and the accumulated deficit to £16 600. The large deficit in 1933 was primarily due to over-expenditure on books for the Library, to replace those destroyed by fire in December 1931. In 1934 and 1935, after the application of the Adamson formula, the University was able to produce a surplus in its annual budget, but thereafter it again slipped into deficit finance, with a deficit of £3 600 in 1936 and £2 100 in 1937.

In a memorandum on 'The Finances of the University' in November 1938, Alexander Aiken explained that expenditure had outrun revenue in the two previous years largely because of new appointments: 'In the years 1936 and 1937 the Council was expecting a material improvement in the Government's grant, and insistent claims on the University for additional staff and services were granted to much too great an extent. The result was a jump in the salary bill which outran the revenue.' By 1937 the University had succeeded in returning to its immediate pre-depression ratio between full-time academic staff members and students of 19.6, the ratio having deteriorated to 21.4 in 1933.

Staff/Student Ratio 1929–1937

Year	Professors	Other Teaching Staff Full-Time	Other Teaching Staff Part-Time	Total Full-Time Staff	Students	Students per Professor	Students per member of Full-Time Staff
1929	36	45	81	81	1 544	42.9	19.1
1930	36	46	83	82	1 609	44.7	19.6
1931	40	45	91	85	1 686	42.1	19.8
1932	40	48	72	88	1 782	44.5	20.2
1933	41	46	94	87	1 863	45.4	21.4
1934	40	50	105	90	1 887	47.2	21.0
1935	42	57	96	99	2 040	48.6	20.6
1936	43	67	94	110	2 132	49.6	19.4
1937	45	71	99	116	2 279	50.6	19.6

For 1937 the University's salary bill for academic staff was £102 000, as against £66 500 in 1932, the year of the salary cuts.[13]

Aiken's objective in his memorandum at the end of 1938 was to attempt to contain staff expansion, as the salary bill for the academic staff was by far the largest single item in the University's expenditure while it was clear that the subsidy from the state had effectively ceased to grow. 'I am convinced', he contended, 'the conclusion is this: the Council has expanded its activities beyond its means, and a definite stop should be placed to creating any new post, still less any new department, but all efforts should be concentrated on improving the efficiency of those departments which are already established, and that can only be as funds permit.' Nevertheless, in 1939 the number of academic staff was increased to 250, of which 150 were full-time. The salary bill for 1939 was to be £112 500.

Despite the expansion in academic staff at Wits in the post-depression years, the University still spent decidedly less on academic salaries by 1939 than did the University of Cape Town. In 1939 U.C.T. devoted £121 800 to salaries for an academic staff of 300, 179 of them full-time. Where Wits greatly outspent U.C.T. was on administration. The expenditure on administration at Wits in 1939 was £28 000, including £13 000 for salaries; at U.C.T. the expenditure on administration was £13 400, of which £7 000 was devoted to salaries.[14] The Registrar's office at Wits continued to complain that it was overburdened, but the Library had acquired a substantial staff and faculty deans had been provided with secretaries.

During the depression years major cut-backs at the University had been suffered in equipment and laboratory supplies. In 1932 and 1933 the

University bought no new equipment, and token purchases only were made in 1934. To cut down on the consumption of laboratory supplies, students were made to work in pairs. The faculties most affected were engineering, medicine, dentistry, and science, of which the first two were precisely the faculties where the growth of student numbers in the thirties was concentrated. Both faculties became grossly overcrowded, desperately in need of more space, equipment, and staff. The medical school was the worst off for equipment as engineering had been reasonably well provided for in the twenties, and was making full use of its available space, whereas the medical school had not been adequately equipped before the depression struck. When the northern wing of the medical school was completed at the beginning of 1930, the University found it had no money for equipment.

More accommodation became major priorities in the thirties for both engineering and medicine. The disastrous central block fire of December 1931, combined with the needs of these two faculties, provided the impetus behind the University's plans for fund-raising and building in the thirties.

III

In the early hours of Thursday 24 December 1931 the University's central block was gutted by fire. The fire was first noticed by a motorist passing along Jan Smuts Avenue, about 200 metres to the east of the central block, and he telephoned the Central Fire Station at 3.07 a.m. Four fire engines were rushed to the University, and they arrived on the road immediately in front of the central block.

The fire, which had been raging for a considerable time before the alarm was given, had gained a strong hold, and the flames were being fanned by a stiff breeze. The fire brigade forced a way through the main entrance doors, which were burning, when the entire central portion of the building, a temporary wood and iron structure, collapsed, almost trapping Chief Officer F. Jeffreys. 'The din was deafening', the *Rand Daily Mail* reported, 'and as the flames continued their fierce attack the stairway crashed down in a huge cloud of feathery sparks. A fire extinguisher, which had apparently burst in the intense heat, was thrown 50 yards out of the front entrance, while great steel girders were buckled, and red-hot sheets of corrugated iron, amazingly twisted, fell like leaves on the burning debris below.'

With blazing debris from above barring their way through the building, the brigade moved to the rear of the central block to fight the fire. In the opinion of the assessors' report, had the brigade gone to the rear of the building in the first instance they would have given themselves a better opportunity to locate the seat of the fire and would have saved valuable time. Unfortunately the janitor, Mr Robson, had been asleep in his quarters in the grounds, and was not on hand to advise the brigade: 'Had he noticed the fire at 3.0 a.m., or been aroused by the Brigade on their arrival, he could, in our opinion, have directed the efforts of the Brigade to better advantage.' Another major complicating factor was that there were no hydrants in the University grounds, and the brigade had to use those on Jan Smuts Avenue. Owing to their distance from the fire, pumps had to be employed to maintain the water pressure. 'We could not obtain sufficient power from the streets', Chief Officer Jeffreys explained to the *Mail,* 'and were forced to suck the water up through steel hoses and then into our machine. We sucked the water up at a pressure of 40 lbs. and then from the machine we were able to play on the fire at a pressure of 70 lbs.' When asked by the insurance assessors why no use was made of the hydrants within the central block, each equipped with nozzle and cradled hose ready connected, Chief Officer Jeffreys replied that having made connection with the public hydrants, additional connections would have affected the pressure. In the opinion of the assessors' report, use of the central block hydrants would also have saved valuable time.

It took the sixty firemen in attendance some three hours to bring the blaze under control. Apart from the top floor of the west wing, which was completely gutted, they largely succeeded in their chief objective, which was to protect the wings from the destruction that had engulfed the central portion of the building. The central portion was completely burnt out, even to the basement. The fire had penetrated to most rooms in the wings of the north front, and virtually every room that survived was affected by heat, smoke, and water. A large part of the electrical installation and central heating installation was destroyed. The assessors reported that: 'The fire will necessitate the rebuilding of the Central Portion and top floor of the West Wing, the replacement of more than fifty per cent of the joinery in the East and West Wings, replacement and patching of plaster throughout, replacement of windows and glazing in each wing and entire redecoration.'

It was evident afterwards that the fire had originated in the central portion above the ground floor, and had then spread downwards and along the corridors connecting to the wings of the north front. 'Owing to the strong wind', the Registrar stated in his report on the fire, 'the corridors acted as funnels for the smoke and flames, the result being that all the woodwork and combustible material in the corridors themselves as well as in the lecture rooms, offices and private rooms of the staff abutting on them, caught fire and spread the conflagration throughout the whole building.' Chief Officer

(Photographs courtesy of the *Rand Daily Mail*)

The central block fire

Jeffreys told the *Mail* he had always feared the fire hazard of the temporary portion: 'Being only temporary, it is made of wood and iron.' Housing the Library, the anthropological museum, and the Departments of Geography and Law, it had been erected to serve until such time as the University found the funds to complete the central block, and it had been considered a waste of money to build it with fire-resistant materials. How precisely the fire started in the central portion was never resolved. The assessors concluded: 'The cause of the fire remains a matter for conjecture and, with the admitted relaxation of discipline owing to the vacation and the imminence of Christmas, the most probable theories are that the fire was caused by a careless smoker or by an electric kettle left connected and forgotten.'[15]

The real damage caused by the fire was not so much to the permanent structure as the contents of the central block. The Library, on the top floor of the central portion, was completely destroyed, as was the Law Library and Mrs Hoernlé's ethnology museum, including C. van Riet Lowe's collection of the remains of primitive man in South Africa. Professor Wellington's research materials and instruments were also destroyed, but Professor Kirby's collection of African musical instruments was largely undamaged. The contents of the administrative offices, though damaged, were largely salvable, and the records office, in which the end of year examination papers had been lodged, somehow survived intact. All the records of the University, except the correspondence files before 1930 which were stacked in the basement, were saved.

The most grievous loss was undoubtedly the Library, with its special collections. In 1929, encouraged by the Carnegie Corporation of New York which donated £5 000 for the purchase of books for the Medical Library on condition that the University appoint a professionally trained librarian to handle its library facilities, the University had finally appointed a Librarian, Percy Freer, sub-librarian of the South African Library in Cape Town. Educated at the Universities of Birmingham and Heidelberg, Freer had been assistant librarian at the Norfolk and Norwich Library before coming out to Cape Town in 1926. In taking up his appointment at Wits, he became the first full-time professional university librarian in South Africa. A man whose first loves were languages and books, he was to serve as University Librarian until his retirement through ill-health in 1954. His first tasks on appointment had been to create a genuine library for the University, and to train a library staff. By December 1931, through purchases, donations and the voluntary amalgamation of departmental libraries, the Students' Central Library had acquired a stock of 30 000 volumes, spread among the rooms and corridors of the top floor of the central block, chiefly the central portion, while a card catalogue using the Library of Congress classification had been established. Freer's assistants included Elizabeth Hartmann, who was to succeed him as University Librarian, and Isaac Isaacson, who in 1970 was made archivist and undertook responsibility for establishing and organizing the University Archives.

The prize possession in the new Library was undoubtedly the Gubbins collection of Africana, acquired by the University in 1930. John Gaspard Gubbins, a Cambridge graduate whose farm in the Ottoshoop district of the Western Transvaal contained a rich fluorspar mine, had for some eighteen years used the profits from his mine to build up a large collection of Africana. His ideal had been to establish a collection that would illustrate every phase and aspect of South African life and culture. The collection was initially housed in a special building on his farm, but because he feared that it was vulnerable to fire, Gubbins decided in 1930 to transfer the books and manuscripts to Wits. In an agreement signed in October 1930, the University purchased the entire Gubbins book collection and undertook that 'the Gubbins Library shall forever be maintained by the University as an independent unit, shall be accessible to all members of the community and shall be enlarged and developed by further acquisition of similar material from time to time'. Gubbins had not quite finished transferring his library when the larger part of it was destroyed in the central block fire. Another major, and quite irreparable, loss were the Philip Papers, the letters of Dr John Philip that had provided the basis for Macmillan's work in the twenties and that had likewise been placed by him in the Library for safekeeping. A valuable collection of eighteenth-century works on Roman and Roman Dutch Law was lost in the destruction of the Leonard Memorial Law Library, which had been founded in 1926 with funds from the estate of J.W. Leonard.

J.G. Gubbins

To compound the sense of disaster caused by the destruction of the Central

Library and the Law Library, the Gubbins collection apart, their contents were uninsured. As the fire made all too evident, the University was underinsured. Buildings, furniture, and equipment were the only items insured, and buildings were supposedly insured for a third of their value in a formula based on the assumption that they were fire-proof. Generally they were insured for somewhat less than a third of their value. The University's entire insurance policy was for £178 500, including £155 000 for buildings. The central block building, the main structure of which had cost £70 000 to construct, was insured for £25 000, its furniture and equipment for £2 000. As the condition of average did not apply, the assessors awarded the University £18 000 for damage done to the central block and the full £2 000 for furniture and equipment destroyed, the real value of which was over £6 000. In respect of books, as the University's annual report put it, 'the Council had to face a considerable loss, having been quite unaware to what extent the vulnerability of the central portion would, in unfavourable climatological circumstances, such as prevailed during the night of the fire, affect the contents of the permanent portions of the structure'. At a conservative estimate, the Librarian put the value of the books destroyed as £5 000.

For the University, the central block fire could not have come at a worse time. As Aiken had told the annual meeting of the Witwatersrand Council of Education a few days earlier the University was already experienceing 'heavy weather' financially, owing to government cut-backs. The government was simply unable to assist reconstruction after the fire. In response to Sir William Dalrymple's plea for a government loan towards the building of a fire-proof library, the Minister of Education regretted that 'under the present financial stringency' it was not possible to provide loan moneys.[16]

The immediate task confronting the University in the wake of the fire was to attempt to reorganize and restore teaching facilities before the beginning of the 1932 academic year in early March. Raikes was absolutely determined that the fire should not be allowed to disrupt the University's teaching, and thanks to some rapid work by John Barrow, the contractor responsible for most of the University's buildings, the main structure of the central block was restored in time for the opening of the academic year. Raikes was also determined that the University should not rebuild the temporary central portion, and accommodation for a temporary library, the Department of Law, and several Arts departments was consequently found in other buildings. As the University almost entirely lacked lecture rooms capable of taking large classes, it was decided, instead of replacing the central portion, to construct a large lecture theatre, which would accommodate an audience of two hundred in the central block.

The University's 'crying need', as Raikes saw it in assessing the situation after the fire, was for a permanent library building. Even before the fire this had been recognized as a pressing requirement, and in 1930 the Council had approached the government for a loan of £50 000 for a library building. The loan had been refused, and Raikes rightly blamed the destruction of the Library by fire on the over-all lack of finance: 'The principal cause of this disaster was lack of funds. Had the Council had at its disposal sufficient money, it would not have been forced to construct a temporary centre to the Main Block.' Although some thought 'it is now too late to build a library as we have no books to put in it', Raikes campaigned hard for the immediate construction of a fire-proof library building. As he advised William Cullen, secretary of the University's London committee: 'I believe we can do quite a good Phoenix act and, provided we have a really proper fire-proof library, we can accumulate a new Library in a very short time.'[17]

Although, as Raikes told a public meeting at the City Hall on 11 January 1932, it was not a good time to be asking the public for money, he fully appreciated that the sense of calamity evoked by the fire needed to be exploited while it was still fresh, and he wasted little time in appealing for help. On 7 January, barely a fortnight after the fire, he asked for donations of money and books to restore the University's book collection, and eleven days later he launched an appeal for £80 000 for the construction of a permanent library, the completion of the central block, and the acquisition of books. As Raikes impressed on a public meeting at the City Hall, the University was not appealing for money to make good its losses, but to fund new construction: 'We want to put the University in such a position as to prevent a recurrence of the disaster of the fire.'[18]

This was the second fund-raising campaign with which Raikes had been associated. The first, the University Development Fund of 1928, had been designed to raise money for out-of-class activities at the University, including the construction of a swimming pool, playing-fields, an open-air theatre, and library accommodation. The campaign was a limited success, and did finance the swimming pool that was opened in 1930. The University of the Witwatersrand Appeal, as the 1932 campaign was called, was launched in the midst of a major depression, and the response, as the University's annual report expressed it, was only 'moderately successful'. The appeal fund raised £21 000, the chief contributions coming, as in the past, from the Johannesburg municipality, the Chamber of Mines, and the Witwatersrand Council of Education. Otto Beit, the brother of Alfred, who had died in London in December 1930, had bequeathed £10 000 to the University. This was automatically put into the fund for the Library building. These funds, and

Opening of the new Library, 12 March 1934

other moneys the University was able to put together, fell far short of the amounts required for building and fitting an adequate library, and no loans could be raised from the government. The University consequently had to resort to the Witwatersrand University Committee for another major loan, this time of £17 000.

At the end of 1932 the Council awarded the contract for construction of the new Library to John Barrow. His tenders were the lowest, £42 800 employing African labour and £45 600 employing white labour. The University architects, Messrs F. Williamson and N.T. Cowin, recommended the acceptance of his first tender. The Council adopted this recommendation, 'subject to the condition that, if the Department of Labour should be found willing to pay the extra amount of £2 775, European labour may be substituted for Native labour'. The Department of Labour, anxious to combat white unemployment, duly undertook to meet the difference, and Mr Barrow was instructed 'to use European labour instead of Native labour'.[19] The University treated this arrangement as a propaganda asset, and newspaper items emphasized how work on the Library served to relieve unemployment. The Department of Labour's £2 800 represented the government's total contribution to the building of the Library.

The foundation stone for the new Library was laid by the Governor-

General, the Earl of Clarendon, on 10 April 1933, and it was officially opened on 12 March 1934 by Prince George, Duke of Kent, during his visit to South Africa. The total cost of the building, including fittings, was £55 000. Situated below the North West Engineering block, it was constructed of pre-cast concrete blocks, and consisted of a fire-proof basement and two main floors. The basement, equipped with three low floors, contained book stacks; the ground floor boasted a large reading room capable of seating some 300 students and smaller rooms for special collections; and the first floor consisted chiefly of office and seminar rooms. Given the pressure on accommodation elsewhere in the University, these last were pressed into immediate use as lecture rooms, classrooms, and offices for various staff members. The Library was designed to house three quarter of a million books. On the day of opening of the Library the *Star* commented: 'It is considered that the Library should meet the needs of the University for at least the next 100 years. It would have been false economy to erect a building which would have been found inadequate after 25 years.'

Simultaneously with its campaign for funds to construct a library building, the University appealed for money and books to stock the new Library. The Carnegie Corporation of New York donated $25 000, that is slightly more than £5 000 for books, and it also provided $2 000 for Freer to visit the United States, Canada, and Britain to study at first hand modern systems of library management and control. In England William Cullen organized a major appeal for books. A University of the Witwatersrand Library Appeal Committee was established on 9 May 1932, with the Earl of Athlone as chairman and Cullen as secretary, which altogether collected and dispatched 32 300 volumes to the University. These included gifts from individuals, learned and scientific societies, universities and firms, with special contributions coming from the British Association for the Advancement of Science, the London School of Economics and Political Science, and Imperial Chemical Industries.[20] In addition, a large quantity of material was presented by all the leading missionary societies with mission stations in South Africa, and J.G. Gubbins undertook a tour of the United Kingdom, Europe, Java, and Australia to find Africana material to replace what had been destroyed in the fire. An exhibition of the most interesting books and objects he collected was staged at South Africa House, London, in July 1933. In December 1933 the University awarded Gubbins an honorary D.Litt. Cullen already possessed an honorary LL.D. from Wits, but in 1974 he was honoured for his role in reconstructing the Library when the building was named after him.

In all, as Raikes had anticipated, the Library had done a remarkable 'Phoenix act' by the end of 1934. The University had acquired for the main

Library some 60 000 volumes, about half of them donated, and there were about 4 000 volumes in the Gubbins Library of Africana, which had its own room on the ground floor of the new building. Shortly before his death in 1935 Gubbins was able to assert: 'I think it is generally recognized that I have got the library back to a much better state than it was at the time of the fire.' In 1937 the Gubbins Library received another major addition when the Church of the Province of South Africa gave its Central Record Library to the University on indefinite loan to 'form part of the Gubbins Collection of Africana'.

Though the University's appeal of 1932 had served to put the Library on a sound footing, the amount raised had fallen well short of the target set. Given the economic depression, this was understandable. In November 1934 Council decided that the moment was opportune to mount another major fund-raising campaign. Two factors encouraged them in this decision. One was the advice received from the Minister of Education in August 1934 that the government would in future make out-and-out building grants to universities up to one half of the cost of buildings approved by it, and on condition that a university had the other half already available or guaranteed when application for a grant was made. The other was the economic recovery in South Africa following its abandonment of the gold standard at the end of 1932. C.S. Richards, the Professor of Commerce, who together with J.Y.T. Greig, the Professor of English, initially proposed a fund-raising campaign to Council, was firmly convinced by mid-1934 that economic conditions favoured such an appeal. As he impressed on Raikes: 'At the present moment, Johannesburg is probably the most prosperous city in the world, and I think will remain so for many years. There are enormous funds available in the country, particularly in Johannesburg and the Witwatersrand district generally. Large numbers of individuals have made considerable sums and indeed are making them every day from gold mining transactions and other connected both directly and indirectly with gold mining.'[21]

The University of the Witwatersrand Appeal, as the campaign was once again called, was launched in August 1935 by the Governor-General, the Earl of Clarendon. Its organizer was Professor J.Y.T. Greig, who had previously been Registrar of Armstrong College, Newcastle-on-Tyne, where he had been responsible for two major fund-raising drives. The target of the appeal was £500 000 in capital, or the equivalent in income, to be used to improve staffing at the University, to complete the central block by building a university hall and adding two wings, to provide increased accommodation for engineering and the medical school, and to construct a students' union building.

As with its predecessors, the 1935 appeal was only moderately successful,

Central block in 1937

and the University again depended heavily on the contributions of the Johannesburg municipality and the Chamber of Mines. The City of Johannesburg increased its annual grant-in-aid by £7 000, from £13 000 to £20 000, and this was represented as the equivalent at 3½ per cent of a capital donation of £200 000. The Chamber of Mines contributed £37 500, African Explosives and Industries £15 000, and the Victoria Falls and Transvaal Power Company £7 500. The two major banks, Barclays and Standard, gave £1 000 each. By early 1936 the appeal, including the capitalized amounts, had raised almost £320 000.

The money received in annual grants, notably the increased grant from the City of Johannesburg, was used to improve the University's staffing position. Twenty-five new posts, representing a 10 per cent increase, were approved in 1936. In utilizing the capital sum collected, priority was given to additions to the central block, particularly the construction of a university hall. It was claimed that the development of the central block would mitigate the congestion in all faculties at Milner Park, including the first year of medicine, and that a university hall would release the temporary assembly hall in the North West Engineering block for use by the engineers, who were especially hard pressed for space.[22]

In a survey of its building and financial needs made in 1936, the University calculated that the cost to complete the central block, and necessary subsidiary construction, would reach £230 000, and that the appeal would fall somewhat short of raising half that amount in capital sums. Council consequently decided to proceed with extensions to the central block up to £160 000, and requested the government to provide its half share. The government duly agreed to vote £80 000, of which £30 000 would be made available in the estimates for 1937/8.[23] For drawing up plans for the completion of the central block, Messrs F. Williamson and N.T. Cowin were again appointed associate architects, and Professor Pearse was made consulting architect. According to Pearse, Council had been reluctant to appoint Williamson and Cowin, but had done so when Pearse advised that as their firms, Emley and Williamson and Cowin and Powers, were the original architects for the central block, it was doubtful whether another firm could or would accept the commission. The proposal that Pearse be appointed as associate architect was turned down by Williamson and Cowin, but after consideration they agreed to accept him as a consultant.[24]

In September 1936 the architects submitted plans for completing the central block at an estimated cost of £225 000, £93 000 for the central portion and hall and £66 000 for each of the two wings, east and west. The estimate included excavation, air-conditioning, and architects' and quantity surveyors' fees. For the actual construction of the central block John Barrow submitted a tender in 1937 for £160 000, substantially lower than anyone at the University had anticipated, and it was consequently calculated that the building could be completed at a total cost of £185 500.[25] This lower cost for the central block, together with the fact that by mid 1937 the capital sum raised by the University had increased to £105 000, encouraged Council not only to contract Barrow to undertake the whole of the central block building scheme but also to approach the government for an increase in its building grant. On 14 October 1937 a deputation saw the Minister of Education, presenting him with building plans for £204 600, including £8 000 for a research laboratory for the newly founded Bernard Price Institute of Geophysical Research as well as the new sum for the central block. Hofmeyr, with the consent of the Treasury, duly agreed to increase the government's building grant from £80 000 to £102 300, in accordance with the 50 per cent principle, with the additional amount to be paid in the year 1939/40.[26]

The contract for building the research laboratory for the Bernard Price Institute at Milner Park had already been given to Barrow. Established at the beginning of 1937, the Institute was founded by Bernard Price, the general manager and chief engineer of the Victoria Falls and Transvaal Power Company and a member of Council, and the Carnegie Corporation of New

York. The laboratory, which could accommodate ten research workers, was completed early in 1938 and opened by General Smuts on 21 October.

Although the completion of the central block, scheduled for December 1939, would ease some of the overcrowding in the engineering faculty, Council was none the less distressed that it had not succeeded in raising funds to undertake building specifically for engineering and the medical school, where the problem of overcrowding was becoming chronic. Indeed, the deputation to the Minister of Education in October 1937 had requested that the government depart from its new procedures and extend a special loan for increasing accommodation at the medical school. This request had been refused. Engineering proved more fortunate. On 6 September 1938 Raikes announced to Council that Mr Wolf Hillman, a member of Council, and his brother Hirsch, leading Johannesburg timber merchants, had offered to defray half the cost of a new building for engineering, the other half coming from government, and to contribute towards the cost of equipping it. Work on the building was commenced in 1939, and completed early in 1941. The Hillman building, to the west of the central block and providing accommodation for the Departments of Civil Engineering and Mining and Surveying, and a research laboratory for organic chemistry, was officially opened by Smuts as Prime Minister on 18 June 1941.

The central block was finally completed in May 1940, though portions of the east and west wings had already been occupied during 1939, with the administration moving into the ground floor of the west wing. The centre of the block contained the Great Hall on the ground floor, and above an examination hall, which was also intended for large classes and for dances. On 10 June 1940 the Great Hall was officially opened by the Governor-General, Sir Patrick Duncan, and the Department of Music presented an operetta, 'The Music Man' by Pergolesi upon the new stage. A feature of the Great Hall, which was capable of seating 1 100 persons, was its acoustic design, which had been worked out by a French consultant, M. Francois Carpentier. Professor Kirby claimed that the acoustics were perfect for speech and for solo performers, but rather different for an orchestra when it had to play on the stage, and not in the well: 'For though the results were reasonably satisfactory from the point of view of the audience, they were not from that of the players, who missed the "blend" that an orchestral player expects to feel, and they felt "acoustically naked" on the stage. The reason for this was the shortness of the period of reverberation for which the Hall had been designed, in opposition to my ideas.'[27]

With the construction of the Great Hall and the completion of the central block, basically the original building programme for Milner Park had been

Milner Park campus, 1939, looking north

Milner Park campus, 1939, looking south

carried out. At Milner Park the University possessed six major buildings that were now complete, Botany and Zoology, Chemistry and Physics, the central block, the South West Engineering block, the North West Engineering block, and the Library. In addition, the Hillman building was under construction, and the University possessed buildings for the Yale Observatory and the Bernard Price Institute of Geophysical Research. For student accommodation, there were three residences, College House and Dalrymple House, which had been built in the twenties, and the Women's Residence built in 1930 with funds from the sale of Sunnyside. For students, what the Milner Park campus still sorely lacked was a students' union building.

IV

From the financial standpoint, the thirties had been a difficult decade for the University, but it had come through it tolerably well, and in some senses was in a sounder position by 1939 than it had been when Raikes took over the principalship. In particular, the new system for financing construction meant that, even though the University had built extensively after 1933, its interest and redemption charges had remained fairly static. In 1933 the University's total indebtedness on loan account was £593 000, the total expended on University buildings and grounds was £708 000, and its interest and redemption charges amounted to £33 000. By the end of 1939 total indebtedness stood at £672 000, whereas the total expended on University buildings and grounds had risen to £940 000. The University's interest and redemption charges in 1939 amounted to £36 000, of which about £10 000 went to the Witwatersrand University Committee. In that year the executive decided to wind up the Committee, and its assets, liabilities, and functions were transferred to three trustees, the chairman of Council, the chairman of the finance committee of Council, and the Principal of the University. The Committee's assets totalled £180 000, of which £163 500 was on loan to the University.

Another positive feature about the University's finances at the end of the thirties was that they were beginning to benefit from the growing prosperity of the Witwatersrand. The two major fund-raising appeals that were mounted in the thirties were only moderately successful, but some very substantial donations and bequests were made towards the end of the decade. The Hillman brothers put up £35 000 for the new engineering building, and in 1938 A.E. Capelli, a local builder with no previous contact with Wits, bequeathed £50 000 to the University. This sum was added to the University's endowment fund, which had previously stood at the rather small amount of about £100 000.

For the immediate future the truly worrying feature of the University's finances was that its state subsidy had been fixed at £100 000, thereby curbing the possibilities of further development and forcing the University to become even more dependent on fee income, and thus the vagaries of student enrolment. A reduction in student numbers would cause the University acute financial embarrassment. By 1939 the University was again feeling itself to be under distinct financial pressure. In a letter to all heads of departments at the beginning of the academic year, Raikes urged 'the necessity for the strictest economy in all directions', and stated that no new developments could be contemplated unless they were self-supporting: 'However sound a new development may be in theory, we cannot consider financing it if this is to mean taking away money which would otherwise go to Faculties and Departments which are starved at the present time.'[28]

After the flurry of activity and expansion in the post-depression years, the University had apparently entered a new period of consolidation.

Notes

1. Paton, *Hofmeyr*, 143.
2. R.D.M., 25 March 1935.
3. Presidential address, Associated Scientific and Technical Societies, 17 Nov. 1948.
4. Thomas to Raikes, 21 Feb. 1935, Thomas file, University Archives.
5. Council minutes, VII, 26 Feb. 1954.
6. *House of Assembly Debates*, XVII, 3019–37.
7. Ibid., 3037–46.
8. *Report of the Committee of Enquiry into Subsidies to Universities, University Colleges, and Technical Colleges*, U.G. No. 8 of 1934.
9. Ibid., 11.
10. *University of the Witwatersrand, Johannesburg, Annual Report 1935*.
11. The statistics are taken from the annual reports of the Department of Education.
12. 'Memorandum by the Principal on University Finance', 3 May 1932, Finance Committee Misc./21/32.
13. 'Memorandum on University Finance', Sept. 1937, Finance Committee Misc./64/37; 'The Finances of the University', 1938, Council Misc./75/38.
14. *Report of the Union Department of Education for 1939*, U.G. No. 50 of 1940, 47.
15. R.D.M., 24 Dec. 1931; 'Memorandum by the Registrar on the Fire in the Main University Building', 28 Dec. 1931, Council Misc./76/31; Assessors' Report on 1931 Fire.
16. Secretary for Education to Dalrymple, 3 June 1932, University Archives File 143.
17. Raikes to Cullen, 6 Jan. 1932, Ibid.
18. *Star*, 19 Jan. 1932.
19. Executive Committee minutes, I, 4 Jan. 1933.
20. Final Report of the Executive of the Library Appeal Committee, Dec. 1934, University Archives File 143.

21. Richards to Raikes, 25 July 1934, University Archives File 144.
22. *R.D.M.,* 20 Feb. 1936; 'Memorandum for the Minister of Education', 13 Oct. 1937.
23. Council minutes, IV, 19 Feb. 1937.
24. Pearse, 'Notes on the site and buildings of the University of the Witwatersrand' (unpublished typescript, University Archives), 32.
25. Building Committee minutes, 1, 23 Sept. 1936, & 10 Aug. 1937.
26. Secretary for Education to Raikes, 20 Oct. 1937, U.O.D. E6/66/17.
27. Kirby, *Wits End,* 166.
28. Raikes to heads of departments, 9 Feb. 1939, Finance Committee minutes, III.

8
ASCENDANCY OF THE PROFESSIONS

I

Between 1928 and 1939 student numbers at Wits expanded by about 40 per cent, from 1 476 to 2 544. The most dramatic growth was in the Faculty of Engineering, including architecture, from 267 to 829, and the Faculty of Medicine, from 231 to 740. Dentistry slightly more than doubled, from 23 to 57. Arts and law, by contrast, experienced an actual decline in numbers. From an enrolment of 571 in 1928, Arts dropped to 445 in 1935, recovering to 539 by 1939. Law declined from 45 in 1928 to a low of 31 by 1939. Enrolment in commerce was extremely erratic. From a peak of 205 in 1928, numbers dropped to 186 in 1931, attained a new peak of 294 in 1934, and had fallen back to 206 by 1939. Science experienced a very slight growth, from 134 in 1928 to 143 in 1939.[1]

Despite financial constraints, the thirties were not without significant new developments at the University. Arts was the most active faculty in promoting developments. The Departments of Bantu Studies and Afrikaans and Nederlands gained chairs; a new degree of B.A. in Social Studies was instituted in 1937, and for it was created a Department of Sociology and an independent Department of Psychology with its own chair; a four-year course for the B.A. Honours in fine arts was introduced; and a two-year diploma in logopedics initiated. In other major developments dentistry had become a separate faculty in 1929, acquiring a chair of dentistry in 1931; the chair of accounting was converted into a chair of commerce in 1930; and law received a second full-time chair in 1935. In engineering, electrical engineering gained the status of an independent branch for the B.Sc. (Eng.), and in 1936 mining geology was established as a new branch for the degree. At the medical school a diploma of nursing was established in 1937, and in 1939 a diploma in massage, medical gymnastics, and electrotherapy, the forerunner of the diploma in physiotherapy, was introduced.

In the latter half of the thirties, once the University's finances began to recover from the depression, there was a quite considerable increase in the teaching staff, and generally staffing increases reflected those in student enrolment. The University's academic staff increased from 195, including 90 full-time, in 1934 to 250, including 150 full-time, by 1939.[2] The spread of staff among the faculties was as follows:

	1934	1939
Arts	36	44
Science	26	36
Commerce	7	12
Law	7	9
Engineering	19	31
Medicine	87	97
Dentistry	13	20

Several of the new posts in the Faculty of Science were to cater for the duplication of first-year classes for engineering and medical students. A feature of the staffing in the medical school was the introduction of full-time appointments to assist the part-time professors in the clinical departments.

In the thirties, while the Faculty of Arts still possessed more full-time staff, and continued to produce more graduates, than any other faculty, it lost the position it had held from the inception of the University as possessing the largest student enrolment. Instead engineering and medicine surged ahead. In terms of student numbers, they were in the ascendant. The complaint sometimes voiced in the twenties, that Wits was not attracting students to the two faculties Johannesburg was most suited to provide, was no longer heard. Instead, the main complaint became that facilities in engineering and medicine were quite inadequate to cope with the vast numbers of students.

II

The increased enrolment in all branches of engineering, but most especially in mining and civil engineering, accurately reflected the dramatic advances in the South African economy, notably from 1933 onwards. Following South Africa's abandonment of the gold standard in December 1932, the country experienced a period of continuous economic growth and prosperity up to the outbreak of World War II. In all, the national income rose from £234,7 million in 1932/3 to £394,8 million by 1938/9, an increase of 68,2 per cent. In the opinion of Professor D. Hobart Houghton, the upsurge in the six years after 1933 marked South Africa's 'take-off' into sustained economic growth.³

Gold mining boomed. After the gold standard had been abandoned, the price of gold had jumped immediately from 85s. an ounce to 120s., and by 1939 it had reached 154s. The result was a considerable increase in mining activity, with previously sub-marginal deposits coming within the pay limit. The number of producing mines rose from 31 in 1933 to 43 in 1939. Of great long-term significance was the fact that the high earnings from gold provided the foreign exchange to finance a major expansion of secondary industry. Capital investment in manufacturing totalled £17,7 million for the period 1932/3 to 1938/9, and the gross output of secondary industry rose rapidly from £90,9 million to £199,6 million in the same period. The clothing and textiles, metals and engineering, and stone, clay, and bricks groups of industries, all more than doubled their output. Particularly rapid was the expansion of the metal engineering industries, supplied after 1933 by the now productive iron and steel mills of ISCOR. The explosives and chemical industry in South Africa, dominated by the giant African Explosives and Industries Limited, thrived as a direct consequence of the gold mining boom. Another major feature of the period was the development of the country's transport network, including railway electrification and the creation in 1935 of the National Road Board, which in the next year launched a comprehensive five-year programme for national road construction.⁴ Civil and chemical engineers, as much as mining and mechanical engineers, were in new demand.

From the beginning of Raikes's principalship there had been a marked increase in enrolment in the Faculty of Engineering, but after 1934 the forward movement became a surge. Because of the massive financial constraints the University had operated under during the depression years, the faculty found itself both under-staffed and under-equipped to cope with the surge. The two crisis areas were first-year classes, and drawing offices and laboratories for first- and second-year students.

First-year engineering students were required to take the basic courses in mathematics, applied mathematics, physics, chemistry, and mechanical engineering design and drawing. In 1937 the University resorted to the expedient of duplicating these classes. On average in the thirties, the failure rate among first-year engineering students was about 45 per cent, which was not considered unacceptably high. At U.C.T., with far fewer students, the failure rate averaged over 50 per cent. 'Our results are no worse than Cape Town's', Principal Raikes commented in a memorandum in 1938, 'though our standard is not lower and our staff considerably more over-taxed.'⁵

Laboratory facilities in the engineering buildings had originally been designed for about 100 students. By 1939 they were required to accommodate well over three times that number, those who had progressed beyond the first year. Because of inadequate space and staff, laboratory classes had to be duplicated and even triplicated. As early as 1933 W.J. Walker, the Professor of Mechanical Engineering, had complained that engineering students were too much exposed to lectures, and too little to laboratories, precisely because there were too many students and too few laboratories and staff. 'It is my own conviction, borne in upon me by experience', he stated in his presidential address to the South African Institution of Engineers in July 1933, 'that an engineering student's best training is to be found in the laboratory and drawing office, coupled with a liberal application of directed self-study, and the absolute minimum of lectures.'[6]

Comparatively speaking, mechanical and electrical engineering were well provided with laboratories and workshops: Orr and Walker had seen to that when the move from Plein Square to Milner Park was planned and made. Much of the machinery was old, some of it going back to the Kimberley School of Mines, but was generally satisfactory for undergraduate teaching purposes, though not for research. Distinctly less well off was civil engineering, which Orr had treated as a mere appendage of mechanical engineering. It was not until the opening of the Hillman building in 1941 that civil engineering acquired its own laboratories. Yet in the late thirties civil engineering had come into its own, and by 1939 possessed almost as many students as mechanical and electrical engineering combined.

The possibility of limiting entry into engineering, as well as medicine, was seriously considered by the University at various points during the thirties. The advice given by Jan Hofmeyr, as Minister of Education, and by the University's legal advisers, was that this would require amendment to the University's Act or statutes, and no such amendment was prepared prior to 1939.[7] The economy, especially mining, in fact required more, not fewer, engineering graduates. In 1937, in negotiations between the University and the Chamber of Mines, it was established that in the immediate future the mining industry would require at least 45 to 50 locally-trained mining engineering graduates per year, whereas Wits was then producing only about half that number. To help make it possible for Wits to increase the number of mining graduates, the Chamber decided at the beginning of 1938 to grant the University £5 000 per annum for 'the provision of facilities for the training of graduates in Mining Engineering'.[8] The sum was used to establish six new posts in mining engineering, surveying, metallurgy, electrical engineering, and geology, all of which were required by mining students.[9]

In student enrolment, mining and metallurgy led the way after 1934. This owed far more to career prospects than to the leadership offered in the two departments. The Professor of Metallurgy, G.H. Stanley, had occupied the chair since 1905, and by the thirties he was beginning to show signs of having lost interest in teaching. At the end of 1934 G.A. Watermeyer retired as Professor of Mining, though he continued to serve as Professor of Surveying until 1939. With very few students of its own, surveying remained mainly a service department for mining. Watermeyer's successor in the chair of mining was C.W. Biccard Jeppe, who assumed duty in 1936. He was generally competent, but not particularly dynamic, and by the time of his retirement in 1954 he had allowed the department to run down.

C.W.B. Jeppe

Jeppe was undoubtedly a very able person, but was something of a dilettante. A member of a wealthy local family, he had been an underground manager for Crown Mines before his appointment to Wits. In 1930 he had been awarded the University's M.Sc., but in 1936, after he had assumed the chair, he failed in his candidature for a D.Sc. The examiners were divided over his thesis, and he finally resolved the issue by withdrawing it.[10] His appointment was a very controversial one. The selection committee's initial recommendation of him in November 1934 was referred back by Senate, and a condition of his appointment was that before assuming duties he should travel overseas to acquaint himself with modern developments in the teaching of mining and in the mines themselves. This he did in 1935, visiting Britain, Canada, and the United States.

As a lecturer, Jeppe was reasonably entertaining, but his approach was basically descriptive rather than scientific. In later years the main complaint against him was that he failed sufficiently to exploit the boom in mining engineering enrolment in the late thirties to secure more staff and laboratories for the department. In 1939 the department's staff consisted of himself, and S.N. Hoffenberg and P.A. Creewel as senior lecturers. Jeppe was not particularly concerned about limited laboratory facilities at the University as his attitude was that the mines themselves provided the students with their best laboratory experience.

In research, Jeppe's chief interest was ventilation. His major published work was a two-volume textbook on *Gold Mining on the Witwatersrand,* which appeared in 1946. Commissioned by the Chamber of Mines, it was designed to review mining practice on the Witwatersrand as it had developed since Watermeyer and Hoffenberg had published their text, and South Africa had abandoned the gold standard, in 1932. The book was clear, systematic, and exhaustive; its critics claimed that it did little more than assemble the work of others. In 1943 Jeppe was elected President of the Chemical, Metallurgical, and Mining Society of South Africa.

Jeppe was the only new professor appointed to an engineering department in the thirties. Otherwise leadership in the faculty remained in old hands; Walker in mechanical engineering, Randall in electrical engineering, Sutton in civil engineering, Watermeyer in surveying, and Pearse in architecture. Chemical engineering remained the responsibility of the Department of Chemistry, under Stephen after Wilkinson's retirement in 1933.

In the thirties two new branches for the B.Sc. (Eng.) were recognized; electrical engineering, previously combined with mechanical engineering, and mining geology, an entirely new creation. The four-year course in mining geology for the B.Sc. (Eng.) was introduced in 1936. The course was based on the Department of Geology, under its new head, Professor T.W. Gevers. The expansion in gold mining activity with the increased price of gold had involved not only mining previously unpayable ore in existing mines, but finding new reserves, at greater depths and to the east and west of the old goldfield. There was a new emphasis on locating previously hidden deposits, and the purpose of the new course was to produce the highly-trained mining geologists required for mining exploration.

The strongest team in engineering in the 1930s was undoubtedly in mechanical engineering. By 1939 it included two very able long-serving senior lecturers in S.F. Gimkey, Walker's successor as Professor of Mechanical Engineering, and A.E. Jensen, a student of John Orr's in the old South African School of Mines and Technology; the lecturers were R.L. Straszacker, who had gained his B.Sc. and M.Sc. in mechanical engineering from Wits and who was later to become chairman of the Electricity Supply Commission (ESCOM), and J. Drysdale; and the junior lecturer was A.J.A. Roux, who secured both his M.Sc. (1937) and D.Sc. (1943) from Wits and who was to become director of the Atomic Energy Board.

Altogether by the end of 1939 Wits had produced 723 B.Sc. graduates in engineering — 238 in mechanical and electrical engineering, 214 in mining and metallurgy, 180 in civil engineering, 80 in chemical engineering, 9 in land surveying, and 2 in mining geology. They were to make a major mark on the economy. Up to the outbreak of World War II, the mining and engineering industries in South Africa were headed almost entirely by immigrants and a few South Africans who had trained abroad. But Wits graduates were to be found in virtually all the major mines and engineering firms, as well as in the public services and state enterprises. After the war leadership gradually passed into the hands of graduates of South African universities, and the majority came from Wits.

In the 1920s Wits had produced engineers of the calibre of F.G. Hill, later technical manager of Rand Mines and later still chairman of the University Council; W.E. Kirkwood, managing director of Dorman Long; the Roberts brothers, Andrew and Douglas, founders of the Roberts Construction Company; and I. de Villiers, chief engineer of ESCOM. Engineering graduates of the 1930s included A.A. von Maltitz, later technical director of Anglo-Transvaal; T.L. Gibbs, government mining engineer; C.M. Kruger, managing director and general manager of ISCOR; T.F. Muller, chairman of ISCOR; D.F. Krige, group financial engineer for Anglo-Transvaal; W.M. Neale-May, chief chemist for SASOL; Brian Loffell and Eric Hall, in succession city engineers of Johannesburg; N. Troost, chief engineer of ESCOM; C. Boyce, chief engineer of the Post Office and deputy Postmaster-General; N. Stutterheim, deputy chairman of the C.S.I.R. and a future chairman of the University Council; H.O. Collett, chief engineer of the S.A.B.C.; C. Skeen, managing director of Roberts Construction; S.C. Newman, managing director of Lonrho (South Africa); and R.J. Laburn, chief engineer of the Rand Water Board. In the 1930s Wits also produced several graduates who were themselves to become engineering professors — J.E. Jennings (civil engineering), G.B. Lauf (land surveying), and G.R. Bozzoli (electrical engineering), all of whom occupied chairs at Wits, the latter becoming Vice-Chancellor of the University; D.W. de Vos, Professor of Civil Engineering at the University of Pretoria; and R.A. Gorges, Principal of the Camborne School of Mines in Cornwall.

In architecture, as in the other departments in the Faculty of Engineering, enrolment boomed in the thirties, and for a similar reason. By 1939 Wits possessed 101 architecture students, 50 of them studying for the degree, and the remainder for the diploma. Since 1934 there had been a phenomenal upsurge in building activity in South Africa's urban centres, but most particularly in Johannesburg. Between 1934 and 1937 the value of the building plans approved by the Johannesburg City Council nearly trebled. 'These were golden days of opportunity for architects in Johannesburg', Gilbert Herbert had written. 'Vast projects were launched, which were to alter the whole scale of the city.'[11]

In its personnel, the Wits architecture school was especially strong in the

Final-year engineers, 1930

Front row: H.B. Brown, Prof. Wilkinson, Prof. Randall, Prof. Walker, Principal H.R. Raikes, Prof. Stanley, Prof. Watermeyer, Prof. Sutton, Prof. Pearse
Second row: D.G. Roberts, E.L. Margo, P. Kirsch, H.V. Lawrance, Mr S.F. Gimkey, R.H.A. Paley, Mr A.E. Jensen, J. Coulter, L.L. Cohen, R.J.J. Dawson, F. Duthie
Third row: E.A. Macdonald, C.L. O'Byrne, C.M. Krüger, H. Hallam, T.F. Deane, E.D. Lyons, E. Witt, M.K. Edmeades, L.X.H. Maynier, N.J. Palmer
Back row: N.W.J. Murray, G.H. Legge, W. Heunes, R.G. Weavind, H.J.E. Freyer, J.W. de Villiers, E.A. MacWilliam, S. Liebenberg, C. McLauchlan

thirties, and it emerged as a leader in architectural trends in South Africa. For this, Rex Martienssen was primarily responsible. 'For a few brief years', Gilbert Herbert has observed in his study of Martienssen and his contribution to architecture in South Africa, 'the Witwatersrand University and its school of Architecture stood at the epicentre of architectural development in the Transvaal . . . And at the heart of the School stood Rex Martienssen.'[12]

A graduate of the Wits school in the twenties, Martienssen first joined the staff in 1931 on a temporary basis, and from 1934 to his premature death in 1942, he was a member of the permanent staff. Herbert has described him as essentially an educator and teacher rather than an architect: 'He did not have the architect's passionate compulsion to build.' His passion was modern

Rex Martienssen

architecture, and his commitment was to proclaiming and disseminating the new style by word, written and spoken, rather than by deed. A charismatic teacher, who built up a loyal following of talented students, he was also an editor of the *South African Architectural Record,* which he revolutionized and used to communicate his ideas.

Modern architecture would have reached South Africa without Martienssen, but his historic role was to create locally a modern movement in the thirties, and to establish international affiliations for it, notably through his personal contact with Le Corbusier in France, whom he saw as 'the greatest single influence in contemporary architecture'. Martienssen, two of his friends in the profession, Gordon McIntosh and Norman Hanson, and his disciples among his leading students in the early thirties, John Fassler, Bernard Cooke, Monte Bryer, and W. Duncan Howie, constituted the core of the so-called Transvaal group, 'a closely-knit and formidable phalanx, crusading for the new order in architecture'.[13] Fassler and Howie, later Professors of Architecture at the University, joined Martienssen on the staff at the architecture school soon after qualifying. Pearse, though not himself a proponent of modern design, protected its advocates in his school.

In 1939 Martienssen was awarded the University's M.Arch. degree for his thesis on 'Constructivism', thereby becoming the first South African to receive a higher degree in architecture. Two years later he was awarded a D. Litt. for his thesis, subsequently published, on 'The Idea of Space in Greek Architecture'. In July 1942, at the age of 37, he died of coronary sclerosis. Never since has the Wits school of architecture been quite so influential as a nursery for revolutionary new trends in the profession.

By the end of 1939, the Wits school had produced 46 architects with degrees, and 64 with diplomas. This was not a great number, but they made a considerable impact on the profession in the Transvaal. Many of the graduates of the thirties were attracted to the *avant-garde* offices. Others again joined the more established practices and, in the assessment of Herbert, 'brought with them the vitality of youth and the freshness of a new outlook which helped to loosen the strictures of conservatism'.[14] By 1939 buildings in the new idiom were being constructed on a substantial scale in Johannesburg and along the Witwatersrand.

III

In medical education, the thirties were of the greatest significance in South Africa. Already at the end of the twenties, the country's two medical schools, at Cape Town and Wits, were beginning to produce a considerable proportion of the new doctors registered in South Africa. By the end of the thirties the proportion of new registrants with South African qualifications was as high as 80 per cent. In two decades South Africa had become virtually self-dependent for its supply of doctors, something it had not achieved in engineering.

By 1939 there were 3 100 medical practitioners in South Africa, slightly fewer than there had been ten years previously. At the end of the twenties the profession was evidently over-supplied in relation to the number of fee-paying patients, and the depression years effected a major decline in the number of registered doctors. From a peak of 3 300 in 1929 the number had dropped to 2 275 by 1932. Thereafter there was a steady annual increase. At the end of the decade it was accepted that South Africa was generally well supplied with doctors in relation to the number of fee-paying patients, estimated at very much less than two million in a total population of nearly ten million. 'The cities undoubtedly have very good medical attention', Professor Dart stated in an interview in February 1937, 'but the country districts and the native territories do not.'[15] According to the statistics provided by the Botha Committee on medical training in South Africa in 1939, the median number of whites per private practitioner in the Union was 1 100, and for the entire population it was 6 400. In the reserves, there were 21 500 persons per doctor.

In England, by way of comparison, there were approximately 1 500 persons per doctor.[16]

By the end of 1939 the Wits medical school had produced 500 new doctors, slightly fewer than Cape Town. Given that no limitations were placed on student numbers in the medical school, and no special qualifications demanded of entrants, the failure and drop-out rate in the first two years of the course was fairly high, over 30 per cent in the first year and about 15 per cent in the second. There were few failures thereafter. In 1939, 80 students were awarded the M.B., B.Ch., as against 18 in 1930.[17]

In the thirties, leadership in the major pre-clinical departments remained with the established figures of Watt in pharmacology and Dart in anatomy, and one relative newcomer as a professor, A.D. Stammers in physiology. In June 1927 Stammers had been appointed as Otto Beit Professor of Physiology in succession to Cluver. Born in England, he had first come to Wits in 1921 as senior lecturer, with an M.A. degree from Cambridge. In 1926 he was awarded a D.Sc. by the University of South Africa. He remained at Wits until his retirement in 1949.

A.D. Stammers

Stammers was a man of wide interests, of which physiology was one. A first-class organist, with a comprehensive knowledge of church music, he was also a competent amateur actor, producer, and broadcaster, and was keenly interested in sports, helping to found the University rowing club. He was especially popular among students. A marvellous storyteller, full of anecdotes, he could be outspoken in debate, and possessed a caustic wit. His senior lecturer was Tommy Osborn, a Rhodes scholar, who was in charge of biochemistry, which he taught with skill and inspiration. In 1947 he was elected Labour M.P. for Benoni. In 1937 Dr Ellen Radloff, who had received her Ph.D. from Yale University, joined the staff as junior lecturer, and in 1939 she was joined by Sonia (Higham) Walker. Radloff later became the first Professor of Physiology at Fort Hare. Walker, who was made an associate professor, retired from Wits in 1977.

Anatomy, under the energetic leadership of Dart, was undoubtedly the strongest of the pre-clinical departments. It included some outstanding men on its staff, and developed an enviable reputation for research. Among Dart's staff in the thirties were Alexander Galloway, later Professor of Anatomy and Dean of the Faculty of Medicine at Makerere University College in Uganda, who was awarded the University's D.Sc. in 1938 for his thesis on 'Human Skeletal Remains from the Ancient Settlements of the Limpopo'; Joseph Gillman, a future Professor of Physiology at Wits, who was responsible for histology, and proved himself a prodigious researcher and writer; and L.H. Wells, who later became Professor of Anatomy at U.C.T., and who made regular research contributions in a number of diverse fields. By contrast with anatomy, physiology appeared insignificant, and pharmacology rather backward. The new era that was opening up in the pharmaceutical industry, with the manufacture of synthetic compounds, did not impinge on Wits.

The other major pre-clinical department, the Department of Pathology and Bacteriology, continued to be based at the South African Institute for Medical Research. Sir Frederick Spencer Lister, the successor to Watkins-Pitchford as director of the Institute, served as honorary professor from 1926 until his death in 1939. Under the initial arrangement with the Institute, members of its staff had been appointed as part-time lecturers paid by the University, but in 1926 it was agreed that the University would in future subvent the Institute to the extent of £1 600 per annum, and the Institute would pay the lecturers. This arrangement enabled the Institute to employ A. Sutherland Strachan and J.G. Becker, both graduates of Glasgow, as senior lecturers in pathology and bacteriology respectively. With the need for additional staff because of increased student enrolment, the University in 1935 appointed two professional assistants whom it paid directly: B.J.P. Becker and C.B. Chatgidakis. Strachan served as head of the department in the thirties and forties, both Beckers were later given chairs, and Dr 'Chat' lectured at the medical school until her retirement at the end of 1975.

The large enrolments of the thirties placed a great strain on the pre-clinical departments, particularly their laboratory facilities. In histology, pharmacology, physiology and biochemistry, and bacteriology and pathology, laboratory classes had to be duplicated. The greatest strain, however, was felt in the clinical departments, which were manned predominantly by part-time and honorary staff. A staffing system better suited to the small classes of the twenties was under enormous pressure by 1939.

The professors in charge of the clinical departments, medicine, surgery, and obstetrics-gynaecology, were all part-timers. Initially, obstetrics and gynaecology were separate chairs, but when J. McGibbon, Professor of Obstetrics, returned to Britain in 1929, the two chairs were combined under

Gordon Grant. After his retirement in 1938, he was succeeded by James Black, who had been a member of the department since 1929. Professor I.W. Brebner, appointed in 1931, and Professor W.H. Craib, appointed in 1932, held the chairs of surgery and medicine during the thirties.

The part-time professors were expected to administer their departments and take an active role in the business and committees of the Faculty of Medicine and Senate, to teach their students, perhaps undertake some research, and maintain a private practice as their annual salary amounted to no more than £750. At the beginning of the thirties, the teaching staff under them was entirely part-time or honorary. They were drawn from the honorary staff of the Johannesburg General Hospital. The responsibility for paying part-timers for their teaching services rested with the University. Senior clinical lecturers, the heads of 'firms' at the Hospital, were paid £100 per annum, the lecturers £50. Assistant lecturers were honorary.

Under the appointments system that operated initially, the clinical professors were selected by a committee of the University, and on appointment they automatically became members of the honorary staff of the Hospital. The remaining clinical appointments were made by the Hospital Board, on the recommendation of its appointments committee, which contained two University representatives. Following the controversy caused by the appointment of Craib, who had not previously served on the Hospital staff, it was agreed in 1935 that in future the Hospital Board should have equal representation with the University on the selection committee for clinical professors. Appointments would remain vested in the University, but would be made only on the recommendation of the selection committee.[18] For clinical services provided by the Hospital the University paid £1 500 per annum.

The clinical teaching staff consisted of the leading practitioners in Johannesburg in their respective fields. As most of them had been trained in either London or Edinburgh, their teaching was very much in the British tradition. Some of the distinguished specialists on the staff during the thirties included A.J. Orenstein in tropical medicine, I. Gluckman in skin diseases, G. Spence Smyth, G. Drury Shaw, and C.F. Krige in obstetrics, the physicians A. Bloom, I.J. Balkin, C.F. Beyers, L.I. Braun, R.L. Girdwood, H.L. Heimann, and Mary Gordon, the paediatricians B.G. Melle and S.C. Heymann, and the surgeons W. Welchman, J.J. Levin, and J.M. Edelsteirr.

For students in the thirties, the dominant figures on the clinical side were the three part-time professors: Gordon Grant, Brebner, and Craib. Gordon Grant, a Scot and a graduate of Aberdeen University, was the doyen of gynaecologists in South Africa. He had come to South Africa in 1904, and was appointed gynaecologist to the Johannesburg General Hospital and the Queen Victoria Maternity Hospital. A strong but dour man, and a skilled surgeon, he was often feared by subordinate staff and students.

Brebner and Craib were both South African by birth, though they had trained overseas. Born in the Free State in 1891, Brebner was a graduate of Edinburgh University, and maintained a general practice in Turffontein before specializing in surgery. In 1923 he joined the staff of the Department of Surgery under Ritchie Thomson, and in 1925 returned to Edinburgh to qualify for the F.R.C.S. His special interest was chest surgery, and in 1938 he was to perform the first lobectomy in Johannesburg. He was a big man, with a powerful presence, but he was also very kind, particularly to students. He taught them surgery in the tradition of the Scottish medical schools; he gave them the facts, and indicated how they were to act in certain given circumstances. Theory and research held little interest for him.

W.H. Craib

Craib, the centre of many a controversy in his lifetime, came to the chair of medicine with a strong reputation for research. Born in Somerset East in 1895, he had originally planned to become an engineer, taking his first degree in physics and mathematics through the South African College, Cape Town. After serving in South West Africa and France in the Great War, he proceeded to read medicine at Caius College, Cambridge, and Guy's Hospital, London. In 1925 he was awarded a Rockefeller Fellowship for research at Johns Hopkins University, Baltimore, where he embarked on his revolutionary investigations into the electrical currents generated by the heart. Contemporary electrocardiographic theory held that when the heart became excited it gave rise to a purely negative potential; Craib's experiments demonstrated the existence of both a positive and a negative component. His doublet-dipole theory of cardiac action currents, as opposed to the entrenched negativity theory, was first announced by him at conferences in Atlantic City and Stockholm in 1926, and immediately encountered fierce resistance from the medical establishment. Craib continued his work in London in Sir Thomas Lewis's laboratory, setting out his conclusions in papers published in *Heart* (1927) and the *Journal of Physiology* (1928), and in a special report of the British Medical Research Council (1930). Continued fierce opposition to his findings from most leading cardiologists, and a deteriorating relationship with Lewis, led Craib to abandon his research and return to South Africa. In the 1930s the work of the eminent electrocardiologist, F.N. Wilson, and others in the field confirmed Craib's conclusions. Craib himself did no more research after taking the chair at Wits.[19]

The appointment of Craib as Professor of Medicine, as is explained in chapter 9, proved highly controversial, leading to the resignation of four members of the Department of Medicine who believed that any one of them was more deserving of the chair.[20] Always clear in his ideas and firm in his demands, Craib remained a controversial figure at the University until his departure in 1946. Twenty years later the University bestowed on him the honorary degree of Doctor of Medicine.

Craib was a man of very considerable ability. Despite the limited extent of his clinical experience prior to his appointment at Wits, he proved a superb clinician, and an equally superb teacher, clear, challenging, and yet sympathetic. His students idolized him, and he greatly respected them. 'I can conceive of no group of medicals anywhere', he afterwards wrote, 'with a finer sense of priorities in a university environment, or a stronger sense of responsibility in the care of the sick in the hospital wards.' What troubled Craib at the time was his sense that the students were receiving an inadequate clinical training, owing to the absence of full-time staff, and particularly full-time professors in command of the clinical departments. Medical students at Wits arguably received an outstanding pre-clinical training, but he believed that in the clinical years it was impossible for the small, overworked, part-time staff to provide them with a comprehensive training.[21]

Soon after taking up their chairs, both Craib and Brebner had discovered that the existing staffing system rendered it virtually impossible both to provide proper instruction in their departments and to maintain their own private practices. Given the circumstances of economic depression, they also appreciated it would be financially impossible for the University to institute a whole series of full-time clinical appointments, including full-time professors. The compromise they suggested in 1933 was that they be provided with full-time clinical and laboratory assistants. Under the threat of Brebner's resignation this was agreed to.[22] J.H. Gear, the third of the medical

Gear brothers who graduated from Wits in medicine, was appointed as the full-time clinical assistant in medicine, and A. Lewer Allen, the first of the surgeon brothers, as the full-time assistant in surgery. These appointments led to an immediate improvement in the efficiency of the two departments, but the continued increase in student numbers served to intensify the strain on the part-time professors. In recognition that they could not maintain a remunerative private practice and also satisfactorily perform their medical school work, the University in 1938 agreed to increase their salaries from £750 to £1 100 per annum, the amount received by a full-time professor at Milner Park, but it was not until 1946 that the University decided to institute full-time clinical chairs. It did so under intense pressure from Craib, who during the war years bombarded Senate and Council with statements on the maltreatment of the medical school by the University authorities, indicating how moneys derived from the medical school were diverted to finance less successful faculties. The part-time professors were, however, required to re-apply for their chairs on a full-time basis, an indignity none of them was prepared to accept. As Brebner and Black were at or near retiring age, they were little affected, but Craib, at 51, found his academic career prematurely ended.[23]

Except in obstetrics, where each student was required to attend twenty deliveries before qualifying, there does not appear to have been any shortage of clinical material during the thirties. Owing to the shortage of obstetric material, the 1937 class did not complete its work until March 1938, and the 1938 class until June 1939. In addition to using every available case at the Queen Victoria Maternity Hospital, the University also used all cases available at the Bridgeman Memorial Hospital, Johannesburg, the Krugersdorp Hospital, the Moedersbond Hospital and General Hospital, Pretoria, and three hospitals in Natal. In medicine and surgery the students were distributed among four 'firms' for bed-side instruction at the Johannesburg General Hospital. Between 1933 and 1938 the size of these 'firms' doubled, from 11 to 22 in medicine and from 9 to 18 in surgery, but from 1936 onwards each 'firm' was subdivided, 'one half working in the European part of the Hospital and the other in the Native part'.[24]

In 1939, on the initiative of Professors Black, Brebner, and Craib, the University established a dispensary in Alexandra Township in conjunction with the Alexandra Health Centre for the purposes of assisting the centre and providing final-year medical students with the opportunity for dispensary and district practice. The 1920s and 1930s had witnessed a very considerable growth of the permanent black population of Johannesburg, and medical and health facilities for that population were minimal. The Non-European

Hospital in town was chronically over-crowded, and there were no hospitals in the townships themselves, nor any other access to expert medical services. In March 1939 a medical service for the four municipal townships of Orlando, Pimville, Western Native Township, and Eastern Native Township, was finally instituted with the appointment of three doctors to attend the 84 000 people of these townships.

Since at least 1934, with the formation of the Society for the Study of Medical Conditions among the Bantu, convened by Sidney Kark, members of the Wits medical school had shown an interest in the problems of health and disease among the black population of Johannesburg, and in 1935 the *Leech,* the student medical journal, had recommended the establishment of clinics in the townships. In his memorandum of July 1939, after the clinical professors had been conducted round the municipal townships, Black strongly urged the establishment of clinics in all townships, beginning with Alexandra to the north of Johannesburg: 'I think I can say that we were all impressed with the vastness of the problem, with the crying need for the establishment of an adequate Medical Service in these areas and with the splendid opportunities for our students obtaining a most excellent experience which would be invaluable to them after graduation. At the same time students would be rendering valuable services to the Natives.'[25] In 1940 the University decided to put its Alexandra clinic on a permanent basis and make 'attendance on Dispensary practice' a compulsory requirement for the medical degree. The University Clinic in Alexandra has remained in operation ever since.

For laboratory work in the clinical departments, the University maintained several laboratories at the General Hospital and its branches. In 1938 these were organized into a separate Department of Clinical Pathology. George Buchanan, superintendent of the routine division of the South African Institute for Medical Research, was appointed as senior lecturer and Head of the Department of Clinical Pathology. It was a small department, and made little impact.

The minor courses in the clinical years, forensic medicine, psychiatry, and public health, were all offered by honorary and part-time staff. The Professor of Forensic Medicine from 1934, until his retirement in 1957, was R.H. Mackintosh; in 1935 W. Russell replaced J.T. Dunston as Professor of Psychiatry and Mental Hygiene, remaining in the chair until 1945; and in 1939 the versatile E.H. Cluver succeeded Sir Edward Thornton as Head of the Department of Public Health.

In all, the picture that emerges of the medical school in the thirties is one of cramped and inadequate facilities, and an overburdened staff engaged overwhelmingly in the training of undergraduates. Outside the Department of

Anatomy, little was undertaken by way of research. Higher degrees were offered in medicine and surgery, and by 1939 nine candidates had been awarded the M.D. degree. Several were for theses relating to health problems among miners, and diseases among Africans. The school also offered higher diplomas in public health, tropical medicine and hygiene, and psychological medicine, and by 1939 had awarded some 80 diplomas. The training of specialist surgeons and physicians had not yet been embarked upon. 'The University is strongly in favour of the development of properly organised postgraduate specialist training', the medical school advised in its submission to the Botha Committee into medical training in South Africa in 1938, 'but to date has been so embarrassed with the problems of undergraduate training as to be unable to proceed.'[26]

For students, the training offered by the medical school was haphazard, if judged by later standards. In the description of Professor W.H. Craib, the medical school was a loosely-knit, somewhat disorganized teaching institution, in which co-ordination was minimal. 'What was locally described or thought of as "the Medical School"', he has written, 'was in fact an extremely complicated arrangement born of expediency and dependent largely upon the almost charitable good will of several entirely autonomous organisations already in existence and not originally established with the requirements of a medical school specifically in mind.' These institutions included the Johannesburg General Hospital and its branches, and the South African Institute for Medical Research. The teaching staff drawn from them were provided with little central guidance as to the ideal training of general practitioners; each gave his personal and independent best in providing what each of them felt any reasonable general practitioner should be required to know.[27] Inevitably, the standards required of students were not especially high.

The students at the medical school were drawn from all the major groups in white South African society; English and Afrikaans-speaking, and Jewish. According to the report of the Botha Committee in 1939, 42 per cent of the medical students at Wits were Jewish, 36 per cent English, 20 per cent Afrikaans, and 2 per cent 'other', including a handful of blacks.[28] By 1939 approximately 18 per cent of the medical students were women; 130 out of a total of 740.[29] The large majority of the students who qualified set up practice in the urban areas, mainly in Johannesburg and along the Witwatersrand. Some of the Afrikaans graduates returned to the country areas.

For all its problems and shortcomings, the Wits medical school prior to World War II produced a significant number of graduates who were to bring distinction both to themselves and the University that had trained them. These

Pharmacology department, 1930

Front row: I. Norwitz, Miss L. Chapman, C. Adler, Miss E.L. Morris, Prof. J.M. Watt, Dr F.V. Stephen, G.J. Moss, Miss B. von Maltitz, E.L. Fisher
Second row: J.D. Raftery, J. Pillemer, A.H. Folb, J. Rudolph, J. Berjak, I. Kessler, J. Gillman, H. Gordon, G.W. Brammer, H. Pillemer, S. Michelson, W. Goldin
Third row: D. Harwood-Nash, F.J. Snell, E.G. Lewis, L. Saitowitz, J. Helman, W. Josselsohn, B.L. Bernstein, H. Bodenstab, J.A. van Rooyen, P.W. Esterhuysen, J.T. du Randt, D.J. de Kock
Back row: J.H. Gear, A. Kessel, A. Pekarsky, J. Cohen, A. Brink, E.L. Nolan

included Lawrie Adler, who became Chief Medical Officer of the Mines Benefit Society; I. Frack, later superintendent of Baragwanath Hospital; P. Menof, principal physician at the Johannesburg General Hospital; the Gear brothers, Harry, who served as Assistant Director-General of the World Health Organization, James, who became director of the Poliomyelitis Research Foundation and later of the South African Institute for Medical Research, and 'Jock' (John), who taught in the University's Department of Medicine for nearly 40 years and was appointed associate professor; Cyril Adler, founder and director of the Museum of the History of Medicine in Johannesburg; Maurice Shapiro, who became director of the South African Blood Transfusion Service; C.A.M. Murray, who became South Africa's Secretary for Health; and J. Wolfowitz, the first Wits graduate appointed senior surgeon at the Johannesburg General Hospital. Those who were later to occupy chairs at Wits included J. Penn, Professor of Plastic Maxillo-Facial and Oral Surgery at the dental school; J. Gillman, Professor of Physiology; B.J.P. Becker, Professor of Morbid Anatomy and Histopathology; H.B. Stein, Professor of Chemical Pathology; and M.B. Feldman, Professor of Psychiatry. Those who were later to hold chairs at other universities included L.H. Wells, Professor of Anatomy at U.C.T.; S.L. Kark, Professor of Social and Preventive Medicine at the Hebrew University, Jerusalem; J. Wolpe, Professor of Behaviour Therapy at Temple University, Philadelphia; P.J. Kloppers, Professor of Medicine at Pretoria University; H.W. Snyman, Professor of Medicine at Pretoria University and sometime president of the South African Medical and Dental Council; G.W.H. Schepers, Professor of Anatomy at Pretoria University; P.M.S. Fischer, Professor of Paediatrics at the University of the Orange Free State; and S. Joel Cohen, Professor of Obstetrics and Gynaecology at Tel Aviv University.

In the thirties dentistry, which had gained the status of an independent faculty in 1929, remained relatively small, and the part-time staff remarkably stable. Until 1939, when Julius Staz was appointed senior demonstrator in dental surgery, the clinical staff under Middleton Shaw was entirely part-time. Born in Johannesburg, Staz had qualified as a dentist in England, and served

Dental school, Bok Street

the dental school in a part-time capacity for much of the thirties. Encouraged by Shaw, he also undertook research into 'the dental conditions of African Negroids', and in 1937 the University awarded him the D.D.S. for his thesis 'Minute Structure of the Teeth of South African Bantu'. In 1948 Staz was to be appointed to the second full-time chair in dentistry, and in 1958 he succeeded Shaw as director of the Oral and Dental Hospital.

Despite the stability of the part-time staff, in dentistry, as in medicine, the co-ordination of clinical teaching was not easy to achieve. The main emphasis in the dental school was on practical and clinical skills.[30] Classes were small, and graduates few. By the end of 1939 the Wits dental school, which remained the only institution providing a dental education in South Africa, had produced a total of 51 B.D.S. graduates.

IV

Whereas engineering, medicine, and dentistry all increased their student enrolment in the thirties, numbers in the law school fell off towards the end of the decade. The explanation for the decline in undergraduate students was the unpopularity of the University's classes for Law Certificate candidates. These came to be considered far too 'academic' for students primarily interested in a 'cramming' course.[31] It also seems that the provisions of the Attorneys, Notaries, and Conveyancers Admission Act of 1934 served to discourage aspirant attorneys from sitting the LL.B. Under the terms of the Act, articled clerks were to undertake five years' training, instead of three as in the past, for admission as an attorney, and LL.B. graduates were required to serve two years' articles instead of gaining automatic admission. It had traditionally been the case that the majority of attorneys in the Transvaal had qualified via articles and the Law Certificate examination, considered perhaps the easiest professional examination in the country, rather than by taking the LL.B., but the sense in the University was that the new legislation 'unduly penalized candidate attorneys seeking to obtain the degree of LL.B.'.[32] But even more effective in discouraging students from embarking on the LL.B. was the University's own requirement, introduced in 1936, that they devote at least three years to the LL.B. Previously students who had taken either a 'legal' B.A. or B.Com. had been permitted to complete their LL.B. in two years.

In 1935 enrolment in the law school was 51, near the peak for the decade; 19 full-time, and 32 part-time, 17 of the latter graduate and 15 undergraduate. By 1939, when enrolment was down to 31, only one student was classified as undergraduate.³³ The University had effectively ceased to cater for the Law Certificate.

Apart from a decline in numbers, the main problem experienced by the law school in the late thirties related to the appointment in 1936 of Dr Elemer Balogh to the second full-time chair of law. He proved eminently unsuitable, and both he and the law school suffered as a consequence.

In 1934 the law school was granted a second full-time chair. The main responsibility of the new professor was to be the teaching of Roman Law. In 1935 L.C. Hoffmann, a Hollander and an able man, was appointed to the chair, but he left after serving only one year. He died during World War II in a Nazi extermination camp. In 1936 the University appointed Balogh, another overseas applicant, and it did so without first requiring that he be interviewed by the University's London committee. The man's record seemed impeccable and his testimonials brilliant. A Hungarian by birth, Balogh had received his LL.D. from the University of Budapest in 1903, and a decade later had been made Professor of International Private Law and Comparative Law at Budapest. From 1922 to 1928 he was Professor of Roman and Comparative Law at the University of Kovno in Lithuania, and from there he had moved to the University of Berlin, where he lectured on comparative law. In 1933 he had fled Germany and the Hitler regime for Paris, where he worked at the Institute of Comparative Law with the help of a Rockefeller grant. The author of over thirty publications, in six languages, he was given glowing testimonials by none other than Professor W.W. Buckland, Regius Professor of Civil Law, Cambridge, and Professor Jean Escarra, Professor of Law at Paris.³⁴ No other candidate for the chair possessed credentials that could in any way rival Balogh's. He was therefore appointed without an interview.

Even before Balogh arrived in Johannesburg it was made evident to the University authorities that they had blundered. When he passed through London he was interviewed by William Cullen, the secretary of the University's London committee, and Cullen was simply appalled by what he saw and heard. In a letter to Raikes, Cullen conceded that Balogh was no doubt very erudite and thoroughly competent, but his 'eccentric pronunciation and enunciation' rendered him absolutely impossible to understand. 'Frankly', Cullen advised, 'I cannot visualise him either as a lecturer or as a teacher.' The London committee, he added for good measure, would never have recommended him, 'but the matter is entirely out of our hands'.³⁵

The apprehensions aroused by Cullen were rapidly confirmed after Balogh's arrival at the University. He was unkempt, suffered from both a stammer and a stutter, and was sometimes ignorant in the areas in which he taught. McKerron took an instant dislike to him, and the students were soon in revolt.

Two main theories were postulated to explain the phenomenon of the new professor of law. The one was that he was an imposter, masquerading for the real Balogh or pretending to be someone who had in fact never existed. The other was that he was indeed genuine, and had once been competent, but had since lapsed into premature senility.

At the end of Balogh's statutory two-years' probation, Council decided to extend his probation for another year, but in the latter half of 1938 it had finally to face up to the question of whether he was to be confirmed in his appointment or not. The recommendation of McKerron, as Head of the Department of Law, was most definitely that his appointment not be confirmed. In a letter to Raikes on 1 July 1938, McKerron detailed various complaints about Balogh's lectures, the elementary nature of his examinations, and his lack of research while at Wits.[36] McKerron's recommendation placed Council in a novel situation, with no precedents to guide it. On the one previous occasion it had been due to receive an unfavourable report on a probationary member of staff, the Principal had persuaded the person in question to resign, and only his resignation had come before Council. At its meeting on 5 August Council decided to appoint a special committee to consider the position of Professor Balogh. Principal Raikes, Aiken, S. Suzman, the four Senate representatives on Council, Professors Le May, Maingard, Sutton, and Stammers, and Advocate Tilson Barry, K.C., representing the legal profession, comprised the committee.

E. Balogh

Altogether the committee held six meetings. McKerron addressed it on three occasions to substantiate his case for Balogh's non-confirmation, and he also submitted 'certain lecture-notes', a letter from Professor Colin Murray, and a statement by Mr Ian Murray, a part-time lecturer in the department and son of Professor Murray, as evidence against Balogh. Although Balogh was given the right to be heard in reply, he was in such a condition he could not state his case. On his nomination Professor J.Y.T. Greig was brought in to represent him before the committee. Much of Greig's thrust was that McKerron's claims against Balogh were mere 'hearsay', but at the same time he resisted the cross-examination of students on the ground that 'such procedure would be extremely distasteful to most members of a university staff'.[37] McKerron, apparently, handled his case badly. In the end, after prolonged hearings and deliberations, the committee found it impossible to come to a unanimous decision, and the full range of its opinions was reported to Council. Evidently, there was a strong feeling that Balogh could not be confirmed in his existing position, but that it would none the less be unacceptable for the University simply to terminate his services. The man was already 55 years of age, with no real prospects of alternative employment; he had given of his best, working up some material from scratch, including an entire course on the history of South African law; he had done nothing positively wrong nor was in any way derelict in his duties; and it was the University that had erred in the first instance in appointing him without properly investigating his abilities and potential to teach in a South African university. To abandon him now would be to invite criticism of the University, both at home and abroad. The only positive recommendation of the committee was that the Principal should 'explore the possibilities of new conditions of appointment'. In his report to Council, Raikes advised that the renewal of Balogh's appointment in a subordinate position to McKerron would lead to a breakdown of the department, but that not to renew his appointment would produce a certain amount of criticism of the University, and might also affect 'the confidence of the Professoriate in the Council'. He therefore recommended a compromise, either by dividing the Department of Law into three divisions, under Professors McKerron, Murray, and Balogh respectively, with a colleague to advise Balogh, or the conversion of Balogh's post into 'an independent research appointment'.[38]

In his report, Raikes added that he had taken legal advice, and that there was no necessity for Council to secure the consent of the Minister of Education before refusing to renew Balogh's appointment. As early as 30 June, indeed, Raikes had written to the Secretary for Education, advising that Balogh was unlikely to be reappointed, and asking whether the minister agreed that his consent was not required as Balogh's position was probationary. The minister properly declined to act in 'the capacity of legal adviser' to the University. 'If he were to express an opinion now', the Secretary for Education informed Raikes, 'he would compromise himself beforehand and would find it rather embarrassing if the professor concerned should disagree with your interpretation of the regulations and appeal to the Minister.' The secretary therefore recommended that Raikes obtain legal advice, which he did. The opinion given by Advocate R. Stratford was that no application to the minister for his consent was necessary, not because Balogh's appointment was probationary, but on the ground that the contract had come to an end: 'The University in declining to renew the engagement of Professor Balogh after February 1939 will neither be dismissing him nor terminating his contract by due notice.'[39]

When Council convened for a special meeting on 6 September to consider the reports on Balogh, another major point of procedure was raised; the right of Senate to be consulted. Professor Maingard moved 'That in accordance with section 11, subsection (2), of the Act, the matter be referred to the Senate for investigation and report'. As the majority on Council was disinclined to refer the matter to Senate, the Principal was consequently instructed to obtain legal opinion on the question of whether there was a statutory obligation on Council to consult Senate. The opinion given in this instance by Stratford was that if Council decided not to renew an appointment it need not consult Senate, but before renewing an appointment it was required to consult Senate. Renewal of appointment constituted a fresh contract, and would consequently be an 'appointment' in respect of which Senate was entitled to be consulted.[40]

At its next meeting on 23 September, Council finally reached the decision not to renew Balogh's appointment in his present capacity, and appointed a committee to 'explore the possibility of finding some other employment for Professor Balogh'. The committee's recommendation was that the second chair of law be placed in temporary abeyance, that Professor Balogh be given a special research appointment for two years, and that the contribution from University funds to his salary should be £400 per annum, with anticipated contributions from private sources raising the total to £600.[41] As a new appointment was envisaged, these proposals were referred to Senate, which approved them while adding two suggestions. Balogh's appointment was to be for five years, taking him up to retiring age, and his salary was to be that of an ordinary professor. Council, at its meeting of 25 November, resolved to inform Senate that, in view of the financial considerations, it was unable to accept Senate's suggestions.

In 1939 Balogh was duly appointed to a special research chair of comparative law, and the Minister of Education was simply informed that he had not been reappointed to the full-time chair. By the time Balogh's two-year appointment expired, war had broken out in Europe, and Council decided that 'in view of the difficult circumstances arising from the war' it should continue to reappoint him on a year by year basis. This it did until the end of 1946, when Balogh had reached the age of 65 and the University had found itself compelled to take the second full-time chair of law out of abeyance. Balogh returned to Europe, and died in Paris on 5 September 1955.

In the history of the University, the real significance of the Balogh case was in raising the question of procedure in instances of non-confirmation. It was, in that sense, the counterpart of the Stibbe affair, which had raised issues of procedure over dismissal. Balogh was infinitely better treated by Council than Stibbe. He was informed of the case for his non-confirmation, he was allowed a hearing before Council's *ad hoc* committee, and a special post was created for him. Senate, however, had been excluded from any direct participation in the non-confirmation process, and that perturbed it. At its meeting of 14 November it voted to request Council to appoint a joint committee to consider the procedure to be adopted in cases of non-confirmation, but Council refused the request. Senate was advised: 'The Council is satisfied that the responsibility of refusing to confirm an appointment has been advisedly imposed on the Council alone, and considers that the attitude of Senate will be adequately represented by the Principal and four members elected by Senate to the Council.'[42] Ever since the Balogh case, Council has excluded Senate, as a body, from non-confirmation proceedings, although it has come to rely almost entirely on the advice of confirmation committees composed overwhelmingly of academics.

The fiasco in the thirties over the second full-time chair of law meant that the law school was obliged to continue to rely heavily on part-time assistance. All classes were given either in the early morning or late afternoon, for the convenience both of part-time lecturers and students. Many of the part-time lecturers were distinguished men in the profession, most notably Walter Pollak, one of the greatest advocates South Africa has produced, and a scholar and writer of distinction. By the end of the thirties part-time LL.B. students considerably outnumbered the full-time students, largely as a consequence of the requirement of the 1934 Attorneys Admission Act that LL.B. graduates serve two years of articles before admission as attorneys. Most preferred to serve articles and simultaneously study part-time for their LL.B.

In all, by the end of 1939, the Wits law school had produced 143 LL.B. graduates, the majority of them becoming attorneys rather than entering the Bar. Indeed, prior to World War II, the practice remained common for aspirant advocates to read law at Oxford or Cambridge rather than locally. Some distinguished silks none the less emanated from the Wits law school, including Arthur Suzman, South Africa's present senior silk. Several became Supreme Court judges, among them H.J. Vieyra, S.M. Kuper, C.S. Margo, G. Gordon, P.M. Cillie (Judge President of the Transvaal and then a judge of appeal), and H.C. Nicholas. The number of Supreme Court judges produced by the Wits law school was disappointingly small, and some attributed this to a concern in government circles to limit the number of Jewish judges. I.A. Maisels, Q.C., one of South Africa's most eminent silks, was in 1961 appointed Judge of the High Court of Southern Rhodesia. Other pre-war graduates of the Wits law school who were to gain prominence included B.L. Bernstein, chairman of Anglo-Transvaal who was elected Chancellor of the University in 1975; H.R. Hahlo, who was appointed Professor of Law at Wits in 1946; P.C. Pelser, a later Minister of Justice; and S.J. Marais Steyn, a later Minister of Indian Affairs and Community Development.

V

In the Faculty of Commerce in the thirties, leadership was provided chiefly by C.S. Richards, who was appointed Professor of Commerce in 1931. He was made Dean of the Faculty of Commerce in 1935, a position he retained until his retirement from the University in 1964.

The chair given Richards in 1931 was a new creation, replacing the chair of accounting held by Findlay. The change reflected the new provisions for the B.Com. degree, and with them the extension of the teaching responsibilities of the old Department of Accounting well beyond accounting and auditing. Under the regulations for the B.Com. adopted in 1929, the course for the degree, which was part-time, was extended from three years to four, and provision was made for specialization in the final year in one of five groups: accountancy, banking and finance, inland transport, trade, and industry. The B.Com., in other words, was to cease to be almost entirely a degree for accountants. The special subjects were all offered in what became the Department of Commerce.

Several accountants applied for the new chair, but in appointing Richards the University decided in favour of an economist. Born in Jarrow in the north of England, and of working-class origins, Richards had received his B.Com. from the University of Durham in 1922, had been admitted to the M.Com. in 1925, and in 1928 had studied at the London School of Economics. According to his curriculum vitae, he required 'one term's further residential qualification only' for a London Ph.D., but the degree never materialized. Since 1923 he had served on the staff of the Natal Technical College, and since 1925 he had also lectured in economics at Natal University College. Among the other applicants for the chair were D. Liddell, later Professor of Commerce at Rhodes University, and H.A. Shannon, who in 1935 took up an appointment as senior lecturer in the Department of Economics at Wits. From the evidence of the selection committee papers, there is no truth in the story, sometimes used to deride the University for its choice of Richards, that John Hicks was passed over for the chair. Hicks, later Professor of Political Economy at Oxford and one of the leading economic theorists of this century, had come out to Wits in 1928 to assist the Department of Economics following the sudden death of Lehfeldt, but he was not a formal applicant for the University's chair of commerce.

C.S. Richards

From all accounts, Richards proved an exceptionally difficult man, apparently suffering from a considerable inferiority complex. His critics, and they became legion, thought him to be extremely selfish and egotistical. Although he occupied positions in the University, such as Dean of the Faculty of Commerce and for a while as Senate representative on Council, that required him to adopt a broad view, the sense was that he never managed to look beyond his own interests, or at best those of his own department. He quarrelled endlessly with colleagues in the University, and became a particular thorn in the side of S.H. Frankel, the Professor of Economics, whom he seems to have perceived as a rival. According to the University's folklore, relations between the two men deteriorated to such an extent that they communicated only by way of notes.

An enterprising, hard-working man, Richards was generally very able as a teacher. His lectures were well prepared and regularly revised; and in his first years he virtually carried the department. As an economist he was never particularly highly regarded, and on two notable occasions his judgement was brought seriously into question. The first was in 1932, when he joined six other economists in issuing a press statement advising that South Africa should remain on the gold standard. In his obituary of Richards, W.J. Busschau recalled: 'The experience of being one of the Seven Foolish Virgins, as the economists of the statement were called by the Press, had a chastening effect on C.S., and he never thereafter gave a hasty opinion to the Press.'[43] The second was the publication in 1940 of his book *The Iron and Steel Industry in South Africa,* based on the thesis that earned him the University's first D.Sc. (Econ.). Richards was a committed advocate of free enterprise, and his study was highly critical of ISCOR, which he attacked as 'virtually a Government monopoly' that exploited the artificial protection given it to foist unnecessarily expensive steel on the country.[44] 'Unfortunately for his book', as Busschau delicately phrased it in his obituary, 'the outbreak of World War II had made a considerable change in the position of ISCOR.' The Witwatersrand business community apparently took little notice of Richards, and resented the fee charged whenever it did approach him. 'As a Northcountryman', Busschau commented, 'he had a healthy respect for money, and sometimes surprised those who consulted him by the height of the fees he charged.' His main academic contribution at national level was as chairman of the board of management of the *South African Journal of Economics,* launched in 1933, and after 1946 as an editor of the journal. He did an immense amount of work for the journal, and was responsible for its survival during the difficult years of World War II.

In the thirties, Raikes evidently found Richards rather a trial. From the documentary record, it is clear that Richards fought hard for his department, and his incessant demands irritated a Raikes already harrassed by the parlous state of the University's finances. In November 1935 a squabble over who would pay for the typing of a paper got out of all proportion, and provoked Richards to complain that 'every time anything connected with the Department of Commerce arises, it seems to me to be viewed in what I can only characterise as an ultra critical spirit, while the Medical Faculty as an instance seems to spend freely'. The Faculty of Commerce, and his department, he alleged, were treated as 'the cinderella of the University', and his own work was not appreciated. Raikes replied: 'I would only say that while I do not agree with all you say I am entirely willing to agree that you have worked hard for your department. Sometimes I feel that the University does not bulk very large in your mind, but perhaps I am mistaken.'[45]

Richards's main achievement in the faculty in the thirties was to secure the introduction of a full-time B.Com. Previously, students had been able to take the first year full-time, but the three years thereafter had all been part-time. In 1931, at Richards's instigation, the Faculty of Commerce agreed to a full-time three-year course for the B.Com., and in the next year H. Greenwood, later Professor of Accounting at U.C.T., was appointed full-time lecturer in accounting. As the number of full-time B.Com. students rose steadily from 22 in 1931 to 85 by 1935, Richards strongly believed he was entitled to more full-time staff, stressing that full-time students, who paid higher fees, were themselves entitled to have their classes during the day.[46] In 1936 John Reedman, another economist, was added to the Department of Commerce as a full-time junior lecturer. Thereafter a decline in the number of full-time students, down to 51 by 1939, ensured that Richards got no more full-time members of staff, though Reedman, a fine scholar and teacher, was promoted to lecturer.

The other major development in the commerce faculty in the thirties, one in which Richards played an important role, was the negotiation of an agreement in 1931 with the Transvaal Society of Accountants whereby the University undertook to provide 'such teaching as may be considered necessary for students preparing for the professional examinations in Accounting' in return for an annual grant from the Society. In 1932 a total of 88 'professional' students enrolled for the instruction, 63 preparing for the professional examinations conducted by the General Examining Board and 25 for those of the English Society of Incorporated Accountants and Auditors. At the end of the year 41 University candidates sat for the examinations of General Examining Board, and 36 passed. All 8 candidates for the Incorporated examinations passed. Despite these 'gratifying' results, the enrolment for the professional courses in 1933 was slightly down, and thereafter the Transvaal Society had to be constantly urged 'to make every effort to induce the enrolment for attendance at the University of all articled and other clerks eligible for admission to the Society's examinations.'[47] From 1934 onwards all 'professionals' were prepared for the examinations of the General Examining Board, as these were now recognized by the Incorporated Society.

The Transvaal Society's main complaint against the University in the thirties seems to have been that undue pressure was placed on the professional students to enrol also for the B.Com. degree. Richards denied such pressure, but insisted: 'He did not think that the University could reasonably be expected to dissuade students from becoming candidates for the degree, particularly since the degree curriculum was revised in 1930 in consultation with the representatives of the Transvaal Society of Accountants, so as to meet the needs of the Accounting Profession.'[48] As the decade progressed, the proportion of professional students who enrolled for the B.Com. increased.

Between 1936 and 1939 the over-all number of students in the Faculty of

Commerce, however, declined steadily. The decline was evident in virtually all categories, but was most marked among the professional students:[49]

	1936	1937	1938	1939
B.Com. Full-time	67	62	51	54
B.Com. Part-time	88	78	64	73
B.Com. and Professional	13	15	27	22
Total B.Com.	168	155	142	149
Professional	95	71	50	46
M.Com.		8		12
Occasional	23	9	22	12
	286	243	214	219

In commerce, as in law, real growth in student numbers came only after the end of World War II.

VI

Although numbers in the Faculty of Arts dropped in the thirties, and the Faculties of Engineering and Medicine both surpassed it in total student enrolment, Arts continued to teach more students, and produce more graduates, than any other faculty. As the B.A. was a three-year degree, Arts had a more rapid turnover of students than either engineering, with a four-year first degree, or medicine, with a six-year first degree. Between 1928 and 1939 the Faculty of Arts produced 831 B.A., 139 B.A.Honours, 45 M.A., 5 Ph.D., and 4 D.Litt. graduates.

One of the reasons for the drop in student numbers in the Faculty of Arts after 1932, when enrolment had reached its pre-war peak of 664, was a change in the system for training teachers. In 1933 the old T^2 and T^3 certificates were replaced by the Transvaal Teachers' Diploma, which required only one year's study at a university and two at a training college. It was soon recognized that the new system was inferior to the old, in that it significantly reduced the academic content in the three-year programme for trainee teachers. In 1935 the Transvaal Education Department summoned a Regional Committee on Teacher Training, and it recommended a return to the old system whereby trainee teachers divided their time in their second year between academic and professional courses. The committee also recommended that 'every facility' be given to aspiring teachers to obtain in four years a degree as well as a diploma.[50] The committee's recommendations were duly implemented in the next year, and thereafter enrolment in the Faculty of Arts began to recover from its low point of 445 in 1935.

In the thirties, the University in general, and the Faculty of Arts in particular, gave serious thought to the whole question of the relationship between the University and the secondary school system in the Transvaal. There was a sense that English-medium secondary education in the Transvaal was entering a period of crisis. As Raikes explained it, the teachers the Milner regime had imported from Britain at the end of the Anglo-Boer War were moving into retirement and there were insufficient 'young English-speaking men' coming forward to replace them. 'Unless active steps are taken', Raikes told the annual S.R.C. dinner in November 1935, 'we shall soon find ourselves with no English-speaking teachers at the top and a mere dribble coming in at the bottom.' There was also a strong awareness that the high schools were not providing an adequate training ground for students who proceeded to university. The matriculation examination and its equivalents served both as a school-leaving and a university entrance qualification, and the belief in the University was that 'the interests of the Universities and their students have been sacrificed to enable Matriculation to function as a dual-purpose qualification'.[51] The schools, in short, paid insufficient attention to their university responsibilities.

Two proposals for improving teaching in the schools, and for bridging the gap between school and university, were considered in the thirties. One was for universities to take responsibility for teacher training by absorbing the normal or training colleges. Recommended in 1930 by an *ad hoc* committee convened by the Administrator of the Transvaal, and in 1934 by the Roos Commission on Provincial Finance, this suggestion enjoyed considerable support at Wits.[52] In 1937 Council authorized that plans be prepared for the transfer of the Johannesburg Training College for Teachers to Milner Park in the expectation that by 1940 the University would become entirely responsible for teacher training. Differences between the University and the Province over particular sites, and the style of the proposed new buildings, followed by the outbreak of World War II, ensured that the transfer did not take place.[53] The University's Department of Education, re-established in 1938, after a lapse of two years, under Professor Thomas Williams, the new Principal of the Training College, consequently continued to have nothing to do with teacher training, offering only supervision for the M.Ed.

The other major proposal contemplated was for Wits to institute a four-year B.A. and B.Sc., with the first year serving as a bridging or preparatory year for training in method. The proposal was first put forward to a special joint meeting of the Boards of the Faculties of Arts and Science in 1936 by J.Y.T. Greig, the Professor of English. In his supporting memorandum, Greig contended that South African universities should frankly recognize that 90 per cent of their first-year students were in their scholastic attainments a good deal below sixth-formers in English secondary and public schools, and that in arts and science they should consequently abandon the English three-year for the American four-year degree. 'Conditions in America', he argued, 'closely resemble conditions in South Africa; and American universities were forced long ago to lengthen their courses in arts and science from three to four years, making their "freshman year" roughly equivalent to what in Europe is done at school.' The proposal was referred to a committee, where it seems to have died.[54] In the next year, in response to investigations by the South African Council for Educational and Social Research on the problem of the relationship between secondary and university education, Senate established a small committee on secondary education. In its report, sanctioned by Senate, the committee recommended 'the extension of the curriculum in Arts and Science by the prefixing of an extra preliminary year at the University'. The committee pointed out that 'the cost of such a measure could not be met except by special Government subvention', but no approach was made to the state.[55]

Despite this awareness that the relationship between the universities and the secondary schools was badly in need of improvement, nothing positive was achieved in the thirties. The schools continued to be largely oblivious of their university responsibilities, and Wits failed to provide incoming students with special assistance to help bridge the gap from school. As departments in the Faculties of Arts and Science were also generally reluctant to fail students in large numbers, the inevitable consequence was that standards suffered.

On the whole, the quality of the academic staff in the Faculty of Arts improved in the thirties, primarily as a result of the employment of promising or well-qualified junior staff. In the twenties, junior staff at Wits had often been woefully weak. In the thirties, as the University became more established, producing some fine graduates of its own, and as depressed economic conditions restricted academic opportunities overseas, Wits was able to employ junior staff of a distinctly higher calibre. This was certainly true of the Faculty of Arts. The Department of English, as a notable instance, was virtually transformed as a result both of the appointment of J.Y.T. Greig as professor, and his recruitment of two excellent lecturers in Dr A.G. Hooper, a graduate of Leeds University, and Harold Jenkins, a graduate of London University. Hooper, who was responsible for phonetics and middle English, was later to become Professor of English at Stellenbosch, and Jenkins established the reputation for himself as a foremost Shakespearean scholar. A local product, Vincent Swart, whose qualities as a student and poet had been recognized by Greig, served as junior lecturer in the late thirties.[56]

The appointment of Greig in 1932 as successor to Drennan was the most important in the Faculty of Arts during Raikes's first decade as Principal. Greig, and the staff he attracted, succeeded not only in establishing a fine local reputation for the Department of English at Wits, but in gaining international recognition for it. Before Greig's retirement at the end of 1951, his department had produced a number of exceptional students, several of whom proceeded to establish distinguished reputations for themselves. Students of his in the thirties included Vincent Swart and Phyllis (Goldfain) Lewsen, the biographer of John X. Merriman.

J.Y.T. Greig

The eldest son of a Scottish medical missionary, Greig was born in Manchuria in 1891, and was educated at the Greenock Collegiate School, the Glasgow Academy, and Glasgow University, where he obtained an M.A. in 1913, and a D.Litt in 1924 for his thesis 'The Psychology of Laughter and Comedy'. After serving with the Northumbrian Fusiliers in World War I, Greig joined the staff of Armstrong College, Newcastle-upon-Tyne, as lecturer in English, psychology, and philosophy, and later became Registrar. In 1929–30 he was Carnegie Visiting Professor of English at Vanderbilt University, Nashville, Tennessee, where he formed a very favourable impression of American students.

At Wits, Greig showed himself to be a totally committed teacher. In the estimate of one of his former students, Professor Phyllis Lewsen, Greig shared his father's missionary impulse; he was a missionary for good teaching practices. A fine teacher himself, who saw it as his duty to bring out everything there was in a student, he not only inspired his students, but also his staff. He conveyed to them a strong feeling of dedication and a sense that teaching was every bit as important as scholarship. Within the University, he was a pioneer in teaching practices. Although he devoted considerable attention to his lectures, which were always original and thought-provoking, he believed that the writing of essays and tutorial discussion were more important for the student, and developed a tutorial system. His concern was that students should learn to think for themselves, and communicate effectively and clearly. Few departments in the thirties followed the lead he offered. Lectures, still very often virtually dictated, remained overwhelmingly the dominant ingredient in the system.

Ideally, universities expect their senior academic staff to contribute as teachers, scholars, and administrators. Greig fitted the ideal. He was not only one of the best teachers that the University has ever possessed, but was a fine scholar in his own right, and as a former university college registrar, an adept administrator. In the latter regard, he ran his department very effectively, took charge of the University's fund-raising campaign in 1935, was Dean of the Faculty of Arts for three spells, 1934–5, 1938–40, and 1947, and informally did much to assist Raikes.

Before coming to Wits, Greig had already established a reputation as a scholar with the publication in 1931 of his biography of David Hume, the eighteenth-century Scottish philosopher. This was awarded the James Tait Black memorial prize for the best biography of the year. In the next year was published in two volumes his edited *Letters of David Hume*. Greig's major scholarly undertaking while at Wits was a critical biography of W.M. Thackeray, the Victorian novelist, published in 1950 as *Thackeray: A Reconstruction*. Greig was unfortunate in that he was not given access to Thackeray's private papers, but the study was of such calibre that it continues to be referred to. Arising out of his concern for English usage, Greig also produced while at Wits two textbooks on the English language, *Language at Work* (1943), and *Structure and Meaning* (1950). Under the pseudonym of John Carruthers he wrote a number of bad novels.

Greig was also prominent outside the University. He was greatly esteemed in the teaching profession, with which he developed extensive contacts, serving on the Joint Matriculation Board, as joint examiner in English for the Transvaal Secondary School Certificate, and as chairman of the English Committee of the Transvaal Board of Moderators. To thousands of radio listeners, his was a familiar voice. Each week he was to be heard on the S.A.B.C. talking about books.

Greig left the University in 1951 in bitterness. When he reached the age of 60, Council would only renew his appointment thereafter on a year by year basis, as was normal practice, and not for another five-year term, as Greig demanded. Greig chose instead to take up the post of Professor of English at Otago University in New Zealand. Some of his colleagues at the University were not entirely sorry to see him go. A forthright, outspoken man, who said what he believed and generally scorned the ways of diplomacy, he was bound to make enemies, particularly as he was consistently critical of the dominant teaching practices in the University. Some students were also wary of him as he could be severely sarcastic.

In 1957 Greig returned to South Africa, and lectured for a short spell at Rhodes University. He died in 1963.

Another department that was well served by its junior staff, though not as well by its head, was history after the departure of Macmillan in 1933. Macmillan's successor, Leo Fouché, was in many ways a surprise choice. He had the advantage of experience for since 1909 he had been Professor of History at the Transvaal University College, later the University of Pretoria. He had also published, having edited the diary of Adam Tas, who led the free burgher protest at the Cape in 1705–6 against Governor Willem Adriaan van der Stel, and was responsible for the official account of the rebellion of 1914, published as the *Report of the Outbreak of the Rebellion and the Policy of the Government with Regard to its Suppression*. But Fouché was rather pedestrian, and the selection committee deliberated for a long time before recommending him. Senate only supported the recommendation after a ballot. Margaret Hodgson, then senior lecturer at Wits, was apparently placed second to Fouché, and other strong candidates in a large field included such promising younger historians as C.W. de Kiewiet, J.A.I. Agar-Hamilton, and J.S. Marais, who was to become Fouché's successor. It was suggested at the time that Fouché owed his appointment to the influence of Smuts, whom he had nominated as one of his referees. A close associate of Smuts's, Fouché was anxious to move from the University of Pretoria, as he had come to find the political atmosphere there intolerable. 'I don't want to say too much', he wrote to Margaret Hodgson on hearing that he had been given the chair at Wits, 'but perhaps you have heard how two notorious firebrands have been pitchforked into my Department, "to strengthen it", and to teach History according to a new principle, laid down

L. Fouché

officially: *History is not a neutral science!* No one with a shred of self-respect could have continued under such circumstances.'[57]

A disciple of the German school of historical studies, Fouché believed history was, or could be, a 'neutral science'. His main concern as a teacher was to convince students that history could be objective and to train them in the techniques whereby historians established facts from their documentary sources. He did not fully recognize the role of interpretation in the writing of history, and consequently failed to alert students to problems of interpretation. A perfectionist, who was not easily satisfied, he did not write much, and refused to recognize that what he did write reflected his own bias. His blue book on the rebellion of 1914 was presented as an 'objective' narrative, but it was widely criticized for its partiality to the government. His own prejudices strongly coloured his introduction to the diary of Adam Tas. In a notorious passage, he attributed the deficiencies and troubles of Willem Adriaan van der Stel to his mixed blood. 'As is frequently the case with persons of mixed blood', he wrote, 'the throw-back had occurred in the third generation.'[58]

For history at Wits, Fouché was a distinct let-down after Macmillan. Whereas Macmillan was a man of broad education and outlook, capable of stimulating the interest of students in the European Middle Ages as well as in the history of South Africa, Fouché was narrow in outlook and uninspiring in approach, and this was reflected in changes made in the syllabus. His interests did not extend beyond South Africa. While at Wits he undertook little new research. For the University of Pretoria he edited a volume *Mapungubwe: Ancient Bantu Civilization on the Limpopo*, containing reports on the archaeological excavations at Mapungubwe in the Northern Transvaal, and he contributed a chapter on the rule of the Dutch East India Company at the Cape to volume eight of the *Cambridge History of the British Empire*. He retired from Wits at the end of 1942, becoming chairman of the S.A.B.C. and assisting Smuts with intelligence work during the remaining years of World War II. He died in 1949, after a brief spell as ambassador to the Netherlands and Belgium.

When Macmillan had learnt that Fouché was his successor, he had indicated his disapproval to Hoernlé, a member of the selection committee. Hoernlé reassured him: 'On the whole, I think we did the best we could; and Miss H. will keep *your* flag flying in the Department.'[59] Miss Hodgson, however, was not allowed to keep it flying for very much longer. At the end of 1935, as a consequence of her marriage to William Ballinger, she was retired. Her successor was Arthur Keppel-Jones, a promising young graduate from Cape Town and Oxford, who was later to become Professor of History at

Natal University and then Queen's University in Canada. In 1939 Dr Joan Searle, who had undertaken her post-graduate work at the London School of Economics, was appointed junior lecturer, and together with Keppel-Jones gave the department a sense of inquiry and liveliness.

With the departure of both Macmillan and Margaret Ballinger, the Department of History lost its standing as the forcing-house of liberal scholarship and ideas in the University. There was no successor to it, though the Department of Economics, under one of Macmillan's former students, S. Herbert Frankel, and the new Department of Social Studies, under John Gray, did pick up some of the slack.

After serving for a few years as senior lecturer, Frankel was appointed to the chair of economics in 1931. At 27 years of age, he was very young for such a position, but he was exceptionally well qualified. After completing his B.A. and M.A. at Wits, he had proceeded to the London School of Economics, where in 1928 he was awarded a Ph.D. for his thesis 'The Railway Policy of South Africa'. A member of a well-known Jewish business family, he possessed and developed

S.H. Frankel

extensive connections outside of the University, including the mining industry, which often turned to him for advice on economic matters. His considerable status outside the University assisted his standing within it, but also provoked the jealousy of C.S. Richards. Frankel remained at Wits until 1946, when he moved to Oxford University to the chair in colonial economic affairs.

Frankel, from all accounts, made a good head of department. He was conscientious and efficient, and an ebullient personality who got on well with his staff. To his undergraduate students he offered well-prepared lectures, but he was probably better with his post-graduate students, whom he nurtured very carefully, helping to produce some very fine economists, most notably L.M. Samuels. As he built up the department he was able to expand his staff. For most of the thirties he was ably assisted by Hansi Pollak. Herself a Wits graduate, Pollak was an exceptionally good lecturer, and one of the major personalities in the University. She later became Professor of Sociology and Social Work at Natal University. From 1935 to 1937 H.A. Shannon was senior lecturer in the department. An able scholar, he wrote several important articles on the South African economy. His special responsibility was the series of new courses in the economics of local government and public administration, financed by a special grant from Reef municipalities.

As an economist, Frankel's primary interests in the twenties and thirties were the place of maize, railways, and gold in the South African economy, and the role of European capital investment in Africa. In the twenties, he published two books based on his M.A. and Ph.D. theses, *Co-operation and Competition in the Marketing of Maize in South Africa* (1926), and *The Railway Policy of South Africa* (1928), both of which reflected his freemarket philosophy. In the latter study, undertaken in the first instance at the request of the Gold Producers' Committee of the Transvaal Chamber of Mines, he provided a sustained critique of the political and non-economic considerations that had come to determine the financing and tariff policies of the South African Railways and Harbours Administration. 'The hope', he contended, 'that the South African State Railways would be managed on commercial principles, and not as a mere State Department on bureaucratic lines, has not been fulfilled.' According to his calculations, the differential rates imposed by the railways cost the Witwatersrand gold mining industry an additional £1 million each year. 'The present suicidal and uneconomic rate policy', he concluded, 'instead of doing everything possible to foster, actually restricts the development, shortens the life, and hinders the activities of this vitally important area.'[60] In 1938 Frankel published his next major book, *Capital Investment in Africa*, in which he examined the extent and nature of European capital investment in Africa, and its impact on the African social order. 'The greatest social and economic fact in the modern penetration of Africa', he asserted, 'is without doubt the universal dependence upon black labour.' European economic enterprise in Africa was based overwhelmingly on systems of 'forced labour', but as Frankel perceived it, a more balanced economic development in the future would require the free movement of all the factors of production, including labour.[61]

Frankel's main contribution to liberal thought in South Africa prior to World War II was in developing the argument that the country's reliance on exploited, unskilled labour was a major obstacle to its economic advancement. In a paper on 'The position of the Native as a factor in the economic welfare of the European population in South Africa' delivered in Port Elizabeth in 1928, he put the case for freeing black labour of the restrictions designed to keep it unskilled and cheap. In his contention:

> The choice that lies before the white people of South Africa is between having a prosperous economically assimilated native population (contributing largely to the economic advancement of the country in general) but separated from them socially and politically, if necessary, and, on the other hand, having a discontented, inefficient largely useless mass of natives, an obstacle in the way of advancement, a constant danger to white civilisation, and necessitating continually revised native legislation as economic conditions change.

His arguments were repeated in his contributions to *Coming of Age,* a series of studies in 'South African citizenship and politics' that he and other liberal intellectuals produced in 1930 to mark the twenty-first year of the Union of South Africa, and in the evidence he gave to the Native Economic Commission in 1932. In the twenties, liberals had often made the point that the state was uninformed in its policies; the Native Economic Commission marked a new departure, with the summoning of liberal intellectuals such as Macmillan and Frankel to give expert evidence.

Unlike Macmillan, Frankel was not active politically, though in 1938 he did join John Gray, the Ballingers, Keppel-Jones, Hansi Pollak, and Glyn Thomas in the formation of the Libertas Bond, which pressed Hofmeyr to lead a Liberal party. Since his student days Frankel had been a great admirer of Hofmeyr's, and during World War II he was to undertake an enormous amount of backroom work for Hofmeyr, assisting the Minister of Finance in the preparation of several budgets.[62] From its inception in 1933, until he left South Africa, Frankel was joint editor of the *South African Journal of Economics*.

John Gray, the first Professor of Sociology at Wits and Head of the Department of Social Studies, was a Scot, who brought with him to South Africa attitudes strongly opposed to racialism. He arrived in Johannesburg in November 1936, and soon established himself as one of the active liberals at the University. In 1938 he was the leading spirit behind the formation of the Libertas Bond. A colleague said of him after his tragic death by drowning in 1947: 'He held strong views on many social and political questions and did not hesitate to express them and, as far as possible, act on them; and he will always be remembered for his uncompromising opposition to all forms of racialism. But no one, I believe, ever felt that he forced his views on others. He was too conscious that they had a right to think differently from him. Gray was a liberal in the best tradition.'⁶³ Enormously interested in African art and music, as well as African society, Gray developed a wide range of personal relationships with blacks. Unlike many contemporary liberals, his attitude to blacks was genuinely equalitarian, rather than paternalistic.

Although he lacked a higher degree, and was only 33 when he assumed the chair of sociology, Gray immediately made the new Department of Social Studies one of the most important at the University. He was a highly skilled sociologist, very much in the new scientific mode, having previously lectured in social science and social psychology at the London School of Economics. Shortly before coming to South Africa, he had carried out large-scale intelligence tests on 10 000 children in the London area, the results of which were published as *The Nation's Intelligence*. The book was accorded a two-column review in *The Times* by Sir William Beveridge, then Master of University College, Oxford. A cultured, educated man, as well as a strong scholar, Gray rapidly emerged as a driving force in sociology in South Africa. Even among South African universities, Wits had been slow in instituting courses in sociology and social work; Gray put the University in the forefront.

John Gray

An attractive personality, Gray was a magnificent lecturer, who got on particularly well with students, taking a close personal interest in them. He was also a very capable administrator, and served as Dean of the Faculty of Arts in 1944–6. It was a major loss to the University when on 29 January 1947 he was drowned with the sinking of the S.S. *Samwater* in the Bay of Biscay.

The idea of providing a specialized education in social studies and training in social work at Wits had originated with Hoernlé in 1933. Since 1930 the Faculty of Arts had offered a B.A. in Social Sciences, requiring majors in two of three subjects, history, economics, and social anthropology, but it had been left to the Universities of Cape Town, Stellenbosch, and Pretoria to take the lead in developing courses in sociology and social work. The publication in

1932 of the Report of the Carnegie Commission of Inquiry into the Poor White Problem, which stressed the need for trained social workers and for a state bureau of social welfare, provided the immediate inspiration for Hoernlé's proposal to begin courses at Wits for social workers. In a memorandum of July 1933 he stated that a major movement had emerged in the country for training and research in social work: 'This movement has come to a head, partly through the publication of the Report of the Poor White Commission, and the weighty recommendations made in that Report; partly owing to the depression which had made the problems of poverty and unemployment more acute and which has scarcely been touched by the gold premium; partly owing to the fact that, for years past the problems of vocational testing and guidance, of social maladjustments in children, juveniles, adults, and, in general, of what may be called "human engineering" have attracted increasing attention, until now the demand for action is loud and insistent.'[64] A committee appointed by Raikes subsequently recommended the institution of a post-graduate diploma in social work, but added that it would have to be financed by an additional special grant from the government, and not out of the University's general purposes grant. As no special grant was forthcoming, the diploma was not instituted. In 1935, on the initiative of the Social Welfare Committee, forerunner of the Johannesburg Co-ordinating Council of Registered Social Welfare Organizations, the proposal to provide courses for the training of social workers was revived.[65] With the improved finances of the University, Council agreed to the establishment of a Department of Social Studies, to be staffed initially by a Professor of Sociology and a lecturer.

In 1937 the Department of Social Studies began teaching, though it was not until the next year that a lecturer was appointed to assist Gray. He was Dr H. Sonnabend, a graduate of the University of Padua, who during World War II was to serve as welfare officer to Italian prisoners of war at Zonderwater camp, near Pretoria. The courses offered by the department were intended primarily for the new four-year degree of B.A. in Social Studies, as well as a diploma in social studies, the curricula for which were approved by the Board of the Faculty of Arts at the beginning of 1937. The department provided three courses in sociology, as well as courses and seminars in social work and social studies, for the new degree, which replaced the B.A. in Social Sciences. Sociology I was also available to ordinary arts students. At first the Union Department of Social Welfare, itself established in 1937 to cater primarily for the welfare needs of whites, was highly critical of the courses and arrangements at Wits for social work. In 1938 Dr Felix Brummer, then a research officer in the Department of Social Welfare, investigated all the universities and training centres engaged in social work preparation, and he reported that only Stellenbosch provided a truly excellent training. In his assessment, the curriculum at Wits paid inadequate attention to social work theory, social field-work, and South African conditions. The Brummer investigation represented the first direct attempt by the state to influence the content, structure, and procedures of social work training programmes, and Wits felt obliged to respond. In April 1939, at the University's request, a meeting was held between officials of the Department of Social Welfare and the Social Studies committee, the result of which was that the Department accepted that the University's courses 'may, from the strictly academic viewpoint, be regarded as satisfactory', while the University accepted the Department's suggestion to appoint an experienced, Afrikaans-speaking social worker for the courses in social work theory and field-work. With the aid of a grant from the Department of Social Welfare a temporary post was created, and in June 1939 Miss E. Malherbe, a graduate in social work from Stellenbosch, was appointed to it. In the next month the Department of Social Welfare accorded 'full recognition' to the Wits social studies degree and diploma for the purposes of government appointments.[66]

In addition to sociology, candidates for the B.A. in Social Studies were required to take economics and psychology as three-year majors. This necessitated the introduction of a third course in psychology, specifically for the B.A. in Social Studies. For the ordinary B.A. psychology remained a two-year major, and for the B.Sc. a one-year course was offered. Together with the Department of Social Studies, the new Department of Psychology began to function in 1937, under Professor I.D. MacCrone, who had previously lectured in psychology in the Department of Philosophy. Dr Simon Biesheuvel, a graduate of U.C.T. and Edinburgh University, was appointed lecturer, and soon proved an inspiring force in the department. In 1940 he left Wits to join the South African Air Force. After a distinguished career as director of the National Institute for Personnel Research of the C.S.I.R., and as personnel director of the South African Breweries Limited, Biesheuvel was to return to the University in 1973 as director of the Graduate School of Business Administration.

Two other major new chairs were established in the Faculty of Arts in the thirties. In 1931 C.M. Doke became the first Professor of Bantu Languages in the University, and in 1933 C.M. van den Heever became the first incumbent of the chair in Afrikaans and Nederlands. Although only 31 years of age at the time of his appointment, Van den Heever had already firmly established himself as both poet and novelist. In the opinion of the *Star*, he was 'one of the most promising members of the younger Afrikaans school'.[67]

Born in a concentration camp in the Free State at the end of the Anglo-Boer War, Van den Heever was educated at the Grey College School and Grey University College, Bloemfontein. After attending the University of Utrecht in Holland, where he passed the examination for the doctorate, he returned to South Africa and presented his thesis, 'Die Digter Totius: Sy Betekenis vir die Afrikaanse Letterkunde', to the University of South Africa. The degree of Doctor of Literature was conferred upon him in 1932, when he was lecturing in Afrikaans at the Grey University College. When he took up his appointment at Wits, he had published several volumes of verse, including *Deining*, as well as novels, most notably *Langs die Grootpad* and *Droogte*. During his long tenure at Wits, until his death in 1957, his status was much more as a novelist and a poet, than as a scholar. Apart from his study of Totius which had been published in 1932, he produced little of scholarly or critical value, although he was otherwise enormously prolific. His reputation has since gone into a decline, but he enjoyed considerable contemporary success, and is of the first importance in the history of Afrikaans letters. In the assessment of J.C. Kannemeyer: 'Literêr-histories is by egter van belang as eerste Dertiger op die gebied van die poësie en as verfyner van die romantiese stylrigting in die Afrikaanse prosa.'[68] As the first of the Dertigers, the group of Afrikaans poets in the thirties that included N.P. van Wyk Louw, Uys Krige, W.E.G. Louw, and Elisabeth Eybers, he reached his pinnacle with *Aardse Vlam* in 1938, but he was more consistently successful as a novelist. In the thirties he published *Somer* (1935), *Kromburg* (1937), and *Laat Vrugte* (1939), which was awarded the Hertzog prize in 1942. Politically, Van den Heever was an ardent supporter of J.B.M. Hertzog, and in 1943 published a biography of the former Prime Minister. It was translated into English in 1946.

C.M. van den Heever

Van den Heever's standing as a poet and novelist helped to attract students to Wits to study Afrikaans, but as a lecturer and an administrator he was not particularly effective. Personally he was very helpful to students, but his lectures were in no sense challenging, as he preferred not to state his own opinion, and he dictated even to his third-year classes. As an administrator he was rather inefficient, with the result that his senior lecturer, Abel Coetzee, virtually took over the department. Coetzee was a much more aggressive personality, and also able to make his own work on Afrikaans language and folklore compelling for students. P.J. Nienaber, the other lecturer in the department, taught the history of the 'Afrikaanse Taalbeweging', and wrote extensively on the history of the Afrikaans language. By far the most notable student produced by the Department of Afrikaans and Nederlands in the thirties was Elisabeth Eybers.

For Doke, in his new capacity as Professor and Head of the Department of Bantu Studies, the thirties was sometimes a difficult decade. The main problem was a shortage of students in the department, with the diplomas in Bantu Studies proving especially disappointing in attracting the anticipated clientele of civil servants. The public service apparently did little to encourage its officers to acquire university qualifications. In all by 1939, only 15 students had qualified for the higher diploma in Bantu Studies, and 4 for the lower diploma. In 1934 it was proposed to introduce a one-year diploma in Bantu Administration, but this was shelved when of all the 'several Departments of Native Affairs' approached, only Southern Rhodesia displayed any interest.[69] In 1939 a two-year diploma in Native Affairs was introduced.

It had always been intended that research should constitute a major priority of the Department of Bantu Studies, but during a decade when the University's financial resources were severely limited, its relative lack of students occasionally made it a target for attack. The most sustained attack was mounted in 1931 by W.M. Macmillan, the Professor of History, who sensed that his department was being deprived of resources in order to cater for the Department of Bantu Studies. In October 1931 he proposed to the Board of the Faculty of Arts that the course in Native Law and Administration be transferred from the Department of Bantu Studies to History 'as better teaching results might be obtained with this arrangement, which would also make possible the retrenchment of the present part-time lecturer in Native Law and Administration and would justify the retention of the part-time lecturer in the Department of History'. In Macmillan's contention the existing course in Native Law and Administration was unsatisfactory, not only because it failed to attract many students, but more importantly because it was quite lacking in historical content. He also made it clear that he did not consider Rheinallt Jones, the part-time lecturer in Native Law and Administration, competent to teach a university course.⁷⁰ In response to Macmillan's proposals and criticisms, a committee on the teaching of Native Law and Administration was set up, and it defended the *status quo* against him. 'I have just been driven off the field', he wrote privately, 'routed in the Committee by four to one on every point.' He regretted having to attack 'poor Rheinallt' as the 'bigger issue is the real thing', but he sincerely believed that Jones had 'too many irons in the fire and is not a real University teacher'.⁷¹ The final paragraph of the report stated, 'The Committee resolved to report that, while it might be considered desirable to have as lecturer a person better qualified academically, the present lecturer was, in its opinion (Professor Macmillan dissenting), the most suitable lecturer obtainable.'⁷² In 1938, following the election of Rheinallt Jones as a Senator, the Native Recruiting Corporation agreed to finance a special lectureship in Native Law and Administration to replace the part-time post. In the next year Julius Lewin was appointed to the lectureship. He was to serve the University until his retirement in 1967, becoming associate professor in 1963.

Apart from Doke, two members of the Department of Bantu Studies served throughout the thirties, the Revd R. Ellenberger, as part-time lecturer in Sotho, and Dr Pierre de Villiers Pienaar, as lecturer in phonetics. Pienaar occupied the lectureship in phonetics from its inception, first on a part-time basis in 1930, becoming full-time in 1935. A graduate of Wits, and a student of Doke's, Pienaar had undertaken his doctoral studies in phonetics and general linguistics at the University of Hamburg in Germany, where he developed an interest in logopedics. He had the foresight to recognize the need for speech therapy in South Africa, and on joining the staff at Wits he was to do pioneering work in both phonetics and speech pathology. In 1936 a second course in phonetics was introduced, making it a major subject for the B.A.; in 1936 the Speech Clinic was established at the University, treating speech-defective children from Transvaal schools; and in the next year a two-year diploma in logopedics was instituted. It owed much to the wisdom of Pienaar that an operating clinic was established before a diploma in logopedics was embarked upon, and that the courses for the diploma looked at both hearing and speech problems, recognizing the relation between the two. In 1944 Pienaar was appointed to the chair of the new Department of Phonetics and Logopedics. In the fifties he apparently found the 'liberal' political atmosphere at Wits uncomfortable, and left the University in 1957 to become Professor of Afrikaans and Nederlands Linguistics at the University of South Africa. Two years later he became the first Professor of Speech Science, Logopedics, and Audiology at the University of Pretoria.

Following Mrs Hoernlé's departure from the Department of Bantu Studies at the end of 1937, Dr Audrey Richards was appointed senior lecturer in social anthropology. Educated at Cambridge and the London School of Economics, and destined to become one of the doyens of social anthropology, she had already established a sound reputation for herself for her detailed work on the Bemba of Northern Rhodesia, *Hunger and Work in a Savage Tribe* (1932). She remained at Wits for three years, during which she undertook field-work among the Tswana of the Northern Transvaal. One other noteworthy appointment in the Department of Bantu Studies was that of B.W. Vilakazi in 1935. The first black to be appointed to the academic staff, he was made a language assistant.

During the thirties, fine arts remained under the aegis of the Department of Architecture, but the one-year course in the history of fine arts given by Pearse was replaced by a three-year course for the B.A., and a four-year course for B.A. Honours in fine arts. Both courses provided for lectures and studio work in architecture, painting, and sculpture; and the latter for studio work in life drawing. W. de S. Hendrikz, the sculptor, was Pearse's main assistant in teaching the fine arts.

In the thirties the Faculty of Arts devoted a good deal of attention to the structure of the B.A. degree. The over-all tendency was to further restrict the freedom of choice available to students. The B.A. remained an eleven-course degree, with two majors, but in 1930 a new scheme of ancillary subjects was devised so as to ensure that 'every student is definitely guided in respect of eight courses'. In addition, students were normally required to take a course in either English or Afrikaans and Nederlands. After 1936 it became mandatory to take at least one course in two languages. The philosophy behind the restriction of choice, particularly once students had decided on their majors, was stated by the 1930 faculty committee on the grouping of B.A. courses:

> (a) The basic purpose of the B.A. degree is to give a general education. Whatever the candidate's purpose in taking the degree, the Regulations are expected to compel such a choice of courses as will lead to a broad culture, even if also to qualification for a profession. It follows that the candidate should have as wide a freedom as possible in the selection of his major subjects . . .
> (b) Ancillary subjects should provide 'parallel' studies to the major subjects and give a background to the more intensive study in the major subjects. Ancillary subjects are desirable concomitants, not essential prerequisites, and should therefore be subjects *related* to the major subjects.[73]

An administrative advantage to be had from 'guiding' students into particular combinations of subjects was to simplify the production of a timetable for classes.

At the postgraduate level, the progress of the Faculty of Arts in the thirties was unspectacular. The 45 M.A. degrees and 9 doctorates awarded in the faculty between 1928 and 1939 did not constitute an impressive total. Several of the doctorates went to members of staff: J.G. Lawrie in English, P.R. Kirby in music, I.D. MacCrone in psychology, and Abel Coetzee in Afrikaans. The Department of History continued to produce a fair proportion of the higher degrees of the Faculty, including a D.Litt. in 1939 for Eric Axelson for his thesis on 'South East Africa, 1488–1530', and an M.A. for L.C.F. Turner for his thesis on 'The Cape of Good Hope and the Trafalgar Campaign'. Nine of the Masters' degrees were in the new Department of Afrikaans and Nederlands, several of them awarded for theses dealing with the history of the Afrikaans language and literature.

VII

By comparison with Arts, the Faculty of Science witnessed few new developments and changes in the thirties. The Department of Geophysics, an offshoot of the Bernard Price Institute of Geophysics, was the only new department, and only a handful of new courses were initiated by the faculty, notably a one-year course in biology and a special psychology course for scientists, given by Biesheuvel. The number of students enrolled in the faculty was generally very stable, building up slowly from 134 in 1928 to a high of 176 a decade later, then falling back to 143 in 1939. Between 1928 and 1939 a total of 317 B.Sc. degrees were awarded, somewhat more than a third of the number of first degrees in the Faculty of Arts. A far higher proportion of science graduates continued with their studies than in arts. In the same period, as many as 113 B.Sc. Honours, 70 M.Sc., and 11 D.Sc. degrees were awarded. But at the undergraduate level, the Faculty of Science remained what it had been in the twenties, basically a service faculty to engineering, medicine, and dentistry.

During the thirties four of the departments based in the Faculty of Science acquired new heads: botany, zoology, chemistry, and geology. In 1931, J.F.V. Phillips, a newcomer to the University, succeeded Moss as Professor of Botany, and in 1933 C.J. van der Horst, previously senior lecturer in the department, succeeded Fantham as Professor of Zoology. They were to maintain the high reputation established by their predecessors for the biology departments at Wits. In chemistry, Stephen succeeded Wilkinson as professor in 1934, and the Departments of Chemistry and Organic Chemistry were amalgamated under him. In 1935 T.W. Gevers, like Phillips a newcomer to the University, became Professor of Geology, following the retirement of R.B. Young.

Under John Phillips the Department of Botany experienced a radical change of direction. The emphasis moved from taxonomic botany, which had been Moss's abiding interest, to plant ecology and soil conservation. Born in Grahamstown in 1899, and a B.Sc. graduate of Edinburgh University, Phillips was initially a forester, spending five years in Knysna as research officer of indigenous forests. He produced several scientific papers and his first book, *Forest Succession and Ecology in the Knysna Region*. In 1928, after gaining his D.Sc. from Edinburgh, Phillips went to what was then Tanganyika (Tanzania) as ecologist and deputy director of tsetse fly research, and there began to formulate ideas about the laws governing the interaction of man and ecosystems. As Phillips perceived, the problem of tsetse involved the whole environment, and he was always thereafter to insist that ecology was the study of an entire environment, the complex interrelations between climate, terrain, and all forms of life, plant, animal, and human. For Phillips, the ecologist investigated the whole biotic community.

J.F.V. Phillips

At Wits, Phillips's primary research interest became field ecology. Soon after his arrival he initiated experiments on grasses at Frankenwald, which was still in the University's possession, and became responsible for establishing the Frankenwald Research Station, officially opened by General Smuts in 1935. In the previous year, 1 269 acres of Frankenwald was sold by the University to African Explosives and Industries for £4 000; the remaining 1 000 acres constituted the Research Station. At the time of Alfred Beit's death in 1906, Frankenwald had been valued at £80 000, but the estate had since been allowed to run down, and the University, desperately short of funds in the early thirties, had become anxious to sell. For Phillips, African Explosives and Industries made a welcome neighbour. As the largest manufacturer of fertilizers in the country, A.E.I. maintained an agricultural advisory department, founded in 1929 under the direction of T.D. Hall, and for a long period the pure scientists of the University and the applied scientists of A.E.I. co-operated in field experimentation. The University itself did not maintain any trained technical assistants or professional research officers at Frankenwald; research there was primarily the responsibility of the academic staff and students of the Department of Botany. 'This lack of trained technical assistants might have been considered a drawback', Eddie Roux has recalled, 'but it is clear that if there had been a permanent trained staff Frankenwald would have been a poorer training ground.'[74] By the late thirties, the Department of Botany was producing a steady stream of postgraduate students, most of whom were employed by either the Department of Agriculture or A.E.I. The truly outstanding botany student of the 1930s, A.H. Bunting, later became Professor of Agricultural Botany at Reading University and an agricultural adviser in East Africa. His M.Sc. thesis in 1938 was on the effect of combined clipping and chemical treatments on the root reserve and development of Highveld grasses. Phillips's own experimentation at Frankenwald in the thirties was chiefly with grass-burning.

Phillips always worked closely with the Department of Agriculture, and in government had a special friend in Smuts, a keen amateur botanist with a particular interest in grasses. It was with Smuts's encouragement at the end of World War II that Phillips set up a course for ex-servicemen to train them in soil conservation and management. Altogether about 120 ex-servicemen were trained as 'donga doctors', and they were to find employment throughout southern, central, and east Africa. In 1948 Phillips left the University, returning to Tanganyika to advise on the ill-fated groundnut scheme. He was later Professor of Agriculture at the University College of the Gold Coast.

A man of considerable enthusiasm, and an able administrator, Phillips played a prominent role in University affairs while also running an efficient department. He was Dean of the Faculty of Science in 1939–40, and together with Stephen, Van der Horst, and Le May came to constitute a powerful grouping which dominated the faculty. The staff in his department in the thirties consisted mainly of women, which was rare for any department at the time: Margaret Moss, Elaine Young, and Dora Weintroub. In 1935 H.B. Gilliland joined the department; he later became Professor of Botany at the University of Singapore.

Cornelius van der Horst, the new Professor of Zoology, had first joined the University in 1928 as senior lecturer. A Frisian, and a graduate of the

University of Amsterdam, where he had initially worked as a botanist under Hugo de Vries, Van der Horst possessed a very fine reputation both as a teacher and as a researcher, though he was not quite of the same calibre as Fantham. What most troubled Raikes about him at the time of his appointment was his difficulty with English.[75] He always retained a heavy Dutch accent, and while some students were inspired by his lectures, others found him only semi-comprehensible. A difficult man, with very strongly-held opinions and a reputation for stubbornness, Van der Horst was none the less consistently fair to students. Those who showed promise were given every encouragement, and he made a big impact on some of them. Eight of his students qualified for the M.Sc. in the thirties, and Nellie Paterson was awarded a D.Sc.

C. van der Horst

A very fine classical embryologist, Van der Horst maintained the Department of Zoology's reputation for research. Before coming to Wits Van der Horst had done some work on brain anatomy, but his primary early interest had been marine biology, where he was a specialist on less well-known marine groups. The animals that attracted him most were the Enteropneusta, and in 1939 he produced the volume on them for Bronn's *Klassen und Ordnungen des Tierreichs*. At Wits, Van der Horst turned to the study of mammalian embryology, focusing on the embryonic development of South African mammals. He wrote a series of papers on the embryology of the spring hare, the dassie, the aardvark, and the elephant shrew, the latter often in collaboration with Dr Joseph Gillman of the Department of Anatomy. The papers on the ovulation and placentation of the elephant shrew gained for him considerable international attention. He also maintained his interest in marine animals, taking students on expeditions to the island of Inhaca in Moçambique. It was chiefly as a result of his work that the Portuguese authorities built a permanent Marine Biological Station there. Although deeply involved in research, Van der Horst never shunned his administrative duties, and in 1941 succeeded Phillips as Dean of the Faculty of Science. Altogether he served as dean for three years. He died suddenly in October 1951.

Van der Horst's department, which had suffered severely from retrenchments caused by the depression, was composed initially of Nellie Paterson, a fine researcher, as senior lecturer, and M.J. de Kock as laboratory assistant. In 1935 Dr G. Eloff, the first geneticist to be appointed to a department of zoology in South Africa, was made junior lecturer. A member of the Ossewabrandwag, he was interned during World War II. In 1939 Mary McEwan, one of Van der Horst's students, was also made junior lecturer, bringing the department's teaching complement up to its pre-depression level. The laboratory assistant, De Kock, was one of the mainstays of the department, and in 1974 became the first person to complete fifty years of service on the University staff.

T.W. Gevers

Under Van der Horst and Phillips there was much greater co-operation between the Departments of Zoology and Botany than there had been under Fantham and Moss. In 1935 the two departments collaborated in launching a one-year course in biology, intended primarily for trainee teachers. Although generally dismissed by the specialist botanists and zoologists, the course was considered of 'definite value' for prospective teachers.[76]

The appointment in 1935 of T.W. Gevers as Young's successor as Professor of Geology caused something of a stir. Not only had Gevers no previous teaching experience, but one of the applicants for the chair had been H.S. Shand, the Professor of Geology at Stellenbosch and an internationally renowned petrologist. Gevers was a field geologist, and the University selected him ahead of Shand precisely because it wanted a field geologist rather than a petrologist. Born in Natal in 1900, and educated at U.C.T. and the University of Munich, where he was awarded his Ph.D. in 1926, Gevers had been a member of the Geological Survey of the Union Department of Mines before taking up his appointment at Wits. For five years he had worked in South West Africa, surveying and mapping a large portion of the territory. He brought with him to Wits an abiding enthusiasm for work in the field.

Gevers was a first-rate geologist, interested above all in his science and his teaching. Administration, and the general affairs of the University, held little appeal for him, and his attitude to administrators was sometimes hostile. He served for but one year as Dean of the Faculty of Science, in 1943. The contribution for which Gevers is best remembered was in making field excursions an integral part of a geologist's training at Wits. Excursions became obligatory for first-, second- and third-year geology students, including those enrolled for mining engineering. Each year an excursion was undertaken to the gold and asbestos mines of the Eastern Transvaal, and other excursions extended as far afield as equatorial Africa. In 1939, while taking his students on a trip to the copper mines of Northern Rhodesia and the Belgian Congo, and the rift valleys and volcanoes of East Africa, Gevers was charged by an irate elephant and seriously injured. He filmed the charge through the windscreen of the car in which he was travelling.

Gevers prided himself on his international interests and connections, and the international reputation he built up for his department. Sometimes referred to by his critics as 'the absentee professor', he travelled extensively, attending international conferences and participating in scientific expeditions. He also made a point of hosting foreign scientific visitors to Johannesburg. He served Wits as Professor of Geology for 34 years, retiring in 1968.

The interests of Gevers required that he have the support of a loyal and reliable second-in-command, and this was provided him by Edgar Mendelssohn. Educated at King Edward VII School, Wits, and Harvard, where he obtained his M.A., Mendelssohn had first been appointed to the staff of the Department of Geology in 1927. He was to serve in the department for 42 years, becoming associate professor in 1957. A modest, reticent man, Mendelssohn was a specialist in economic and mining geology, and it was he who took chief responsibility for the degree course in mining geology introduced in 1936. In 1933 he was appointed honorary secretary and treasurer of the Geological Society of South Africa, and editor of its *Transactions*, and for the next 35 years he virtually ran the society. In 1972 the University awarded him an honorary LL.D.

When Gevers took over the Department of Geology in 1935, its staff consisted of himself, Mendelssohn, and Margaret Welsh, a recent Wits graduate. In 1936 J.U. Swiegers, a mineralogist and petrologist from Stellenbosch, joined the department as junior lecturer, and in 1938 H.B.S. Cooke took over from Margaret Welsh. His main work was as palaeontologist and stratigrapher, and he was later to become Professor of Geology at Dalhousie University, Halifax, Nova Scotia.

The two largest departments in the Faculty of Science were chemistry and physics. In addition to providing service courses for both engineering and medical and dental students, the Department of Chemistry was also responsible for the courses in chemical engineering. When Stephen took over in 1934, and chemistry and organic chemistry were amalgamated under him, the department included four other academic members of staff, J.B. Robertson, O.G. Backeberg, G.J.R. Krige, and B. Segal. By 1939 two posts had been added. S.S. Israelstam, a graduate of Wits, was appointed lecturer in chemistry in 1935, and he was to serve in the department for 43 years, becoming associate professor in 1958. Another Wits graduate, F. Hawke, was made junior lecturer, and together with Segal taught the classes in chemical engineering.

Stephen's main constructive impact on the Department of Chemistry in the thirties was in stimulating research. Between 1935 and 1939 the department produced eight M.Sc. graduates, while among the staff Segal, Backeberg, and Robertson published regularly. In 1934 Backeberg was awarded a D.Sc. for his work on quinoline derivatives. Later Professor of Organic Chemistry and Head of the Department of Chemistry, Backeberg was given an honorary LL.D. in 1972.

The Department of Physics, by contrast, produced very little by way of research and post-graduate students. It was the classic service department, and together with chemistry provided courses for both engineering and medical and dental students. The academic staff numbered six by 1939. Paine had under him G.R.T. Evans and M.A. Cooper as senior lecturers, E.C. Halliday and G.G. Wiles as lecturers, and W.H. Aarts as junior lecturer. Halliday, working on atmospheric physics, was the most productive in research, publishing five articles during the thirties. He left Wits in 1946 to join the C.S.I.R., where he embarked on air pollution research. An important advance in 1937 was the formation of the Physics Club, which was open to anyone interested and which came to facilitate co-operation between the University and industry.

While the Department of Mathematics produced more graduates of its own than did physics, its main function was to provide courses for engineering students. Three years of mathematics were required of students in civil, mechanical, and electrical engineering, with the result that the department had to contend with vast classes in the thirties. The number of academic staff, however, remained constant at five. Constancon, Kerrich, and Young continued to serve Dalton during the thirties, and A.L. Hales lectured in the department from 1933 until he transferred to the Department of Applied Mathematics in 1939. Dalton, Kerrich, and Hales were the most productive in publishing articles.

Remarkably strong in its personnel by 1939 was the Department of Applied Mathematics. In 1931 Le May had acquired the services of A.E.H. Bleksley as lecturer, and he was to remain on the staff for 37 years, becoming Professor and Head of the Department in 1953. A graduate of Stellenbosch, with a keen interest in astronomy, Bleksley taught the courses in astronomy offered in the Faculty of Science as well as courses in applied mathematics. In 1937 he was awarded a D.Sc. by Wits for his thesis, 'The Pulsation Variables: An Analytical and Statistical Study of Stellar Variability'. In 1938 H.O. Oliver, who proved a good teacher, was appointed junior lecturer, and in the next year Hales was a very important capture. He remained in the department until 1945, later becoming Professor of Applied Mathematics at Cape Town, and then Director of the Bernard Price Institute and Carnegie Professor of Geophysics at Wits.

Applied mathematics, like mathematics, offered service courses for engineering students. The only non-service department in the Faculty of Science was geography, but it also received most of its students from outside the faculty: from Arts. Throughout the thirties the department possessed two members of staff, Professor J.H. Wellington and Stanley P. Jackson, who was appointed junior lecturer in July 1930, becoming lecturer in 1934. A graduate of Wits, Jackson's research interest was climatology. In 1937 he was awarded an M.A. for his thesis on the climate of Johannesburg and the Highveld. In 1958 he succeeded Wellington as Professor and Head of the Department of Geography, and later became Deputy Vice-Chancellor of the University.

VIII

By later standards, the University's research achievement prior to 1939 was limited. It included some outstanding contributions, and much of what was done was of a pioneer nature, but productivity in research was generally low. It could hardly have been otherwise, given the heavy weight of teaching and administrative loads, particularly the former. Like the other universities and university colleges in South Africa, Wits was overwhelmingly a teaching institution. As the National Research Council stated in its report in 1939 on *The Research Position in the Universities of South Africa*, 'While teaching and research are allowed, in theory, to be parallel functions of a university, the organization of our universities is almost wholly directed to the former.'

University authorities themselves attributed this state of affairs to the lack of finance for research, and to poor staff/student ratios, with the consequent overloading of university staffs with teaching work. In the view of the National Research Council: 'The crowding of the institutions with immature schoolboys, who have to be educated up to university level is obviously a contributing cause. Another, it may be suggested, is the tendency to expand on the instructional side before consolidating the position already held.'[77]

In the campaign to found a university in Johannesburg, the research advantages of such an institution for industry had been stressed, but no co-ordinated attempt was made during the University's first two decades to fund and promote research. The University was quite without a separate research fund, and there were no standing research committees. Research depended very largely on individual initiative, or in some instances the co-ordination of a department by its head. In the thirties major advances were made in that the University began to provide *ad hoc* funding for special research projects, notably the 1936 Bushman Research Expedition to the Kalahari, and the first research institutes were founded, including the Bernard Price Institute of Geophysical Research.

In the economic boom following South Africa's abandonment of the gold standard in December 1932, new thought was given within and without the universities to their role in research. In 1938 the government established the National Research Council and National Research Board under the Minister of Education. It replaced the Research Grant Board, instituted in 1918 'to meet the demands for research which arose chiefly in the industrial sphere as a result of the Great War', and which had been attached successively to the Union Department of Mines and the Department of Commerce and Industries. Like the Research Grant Board, the National Research Board received annual grants from the government for the purposes of research work, and the funding of university research grants and scholarships designed to promote the training of research workers. For 1938/9 the new Board had £6 860 at its disposal, including £2 460 for grants and scholarships. The intention of the National Research Council and Board was that they would encourage not only scientific research, but also research into the country's human problems and resources.[78]

In the thirties three research institutes were established at Milner Park; the Bureau of Archaeology, the Minerals Research Laboratory, and the Bernard Price Institute of Geophysical Research. The first two were government funded. In 1935 the Bureau of Archaeology of the Union Department of Interior was formally established with its headquarters at Wits. The staff comprised an archaeologist, functioning as director, and a second-grade clerk. The first director, C. van Riet Lowe, a civil engineer turned archaeologist, was made Professor and Head of the Department of Archaeology, although archaeology was not offered as a degree course at the University. In the same year the Minerals Research Laboratory, the forerunner of the National Institute for Metallurgy, was opened by the Minister of Mines, Patrick Duncan. The University provided the site and buildings for the laboratory, and the Union Department of Mines financed the equipment, running expenses, and salaries for the staff. Under Professor G.H. Stanley as director, the staff comprised three research officers, a chemist and assayer, and two laboratory attendants. As was pointed out by Duncan in his opening address, the laboratory represented the state's first venture into mineral and metallurgical research.[79]

B.F.J. Schonland

The Bernard Price Institute of Geophysical Research, formally established in 1937 and officially opened by General Smuts on 21 October 1938, owed its foundation to the interest of the electrical industry in research into lightning. In April 1930 T.P. Pask of the Victoria Falls and Transvaal Power Company had read a paper to the South African Institute of Electrical Engineers advocating the establishment of a lightning research laboratory. Later in the year the Institute had set up a Lightning Investigation Committee, with Pask as chairman. In 1932 Dr Basil Schonland, senior lecturer in physics at U.C.T., was made chairman of the Lightning Investigation Committee's research sub-committee, and it was his work that prompted Bernard Price, general manager and chief engineer of the Victoria Falls and Transvaal Power Company, to take positive steps to create in South Africa an institute for geophysical research. Price personally contributed £10 000 for the venture. The Carnegie Corporation of New York, which had already made generous donations to the University's libraries, contributed £11 000 on the recommendation of the Carnegie Institute in Washington, the famous American centre for geophysical research, and an anonymous donor guaranteed a sum of £1 500 per annum for twenty years to help cover running expenses. In April 1936 the University's Council decided to proceed with the establishment of an institute of geophysical research, to be named after Bernard Price. In addition to undertaking research into lightning, the Institute was to conduct research in such fields as terrestrial magnetism, seismology, rock temperatures, meteorology, and radio communications. It was intended that pure research should be the chief function of the Institute, but that on the applied side its work would be of value primarily to the electrical and mining industries.[80]

One of the conditions laid down by Price in his grant was that Schonland accept appointment as director of the Institute. This Schonland did, commencing duties as director and as Carnegie-Price Professor of Geophysics at the beginning of 1937. Born in Grahamstown in 1896, and educated at St Andrews College, Rhodes University College, and Cambridge, Schonland had worked in the Cavendish Laboratory before taking up his appointment as senior lecturer in physics at U.C.T. At the Cavendish he had studied the scattering and absorption of B particles from radioactive elements, but at U.C.T. developed his interest in atmospheric electricity. He was to become the world's leading authority on lightning. In the opinion of T.E. Allibone in his obituary on Schonland, his contribution to our knowledge of lightning became such that 'his name can be truly classed, alone, with Benjamin Franklin'.[81]

The laboratory building for the Bernard Price Institute was completed in early 1938. At the Institute Schonland had four full-time members of staff. Dr P.G. Gane, a seismologist, was chief assistant, J.W. van Wyk and J.S. Elder were the research assistants, and J. Keiller the mechanical assistant in charge of the workshop. There were also four associates of the Institute. The associate research workers, drawn from the teaching departments of the University, were A.L. Hales and G.G. Wiles. The honorary associates were Professor D.B. Hodges of Howard College, Durban, and Dr D.J. Malan of U.C.T., who collaborated with Schonland in his lightning research.

As Schonland's work on lightning was already in progress, the Institute quickly established an international reputation for itself in the field of lightning. Utilizing the Boys rotating-lens camera, Schonland and his associates examined the lightning flash photometrically, and established the basic mechanism of the lightning discharge. By the outbreak of World War II they had established that all lightning strokes brought a negative charge to ground, with the positive charge going to the upper atmosphere. In 1938 Schonland was elected a fellow of the Royal Society, the first member of the

Wits staff to be so honoured. Before the outbreak of war, the Institute was also engaged in seismological work, particularly with the location of the foci of earth tremors in and around Johannesburg. This was the work of Gane, Hales, and Wiles.[82]

With the outbreak of war in September 1939, Schonland was immediately drafted by Smuts to assist with radar defence, and the B.P.I. became the headquarters for the Special Signals Services. After the war Schonland served for five years as the first president of the Council for Scientific and Industrial Research, before returning full-time to the B.P.I. In 1954 he became deputy director of the Atomic Energy Research Establishment at Harwell, and in 1958 he was made director. He was knighted in 1960.

All in all, by 1939 Wits had made several distinguished contributions in research, and the work of Dart and Schonland had proved of international importance. Council was certainly not unpleased with the University's record in research. In a memorandum of 1940, Council sought to disassociate Wits from the general criticisms of the report of the National Research Council on research in South African universities:

> The University cannot accept the statement in the Report which implies that the research position *in this University* 'cannot be regarded as gratifying'. The encouragement given to research activity, the devotion of our staff to research work, and the volume and quality of the work carried out, are such that the position is with justice regarded as highly gratifying. The University is very proud of its contribution and there is no doubt at all that if the lack of financial resources were remedied by an adequate increase in the grant from Government there would be no other hindrance to further development to a completely satisfactory level.[83]

Notes

1. 'Statistics: Medicine, Engineering, General', University Archives 211.
2. *Report of the Union Department of Education for 1939*, U.G. 50 of 1940, 45.
3. D.H. Houghton, 'Economic Development, 1865–1965', in M. Wilson and L. Thompson (eds), *The Oxford History of South Africa* (Oxford, 2 vols, 1969–70), II, 32.
4. For economic developments of the 1930s see, in addition to Houghton: S.H. Frankel, 'An Analysis of the Growth of the National Income of the Union in the Period of Prosperity before the War', *South African Journal of Economics*, 12 (1944), 112–35; G.F.D. Palmer, 'Some Aspects of the Development of Secondary Industry in South Africa since the Depression of 1929–1932', Ibid., 22 (1954), 148–59; A.B. Lumby, 'Tariffs and Gold in South Africa, 1886–1939', Ibid., 44 (1976), 139–57.

5. Council Misc./15/38.
6. *Journal of the South African Institution of Engineers,* 27 (1933), 26–34.
7. Council minutes, IV, 8 Sept. 1939.
8. See Chamber of Mines file 120 of 1938 on 'University business'.
9. *University of the Witwatersrand, Johannesburg, Annual Report 1938 and 1939.*
10. Faculty of Engineering minutes, III, 5 Feb. & 11 March 1936.
11. Herbert, *Martienssen and the International Style,* 111.
12. Ibid., 247.
13. Ibid., 83.
14. Ibid., 227.
15. *Sunday Express,* 21 Feb. 1937.
16. *Report of the Committee on Medical Training in South Africa,* U.G. 25 of 1939, 5–8.
17. 'Statistics: Medicine, Engineering, General', University Archives 211.
18. 'Memorandum by the Principal on Hospital Agreement', 25 Nov. 1935, Council Misc./60/35.
19. Raymond D. Pruitt, 'Doublets, Dipoles and the Negativity Hypothesis: An Historical Note on W.H. Craib and His Relationship with F.N. Wilson and Thomas Lewis', *Johns Hopkins Medical Journal,* 138 (1976), 279–88; 'Integrity in Science: The Case of William Craib and the Doublet Hypothesis', *South African Journal of Science,* 73 (1977), 98–100.
20. See pp. 317–22.
21. Craib, 'My Removal from Wits — 1946', *Bulletin of the Adler Museum of the History of Medicine,* 5 (Aug. 1979), 2–8.
22. Faculty of Medicine Misc./12/33.
23. Craib, 'My Removal from Wits'.
24. 'Reply to Questionnaire of Government Committee on Medical Training', Faculty of Medicine Misc./54/38.
25. Memoranda on establishment of dispensary services, Faculty of Medicine Misc./123/39, Council Misc./59/39.
26. Faculty of Medicine Misc./54/38.
27. Unpublished recollections of Professor Craib.
28. *Report of the Committee on Medical Training in South Africa,* 49.
29. 'Statistics: Medicine, Engineering, General', University Archives 211.
30. J.F. van Reenen, 'Some Developments in Dental Education at the University of the Witwatersrand, Johannesburg, over the Last 50 Years', *Journal of the Dental Association of South Africa,* 31 (1976), 661–5.
31. Faculty of Law Misc./31/34.
32. See McKerron's memorandum on the 1931 Attorney's Admission Bill, Ibid./36/31.
33. *Report of the Union Department of Education for 1935,* U.G. 55 of 1936, 53–4; Ibid. for 1939, U.G. 50 of 1940, 37–41.
34. For details on Balogh's career see the obituaries in the *Tulane Law Review,* 30 (1955–6), 315–8, and the *American Journal of Comparative Law,* 5 (1950), 174. For his selection see 'Chairs: Applications and Appointments 1932–38', University Archives 313.
35. Cullen to Raikes, 14 Jan. 1936, Balogh file, University Archives.
36. Balogh file, University Registry.
37. Greig to Raikes, 16 Aug. 1938, Ibid.
38. Council Misc./44/38.
39. Raikes to Secretary for Education, 30 June 1938; Secretary of Education to Raikes, 8 July 1938; Raikes to Secretary for Education, 27 Sept. 1938; Balogh file, University Registry.
40. Council Misc./46/38.
41. Ibid.,/57/38.
42. Ibid.,/14/39.
43. W.J. Busschau, 'Cecil Sydney Richards (1896–1974): An Appreciation of his Writings', *South African Journal of Economics,* 42 (1974), 111–17.
44. Richards, *The Iron and Steel Industry in South Africa* (Johannesburg, 1940), chap. 13.
45. C.S. Richards file, University Archives.
46. Faculty of Commerce Misc./119/32.

47. Ibid., 28/33 and 35/34.
48. Ibid.
49. 'Statistics: Medicine, Engineering, General', University Archives 211.
50. Raikes's speech to the S.R.C. dinner, 30 Nov. 1935, University Archives, 692 Raikes; A.N. Boyce, 'The History of the Johannesburg College of Education 1909–1968', (unpublished typescript).
51. Committee on secondary education, 5 Oct. 1937, Senate Misc./147/37.
52. 'Proposed taking over of the Johannesburg Normal College by the University', Senate Misc./87/30; *Provincial Finance Commission,* U.G. 46 of 1934.
53. Council Misc./13/38.
54. Special joint meetings of the Boards of the Faculties of Arts and Science, 18 May and 5 June 1936, Senate Misc./46/36, 50/36, 59/36, and 60/36.
55. Ibid., 147/37.
56. For Swart see M. Leveson (ed.), *Collected Poems: Vincent Swart* (Johannesburg, 1981).
57. Fouché to Margaret Hodgson, 19 Feb. 1934, MS. Ballinger A410/B2.16.1.
58. Fouché (ed.), *Diary of Adam Tas 1705–1706* (London, 1914), xxiii.
59. Hoernle to Macmillan, 11 April 1934, MS. Macmillan.
60. Frankel, *The Railway Policy of South Africa* (Johannesburg, 1928), 19, 46–7, 135 and 233–4.
61. Frankel, *Capital Investment in Africa* (London, 1938), chap. 1.
62. For Frankel's association with Hofmeyr see Paton, *Hofmeyr.*
63. *Star,* 3 Feb. 1947.
64. Senate Misc./51/33.
65. I.R. Hare, 'The Role of the Field Work Consultant in Social Work Education' (unpublished University of the Witwatersrand M.A. thesis, 1973), 66.
66. Ibid., 69–70; B.W. McKendrick, 'The Selection and Training of Social Work Manpower in South Africa' (unpublished University of the Witwatersrand Ph.D. thesis, 1980), 52–64.
67. *Star,* 14 June 1932.
68. J.C. Kannemeyer, *Geskiedenis van die Afrikaanse Literatuur* (Cape Town, 1978), 310. See also D.J. Opperman, *Digters van Dertig* (Cape Town, 1953).
69. Faculty of Arts Misc./30/34.
70. Board of the Faculty of Arts minutes, III, 28 Oct. & 13 Nov. 1931; Faculty of Arts Misc./195/31.
71. Macmillan to Mona Tweedie, Nov. 1931, MS. Macmillan.
72. Faculty of Arts Misc./195/31.
73. Ibid.,/177/30.
74. E. Roux, *Grass: A Story of Frankenwald* (Cape Town, 1969), 5.
75. Raikes to Professor D.W. Thompson, 10 Nov. 1932, Van der Horst file, University Archives.
76. Faculty of Science Misc./175/36.
77. National Research Council and Board, *The Research Position in the Universities of South Africa* (Johannesburg, 1940), 7.
78. Council Misc./73/40.
79. *Annual Report of the Department of Education for the year ending December* 1938, U.G. 59 of 1939, 46.
80. Council minutes, IV, 17 April 1936; Memorandum submitted to the Carnegie Corporation, Council Misc./9/36; T.E. Allibone, 'Basil Ferdinand Jamieson Schonland 1896–1972', *Biographical Memoirs of Fellows of the Royal Society,* 19 (Dec. 1973).
81. Ibid.
82. Ibid.; A.L. Hales, 'Research at the Bernard Price Institute of Geophysical Research, University of the Witwatersrand, Johannesburg', *Proceedings of the Royal Society,* 258 (1960), 1–26.
83. Council Misc./73/40.

PART IV
Students and Special Issues

9

QUESTIONS OF DISCRIMINATION

I

TRADITIONALLY, the Universities of Cape Town and the Witwatersrand have been seen by white South Africans as 'open'. *The Open Universities in South Africa,* published in 1957 on behalf of a joint conference of U.C.T. and Wits held in response to the plans of the Nationalist government to enforce segregated institutions of higher learning in South Africa, stated: 'The University of Cape Town and the University of the Witwatersrand are called the "Open Universities" because they admit non-white students as well as white students and aim, in all academic matters, at treating non-white students on a footing of equality with white students, and without segregation.'[1] In 1959 Parliament passed the Extension of University Education Act, which deprived the universities of South Africa of their autonomy in regard to the admission of black students. The 'white' teaching universities of South Africa were thereafter prohibited from admitting black students, except in special circumstances and only with ministerial permission.

The impression is sometimes given that the Universities of Cape Town and the Witwatersrand, prior to the government's intervention in 1959, had always followed 'open' admissions policies. Such an impression is conveyed by *The Open Universities in South Africa,* which traces the 'open' policies of the two universities back to their respective precursors, the South African College in Cape Town and the South African School of Mines and Technology in Johannesburg: 'At Cape Town the admission of the first non-white students to studies at the post-matriculation level dates from back to the turn of the century; in the case of the Witwatersrand the corresponding date was 1910.'[2] It is true that a handful of 'non-white' students had been admitted by the South African College, and one Chinese student by the School of Mines, and it is also true that the statutes adopted by the University of Cape

Town, and the University of the Witwatersrand, Johannesburg, provided for 'open' admissions. Statute 69 of the University of Cape Town and statute 72 of the University of the Witwatersrand alike stated that 'every person shall be entitled to become registered as a matriculated student of the University' who had obtained the matriculation certificate of the Joint Matriculation Board, or a recognized exemption from the J.M.B. matriculation examination. But the impression should not be gained from this that the two universities followed 'open' admissions policies from their inception.

A study of admissions policies indicates that at its inception Wits very much reflected the prejudices of the society to which it belonged. Only very slowly and hestitantly was it accepted that black students, African, Coloured, and Indian, should be admitted in any substantial numbers. It was not until World War II, when it became impossible for black students to continue to pursue their professional studies overseas, that Wits began to accept black students on any scale at all. Ironically, it did so at the request of government. The wartime Smuts government was particularly anxious that Wits should train black medical students, and made a number of scholarships available for the purpose. The number of black students at Wits consequently rose from 4 in 1939 to 87 by 1945.

While Wits never officially adopted a policy of excluding students on grounds of race or colour, at times it was sorely tempted to do so. The popular campaign launched in 1916 to establish a university in Johannesburg had emphasized that the new university would be for 'Europeans'. That the statutes adopted for the University of the Witwatersrand did not attempt to provide for an exclusive admissions policy owed much to the example of U.C.T., whose Act and statutes were closely followed, and to the influence of J.H. Hofmeyr, who had become Principal of the School of Mines in 1919. Hofmeyr, in his inaugural address as Principal in August 1919, first suggested that as a matter of policy the proposed new university should be open to all who possessed the necessary qualifications: 'It should know no distinctions of class or wealth, race or creed.'[3] In the 1920s and early 1930s the University's Council and Senate seriously contemplated officially adopting a restrictive admissions policy when blacks — first Coloureds and then Indians and Africans — began to apply for admission to the University. In 1926 Council appointed a committee 'to ascertain what procedure is necessary to empower the University to exclude students on the ground of colour'.[4] In the event, the University proved reluctant to take action itself, and sought instead to encourage the central government to adopt the appropriate measures to exclude black students from the 'white' universities, or else to provide separate facilities for blacks at the University, notably at the medical school.

The Hertzog governments of the 1920s and 1930s failed to act on either suggestion. The government's attitude on university admissions at the time was that it was entirely a matter for each university to decide.

As at U.C.T., the medical faculty was the main testing-ground of the University's admissions policies. In theology, education, and law, blacks could study for their degrees at Fort Hare and through the University of South Africa, but Wits and U.C.T. possessed the only medical schools in the country, and practical medical training in hospital wards was an especially touchy area. In 1921 U.C.T. persuaded an Indian applicant to its medical school to go elsewhere, but in 1926 the authorities at the University of the Witwatersrand swallowed hard and agreed to admit a Coloured student to its medical school. Six years later they refused to admit an African student to the medical school on the ground that segregated clinical facilities for him were not available. In 1934, the University Council, rather than continue looking for ways and means of excluding black students, agreed in principle to admit black applicants, though not until World War II were blacks accepted for clinical training at the University's medical school.

Race and colour were by no means the only issues on which the 'openness' of Wits, and its claim to be regarded as a 'democratic' and egalitarian university, were challenged. The place and rights of Jews, Afrikaans-speakers, and women within the University were also key issues raised from time to time during the 1920s and 1930s.

In the 1920s and 1930s, in South Africa as elsewhere, racism was often, in the ascendancy. After 1924, the Hertzog governments adopted an active policy of segregation, first in the economic sphere, where they extended and consolidated the colour bar, and later in the political sphere, where Cape Africans were removed from the common voters' roll in 1936. In Europe, these were the decades of National Socialism in Germany and Fascism in Italy, and in the United States, notably in the 1920s, of an aggressive 'nativism'.

While universities might wish to regard themselves as the leaders of society, often they merely reflect the society round them. In the 1920s and 1930s, universities in the Western world revealed a distinct tendency to mirror the prejudices of the dominant groups in their society. The very strength of assertive and exclusive nationalism and of anti-Semitism in German universities helped to ensure that they would fairly readily fall in behind the anti-Semitic policies of the Hitler regime. In the United States most major universities capitulated to those racial, ethnic, and religious prejudices stimulated by American participation in World War I, and which reached a pitch during the 'tribal twenties'. It was not simply a matter of southern and mid-western universities excluding blacks. Illustrious northern universities such as Harvard,

Yale, Princeton, and Columbia imposed admissions quotas on Jews and Catholics, and severely limited the intake of blacks. At Princeton, blacks were totally excluded.[5]

Not only were many white South Africans at the time opposed to the admission of blacks to the 'white' universities, but they also were hostile to providing them with a university education or professional training. In an economic climate that was often depressed, what was ultimately feared in certain professions was competition from blacks. White workers secured protection for themselves against black competition through the operation of the industrial colour bar; white professionals sometimes sought to achieve the same end by denying or limiting black access to professional training.

For white liberals in the 1920s and 1930s, the main concern with regard to the professions was that blacks should be allowed access to them, and not that they should receive professional training in the same institutions as whites. White liberals in South Africa were by no means committed to the idea of racial integration at all or even most levels, including higher education. R.F.A. Hoernle, the leading liberal intellectual of the inter-war years, insisted in the 1930s that integration did not represent the only response to the problems of a multi-racial South Africa that was consistent with liberal principles. Indeed, according to W.K. Hancock in his biography of Smuts, 'parallelism' was 'the orthodoxy, and not least the Liberal orthodoxy, of that time'. Concerning higher education specifically, Edgar Brookes, in his Phelps-Stokes lectures of 1933, argued 'I would make it clear that in my judgement an indiscriminate mixing everywhere is neither practicable nor desirable in the concrete circumstances of South Africa to-day, and that the existence of a special non-European institution of university standing at Fort Hare is all to the good.' He added the caveat that there should be some contact between blacks and whites in a university environment.[6]

II

In law and medicine, the two 'paying' professions that blacks were most interested in during the 1920s and 1930s, they could attain the basic degree qualifications for the former in South Africa, but not the latter. Blacks could secure their B.A. and LL.B. at Fort Hare and through the University of South Africa, though this by no means guaranteed them access to the legal profession. By refusing articles, and by an almost absolute refusal to admit blacks to the Bar, whites in the legal profession denied blacks entry into the profession. As late as 1943 J.D. Rheinallt Jones, in his capacity as a Senator representing Africans, advised D.L. Smit, the Secretary for Native Affairs, that even an African with an 'unusually good' academic record would find 'it is going to be very difficult to get articles in an attorney's office . . .'.[7] Indians usually found it easier than Africans, particularly among Durban lawyers with important Indian clienteles. With one exception, all black doctors who practised in South Africa prior to World War II secured their training overseas.

The medical profession was undoubtedly the most controversial and problematic on the question of providing blacks with the opportunity of a professional training. Within the profession there was a widely recognized need to train black doctors and nurses to 'serve their own people'. Great resentment, however, was caused in the profession, as in the wider white community, when black doctors dared to wait on white patients. In 1927 the white nurses at Mafeking Hospital went on strike against Dr Silas Molema, a member of the family that had founded Mafeking and a graduate of Glasgow University, when he attended white patients in the hospital, and their action was widely supported by country doctors. 'It is just as impossible for the native to resist the temptation to treat a European', an indignant Dr J.A. du Toit of Victoria West wrote to the *Journal of the Medical Association of South Africa,* 'as it is for our unfortunate and ignorant Europeans not to go to the native for treatment. The native doctor has attractions for the ignorant European by virtue of there being something mysterious about him, something of the "toor dokter".' The immediate consequence of the incident was that the Cape Provincial Administration adopted a new regulation that any registered medical practitioner not on the staff of the hospital in which he desired to attend paying patients would require written permission from the hospital board concerned in order to 'have access to the hospital for the purpose of so attending patients'. Dr H.A. Moffat of Cape Town, youngest son of the missionary John Moffat, dismissed the new regulation as 'a subterfuge, a disguised colour bar'. In a letter to the *Journal of the Medical Association of South Africa,* he asserted: 'If we do want to be unequal in our treatment of people because of their colour, let us say so and not be hypocrites. All sorts of reasons are given for this Regulation — there is only one.'[8]

The Mafeking incident caused considerable disquiet in the medical profession. Doctors, particularly in small towns, sometimes depended quite heavily on the cash trade they did with black patients, and they certainly resented losing white patients to black doctors. 'It is one of the paradoxes of segregationist South Africa', R.F.A. Hoernle told a meeting of the Institute of Race Relations in 1936, 'that Native, and generally non-European, medical men make most of their income from White patients.'[9]

To check the incipient challenge of black doctors to white practitioners the Federal Council of the Medical Association of South Africa, after a 'full discussion' of the question of 'native practitioners in relation to general hospitals', resolved at the end of 1927 that: 'It is eminently necessary that boards of public hospitals be empowered to withhold the privilege of attending upon patients in the hospital, or in any specified section thereof, from any person when, in the opinion of the board, or that of an official duly authorized thereto by a resolution of the board, such attendance may result in, or be likely to cause, difficulty in the efficient administration of the hospital.'[10] In 1928 the Transvaal Provincial Council passed a new Public Hospitals Ordinance which allowed hospital boards to refuse 'to any registered medical practitioner access to any public hospital or to any specified portion thereof, provided that any such practitioner may appeal to the Administrator whose decision in the matter shall be final'.[11] The ordinance was later used to exclude black medical students from the wards of the Johannesburg General Hospital. According to a Senate document of 1954, the presence of the University's first black medical student, J.T. du Randt, at the General Hospital had prompted an official interpretation of the ordinance so as to exclude black medical students from the hospital: 'The term "Medical Practitioner" was, by this interpretation, extended to include "medical student". The power of exclusion, however, was not applied in Du Randt's case.'[12] In 1933 Du Randt duly became the medical school's first black graduate.

In 1928, with the publication of the report of the Loram Committee appointed by the Department of Native Affairs to 'inquire into the training of natives in medicine and public health', the whole question of medical training for blacks became a matter of national debate. Chaired by C.T. Loram, the former chief inspector of Native Education for Natal and a member of the Union Native Affairs Commission, the six-man committee included Professor Raymond Dart of the University of the Witwatersrand. After drawing attention to the inadequate supply of doctors for the black population, to the 'excessively high' rate of infantile and maternal mortality among blacks, and to the rise in the general death rate in 'the more congested and impoverished areas', the committee stated: 'Such a condition of things is a double menace to South Africa. Firstly, there is the immediate danger of the spread of infectious and contagious diseases from areas where they may be said to be practically endemic. Secondly, there is the economic danger of the deterioration and eventual failure of the labour supply, which is already forming the subject of special inquiry in Kenya and the Congo.' To help to rectify the situation, the committee recommended the creation of a government Native Medical Service, and urged that facilities be created in South Africa to train blacks as medical practitioners for the service. Six black doctors, who had gone over to the United Kingdom for their training, were already practising successfully in the Union and Basutoland, and this convinced the committee that, 'there is no doubt but that medical work attracts them [Africans] and that they are capable of completing the course.'[13]

While the committee more or less automatically accepted that blacks would have to be trained separately from whites, it insisted that they be trained to the same standard required of white doctors. In this it broke sharply from the proposal then being canvassed by Colonel Sir Edward Thornton, the Union's senior assistant Health Officer and later honorary Professor of Public Health at Wits, that blacks should be trained, as in French West Africa, not as medical practitioners but as auxiliary medical officers. In the proposal he put to the Loram Committee, he contended that such a scheme would help keep down costs; it would retain the authority in black areas of white medical officers, the district surgeons; and would help to ensure that blacks would not be able to compete with white doctors in urban areas.[14] In a later paper to a Durban conference of the Medical Association of South Africa, called to consider the question of medical training for blacks, Thornton protested strongly against the prospect of 'opening the profession to a specially subsidized invasion by natives.'[15]

When insisting on a full training for black medical practitioners, rather than the institution of a lower-grade diploma for medical auxiliaries, the Loram Committee pointed out that as the problems of health and disease were the same among blacks as among whites, they required the same skilled treatment. It contended that 'the Natives themselves demand the same standard of training and are unwilling to accept anything inferior'. The committee further contended that should black doctors be employed in the proposed government Native Medical Service then this would 'tend to minimize very considerably the likelihood of European patients in other parts being treated by Native doctors, and should thus help to relieve a situation which threatens grave disturbance to South Africa'. The committee urged that the government Native Medical Service should also include 'health assistants' and nurse-midwives, and that as the training of black doctors would be a long and slow process, a crash programme should be launched for training assistants and nurse-midwives.[16]

For the training of black doctors, the Loram Committee recommended the creation of 'a non-European branch of the medical school of the University of the Witwatersrand'. The committee considered the cost of establishing an entirely new medical school for blacks would be 'prohibitive' and 'beyond the present resources of the Union', and therefore an existing school should be utilized. It proposed that blacks should undertake the preliminary year at the South African Native College at Fort Hare, which had been incorporated as an institution of higher learning in 1923, and then proceed to Johannesburg for the remainder of their course. The committee chose Johannesburg largely because of 'the abundance of clinical material' available there, and 'the comparative proximity of Johannesburg to rural Native areas'.[17]

The recommendations of the Loram Committee in essentials accorded with the proposals that Wits had submitted to the committee, and which the University saw as perhaps the most positive way of dealing with the problem posed by black applicants to enter the medical school. In 1925 the question of the admission of blacks to the medical school had first been directly raised when a Coloured student applied for admission for the next year. The University's Council responded by seeking legal advice whether it was entitled to exclude the applicant on the grounds of colour. The legal opinion was to the contrary. H.J. Hofmeyr, in his capacity as solicitor to the Council, advised in November 1925 'that after careful perusal of the University Act and Statutes, he found no provision that would warrant the exclusion from the University by the Council of a non-European student'.[18] This was similar to the legal advice given to U.C.T. in 1921, when an Indian had applied to enter its medical school. The advice was repeated in 1926 when Wits approached Advocates Solomon and Manfred Nathan for their opinion.[19] Council consequently resolved 'that no action be taken' on the Coloured applicant, which meant that he was admitted in 1926.[20]

At the time, the admission of a black student to the University was seen as a truly momentous step. To advise the University on policy for the future on black admissions, Senate appointed a committee, to which Council added four members, including J.H. Hofmeyr in his capacity as Vice-Chancellor. In its report of 19 October 1926, the joint committee recommended that statute 72 of the University be amended to read permissively rather than affirmatively, and that the University seek legal opinion whether under such an amendment 'the Council would have the power to exclude students on the grounds of colour with or without regulations'.[21] The opinion of Solomon and Nathan was that the proposed amendment was 'open to the same objections as the existing Statute'.[22] It failed, in other words, to empower the University to exclude students on the basis of colour. It was in this situation that Council decided, in December 1926, to appoint its own committee, consisting of Alexander Aiken, the chairman of the finance committee, and H.J. Hofmeyr, the University's solicitor, to ascertain the procedures required to empower the University to exclude students on the grounds of colour.

Because Council and its committee were reluctant to enshrine a racist clause in the University's statutes, the procedure recommended by the committee was to attempt to 'induce' the government to 'introduce a General Bill empowering any University in South Africa to exclude students on the ground of colour'. Legislation already existed to empower the colleges associated with the University of South Africa to exclude blacks. Section 17 of the Higher Education Additional Provision Act of 1917, which had applied to the South African School of Mines and Technology, provided that: 'A college authority shall have the right to refuse admittance to the college to any applicant therefor, if it considers that refusal is in the best interests of the college.' The Council of the University of the Witwatersrand, wishing for similar legislation for universities, approached the state to this end, but the government failed to take any action.[23] However, clause 47(3) of the Public Hospitals Ordinance adopted by the Transvaal in 1928, and the official interpretation given to it, enabled the University in future to exclude blacks from its medical school.

A less negative approach on the part of the University to the question of black admissions to the medical school was made possible by the appointment of the Loram Committee in 1927. This enabled the University to come forward with the proposal that blacks should be admitted to the medical school, but with separate facilities to be provided for them entirely at government expense.

In July 1927 Professor Dart, as a member of the Loram Committee, approached the University for a statement of its attitude to the provision of medical education for blacks in South Africa. The matter was referred in the first instance to the Faculty of Medicine, which recommended that the training of black doctors in South Africa should be carried out under the aegis of one of the existing medical schools, and that they should be given the same training as whites. The Faculty stated further:

> That, under the social conditions of South Africa, the training would require to be given in separate buildings.
> That the number of students qualified to pursue the training is unlikely to be sufficient, for many years to come, to justify on economic grounds the establishment of the required buildings, even at existing schools.
> That, although as indicated above, this University could undertake the training, it must be borne in mind that such training is very costly and could not be met except by additional financial provision in the way of both capital and current expenditure.[24]

When these recommendations came before Senate, Professor W.M. Macmillan of the Department of History proposed they be deleted and replaced by a more positive policy statement:

> That this University is prepared to undertake this training.
> That, in so far as, under the social conditions of South Africa, it is expedient to make provision for separate classes, additional expenditure, both capital and current, would have to be incurred.[25]

This new proposal was accepted both by Senate and the Faculty of Medicine.

The matter then went before Council, which at a special meeting on 24 October 1927, approved the resolutions to be presented on behalf of the University to the Loram Committee. These resolutions were:

(a) That, if the Government decides that provision of facilities for the training of Non-Europeans in medicine should be provided, the Council considers that no separate school should be instituted for the purpose, but that the facilities should be offered by one of the existing Medical Schools.

(b) That this University is prepared to undertake the training under the following conditions:
   (i) In view of the strong prejudices of the Community, Non-European students cannot be admitted to the existing medical classes for European students; but they must be taught in separate classes.
   (ii) The same training should be given and the same standard demanded as for European Medical Students.
   (iii) As the finances of this University cannot support the additional burden entailed by the establishment of classes for Non-European Medical Students, full provision should be made for such additional cost, including the necessary buildings and equipment as well as the recurring expenses.

Despite the Loram Committee's recommendations in favour of creating separate medical classes for blacks at Wits, nothing was done to establish such classes prior to World War II. Blacks who wished to qualify as doctors continued to go overseas for their main training.

The economic depression after 1929, with the consequent reduction in government expenditure on education, in part explains the failure to implement the recommendations of the Loram Committee regarding black doctors. But more important was the hostility of sections of the medical profession to the idea of training black doctors in South Africa.

The medical profession in the country was deeply divided. Dr C. Louis Leipoldt, the Afrikaans poet and medical man, as editor of the *Journal of the*

Medical Association of South Africa, adopted a consistently liberal stance. He even questioned the need for separate classes for blacks, and urged that they simply join the existing classes. As he argued in a leading article on 'Medical Training of Natives' on 22 December 1928: 'We work and live alongside of and in close proximity to natives in all phases of our life, and do not find any great difficulty in doing so. Deep down in our hearts we have no real antipathy to the native. Why, as educated University men, do we not act as true citizens of the Universities and throw our portals open wide to anyone, whatever his colour, who satisfies the same conditions as the European?' But the Medical Association was not so broad-minded. In a memorandum sent to the government in 1931 on 'Medical Services for Rural Areas, with special reference to Native Areas and the Training of Native Medical Practitioners', the Federal Council of the Medical Association of South Africa submitted that the government, rather than devote limited resources to training black medical practitioners, would be better advised to train a corps of black male and female 'Nursing Aids' for the 'Native areas'. The memorandum contended that the very limited supply of black matriculants would not 'warrant the large expenditure which would be necessary to enable their training in South African medical schools', the clinical training of blacks in hospitals would raise grave social and administrative difficulties, and it would prove difficult even to confine their training to the black wards as 'the Native wards of the hospital furnish very important material for the training of European students, [and] they are in charge of European Sisters and Staff Nurses'. The Association's memorandum also rejected the proposal that the government should subsidize the training of black doctors abroad on the ground that this would 'offer Natives advantages which would not be available to Europeans'.[26]

As an indignant Dr H.A. Moffat wrote in the *Journal,* the Federal Council's memorandum simply provided the government with an excuse to do nothing about training black doctors. He added: 'The reasons given as difficulties are unworthy of the Executive. European students may be deprived of clinical material! Is such a consideration to be allowed to deprive Natives of a right? It is the old story that the Native is to come in only to the leavings of the European.' The conclusion he came to was that 'The prejudice and fear of competition for the European from the Native doctors are contemptible.'[27]

Even though the Rockefeller Foundation offered to put up £65 000, the government failed to take any steps towards providing special facilities for the training of black doctors in South Africa. In reply to a question by J.H. Hofmeyr in the House of Assembly, the Minister of Native Affairs, E.G. Jansen, stated in 1931 that the time had not 'yet arrived when an institution should be established for the training of natives in medicine'. He explained that very few blacks were interested in training as doctors and that those who did qualify tended not to go to 'the native areas', but rather 'the professional men among the natives prefer to compete with the Europeans by obtaining a clientele in the towns'.[28]

Wits never subscribed to the view that blacks should be denied the opportunity of a medical training within South Africa itself. With the exception of Dr Hans Pirow on Council, the Council, Senate, and Faculty of Medicine, were in favour of providing for the medical training of blacks at Wits, but they all also accepted that classes for blacks and whites would need to be separate. They were convinced that mixed classes might lead to racial friction. As the Registrar, H. van der Brugge, had explained to the Secretary for Education in 1927, while there had been 'little trouble' over the admission of a Coloured student the year previously, 'chiefly owing to the discreet attitude of the student himself', it was none the less 'expected that considerable friction may arise, both amongst the students and also possibly between coloured students and members of the staff, when one of the former should enter the second year of study, which embraces the subjects of Anatomy and Physiology'.[29]

In the years immediately after the Loram Committee's report, the University sought to encourage the government to take action on the question of black admissions to the country's medical schools, preferably in the direction of providing separate facilities for blacks at Wits. But the government did absolutely nothing, and rather than challenge white prejudices at all directly, the University resorted to the policy of refusing blacks admission to its medical school.

In mid-1931 the University received from Mr A. Mtimkulu, of Ndabeni, Cape Town, and 'obviously of native birth', an application for the admission of his son to the Wits medical school for the next year. Laughton Mtimkulu who had matriculated in 1928, had completed the first year course in Arts at Fort Hare, and was then studying the preliminary course for medicine at the same institution. The response of the University's Council and Principal Raikes was to seek an interview with the Secretary for Education, S.F.N. Gie, and possibly even the Minister of Education, Dr D.F. Malan. As the Registrar wrote to Gie:

> The Council is fully aware that the final responsibility for making a decision in a case of this nature rests on its shoulders and does not wish to avoid that responsibility. At the same time it is considered that a matter of this kind is almost necessarily involved with social complications of a possibly far-reaching character, and the Council is naturally anxious to

keep its policy in accord with what must ultimately become the settled trend of Higher Education in South Africa, or at least of the Northern provinces.

Raikes subsequently met the Ministers of Education and Native Affairs, and also the Secretaries for Education, Native Affairs, and Health, and urged that the government should adopt the Loram Committee's recommendation and provide separate facilities for black medical students at Wits.[30] From the evidence it is not clear what happened to Laughton Mtimkulu, but he did not attend the medical school at Wits.

In 1932 another African, R.J. Xaba, who had already completed his pre-clinical training, applied for admission to the Wits medical school. The idea of admitting an African to a clinical training at the University proved unacceptable to the Faculty of Medicine, and Mr Xaba was refused admission. The excuse used to exclude him was that the University could not offer him an adequate clinical training. The Johannesburg General Hospital, while prepared to admit him to the Non-European Hospital, would not allow him into the 'white' wards. At its meeting on 3 May 1932, the Board of the Faculty of Medicine resolved that 'on account of the social difficulties, it is impossible at present to give an adequate medical education to Native students'.

The Faculty of Medicine, in other words, was prepared to take a policy decision to exclude Africans from the medical school, or at least from its clinical training. Senate, however, on the initiative of W.M. Macmillan, resolved that the University should again approach the government on 'the matter of Medical education for Natives'. Macmillan wrote to a friend: 'Senate unexpectedly lively: the medical people having recommended refusing admission to a native on grounds of expense of making "suitable" (and unnecessary) provision for him, I led a fight. Had a grand scrap and got them to agree fairly readily at least to press on the government the need to make the "necessary" arrangements; there was more support than might have been for setting the university against the government.'[31]

On 11 June 1932 Raikes duly wrote to the Secretary for Education, on behalf of the Senate, 'The Senate is well aware of the difficulties inherent in this problem, but at the same time wishes to bring to the notice of the Minister of Education the fact that the number of applications from coloured and native students is increasing, and no definite policy has been laid down indicating a clear line of action for University Councils to follow.' He reiterated that, if the government provided the finance, Wits was prepared to establish separate classes for black medical students. In his reply, Gie advised that the Minister of Education had already made it clear to the University that in 'the existing financial circumstances' it was impossible for the government to provide additional facilities for black medical students, and that it was entirely a matter for the University to decide who it would or would not admit as a student: 'The Department can only state that it is a matter which must be dealt with by the authorities of the University in terms of its Act and Statutes in the best interests of the institution.'[32]

In short, although the Hertzog government was not prepared to provide for the training of black doctors in South Africa, it never took any steps to discourage Wits from accepting blacks into its medical school, and had even resisted suggestions that it should seek to lay down a general policy on the question of admission for universities to follow. The University's own hesitations were responsible for keeping blacks out of its medical school.

Principal Raikes was himself something of a High Tory paternalist, genuinely anxious to provide a medical training for blacks. But he was also apprehensive of offending the government and white public opinion, and was certainly reluctant to challenge white susceptibilities. The formula that Raikes generally used to sum up his position was that he believed in white ascendancy, but not white domination. 'We should endeavour to maintain our ascendancy', he told an S.R.C. dinner in 1933, 'but reaching out always for the further development of the natives at the same time.' The point he appreciated was that the University could not afford to run completely counter to white opinion, and he was consequently anxious to get some sort of lead from government. Like many others at Wits at the time, he truly dreaded racial incidents arising out of the admission of black students, and the medical school was seen as particularly vulnerable. His caution, as well as his concern to placate white susceptibilities, is very evident in the letter he sent to the S.R.C., in June 1932, which, while granting the request that student societies be allowed to invite black visitors from time to time, made them subject to stringent rules, including the provision of separate seating. Raikes concluded that he reserved the right to refuse permission for blacks to attend a meeting when, entirely at his own discretion, he 'should judge that there might be a possibility of racial friction'.[33]

In 1934 the University's authorities took the deliberate decision to adopt a more positive or 'open' policy on the question of black admissions to the University. As was announced in the Council's annual report for 1934:

> In the course of the year several enquiries were received from, or on behalf of, prospective students of Indian, Coloured and Native birth. Since the Act and Statutes of the University do not make mention of differences of colour or race, enquiries were treated without reference to such contingencies and it may therefore be expected that students

belonging to those categories will, in the near future, offer themselves for the various courses of study. It is hoped that the exercise of tact and discretion will avoid the difficulties which are sometimes attendant upon the closer contact of the various races.

1935 was consequently to become a 'landmark' year in the evolution of Wits as an 'open' university. Several blacks were admitted to the University, including an African to post-graduate study at the medical school. Dr M.C.C. Motebang, who had received his M.B., Ch.B. from Edinburgh University, was admitted to the course for the diploma in public health. In 1935 the University also appointed its first black member of the academic staff, B.W. Vilakazi, as a language assistant in the Department of Bantu Studies.

Several factors inclined the University to adopt a more 'open' policy in regard to black admissions. White liberal opinion in South Africa was beginning to press for the admission of blacks to at least some of the country's universities. For instance, in his Phelps-Stokes lectures of 1933, Edgar Brookes urged that 'though non-European students should not be admitted *everywhere*, they should surely be admitted *somewhere* — and this in no spirit of grudging tolerance, but with the hearty and unequivocal welcome of staff and students alike'. He added: 'I should regard the University which succeeded in carrying through such a policy and at the same time keeping the loyalty of its European students of both races, as the first complete University institution in South Africa, destined to lead University education for years to come'.[34] Within the University, Professor R.F.A. Hoernlé served as an articulate champion of this point of view. Important also was the growing pressure from blacks themselves for admission to Wits. In 1934 the University was formally challenged on its admissions' policy by a black educational institution. The Principal of Sastri College, the Indian high school in Durban, inquired whether Indians were admitted as students of the University of the Witwatersrand. A Council committee, chaired by H.J. Hofmeyr, was established in November 1934 to consider the matter, and it resolved to instruct the Registrar to reply:

> I am directed to inform you that the statutory condition laid down for admission is that the candidate shall be in possession of a matriculation certificate of the South African Joint Matriculation Board or of a certificate of exemption issued by the same Board.[35]

In the following year the first Indians to attend the University were admitted to the Faculty of Arts. In 1938 I.M. Bawa and A.H.I. Mulla became the first Indian graduates of Wits, and in 1940 Mulla was awarded the LL.B. degree.

The change in the country's government in 1933 was another factor which inclined the University to adopt a more 'open' admissions policy. In March 1933, following South Africa's abandonment of the gold standard, a coalition government was formed, with Hertzog as Prime Minister and Smuts as Deputy Prime Minister. D.F. Malan, who disapproved of a coalition, left the Cabinet, and was replaced as Minister of the Interior, Education, and Public Health by Jan Hofmeyr. The new Minister of Education, a former Principal and Vice-Chancellor of the University of the Witwatersrand, was a liberal who positively approved the idea that Wits should open its door to black students. Prior to 1933 Raikes, without question, had been reluctant to run counter to the segregationist policy of the Pact and Nationalist governments. The policy of the Fusion government remained segregationist, but it possessed a Minister of Education who was prepared to encourage, and defend, liberal experiments.

By 1934–5, while the University of the Witwatersrand cannot be said to have thrown its door wide open to black students, it had nudged the door ajar. Prior to World War II, black students at the University remained very small in number, and blacks continued to be denied access to a clinical training at the University's medical school.

Undoubtedly the most dramatic development in this context in the mid-thirties was the appointment of an African to the teaching staff in the Department of Bantu Studies. The Department's interests dictated that it should be something of a front-runner on the question of the admission of blacks to the University. In 1925, after some badgering of the University authorities, 'a limited number of selected Natives' had first been admitted to the annual vacation course in African Studies, and in 1931 the Department had enrolled its first black student, J.S. Twala, a clerk-interpreter in the employment of the Department of Native Affairs. He was admitted to the courses for the lower diploma in Bantu Studies, which rarely had more than two or three students. In August 1934 the Matriculation Exemptions Committee of the Senate recommended that Twala be given a 'mature age' exemption so as to be able to proceed to the B.A. degree.[36] In the next year B.W. Vilakazi, who had received his B.A. degree from the University of South Africa, took up his appointment as a language assistant in the Department of Bantu Studies. He also enrolled to study for an Honours degree at Wits.

Professor C.M. Doke, the Head of the Department of Bantu Studies, had strongly urged Vilakazi's appointment on the ground that 'for the proper teaching of Bantu languages at the University, an African Native Assistant is needed'. 'The principle of learning any foreign language from the native speaker of that language', he explained in a memorandum to Council, 'is one which need not be emphasized — French from a Frenchman, German from a German, Zulu from a Zulu.'³⁷ The appointment, sanctioned only after some furious in-fighting in Senate and Council, provoked a storm of controversy once announced. Such was the extent of public criticism that a Senate committee, chaired by Principal Raikes, felt constrained to issue a press statement that the appointment was subject to certain conditions. In status Vilakazi was a language assistant, not a lecturer; no student would be compelled to avail himself of his assistance; and the language assistant would have no disciplinary authority over students.³⁸ Vilakazi, who remained at the University until his death in 1947, was never given a full lectureship. He received his B.A.Hons in 1936, his M.A. in 1938, and his D.Litt. in 1946.

B.W. Vilakazi

The University's authorities had always anticipated that the admission of blacks would expose the University to powerful criticism from segregationists, but the timing of their more 'open' policy meant that the University did have a Minister of Education prepared to defend it against such criticism in Parliament. In 1936, and again in 1937, J.H. Hofmeyr defended both Wits and U.C.T. against their critics in the House of Assembly.

In 1936 the main attack against Wits and U.C.T. was led by the Revd C.W.M. du Toit, the Nationalist M.P. for Colesberg, who wanted to know what had happened to 'our segregation principle in connection with our higher education'. In his reply in the Assembly on 3 June 1936, Hofmeyr made it clear that the question of admissions was a matter of university autonomy and that he had no intention of prohibiting universities from admitting black students:

> All I can do is to prohibit the universities, by means of legislation, from registering non-European students. I do not intend to do that. I do not regard the universities as Government institutions, but as State-aided institutions, and I regard it as part of the policy of the universities, whether they want to register non-European students or not.

He added that he believed that public opinion acted as a major constraint on the universities, and that they would find they could not afford to move too far in advance of white public opinion in opening up their facilities to blacks: 'The universities are, in the first place, responsible to the public, because if they do not get support from the public they cannot get support from us either, and then they cannot continue. Therefore, if the universities do not follow a policy which the public approves of they would very soon feel the consequences.'[39] His statement accurately summed up the sentiments that prevailed at Wits.

In the next year the attack was renewed by J.D. Verster, the United Party M.P. for Zwartruggens, who claimed that not even the Minister of Education would 'like to see a non-European next to him in the street wearing the blazer of his university'. Hofmeyr reiterated that under the law as it stood universities were free to admit black students, and that he was 'not prepared to introduce legislation into the House that will definitely prohibit the universities from registering non-European students'.[40]

Hofmeyr's first term as Minister of Education, from 1933 to 1938, was also of major importance for the question of a medical training for blacks, although his initiative in this regard did not receive general approval at Wits. Soon after taking office Hofmeyr appointed an inter-departmental committee, under the chairmanship of Sir Edward Thornton, then senior Health Officer of the Union, to inquire into 'native medical education'. The Thornton Committee report was not published, but not unexpectedly it recommended in favour of Thornton's own proposal for training black medical auxiliaries, or medical aids as they were called, at least as a temporary measure. The committee declared that there were too few black students available for a full medical course to justify the provision of a separate medical school for them, and it also declared against admitting black medical students to Wits or U.C.T. on the ground of 'insurmountable' racial difficulties. The proposed shortened course for medical aids was to extend over five years, the first four at Fort Hare and a final practical year at the McCord Zulu Hospital in Durban. Those who qualified as medical aids were 'to serve in the Native Territories under the supervision of Medical Practitioners'. At Hofmeyr's request, the Chamber of Mines agreed to put up £75 000 to finance the scheme, which was implemented in 1936.[41]

The recommendations of the Thornton Committee ran completely counter to those of the Loram Committee, and the scheme favoured by Wits. The University remained anxious to establish, at government expense, separate facilities and classes for black students at its medical school, and had used the opportunity provided by the formation of the Fusion government to revive the proposal for parallel medical classes for blacks. In May 1933 Professor Dart persuaded Senate to adopt the motion 'that the Council request the Government to reconsider again the question of founding a medical school for non-Europeans'. In June, Raikes sent a memorandum to Hofmeyr on the subject, and later a deputation from Wits interviewed the minister at his office in Pretoria. From the account provided by Professor W.H. Craib, a member of the deputation, the meeting was in the nature of a disaster: 'I recall particularly how, during the interview, Principal Raikes, greatly incensed by the Minister's somewhat offhand and almost discourteous handling of the deputation, rather rudely upbraided Mr. Hofmeyr for his lack of civility. Indeed, we withdrew rather like a pack of school-boys too big for their boots and summarily put in their place. Hofmeyr and Raikes disliked each other, for good reasons on both sides.'[42]

When the contents of the Thornton Committee report became known in mid-1934, a Senate committee consisting of Raikes, Dart, and Craib was set up to formulate the University's response.[43] The committee declared that it was not necessarily opposed to the concept of black medical aids, as a transition stage only, but it thought that they should be trained in Johannesburg rather than at Fort Hare. Ideally, it believed that a full medical training should be made available to blacks, and the Rand was the most suitable centre for such training.[44]

As part of its investigations, the Senate committee undertook a survey of the attitude among Wits medical students to the training of black doctors. A questionnaire on the 'Medical Education of Non-Europeans' was sent out to the students, who were told that 'In this particular question the attitude of future medical citizens is of prime importance.'[45] The returns to the questionnaire indicated that the large majority of medical students at Wits favoured the medical training of blacks, carried out in South Africa and to the same standard as whites, but that such training should be provided in an entirely new medical school. Should the medical training of blacks be undertaken by Wits, the students indicated most affirmatively that separate buildings and classes for blacks would need to be provided. On the question of where 'fully-qualified native doctors' should be allowed to practise, 74 students indicated they should be confined to 'native territories', 115 that they be allowed to practise in 'prescribed areas', such as locations as well the territories, and 87 that they be permitted to practise 'anywhere they please'.[46]

The Wits questionnaire exercised no visible influence on government policy, and in 1936 Fort Hare embarked on the training of black medical aids. The scheme did not prove a success. As Alexander Kerr, the first Principal of Fort Hare, has recalled in his history *Fort Hare 1915–48*:

> At first there was enthusiasm for the new course and the prospects of employment it offered; but when later it was realized that after three years, the normal length of a degree course, there was no recognized medical or university qualification beyond the Diploma, there began to be difficulty in securing the requisite number of recruits.[47]

After investigation by a committee of the Department of Native Affairs in 1942, the Medical Aid Diploma was scrapped.[48]

The Fort Hare medical aid scheme was designed entirely for Africans, and no special provision had been made for the medical training of Indians and Coloureds in South Africa. In 1938 Wits took the decision to admit three Indian students to the pre-clinical study of medicine at the University; they would be allowed to complete the first three years of study at Wits, and would then have to proceed overseas for the remainder of their training. When in 1939 Mr K.J. Tavaria, the uncle of one of the Indian students, approached Jan Hofmeyr, now Chancellor of the University, to get him 'to try and remove the colour-bar in the Hospital, whereby non-European students are prevented from proceeding beyond the third year of study', Hofmeyr referred the matter to the University's Council, and it refused to take any action. At its meeting on 23 June 1939 Council resolved 'to inform Mr Tavaria that the Council regrets it is unable to take up this matter under present circumstances'. In the next year the Indian students went direct to the Board of the Johannesburg Hospital which, without consulting the University, decided to permit them to attend 'the non-European wards' of the Hospital.[49] A new era had dawned for the University, and for blacks who wished to secure a full medical training in their own country.

The outbreak of World War II in September 1939 transformed the whole situation in regard to the medical training of blacks by making it impossible for them to continue to go overseas for any part of their training. The war, more than anything else, obliged Wits to open its doors more widely to black students. In so far as Wits ever became an 'open' university, it did so as a consequence of World War II.

Prior to the war, U.C.T. rather than Wits led the attempt to bring white and black together in the same classes. The relatively dramatic rise in the number of black matriculants in the 1930s was reflected much more in U.C.T.'s intake than in Wits's. Between 1901 and 1934 some 253 blacks in South Africa had achieved matriculation passes; in the years 1934 to 1937 there were 389 black matriculation passes. There was a sudden jump from 78 passes in 1935 to 124 in 1936. The progress was such that in 1937 Fort Hare ceased to take on new students for the matriculation certificate, and enrolled only those seeking a higher education. There were 115 matriculated students, mainly African, at Fort Hare in 1937; 40 black students, overwhelmingly Coloured and Indian, at U.C.T.; and 10 black students at Wits, 5 African, and 5 Coloureds and Indians.[50]

III

Prior to World War II, as after, the majority of Wits students were English-speaking and nominally Christian; Raikes described them as 'British'. But in the period before the war Wits included many more Afrikaans-speaking students than was the case in later decades, and Jews and Afrikaners constituted substantial minority groups. On occasion there were suggestions, or accusations, of anti-Semitism in the official policy of the University, but it was generally recognized that anti-Semitism had little place in the University, particularly in its official policy. The question of Afrikaners was another matter. In a country that was officially bilingual, language rights were at issue, and the charge sometimes made, especially in the thirties, was that Wits discriminated against Afrikaans students by teaching only in English. The charge related particularly to the Faculties of Medicine and Engineering, for Wits, and U.C.T., both English-medium, were the only South African universities with these faculties.

In the thirties the proportion of students at Wits who were Jewish averaged about 28 per cent, and the proportion of Afrikaans students increased steadily, from under 20 per cent in 1930 to 25 per cent by 1935.[51] The Jewish students were overwhelmingly first generation South Africans, the sons and daughters of immigrants drawn chiefly from Eastern Europe. The main East European Jewish immigration into South Africa had been in the three decades before World War I, but with a substantial inflow in the twenties.[52] However, by the end of the thirties only a handful of the Jewish students at Wits were not South African born. Medicine, dentistry, law and arts provided the most popular faculties among Jewish students, and generally the University provided the Rand's Jewish community with a major channel for upward mobility into the professions. In a generation the University produced a large Jewish professional class on the Rand. Few pre-war Jewish students had themselves been the offspring of professional men. According to the statistics provided in the report of the Botha Committee on medical training in South Africa in 1939, 75 per cent of the Jewish medical students at Wits had fathers in commerce, and only 5 per cent in the professions, yet Jews constituted 42 per cent of the University's medical students.[53]

The University's Afrikaans students were spread among all faculties, but with a distinctly higher proportion in medicine and engineering than the others. A feature of the Afrikaans students was the relatively high proportion, particularly in medicine and engineering, who were drawn from outside Johannesburg. Their entry into Wits reflected the whole process of the urbanization of Transvaal Afrikaners. According to the Botha Committee's statistics, a third of all the medical students at Wits came from outside Johannesburg, but nearly two-thirds of the Afrikaans students were from out of town. A third of the fathers of Afrikaans medical students were farmers.

From the outset, Jewish students were active in student affairs, and the first suggestions and accusations of anti-Semitism concerned student clubs. In 1919 the Biological Society was re-named the Biological and Medical Society to allow more scope to the medical students, but in the University's first year the medical students broke away to form the Medical Students' Society. The latter's committee was strongly Jewish, and it struggled to secure S.R.C. recognition, allegedly because of resentment against a Jewish takeover of medical student organization. Apparently, Principal Hofmeyr had to intervene before the society was recognized. The S.R.C. proved even more reluctant to recognize the Students' Jewish Association. Formed in 1921, it was denied recognition in that year on the ground that it was a religious society confined in its membership to a religious group. While it was free to operate at the University, as was the Students' Christian Association, it could not be given any official standing. In the next year the association re-applied for recognition, claiming that it was not a religious society but primarily a group for the study of Jewish literature, culture, and history. The application was again refused. In 1925 the association was finally granted recognition.[54]

Although the Students' Jewish Association thought that prejudice obstructed its recognition, an important point of principle was in fact at stake. The S.R.C. was not prepared to extend official recognition to societies that were exclusively racial or religious in purpose and composition, and it has retained that position ever since. All recognized student societies are required to be open to all students.

These initial skirmishes aside, Jewish students found little active resistance to their participation in student affairs and activities, and they played a prominent role in the S.R.C., rag, and sports. In the award of scholarships there were occasional allegations of bias against Jews, but it seems evident that the University was free of any major scandal involving discrimination against Jewish students. The one *cause célèbre* that gave rise to allegations of anti-Semitism concerned the appointment of a member of staff. In late 1931 Dr W.H. Craib was appointed Professor of Medicine over the heads of a number of fancied Jewish candidates, and this provoked a major rumpus, leading to the resignation from the Department of Medicine of five prominent Jewish physicians.

As is evident from his own memoir on the incident, Craib was himself convinced that the opposition to him was rooted in a sense that his appointment represented a derogation of the Jewish doctors on the University's clinical staff.[55] However, in the minutes of Senate and the Board of the Faculty of Medicine relating to the incident, no mention was made of allegations of anti-Semitism; the objections to Craib's appointment were couched in different terms. The main complaint was that as the four candidates for the chair, Dr Arthur Bloom, Dr Loswel Israel Braun, Dr Henry Lewis Heiman, and Dr William Hofmeyr Craib, all possessed qualifications that were approximately equal, preference should have been given to one of the three who were 'already members of the Hospital Staff and have served the University as clinical teachers for a number of years'. Craib, who had only recently returned to South Africa from Britain, had no local standing, and little clinical experience. What was unique about him was his scientific background, and it was this that had impressed the selection committee, which was itself composed mainly of scientists rather than clinicians. In a committee comprising of Principal Raikes, Professor R.A. Dart, J.M. Watt, A.D. Stammers, C. Ritchie Thomson, and O.K. Williamson, the retiring Professor of Medicine, Dr A.S. Strachan, Head of the Department of Pathology and Bacteriology, and Dr A.H. Louw, Superintendent of the Hospital, only Ritchie Thomson and Williamson were clinicians.

At its meeting of 25 August 1931, the selection committee decided to nominate Craib for the chair, and this was announced to the Board of the Faculty of Medicine on 8 September. News of the recommendation soon leaked out, and Raikes found himself overwhelmed by threats of resignation from the University's clinical staff at the Hospital. On his own initiative the Principal reconvened the selection committee to reconsider its nomination in the light of 'some additional information that had come to hand', but the committee decided to reaffirm its recommendation. Again acting on his own initiative, Raikes approached Craib and asked him to withdraw his application for the chair. According to Craib's own account, Raikes told him: 'The fact is that quite an explosive situation has developed as a result of your application. A large section of the community, and, moreover, one that has generously supported the University, has threatened to withdraw its support if you are appointed over the heads of three distinguished physicians on the hospital staff who have also applied.' When Craib retorted that the obvious course was simply not to appoint him, an exasperated Raikes informed him:

'Craib, you don't seem to have grasped the dilemma in which we find ourselves. Your application has been placed at the top of the list. My request to you to withdraw is something I am doing off my own bat, entirely on my own, and I do so solely to prevent what I feel will be a calamity from overtaking the institution of which I happen to be Principal.' Craib, by his own account, then agreed to withdraw provided Raikes put his request in writing. This Raikes refused to do. Thereafter several other attempts were made to get Craib to withdraw, including one by J.H. Hofmeyr, the Minister of Education and a relation of Craib's, but to no avail.

When Craib's nomination came before Senate on 6 October, Raikes proposed the appointment of 'a new and independent Committee for the purpose of ascertaining the effect which the appointment recommended would have, considered from the point of view of public policy'. Senate resolved to appoint such a committee, Professors Dart, Middleton Shaw, Stammers, and Williamson recording their opposition. The committee, consisting of Raikes, H.J. Hofmeyr, Professors Young, Dart, Hoernlé, Maingard, and Williamson, and Drs A.H. Louw and A.J. Orenstein, reported back to Senate two weeks later. The main question of 'public policy' considered by the committee was whether the appointment to a medical chair of a candidate who was not a member of the Hospital staff was 'likely to disturb the cordial relationship and co-operation at present existing between the Medical School and the Hospital Staff'. The committee concluded it would be wrong to allow considerations of a non-academic character to influence the appointment: 'The consensus of opinion of the Committee was that in the ultimate selection of a candidate for a University post, the considered judgment of the Committee of experts must prevail, even at the risk of losing the co-operation of a portion of the clinical staff.' With a view to preventing a similar crisis in the future, the committee recommended that Senate should ensure that all interests were properly represented on selection committees for senior appointments, and that the University arrange with the Hospital that clinical and teaching appointments be held on such terms that neither could be resigned without the other.[56]

Endorsed by Senate, the committee's report, together with Senate's nomination of Craib for the chair of medicine, went before Council for its meeting of 23 October. Council also received a letter from a committee appointed by 'a portion of the Clinical Staff of the Hospital', protesting against Senate's recommendation and requesting a hearing. The committee, consisting of Drs A.G. Brinton, A. Campbell, and E.B. Woolf, was given its hearing, but Council proceeded to appoint Craib as Professor of Medicine. He was appointed from 1 January 1932.

With Craib's appointment, five members of the Department of Medicine carried out their threat of resignation. The defeated candidates, Bloom, Braun, and Heiman, all resigned, as did I.J. Block and Mary Gordon, leaving R.L. Girdwood as the only senior clinical lecturer, and I.J. Balkin as the only Jewish clinical lecturer. Nor did Craib find some of his colleagues at the Hospital at all welcoming. He has recalled that on his arrival at the staff dressing room he bumped into the surgeon, Professor J.J. Levin, whose father was Jewish, who told him outright: 'I just cannot understand how you can have fallen so low as to allow yourself to be used as a flail to beat up the Jewish section of the community.'[57] Faced by such hostility, and with hardly any clinical staff, Craib thought of resigning forthwith, but in the event decided to press instead for the appointment of temporary clinical assistants pending the permanent reconstruction of his department. His proposals, put to the Board of the Faculty of Medicine on 8 March 1932, were vigorously opposed by Levin. According to Craib's account, Levin stated: 'I strongly object to the iniquitous proposals we have just heard from Professor Craib. It is his obvious intention to dig an unbridgeable gulf between the Medical School and those members of the hospital staff who have resigned.' There followed prolonged manoeuvres to attempt to appoint temporary clinical assistants, and thereby avert a breakdown in clinical instruction, without at the same time making impossible a reconciliation with the five physicians who had resigned. In early May Raikes finally succeeded in negotiating a settlement. The five physicians agreed to resume clinical teaching with the proviso that 'if reasonable representation of the Hospital on the Selection Committee for the appointment of Clinical Professors were not granted, they would have to reconsider their decision'.[58]

Craib's appointment was an outstanding one, but it is understandable why it caused resentment at the time. It ran counter to the Hospital-based tradition that the Wits medical school had established for itself on the clinical side, and it highlighted the fact that no Jewish candidate had yet been given a chair at the Wits medical school. There was not to be a Jewish professor at the medical school prior to World War II, but there were to be no further allegations of anti-Semitism in the making of senior appointments.

All in all, it seems that Jewish members of the University, students and staff alike, had little reason to complain of discrimination against them. It is arguable that Afrikaans students, by contrast, might have had some reasons for complaint, and that one of the University's great failures in the pre-war period was in its handling of the question of Afrikaans students.

From the outset it was part of the ideal of Wits that it would bring together English- and Afrikaans-speaking white South Africans. In his inaugural address as Principal, Jan Hofmeyr had declared that 'the University of Johannesburg' would seek to build up a 'healthy national spirit' within its walls, and that through 'the frank and friendly intercourse' of its students it would help resolve 'racial' tensions between English- and Afrikaans-speaking South Africans. While Wits never attracted as many Afrikaans-speaking students as U.C.T., generally because Afrikaners in the Transvaal were less well off than those in the Cape, they none the less constituted a sizeable minority from the University's beginning. Apart from the general rule that students were free to answer their examinations in either of the country's two official languages, no special provision was made in the twenties by either Wits or U.C.T. for their Afrikaans students. Nor was there any great demand from the students for such provision.

In the thirties the position of Afrikaans students at Wits and U.C.T. became a major political issue, and the two universities were subjected to heavy pressure from outside to cater more effectively for the special needs of their Afrikaner students. In 1931 Dr D.F. Malan, the Minister of Education in Hertzog's Nationalist government, introduced the Higher Education Control Bill for the specific purpose of forcing bilingualism on Wits and U.C.T. Under the terms of the Bill the minister was to be given a right of veto over university appointments so that he might in future block the appointment of unilingual persons. On the language question, Malan declared himself in favour of an arrangement 'elastic enough to allow that some institutions shall be predominantly English and others predominantly Afrikaans', but he insisted that at Wits and U.C.T., which possessed so-called 'restricted' faculties not available at Afrikaans institutions and which contained significant Afrikaans minorities, 'the right of the minorities shall be reasonably and adequately protected'. His purpose in the Bill was 'to secure adequate protection to minorities, racial minorities, as far as their language rights are concerned in the various institutions, the equal language rights to which they are entitled under the South Africa Act'. After representations from all the universities Malan withdrew the Bill, but on the understanding that the universities themselves would 'take such steps as may be reasonably expected of them to secure that the language rights of both sections of the community, particularly in connection with the so-called restricted faculties, will be adequately safeguarded'.[59]

Representing part of the Hertzog government's drive towards establishing complete equality of language rights between English and Afrikaans, Malan's Bill was proposed at a juncture when the majority of Afrikaans students at Wits no longer had received their secondary education in English. According to the *University of Witwatersrand Magazine* in March 1925, the majority of

Wits Afrikaans students at that stage had been taught in English at high school, but this ceased to be the case in the thirties as a consequence of the movement in the previous decade to separate English- and Afrikaans-speaking pupils at school.

The University's response to Malan's initiative was both cautious and limited. Council appointed a small committee, headed by Raikes, on bilingualism at the University, and it advised against bilingual instruction, with some lectures in English and some in Afrikaans, as well as against parallel classes. As was stressed by the committee, and by the Vice-Chancellor, H.J. Hofmeyr, in his graduation address in 1933, the root of the problem lay in the schools, which were separated along racial and linguistic lines, and in which the second official language was very inadequately taught. 'The causes of our discontent, the disregard of equal rights to both languages', Hofmeyr declared, 'arise from the lack of equal instruction of the child in both languages from the earliest stage of his education.' The schools simply did not produce bilingual students, and this made bilingual instruction at university virtually impossible. The committee on bilingualism at Wits concluded that it would certainly be 'unreasonable' to impose on their English-speaking students the task of following lectures in Afrikaans. Nor did parallel classes seem to offer a satisfactory solution. The main demand for parallel classes was in the restricted faculties, medicine and engineering, but the sense in the University in the early thirties was against instituting them. They would be exceptionally expensive to mount, and would not necessarily be in the best interests of Afrikaans students themselves. In 1934 Raikes advised J.H. Hofmeyr, as Minister of Education, that in his considered opinion students who wanted to become doctors and engineers required to know English, especially in order to have access to the literature, and it would therefore be a mistake to establish parallel classes. H.J. Hofmeyr made the same point even more forcefully in his 1933 graduation address. Speaking as an Afrikaner, he protested against crippling Afrikaans-speaking students by confining them to instruction in Afrikaans. 'Dearly as I love Afrikaans', he declared, 'we must not be swept off our feet by emotion and sentiment.'[60]

The University's own survey in 1931 revealed a fairly limited demand for instruction in Afrikaans. It was requested by 67 students, representing 3,4 per cent of the total student population and less than a third of the Afrikaans-speaking students. The committee on bilingualism consequently concluded that English should be maintained as the ordinary medium of instruction at the University, but that some steps should be taken 'to remove the disability under which Afrikaans speaking students suffer'. In the restricted faculties in particular, the committee recommended the appointment of special tutors qualified to explain in Afrikaans the instruction given in English. The committee also recommended training English-speaking members of staff in Afrikaans, and urged that as the administrative staff came into close contact with parents who were often unilingual Afrikaners, the posts of Registrar, Assistant Registrar, and Accounting Officer should in future be held only by bilingual persons.

Following Council's adoption of the committee's report in August 1931, certain steps were taken to provide instruction in Afrikaans. In January 1934 Raikes reported to the Minister of Education that clinical instruction for medical students was given in the language of the patient in those 'firms' where the head was bilingual, and that in physics, mathematics, and botany tutorials and demonstrations were generally given 'in either language'.[61] Appointment committees in medicine and engineering always took note of the language capabilities of candidates, and before I. Glyn Thomas was installed as Registrar in 1936 he was required to acquire proficiency in Afrikaans. Together with the creation of a chair in Afrikaans in 1933, these sorts of steps met with a degree of approval from the Afrikaans community on the Witwatersrand. An editorial on 'Afrikaans Aan Univ. Raad' in the *Vaderland* in April 1934 concluded:

> Ten besluite wil ons dit graag opmerk dat veel eer seker aan mnr. H.R. Raikes, die prinsipaal, toekom vir die vordering wat Afrikaans in die afgelope jare op die Randse Universiteit gemaak het. Ons wil ons graag aansluit by die blykie van waardering deur die klompie Afrikaners gegee. Mnr Raikes het hierheen gekom as buitelander. Sover ons uit sy dade kan oordeel, het dit nie lank geduur nie of hy het die dinge in die regte verhouding begin sien, en na daardie verhouding toe gewerk. Ons wil hom verseker dat Afrikaners nie onerkentlik is nie, en ons wil hoop dat hy in hierdie rigting sal voortgaan totdat 'n groot ongerymdheid wat vandag nog bestaan, uit die weg geruim is; d.i. dat Afrikaners wat in die geneeskunde en in die tegniese wetenskappe wil studeer, dit aan geneen van die twee doserende universiteite nog deur medium van hul eie taal kan doen nie.[62]

The demand in Afrikaans circles for the creation of medical and engineering faculties at one or other of the universities in which Afrikaans was the chief medium of instruction, Stellenbosch or Pretoria, the latter of which had acquired university status in 1930, became ever more insistent as the thirties progressed. It was actively championed by D.F. Malan's Purified (Gesuiwerde) National Party, which had split from Hertzog over fusion in 1933–4, and by the front organizations of the Afrikaner Broederbond, notably the *Federasie van Afrikaanse Kultuurverenigings* (the F.A.K.) and the *Spoorbond,* the Afrikaans railway workers' trade union.[63] In July 1937 the University of Pretoria itself petitioned J.H. Hofmeyr, as Minister of Education, for a medical faculty, and at the end of the year Hofmeyr appointed a committee under Professor M.C. Botha, the Secretary for Education, to investigate and report upon medical training in South Africa.

Hofmeyr, it appears, was reluctant to see the creation of a separate Afrikaans medical school, and before appointing the Botha Committee he requested from Wits and U.C.T. information as to what arrangements they were prepared to make for providing instruction in Afrikaans in their medical faculties. The response of Wits, on this occasion, was to accept the principle of parallel classes, but also to insist that the government would be entirely responsible for funding these classes. The decision finally reached by Council, after considerable consultation, on 10 September 1937 was that 'the University is prepared to arrange for instruction in Afrikaans in the Faculty of Medicine by instituting separate parallel classes for instruction in that medium of students who so desire, provided the Government is prepared to bear the whole of the extra cost involved'. U.C.T. likewise resolved in favour of parallel classes. This 'eleventh hour' conversion to parallel classes in medicine was dismissed by Dr Theo Wassenaar, chairman of the committee for a Afrikaans medical faculty at Pretoria, as a 'contrived intervention'. For cultural reasons, from Wassenaar's standpoint, it was of the first importance to have an Afrikaans medical faculty in an Afrikaans university:

Die kulturele aspek is vir die Afrikaanssprekende bevolking die vernaamste van die hele saak. 'n Afrikaanse mediese fakulteit sal vir die Afrikaanse kultuurontwikkeling alleen dan van groot waarde wees as dit in 'n omgewing kom waar dit lewensvatbaarheid sal hê, en dit is aan 'n Afrikaanse Universiteit.[64]

The Federal Council of the South African Medical Association and the *S.A. Medical Journal* likewise rejected the idea of parallel classes in favour of a medical faculty at the University of Pretoria. 'From the economic point of view', the *Medical Journal* concluded, 'there is little to be said in favour of parallel classes at the existing faculties, while from the practical and cultural point of view there are grave objections against such classes.'[65]

The recommendation of the Botha Committee, which reported in 1939, was for the creation of an Afrikaans medical faculty at the University of Pretoria. The existing medical schools were already over-crowded, and it did not think parallel classes would prove efficient. The committee also rejected the notion that in the interests of national unity Afrikaans-speaking medical students should not be separated from English-speaking students. Although the committee considered it unfortunate, the country's educational institutions had developed along separate lines, including the universities, which 'may fairly correctly be classified as either Afrikaans speaking or English speaking institutions'. It saw no valid reason why an exception should be made in the case of medicine. In 1943 a medical faculty was finally established at the University of Pretoria.

In retrospect, it seems there was little that was far-sighted in the University's policy towards its Afrikaans students. It proclaimed that it wanted to promote national unity among white South Africans by creating bridges between Afrikaans- and English-speaking students, the country's future leaders, but it never really appreciated that this might require making special provisions for its Afrikaans students. What provisions were made or proposed were done so largely under pressure from outside; few initiatives came spontaneously from within. The proponents of educational separation between Afrikaans- and English-speaking whites knew exactly what they wanted and how to secure their goals; those who governed Wits might have known what they wanted, but they possessed no long-term strategy to realize their goals.

In student politics, the question of Afrikaners at Wits also loomed large in the thirties. In 1933 students at the Grey University College, Bloemfontein, Potchefstroom University College, and Pretoria University, broke from the National Union of South African Students (N.U.S.A.S.) to form the Afrikaanse Nasionale Studentebond (A.N.S.). They were followed in 1936 by Stellenbosch University.[66] A local branch of the A.N.S. was formed at Wits but was denied recognition by the S.R.C. on the grounds that the S.R.C. supported N.U.S.A.S., that the A.N.S. confined its membership to Afrikaans-speaking Protestant Christians, and that it was an illiberal and racial organization. Something of a compromise was reached in 1938 when the A.N.S. was given permission to use University rooms and to put up notices on the student notice boards.[67] In 1939, in another major development, the S.R.C. refused the request of the Afrikaanse Taal- en Kultuurvereniging at Wits to produce an Afrikaans newspaper at the University, and agreed instead to make the existing student newspaper, *Wu's Views,* bilingual, with the appointment of an Afrikaans editor.[68]

All in all, for the period prior to World War II the conclusion seems inescapable that Wits achieved disappointingly little to realize its potential to serve as a bridge between the different groups in South African society, white and black, English- and Afrikaans-speaking. The verdict of C.W. de Kiewiet, the distinguished South African historian who studied at Wits under Macmillan, stands:

The period between the wars saw the active growth of separate Afrikaans-speaking universities. The Afrikaans universities are perhaps more truly South African than the English-speaking universities, which have not always dared escape from a sort of minor British provincialism. Universities in a new land are especially in need of daring and enterprise. In the vital field of race relations there was in the English-speaking universities insufficient enterprise or daring. In the critical period between the two world wars they lost the chance of becoming a common and generous meeting ground where the equal intercourse of eager youth could end the estrangements of the past and seek to dissolve the prejudices of race and colour. Far too heavy a load was placed upon the shoulders of the few men of courage and insight in economics, sociology, and history who laboured to promote the new thought and enterprise out of which South African society could generate the policies and adjustments which were necessary if Afrikaner, English, African, Indian and coloured men were to live harmoniously together.[69]

IV

Women students at Wits were not discriminated against in the period prior to World War II, but women members of the academic staff were. They were paid less, retired earlier, and were liable to have their service terminated whenever they married. When advertising academic posts, the University sometimes specified that it wanted male applicants only. Agitation against these forms of discrimination reached a climax in 1935 when Mrs Margaret Ballinger, formerly Miss Hodgson, was retired following her marriage. In the midst of the agitation Council arranged to equalize pay scales for men and women, but women still remained liable to early retirement, and to the loss of their posts upon marriage.

Among students, women generally constituted about a third of the total student population. They greatly outnumbered men in the Faculty of Arts, they were prominent in the Faculty of Science, and came to comprise almost a fifth of the students in the Faculty of Medicine. Among academic staff, there were very few women, and none held a chair.

From the standpoint of the values and practices of the later twentieth century, it is perhaps easy to deride the University's pre-war policies and attitudes towards women staff. But it should be remembered that women were only then beginning to establish a position for themselves in the professions, that South Africa was rather backward in accepting a positive role for women in society, not granting them the franchise until 1930, and that English-speaking South African women were generally very much less assertive, and certainly less politically and socially-conscious, than Afrikaans women. In an era in which it was virtually unheard of for husbands and wives to share domestic responsibilities, the University's authorities also had a very real point when they claimed that married women could hardly be expected to devote the same time and attention to their academic work as men and single women.

From the first the University inherited a situation in which women members of staff were discriminated against in terms of pay. Discrimination was built into the pay scales under the original formula for government financing of universities, and it was simply perpetuated by the University after the introduction of the general purpose grant. The basic salary scales for lecturers first adopted by the University were:

	Juniors	Lecturers	Seniors
	£	£	£
Men	300-25-350	400-25-500	450-25-650
Women	250-25-300	325-25-425	425-25-525

In 1922 Margaret Hodgson, then a lecturer in history and economic history, protested to Council about the differential salary scales for men and women, but she was told that for the moment equalization was simply not possible. At the end of 1922 the finance committee of Council reported that existing financial conditions ruled out any increase for women members of staff, and that the University could not be expected to take any special initiative in the matter. The committee, headed by Alexander Aiken, contended that equalization 'would involve a departure from the existing policy of South African Universities as previously laid down by Parliament, and that this should not be undertaken by this Institution alone'.[70]

In 1923 Council intensified the discrimination against women when it drew up regulations for their retirement at 55 and their termination of contract upon marriage, unless otherwise agreed by the Council and the individual concerned. Before deciding on the provision with regard to married women, Council instructed Principal Hofmeyr to investigate procedures elsewhere, and he reported that while these varied greatly, there was 'a tendency towards the opinion that female members of the staff should resign on marriage, unless otherwise arranged between the parties concerned'.[71]

In 1924 the Lecturers' Association, which had been founded in 1918, took up the issue of discrimination against women members of staff, particularly in regard to salaries. In August 1924 J.G. Lawrie, the association's secretary, advised Council that the association was 'strongly of opinion that discrimination on the grounds of sex is wrong in principle', and in the next year the association sent a deputation to Council on the matter. In support of equal pay for men and women, Margaret Hodgson, as the deputation's spokesman, urged that as there was no discrimination in matters of training, qualification, or work, there was 'no apparent justification for the implication of professional inferiority underlying the financial inferiority'. She also pointed out that 'South Africa is the only country in which such differentiation exists, and now Grahamstown and Cape Town make no discrimination, leaving Stellenbosch and Johannesburg the only two mixed institutions to maintain this differentiation'.[72]

Mainly at the behest of Professor Dalton, the special committee subsequently set up by Council to consider the equalization of salaries strongly recommended the adoption of 'the principle of equality of pay for equal work, regardless of the sex of the officers concerned', but Council refused to accept the principle. At the Council meeting of 1 May 1925, the committee's recommendation was put to the vote and lost. The debate and the voting was not recorded, but it is evident that the principle of equalization had a very powerful opponent in Alexander Aiken, the chairman of the all-important finance committee. As there were only eight women on the full-time academic staff, equalization would hardly have crippled the University financially, but Aiken was firmly convinced that women did not in fact provide the equal service to warrant the equal pay. As Principal Raikes reported on a later occasion: 'Dr Aiken holds strongly that the work of women is not equal to that of men.'[73]

During the early thirties, when the University was in financial difficulties, it was virtually impossible for the movement to secure the equalization of salaries to make any progress, despite the small amounts involved. The issue was raised from time to time in the Lecturers' Association, but it did not get much beyond the association. In 1935 the whole question of discrimination against women suddenly leapt to the foreground when Margaret Ballinger was obliged to give up her senior lectureship in history.

At the end of 1934 Miss Hodgson, a member of the Department of History since 1920, married William Ballinger, the well-known trade unionist. They had long wished to marry, but had feared she would lose her position. They needed her salary, and she was reluctant to abandon her academic career. At the beginning of 1935 she formally informed Principal Raikes of her marriage, and requested that the saving clause in the conditions of appointment be invoked to allow her to continue as a senior lecturer. As a new academic year was about to begin Raikes had no hesitation in advising that she should remain at her post for 1935, but thereafter she would have to go:

> With reference to your request to be retained in your post, I am afraid that Paragraph 4 of the conditions of appointment is quite clear. It is of

course open to the Council by the saving clause to keep you on, but they have never done so and would, I feel quite sure, not be willing to make a precedent.[74]

Raikes did not bother to refer the request to Council. He considered the matter closed, and in due course initiated the proceedings for the selection of a successor to Mrs Ballinger.

Raikes had not reckoned on the fighting qualities of Mrs Ballinger. As a Natives' Representative in Parliament after 1937 she was to make life difficult for successive governments, so in 1935 she made life difficult for Raikes. The clash between them was one of personalities and prejudices more than principles. Rather isolated at the University, Mrs Ballinger fought the Principal not so much through Wits as through women's organizations.

A very formal, even rigid, person, with a closed rather than an open personality, Margaret Hodgson had formed a very formidable teaching team with Macmillan. The one had almost exactly complemented the other. Where Macmillan's lectures were unstructured and spontaneous, hers were always very carefully prepared, and were virtually dictated. She had hoped to succeed Macmillan as Professor of History, but was placed second to Leo Fouché out of the 39 candidates who applied for the chair. In her struggle to save her position she did not get the support from Fouché she believed she should have. 'I had an idea he'd be glad to keep me not for myself but as an experienced hand to help his tiredness', she wrote to Macmillan on 20 March 1935, 'but I've had inside information today that he will be glad to see the last remnants of the negrophil tradition rooted out of the Dept.'[75]

In May the National Council of Women of South Africa, the South African Association of University Women, and the League of Women Voters indirectly took up Mrs Ballinger's cause by petitioning to discuss the position of women at the University with the Principal and Council. On 20 June a committee of Council, including Raikes, met delegates of the three organizations, who protested against all forms of discrimination against women practised by Wits. Practices at the University, the delegates claimed, were backward even by South African standards, and they protested that discrimination on the grounds of sex was 'fundamentally unjust in modern society based on the principles of advancing civilization'. They further contended that to disqualify a woman for marrying was particularly pernicious as it might deprive the University of talented teachers, and that 'in addition the enforcement of such a rule leads to undesirable relationships, in that it tends to discourage marriage and to subvert the principles of social morality'.[76]

Raikes's response to the pressure from the women's organizations was to urge Council to give way on the pay issue, but to hold firm on early retirement and also retirement on marriage. In a memorandum for Council he stated that women could be every bit as capable as men as university teachers and that they should therefore be put on the same salary scale as men. But he added that he believed that the end of a woman's useful teaching life was probably reached by 55, and he consequently opposed any change in the regulation providing for the retirement of women at that age. On the question of retirement on marriage he was most assertive. 'A University appointment', he argued, 'is a full-time job and a marriage which allows a woman still to give her full service to the University can hardly be a marriage in the true sense.'[77]

At its meeting of 5 July Council agreed, subject to the Minister of Education's consent, to put female members of the academic staff on the same salary scale as men, and to leave the other regulations concerning women intact. At the same meeting it also agreed to appoint Arthur Keppel-Jones as lecturer in history from 1 January 1936 vice Mrs Ballinger, retired.[78]

When Keppel-Jones's appointment was announced Mrs Ballinger increased pressure on Raikes. She wanted to know why Council had not seen her request to retain her position in the Department of History, and demanded a formal ruling from Council. In mid October Raikes finally put the case before Council, which resolved to confirm the Principal's action in advising Mrs Ballinger that she should retire at the end of 1935. The one dissentient, Professor Herbert Le May, a consistent critic of Raikes, requested that his adverse vote be recorded 'as he considered that Mrs Ballinger's case was sufficiently exceptional to merit the special consideration' allowed under the saving clause in the conditions of appointment.[79]

Mrs Ballinger had effectively lost her job, but her case had become caught up in the wider feminist movement in South Africa, and at the urging of the League of Women Voters she appealed to the Minister of Education against Council's decision. She claimed, first, that Council had discriminated against her in the exercise of its powers in that it had retained the services of at least one married woman since the condition about marriage was laid down. Second, her interests had been prejudiced 'by the action of the Principal in failing to submit my request for the continuance of my contract until the Council had accepted a nomination of my successor as if there had been no such request from me, and indeed in ignorance of the fact that such a request had been made'. In a supporting memorandum the League of Women Voters called on the Minister to secure the reinstatement of Mrs Ballinger, and also to get the clause dismissing women on marriage deleted 'in conformity with the procedure of other progressive universities'. The League declared that the clause was too indeterminate, depending for its execution on administration rather than principle: 'As such, it is destructive of the permanent security of women's work, and its application might vary according to the viewpoint of the Council of the moment.'[80]

The appeal to Hofmeyr failed. Despite the furore caused by the enforced retirement of Mrs Ballinger, the provision against employing married women on the academic staff continued to be enforced, though it was relaxed during World War II, largely as a consequence of the scarcity of qualified men. Principal Raikes was even prepared to allow his own wife to lecture in the Department of History from 1943 to 1947.

The allegation has been made that Wits enforced Mrs Ballinger's retirement from the University for political reasons more than anything else. Like Macmillan, she was a known radical on issues of race relations, and the man she married was a fervent trade unionist and 'friend of the native'. William Ballinger, a Scottish trade unionist, had first come out to South Africa in 1928 to help reorganize the I.C.U., the mass black trade union of the 1920s, though the effect of his intervention was to help split the I.C.U. In her biography of Winifred Holtby, the novelist friend of the Ballingers, Vera Brittain makes the charge: 'The real reason for Margaret Ballinger's dismissal was her marriage to a man whose native sympathies did not please an institution which derived financial support from various mining groups in the Rand.'[81]

This is an over-statement. To be sure, Mrs Ballinger was not removed because she was an incompetent lecturer; by the standards of the time, which emphasized teaching ability and efficiency, she was 'singularly competent'.[82] It is also certain that she was not removed for fear of setting a precedent for married women to remain on the academic staff. General policy was in practice for women to be retired on marriage, but married women who had served the University with distinction included Dr Annie Porter in Zoology, Mrs M. Moss in Botany, and Mrs A.W. Hoernlé in Bantu Studies, and the provision against married women could certainly have been applied in the case of Mrs Hoernlé. The fact of the matter is that prejudice against Mrs Ballinger personally, as well as a strong prejudice against married women in an academic career, forced her retirement. Raikes and the majority on Council did have a personal animus against Mrs Ballinger which was partly political, in so far as they disliked the radicals in the History Department and disapproved of William Ballinger's activities. But it was also partly puritan in that they disapproved the Ballingers living together prior to their marriage. Memories of the Stibbe affair ensured that the Council would refrain from acting against Miss Hodgson, but she was punished

Miss V.M.L. Hodgson   Mrs A. W. Hoernlé

retrospectively by being forced to retire on becoming Mrs Ballinger. There is also no question that Raikes and the majority on Council simply did not believe that women could successfully combine marriage and a chair, and that certain members of Council were basically opposed to women in the professions. As Hoernlé had explained to Macmillan when in 1934 the chair of history had been given to Leo Fouché instead of Margaret Hodgson, Council would never have appointed her even if she had been nominated by Senate: 'Partly anti-women complex; partly anti-Ballinger!'.[83]

Raikes handled the whole matter badly, particularly in arbitrarily informing Mrs Ballinger that she would have to resign at the end of 1935 instead of referring her request to be retained as a senior lecturer to Council. Included in the Ballinger Papers at Wits is a detailed hand-written record of Council's initial discussion of the Ballinger case in October, and it is clear from this that everyone was aware Raikes had acted irregularly. He lamely stated *'He thought he had put the matter to Council, and hoped Council would now endorse his action.'* To the claim, made by Van der Brugge in a letter to Mrs Ballinger and repeated in the Council, that Raikes had acted quite legally in his capacity as executive officer of the Council, Professor Le May was able to point out that Raikes was the executive officer of the Senate and not of the Council. When Le May further pointed out that the whole matter had been greatly complicated by the appointment of a successor to Mrs Ballinger, Raikes was quick to argue that 'he regarded acceptance of successor as endorsement of his action'. To the question of what kind of married woman might be retained by the University, Raikes replied: 'Oh, women like Madame Curie – anybody absolutely irreplaceable.'[84]

There was never any question that Council would over-rule the Principal for the majority on the Council were generally hostile to the idea of employing married women. Even the Women's Discussion Club among the students was not so sure that a married woman's place was not in the home rather than the classroom. The Club voted by a bare majority of 14 to 13 votes that it should 'make some definite protest to the University Council against the present regulation which provides for the dismissal of women lecturers in the event of their marriage'.[85] In the next year a general meeting of women students protested to Council against 'the principle of the exclusion of married women from the lecturing staff on the grounds of sex alone', but the S.R.C. itself never picked up the issue.[86] The Lecturers' Association, for its part, investigated the circumstances of Mrs Ballinger's retirement, but took no action.[87]

For Mrs Ballinger her enforced retirement at the end of 1935 proved, in the event, the great turning point in her career. As a teacher and a historian she had built up a solid reputation for herself; as a Natives' Representative in Parliament from 1937 to 1960 she was to establish a formidable reputation for herself. In 1962 U.C.T. conferred an Hon. LL.D. on her, and in 1964 Rhodes similarly honoured her. She died in 1980, without Wits ever having offered her an honorary degree.

Unlike female members of staff, women students at Wits in the period before World War II could not claim that they were discriminated against. As there was no quota system in the University, or any attempt by any of the faculties to limit student numbers, there were no limits on the entry of women students into the University and its faculties. It was only later, when the medical school resorted to selective entry, that women students could claim that they were seriously discriminated against.

Notes

1. *The Open Universities in South Africa* (Johannesburg, 1957), preface.
2. Ibid., 31.
3. *R.D.M.*, 2 Aug. 1919.
4. Council minutes, III, 2 Dec. 1926.
5. M.G. Synnot, *The Half-Opened Door: Discrimination and Admissions at Harvard, Yale, and Princeton, 1900-1970* (Westport, Conn., 1979).

6. See Hoernlé, *South African Native Policy and the Liberal Spirit;* Brookes, *Colour Problems,* 149; W.K. Hancock, *Smuts: The Fields of Force 1919–1950* (Cambridge, 1968), 121.
7. Rheinallt Jones to Smit, 22 Feb. 1943, and Smit to Rheinallt Jones, 2 March 1943, MS. Rheinallt Jones Ja 4.4. For the difficulty of blacks securing articles see also Alexander Kerr, *Fort Hare 1915–48* (London, 1968), 129.
8. *Journal of the Medical Association of South Africa,* 24 Nov. 1927, & 28 Jan. 1928.
9. Hoernlé, *Race and Reason,* 101.
10. *Journal of the Medical Association of South Africa,* 25 Feb. 1928.
11. Ordinance No. 18 of 1928. See also the Hospitals Regulations amendment of 1927, *The Province of Transvaal Official Gazette,* 11 Jan. 1928.
12. Senate Misc./101/54.
13. *Report of the Committee appointed to inquire into the Training of Natives in Medicine and Public Health,* U.G. 35, of 1928, 4–7.
14. Ibid., Appendix 3.
15. *Journal of the Medical Association of South Africa,* 13 Sept. 1930.
16. *Report,* 8–9, & 19–22.
17. Ibid., 16.
18. Council minutes, II, 24 Nov. 1925.
19. J.H. Louw, *In the Shadow of Table Mountain* (Cape Town, 1969), 145; Council minutes, III, 2 Dec. 1926.
20. Ibid., II, 24 Nov. 1925.
21. Ibid., III, 2 Dec. 1926.
22. Ibid.
23. Ibid., 21 Jan. 1927; H.W.J. van der Brugge to the Secretary for Education, 31 Jan. 1927, U.O.D. E68/6.
24. Faculty of Medicine minutes, III, 26 July 1927.
25. Senate minutes, III, 8 Aug. 1927.
26. *Journal of the Medical Association of South Africa,* 24 Oct. 1931.
27. Ibid., 28 Nov. 1931.
28. *House of Assembly Debates,* XVII, 4795–4801.
29. Van der Brugge to Secretary for Education, 31 Jan. 1927, U.O.D. E68/6, vol. 1.
30. Van der Brugge to Secretary for Education, 10 June 1931; S.C. Schoen to Raikes, 21 July 1931; Raikes to Secretary for Education, 11 June 1932, Ibid.
31. Macmillan, *My South African Years,* 218.
32. Secretary for Education to Raikes, 16 Aug. 1932, U.O.D. E68/6.
33. Raikes to Secretary S.R.C., 13 June 1932, S.R.C. minutes, 9 Aug. 1932.
34. Brookes, *Colour Problems,* 149–50.
35. Council Misc./62/34.
36. Senate Misc./75/34.
37. Council Misc./8/35.
38. Senate Misc./48/35.
39. *House of Assembly Debates,* XXVII, 5031–48.
40. Ibid., XXX, 7011–19.
41. For an analysis of the report see K.A. Shapiro, 'The Delivery of Health Care to the Rural Black Population' (unpublished University of the Witwatersrand Hons. dissertation, 1981), 43–5.
42. W.H. Craib, 'Proposed Medical School for non-Europeans Situate in Johannesburg and Oriented to the needs of the Bantu Hinterland', *Bulletin of the Adler Museum of the History of Medicine,* 3 (Oct. 1977), 2.
43. Senate minutes, III, 20 Aug. 1934.
44. 'Report of the Committee on Native Medical Education', 30 Aug. 1934, Faculty of Medicine Misc./94/34.
45. 'Statement and Questionnaire Re Medical Education of Non-Europeans', Faculty of Medicine minutes, Oct. 1934.
46. Ibid.
47. Kerr, *Fort Hare,* 188.
48. For a full analysis of the medical aid scheme and its fate see Shapiro, 'The Delivery of Health Care to the Rural Black Population', 43–8.
49. 'The Training of Non-European Medical Students with special reference to Johannesburg', Council Misc./159/3/47.

50. Statistics from Kerr, *Fort Hare,* 173; *Report of the Committee on Medical Training in South Africa,* U.G. 25 of 1939; *House of Assembly Debates,* XXIX, 4954.
51. Raikes to William Cullen, 6 Jan. 1932, University Archives File 143; 'Statistics: Medicine, Engineering, General', University Archives 211.
52. G. Saron and L. Hotz, *The Jews in South Africa: A History* (London, 1955), 376–8.
53. *Report of the Committee on Medical Training in South Africa,* U.G. 25 of 1939, 53.
54. S.R.C. minutes, 25 April 1922 & 5 June 1924.
55. Craib, 'My Return to South Africa and Appointment at Wits', *Bulletin of the Adler Museum of the History of Medicine,* 5 (April 1979), 6–15.
56. Senate Misc./178/31.
57. Craib, 'My Return to South Africa', and unpublished recollections.
58. Faculty of Medicine minutes, VI, 10 May 1932.
59. *House of Assembly Debates,* XVII, 3024–37.
60. *R.D.M.,* 27 March 1933.
61. Raikes to J.H. Hofmeyr, 23 Jan. 1934, U.O.D. E68/6.
62. *Vaderland,* 17 April 1934.
63. Ibid., 9 Oct. 1937; *Transvaler,* 26 Nov. 1937.
64. *Vaderland,* 16 June & 19 Oct. 1937.
65. *S.A. Medical Journal,* 13 Nov. 1937.
66. See chap. 10, pp. 340–3.
67. *Wu's Views,* 4 Aug. & 22 Sept. 1938.
68. Ibid., 9 March 1939.
69. C.W. de Kiewiet, *The Anatomy of South African Misery* (London, 1956), 26.
70. Council minutes, I, 30 Nov. 1922.
71. Ibid., 4 May & 29 June 1923.
72. Ibid., II, 3 April; Council Misc./32/25.
73. 'Position of Women Members of Staff', Council Misc./33/35.
74. Raikes to Mrs Ballinger, 23 Jan. 1935, MS. Ballinger A410/B.2.16.1.
75. Margaret Hodgson to Macmillan, 20 March 1935, MS. Macmillan.
76. Council Misc./32/35.
77. Council Misc./33/35.
78. Council minutes, IV, 5 July 1935.
79. Ibid., 21 Oct. 1935.
80. Mrs Ballinger to the Minister of Education, 25 Oct. 1935, and draft memorandum from League of Women Voters to the Minister of Education, 2 Nov. 1935, MS. Ballinger A410/B.2.16.1.
81. Vera Brittain, *Testament of Friendship: The Story of Winifred Holtby* (London, 1941), 213.
82. Reference by W.M. Macmillan, 10 Oct. 1933, MS. Ballinger A410/B.2.16.1.
83. Hoernlé to Macmillan, 11 April 1934, MS. Macmillan.
84. Notes of Council meeting on Oct. 16th 1935 re appointment, MS. Ballinger A410/B.2.16.1.
85. *Wu's Views,* Oct. 1935.
86. Council minutes, IV, 26 June 1936.
87. Minutes of annual general meeting of Lecturers' Association, 19 Oct. 1935.

10
STUDENT LIFE

I

FOR STUDENTS, Wits in the twenties and thirties was generally a happy place. The student body was relatively small and familiar, the academic demands made on students were by no means excessive, and the students themselves enjoyed being students. They created a full range of clubs and societies to cater for their extramural interests, and rags, intervarsities, raids, and university dances featured prominently in their lives. They were also very proud of their status as students and their membership of the Rand University, advertising this by wearing their University blazers whenever the opportunity allowed. Politically, they were rather more aware by 1939 than they had been in the twenties, though student political activity was as yet sporadic and individualistic.

Wits students were drawn overwhelmingly from Johannesburg, the Witwatersrand, and elsewhere in the Transvaal, and from the middle classes. In 1939, 53 per cent of the students came from Johannesburg, 11 per cent from other Reef towns, and 18 per cent from elsewhere in the Transvaal. The Orange Free State and the Cape each provided 6 per cent of the student population, and Natal 3 per cent.[1] The University, in short, did not attract many students from beyond its own hinterland. It attracted some, but again not many, from the white working classes. Satisfactory statistics on the social background of students in the pre-war period are, unfortunately, impossible to compile, but it is evident that the University served as a medium of upward mobility chiefly for first generation Jewish South Africans, rural Afrikaners, and lower middle-class English-speaking whites. A large proportion of the 'English' students had fathers in the professions, but outside of engineering, and later medicine, few were from the wealthiest Johannesburg families. Before World War II, it was still common for these families to send their sons to a British university, preferably Oxford or Cambridge.

The large majority of students travelled each day to the University from home, in Johannesburg primarily by bus and tram, and by train from Pretoria and the Reef towns. University accommodation for out-of-town students was provided in three residences, College House and Dalrymple House for men, and Sunnyside (later Isabel Dalrymple House) for women. Altogether they accommodated about 250 students. For the rest, students who did not live at home resided in Training College residences or in private lodgings, mainly in Berea, Auckland Park, and Braamfontein north of Jorissen Street. The white working-class areas south of Jorissen Street were generally shunned by students.

For the quality of student life, the move from Plein Square to Milner Park had represented an enormous improvement. Plein Square had lacked any facilities for student life outside the classroom. Milner Park, with its residences and playing fields on campus, and meeting places, such as the sports pavilion, provided several of these facilities, though it lacked a students' union building and, to begin with, even a library. Despite these inadequacies, and despite the fact that Wits was from its inception overwhelmingly a non-residential university, student leaders in the early twenties were generally happy with the corporate life and spirit which had developed among students at Milner Park. But as the University grew larger, so it was sensed that corporate spirit declined. In 1927 the S.R.C. president, T.W.B. Osborn, after observing that students had become indifferent about ragging, and that there had been a marked falling off of attendance at dances and sporting events, commented:

> Many are very pessimistic about this state of affairs. But it must be realised that the University has now nearly fourteen hundred students, and it is only natural that it should not have the same "corporate spirit" as it had when it was smaller. There are very few students who are not interested in some section of our activities, as is evidenced by the greatly increased membership of almost all our Clubs and Societies; so that where interest in matters concerning the general body has waned – largely on account of greatly increased numbers – a more specialised interest in certain sections of student activities has developed. This latter is a very desirable state of affairs and probably does more good to the University than the one time widespread but less active general interest. It is, however, imperative that both should exist, and we confidently trust that the proper corporate spirit will return with increasing age and traditions.[2]

In the thirties, the fragmentation of the student body became more marked. As a consequence particularly of the great expansion in student numbers in engineering and medicine, a tripartite division of the full-time student body into engineers, medical students, and arts and science students, became more distinct. By the end of the thirties, from evidence in the student press, the rivalry among different groups of students was beginning to take on some ugly overtones, both political and racial, with engineering and residence students especially gaining a reputation for intolerance. In late September 1938 the Diogenes Club, denounced by the *Transvaler* as a Communist society, had its meeting on the Munich crisis broken up by right-wing and conservative students. On 20 October the student newspaper, *Wu's Views,* carried a long letter from I.T. Greig, son of the Professor of English and a member of the S.R.C., expressing concern at the increasing signs of intolerance, racialism, and anti-Semitism among the student body. *Wu's Views* itself declared 'That there is no place at Wits for racialism, inter-faculty bad feeling, anti-hostel and anti-day student bitterness, and the other evils which have been a product of a year of transition and growth.' At the beginning of the 1939 academic year Principal Raikes, in a special address to the student body, felt constrained to make an appeal for greater tolerance and understanding. 'We have, I think, got beyond the stage of branding one another as Rooineks, Boers and Yids', he declared, 'but even so there is still far too little understanding between the three groups.'[3]

II

These differences within the student body were a reflection of differences at the national political level, and were symptomatic of a growth of student political awareness and activity in the 1930s. In the previous decade students had conventionally regarded themselves as apolitical, though on occasion, as in their support for the action of the Smuts government against the striking mine-workers in 1922, this was not the case in practice. None the less politics, and particularly the politics of protest, did not feature prominently in student life in the twenties. There were several reasons for this political indifference. Very few students possessed the vote, which was limited to males over 21, and most students were not inclined to question the society they lived in. The large majority of them belonged to social groups still too intent on establishing their own place in society to concern themselves with the plight of others. Even if they did feel such concern, career opportunities were generally so limited, and competition so strong, that students were unwilling to earn reputations for themselves as rebels. Another reason was that politics was sometimes deliberately shunned by student leaders who feared its divisive impact on student bodies and organizations.

This viewpoint was evident in the discussion over the role of the National

Union of South African Students (N.U.S.A.S.) in its early years. N.U.S.A.S. was founded in 1924. Affiliated to it were the eight teaching universities and university colleges in South Africa, and the intention was that it should weld both English- and Afrikaans-speaking students together. At a time when the major issues in white politics concerned the divisions within white society, between capital and organized white labour, and between English- and Afrikaans-speakers, it was appreciated that these issues needed to be averted or skirted if N.U.S.A.S. was to succeed in encompassing all white students. Simultaneously, it was the objective of Leo Marquard, of U.C.T., the founder and first president of N.U.S.A.S., that the student organization should play a genuinely educational role in the universities, assisting in that 'free discussion of the vital questions of the day' which was 'a necessary part of student life', and that it should even take its 'place in the formation of, and influence on public opinion'. This it could not do if the Union restricted itself to 'safe problems'. The formula resorted to was that N.U.S.A.S. would encourage in students a lively interest in political questions, but that it would not itself become a 'political' body, adopting an official stance on major political issues. As specified in the Union's constitution, it was 'To promote the educational and social interests of students in entire independence of all religious and political propaganda.'[4]

In the event, N.U.S.A.S. played a major politicizing role at Wits, and on other campuses, primarily through its Bantu Studies Department and its Student Parliaments. The Bantu Studies Department, founded in 1927, was designed to help students become better informed about 'the Native problem', and the Student Parliament represented an explicit attempt to heighten the political awareness of students. First staged in Durban in 1927, the Student Parliament became an annual event after 1929, when it was organized along party political lines, with 'parliamentary' elections at the various campuses. 'You must stimulate interest in politics in your universities', Leo Marquard urged upon the first Student Parliament, 'you must study politics, you must have something to contribute to government.' He concluded: 'If you accept this challenge, you will revolutionise our universities, and will leave a mark on the history of our country.'[5]

In 1933 a heightened political consciousness among Afrikaans student leaders led the S.R.C.s of Grey University College, Bloemfontein, Potchefstroom University College, and Pretoria University to secede from N.U.S.A.S., and to form the Afrikaans Nasionale Studentebond (A.N.S.). Stellenbosch University joined them in 1936. Assertive Afrikaner nationalism, together with a distrust of 'liberal' tendencies in N.U.S.A.S., provided the basis for the secessions and the formation of a purely Afrikaans student organization. The lead was taken by Grey University College in August 1933. The students of Grey, P.J. Meyer, later chairman of the S.A.B.C., informed the N.U.S.A.S. executive, had decided to withdraw from the Union 'because of its un-national, un-Afrikaans and liberal spirit'.[6] By contrast, the new A.N.S. asserted an Afrikaans nationality. As three A.N.S. delegates from Pretoria University explained to the Wits S.R.C., this comprised Christian Protestantism, the Afrikaans language, and 'a National Cultural basis of Afrikaans life'.[7]

This secession of the Afrikaans centres from N.U.S.A.S. coincided with the emergence at the English-speaking universities of some articulate liberal students, who began to make their presence felt in student affairs. Indeed it was probably a matter of genuine concern to student leaders at the seceding centres that in the early 1930s liberal groups in N.U.S.A.S. had become more assertive. The complaint of P.J. Nienaber, the president of the Grey S.R.C., and later lecturer in Afrikaans at Wits, was that N.U.S.A.S. was 'too negrophilistic', and very much influenced by 'socialistic-international-minded Jews'.[8] But the liberals were by no means in control of the Union. In 1929 a memorandum prepared by the Bantu Studies Department had recommended in favour of the admission of blacks to the Wits and U.C.T. medical schools, but the response of the N.U.S.A.S. Council had been to defer the issue.[9] In 1933, again, on the initiative of Max Gluckman in the Wits S.R.C., the Wits delegation on the N.U.S.A.S. Council had proposed that the possibility of admitting Fort Hare to the National Union be investigated, and a commission was duly appointed, but in early 1934 it reported against Fort Hare's admission.[10]

The secessions from N.U.S.A.S., and the subsequent reorganization of the Union, together with developments in the outside world, including the passage of the Hertzog Native Bills, the emergence of a liberal wing of the United Party round Jan Hofmeyr, the accelerating pace of black urbanization, the systematic racism of the Nazi regime in Germany, and the drift towards war in Europe, all served to heighten political awareness among students at Wits, as elsewhere, and to swell the numbers who might be described as liberal. The late thirties also witnessed the emergence of vocal radical groups, some socialist and some communist. To an extent not rivalled by later generations, politically-aware students in the thirties were deeply concerned about international affairs, particularly from the outbreak of the Spanish Civil War in 1936 onwards, and the communist attempt to construct a united front against Fascist aggression helped to produce a sudden leap forward in interest in communism among students on the left in South Africa, as elsewhere in the Western world.

The immediate effect of the secessions from N.U.S.A.S., and the foundation of the A.N.S., was to force student leaders at the English-speaking universities to define where they stood on certain key issues, and to grapple directly with some of the political and ideological divisions within white society. At a juncture when at the national level the main drift seemed to be towards consensus, with the formation of the Hertzog/Smuts Fusion government and the United Party, students had to contend with the cleavages among themselves. It was instructive that the Student Parliament of 1933 failed to continue to mirror national politics, and did not produce a fusion government. Disagreements over the future of the African franchise in the Cape prevented any such government being formed.

The first response of N.U.S.A.S. to the secessions had been to seek to restore co-operation with the Afrikaans S.R.C.s by way of some *modus vivendi* with the A.N.S. To this end N.U.S.A.S. continued to decline to take any steps to admit Fort Hare, though it refused the proposal made by Stellenbosch University that it be inserted in the constitution 'that no native, coloured or Asiatic person be admitted to membership'. In 1935 N.U.S.A.S. Council instructed its executive to 'do everything in their power to get in touch with the A.N.S. executive with the object of introducing double membership', and in 1937 the executive was instructed to 'go into ways and means of co-operating with the A.N.S. in the matter of tours and conferences'.[11] The attitude the Wits S.R.C. adopted towards the A.N.S., and exclusive Afrikaner nationalism, was far less compromising. In September 1935 it unanimously resolved:

> This Council considers that the A.N.S., insofar as it departs from the purely cultural sphere and bases itself on principles of narrow nationalism and religious antipathy, is radically opposed to the fundamental principles of N.U.S.A.S. as an organisation representing freedom of thought and opinion among South African students, and as embracing all shades of student opinion.
>
> Accordingly, this Council considers that the time is ripe for N.U.S.A.S. to take a definite stand towards A.N.S. in an effort to combat its pernicious effect on liberal thought, and instructs the delegates to N.U.S.A.S. Council Meetings to insist that N.U.S.A.S. refuse to accord any recognition to A.N.S. unless and until that body is prepared to modify its principles so as to be compatible with the ideals of N.U.S.A.S.

In 1938 N.U.S.A.S. Council finally accepted that co-operation with the A.N.S. was 'impossible', and that 'nothing could be achieved from any further overtures by N.U.S.A.S.'[12]

The withdrawal of the Afrikaans S.R.C.s from N.U.S.A.S. proved a deathblow to the Student Parliament, the last meeting of which was held in 1935. By then it had been reduced to a farce. As stated by Sydney Kark, in proposing the motion in the Wits S.R.C. in June 1935 that the Student Parliament be abolished, 'the N.U.S.A.S. Parliament had failed in its objects, which were to pull politics out of the rough bickering into which it had fallen, not to give rugby-players and cheerleaders a cheap holiday'.[13] In the subsequent reorganization of N.U.S.A.S., and the formation of the South African Students' Liberal League, liberal and radical students began to occupy more prominent positions in student politics and organization at the English-speaking universities and university colleges.

Within N.U.S.A.S., the Student Parliament was replaced by a Department of Social Research, to embark on research on problems of national importance, including poor whites, Bantu affairs, and international affairs. On each campus a local branch of N.U.S.A.S. was formed to co-ordinate research, the results of which were to be collated and discussed at the annual conference. It was through these local committees, formed for the express purpose of examining political problems and issues, that the left was ultimately to move into control of N.U.S.A.S. The S.R.C.s ceased to dominate the N.U.S.A.S. Council, but instead shared representation with the local committees. In the late thirties, and more particularly during World War II, the local committees were taken over by left-wing students.[14]

The formation of the South African Students' Liberal League in July 1937 represented the first attempt by English-speaking South African students to establish an overtly political national student organization. It was preceded on the Wits campus by the Democratic League, founded in 1935 following the last Student Parliament and refused recognition by the S.R.C. because of its 'political' nature. The prime mover behind the Democratic League was Guy Routh, a politics student and a committed humanitarian. He was evidently the most active organizer of radical student groups at Wits in the late thirties. After the war, in which he fought, he was to become active in the trade union movement in Britain, and was later made Reader in Economics at Sussex University. In 1937 he was a key figure in organizing the South African Students' Liberal League, becoming its national secretary. The local secretary at Wits was Brian Bunting, an arts student and son of Sidney Bunting, a key figure in the founding of the Communist Party of South Africa. After the war, in which he served, Brian Bunting edited the *Guardian* and its successor publications, including *New Age,* until finally prohibited from publishing in 1963. In 1952 he was elected to Parliament as a Natives' Representative, but in the next year he was expelled under the Suppression of Communism Act.

Prior to Bunting, there had been students at Wits who had belonged to the C.P.S.A., notably Eddie Roux in the twenties, but Bunting was the first to become actively involved in student politics and affairs, serving as president of the S.R.C. and editor of *Umpa*, the student magazine.

In a statement to *Wu's Views*, Routh explained the objectives of the South African Students' Liberal League: 'The S.A.S.L.L. has been formed to organise and express student opinion, and to bring its weight to bear on the politics of South Africa, to combat generally retrogressive tendencies in the legislation of the country: to this end it asks for freedom for political discussion in the universities.' Jeanette Jaff made it clear that for Wits students, a major purpose of the League would be to protect and advance the position of Africans. 'Let those who desire to suppress natives', she stated, 'do it in the name of cheap labour; to pretend it is for the sake of art, morality and culture is not only a contradiction in terms, but unpleasant hypocrisy.'[15]

The South African Students' Liberal League did not prove a success, and it was dissolved in the next year following a disagreement between the Wits and U.C.T. branches 'over the native question'.[16] In 1938 the Democratic League at Wits was also dissolved, as a consequence of its continuing failure to receive S.R.C. recognition. Arthur Bunting, the elder brother of Brian and president of the S.R.C. in 1937, explained to the *Star:* 'The council as a whole felt that it was against the best interests of university life to allow the divisions and recriminations of active outside politics to enter into the activities of students and their organisations'.[17] Before capitulating, the Democratic League published two numbers of its journal, *Wits Laager*. It included articles on economics by staff members John Reedman and Hansi Pollak, who did not share the *laissez-faire* philosophy of Frankel and Richards but advanced instead social welfare views, and also on new trends in modern literature by Fanny Klenerman, the left-wing bookseller, as well as a 'Letter from Russia'.

In April 1938 at a crowded student meeting which dissolved the Democratic League, it was decided to form in its stead the Diogenes Club to discuss political issues 'impartially'. The club was to profess no political attitude itself, and in this way it was hoped to gain S.R.C. recognition. H.C. Nicholas, the S.R.C. president in 1936 and later a Supreme Court judge, opposed the move as a 'subterfuge to try to bluff the S.R.C.' He also apparently thought the club would be a waste of time. According to the report in *Wu's Views* he stated: 'Every South African student should be prepared to act militantly. Discussion among the faithful was useless.' Despite the reservations of Nicholas, the new club was given S.R.C. recognition.[18]

In September 1938 it was Nicholas, a brilliant speaker, who was due to address the meeting of the Diogenes Club on the British government's handling of the Munich crisis. Rowdy right-wing and conservative students in the audience that packed the Chemistry Lecture Theatre, refused him a hearing, and the meeting was terminated without any discussion taking place.

A year later Britain and South Africa were at war with Hitler's Germany. Many of the students who had howled down Nicholas immediately volunteered to serve; others, chiefly Afrikaans-speaking, remained fundamentally opposed to South African participation in a war with Germany. More than anything before, the war opened wide cleavages in the Wits student body. The war was also to prove the start of a new era in student interest and involvement in politics.

III

Principal Raikes, the majority of the University staff, and many on the S.R.C., watched with concern the growing involvement of students in political issues and movements. They feared the divisive impact of politics, and disliked the idea of students ruffling public sensibilities. They consequently sought to ban the distribution of political literature on campus, and to discourage students from adopting a high profile in outside political activities. The *Students' Handbook,* issued by the S.R.C., came to include the statement:

> The S.R.C. disapproves strongly of students attending external political meetings and demonstrations in University blazers, as such actions invariably bring the University into disrepute. It must be pointed out that the University blazer is a sports blazer and should be worn on the sports field only. It is bad to wear it to lectures, but very much worse to wear it in public at political meetings. Students may, of course, attend political meetings and take part in any other external activities in their capacities as private citizens. But it must be made clear again that should students even then come into conflict with the police, or be brought before the courts, the Principal must necessarily take cognisance of the fact.

In a way that had simply not happened in the twenties, the S.R.C. in the thirties found political issues impinging on its discussions and deliberations. The question of the recognition of the A.N.S., of the Democratic League, and of the Diogenes Club, the place of political activity and debate on campus, and the admission of Fort Hare to N.U.S.A.S., all came to feature in S.R.C. discussions. In 1939 politics even impinged on the S.R.C.'s handling of the annual intervarsity with Pretoria University.

The 1939 intervarsity was a bad-tempered affair. The rugby game was marred by a brawl between Wits and Tucs students in the crowd and by anti-Semitism in some of the cheer-leading. The athletic and hockey competitions were cancelled, and the law moot was called off. The secretary of the Wits Law Students' Society was an Indian, A.H. Mulla, and the Pretoria University students refused to correspond with him. At first the Wits S.R.C., chaired by Brian Bunting, attempted to dodge some of the main issues arising out of the intervarsity, but at the insistence of Basil Shtein, a law student, it eventually carried the motion 'That the S.R.C. is not prepared to accept the position that future communications between the two S.R.C.'s shall be subject to any condition involving colour, or creed, in regard to any student official or member of any society'. It also passed the motion 'That this S.R.C. objects to the introduction of politics into sport'.[19]

Political issues confronting the S.R.C. were none the less still episodic, and did not constitute a central part of the council's debate and activity. The S.R.C. remained as it had been in the twenties, essentially an administrative body for co-ordinating and financing student societies and clubs, and general student activities.

The Students' Representative Council was founded in 1905, in the days of the Transvaal Technical Institute. It was elected annually by the general body of students to represent them 'in all matters concerning their interests'. According to the constitution adopted for the S.R.C. when the University was established, it was to serve as the official means of communication between students on the one hand and Council and Senate on the other, to authorize all student functions, to be the ruling body over all recognized societies, clubs, and committees, to control and regulate the sale and wearing of all University colours and badges, to be the ruling body in all matters pertaining to meetings, collections, and petitions organized by students, to ensure good conduct at student entertainments, and generally to control all matters affecting the general interests of students, with the proviso, required by Council and Senate, that its functions should in no way conflict with the powers vested in Council and Senate. In the performance of its routine work, the S.R.C. operated chiefly through a series of sub-committees, which came to include the finance committee for recommending grants and loans, the students' union committee for arranging or authorizing social functions, the all sports committee for looking after the interests of sporting clubs and recommending the award of colours, the pavilion and grounds committee to supervise the maintenance and use of the sports grounds and the change rooms at the pavilion, the rag committee to arrange and control the annual rag, and the Students' Benefit Society, a compulsory insurance society for all students other than medical students.

STUDENT LIFE

Front row: Miss M. Janisch, R.W. Talbot, I. Liknaitzky, A. Goldstein, I. Frack, L.D. Adler, Miss B. Liknaitzky; Second row: W.H. Evans, Miss J. Mayne, B. Bessarabia, J.A. Lindenberg, E.B. Gascoigne, L.A. Moses, A.S. Wakefield, C. Duthie, Miss E. Franks; Back row: M. Franks, A.E. Ettlinger, K.E. Acheson, C.W. de Kiewiet, T.L. Davis; Insets: L.I. Cohen, G.C. Thomson

Front row: M.G. Rabinowitz, Miss H. White, L.P. Badenhorst, L. Frenkel, G.D.G. Davidson, H. Nicholas, F.R. Chamberlain; Second row: J. Unterhalter, D.H. Russell, J.C. Dunne, J. MacKintosh, D.P.S. O'Keeffe, M. Levin, M.A. Millner; Back row: S.L. Kark, J.N. Benjamin, E.W. Schultz, A. van Niekerk, J. O'Meara, D.P. Jones, C. Sinclair; Upper insets: R.F. Amm, T.A. White; Lower inset: W. Bryer

Students' Representative Councils, 1922 (top) and 1935 (bottom)

347

The members of the S.R.C. were elected by faculties. In the University's first year, an S.R.C. representative was returned for every 40 students in a faculty, but by 1939 the basis had been changed to one representative for every 140 students. This meant that the size of the S.R.C. was kept to about 30 members, and that in the thirties it came to be dominated by arts, medical, and engineering students, with a notable number of its presidents coming from the medical faculty. Despite the fact that the medical school was separate from the main campus, medical students prior to World War II were closely involved in the general affairs of the University. A medical training did not as yet consume all their time. L.D. Adler (1924), S.C. Heymann (1926), T.W.B. Osborn (1927), J. Schwartz (1929), C. Adler (1931), and L. Frankel (1935) were all S.R.C. presidents drawn from the medical school. A.C. Backeberg, in 1925, was the only engineering student to become president of the University S.R.C.

Uniquely among South African universities, the Wits S.R.C. managed its own finances. Included in student fees was a compulsory S.R.C. levy. In 1922 the levy was still £1 per annum, the amount agreed to by Council in 1911, but a decade later it had been increased to £2 10s., largely to help finance the provision of new sporting facilities, notably the swimming pool. Half of the revenue obtained from the increased levy was handled independently by the S.R.C. for financing various student activities; the other half was paid into the Development Fund, established in 1928, for capital expenditure in providing sporting and other student facilities.

A good deal of discussion in the S.R.C. was devoted to the allocation of financial grants, as well as to the recognition of new clubs and societies wanting S.R.C. funding. Questions relating to the award of sporting colours, the arrangements for rags, N.U.S.A.S. conferences, intervarsities and other sports meetings, and the administration and condition of the men's and women's common rooms, were the other main items on the agenda for S.R.C. meetings. In the University's first year, the S.R.C. resolved that 'heraldic blue' should serve as the colour for the University's blazer.[20]

Two issues that for long preoccupied the S.R.C. were initiation and Sunday sport. After what was widely described as the 'barbaric' initiation ceremony for freshers in 1923, a major campaign was mounted in the public press and within the University for the abolition of initiation. At first the S.R.C. proved reluctant to abandon the ceremony, and the 'spirit' that prompted it, but in 1925, under the chairmanship of A.C. Backeberg, it finally recommended in favour of abolition. At a general meeting held in the Chemistry Lecture Theatre on 14 September 1925, Backeberg informed the student body that the S.R.C. had come to the conclusion that the practice of initiation 'was not in accordance with the dignity of a great University'. The S.R.C. consequently

STUDENT LIFE

Initiation, 1923

recommended that no initiation ceremony be held in future, and that freshmen be required simply to wear some distinctive badge for their first term. When put to the vote, the recommendations were adopted virtually unanimously.[21]

Several attempts were made thereafter to revive initiation. The last major effort, it seems, was in 1934 when Lennie Rabinowitz proposed to the S.R.C. that it be reinstated. He contended that initiation served both to create unity among the freshers and to bring them 'at once into the spirit and social life of the University'. Although a committee was appointed to 'devise a system for fresher introductory ceremonies', it failed to recommend any kind of initiation ceremony. Instead it recommended the introduction of a card system designed to oblige freshers to join a certain number of University clubs.[22] In the men's residences, initiation ceremonies continued to be practised until after World War II.

The question of Sunday sport was raised repeatedly in the S.R.C. in the twenties and thirties. As soon as playing fields and tennis courts had been constructed at Milner Park, Council had imposed a total ban on their use on Sundays, and University clubs were also prohibited from playing matches at other venues on Sundays. This was resented particularly by students in residence, who were consequently often at a loose end on a Sunday, and by those students who played sports, such as hockey, the local leagues for which were organized on a Sunday. On their behalf, the S.R.C. consistently pressed for the ban on Sunday sport to be lifted, or at least modified.

Certain concessions were in fact made to allow residence students to play tennis and to use the swimming pool on Sunday afternoons. Permission for residence students to use the tennis courts on Sundays was first granted by Council in 1925, but at the end of the year it was withdrawn following a conference between Council and the Witwatersrand Church Council. In 1931 permission was restored. Two years previously Principal Raikes had written to the Minister of Education, Dr D.F. Malan, to sound out his views on allowing 'the playing of tennis, net practice for cricket and kicking about of footballs', at the University on Sunday afternoons. 'I wish it clearly to be understood', he advised Malan, 'that I am not asking the Minister to express direct approval of the scheme, but I feel that if he considers that the scheme outlined would be counter to the policy of the Government or might be liable to cause inconvenience to the Government, it would be essential for the Council of the University to take this decision very carefully into consideration quite apart from any local considerations.'[23] Malan made it equally clear that he disapproved, and the proposal was temporarily shelved. In 1930 the S.R.C. petitioned that 'Sunday Sport should be sanctioned', and in response Council in the next year agreed to allow students in residence to play tennis and swim on Sunday afternoons. The concession was strongly opposed by Jan Hofmeyr, who demanded that his adverse vote be recorded.[24] Despite further petitions from the S.R.C. to permit full sporting activities on Sundays, Council refused to 'alter its general policy whereunder certain limited facilities for Sunday recreation are allowed to students in residence only'.[25]

Two other issues of general concern to students that featured from time to time in S.R.C. deliberations were the questions of student dress and behaviour. On occasion the S.R.C. would become quite as agitated as the University authorities about 'unbecoming' dress among students, and the S.R.C. of 1925, in addition to abolishing initiation, went so far as to recommend that the University make it compulsory for students to wear gowns to lectures. 'The S.R.C.', the secretary, S.C. Heymann, wrote to the Principal, 'feel that this would be a procedure which would lend dignity to the University activities . . .'[26] The University thereupon adopted the rule that students were required to wear gowns at all academic functions and at all ordinary day-class lectures, unless exempted by the head of the department. The provision about gowns was withdrawn in 1934, and no new rule on student dress at lectures replaced it. The regulating of student dress, it appears, was left to the Principal and individual heads of departments. Guidelines about dress were set down in the student handbook:

> Men Students should wear a lounge suit, or a sports coat and grey flannels, together with a collar and a tie, when attending lectures or other normal University functions. Women Students, correspondingly, should wear conventional dress with stockings. All such irregularities as, on the part of men, lumber jackets, open necked shirts, shorts, and University blazers, and on the part of women, the not wearing of stockings, are frowned on by the authorities. Students should respect their professors and lecturers and the administrative staff by adopting respectable forms of dress.[27]

Of particular concern to the S.R.C. was the wearing of University blazers to lectures, but attempts to stamp out this practice do not seem to have succeeded.

As prescribed by its constitution, one of the functions of the S.R.C. was 'To take steps for the preservation of order at the University's entertainments and for the ensuring of good conduct at other approved social meetings of the Students'. In some instances, as after the break-up of the Diogenes Club meeting on the Munich crisis, the S.R.C. took the initiative in dealing with questions of student disorderliness or misbehaviour, but normally the initiative came from the University authorities seeking S.R.C. support. The establishment in 1937 of the standing committee on student discipline as a committee of Senate led almost immediately to an attempt to co-opt the S.R.C. in the effort to improve student behaviour at rag and other functions. In September 1938, following complaints from members of the public about 'acts unbecoming to students' during rag, and reports of student misbehaviour at the annual N.U.S.A.S. conference, the standing committee on student discipline, chaired by Raikes, recommended that the Principal summon the S.R.C. to meet him to discuss the question of student behaviour. The S.R.C.'s response was that the reports received by Senate of bad student behaviour had been greatly exaggerated, but that none the less it would do 'all in its power to raise the standard of student behaviour'. With regard to rag, the S.R.C. seemed to think that the rag committee had always 'exercised a strong censorship of floats and costumes', but gave the assurance it would do so 'even more strenuously in the future'. With regard to the suggestion that when teams and other parties travelled out of town, one or more students be made responsible for the behaviour of the group, the S.R.C. replied: 'It is considered impossible to make any one person responsible for the behaviour of a team or party of students while travelling; but in every case a responsible member will accompany the group, who shall be instructed before departure of the team or group, of the need for maintaining a high standard of behaviour.'[28]

Prior to World War II, the S.R.C. was never very assertive in its dealings with the University authorities. The two attempts it did make to advance its own position, and the role of students, in the government of the University, were easily brushed aside by the University authorities. In the framing of the Act and statutes of the University, the S.R.C.'s request for statutory recognition was ignored, and in 1927 the suggestion that students be given representation on Council and Senate was turned down. In his president's report for 1927, Tommy Osborn complained: 'One of our most ambitious hopes – that of obtaining some representation on the ruling bodies of this University – has met with no success at all, and we feel that we have been treated somewhat curtly in this matter.'[29] After the war, the University authorities were to find it less easy to dismiss such approaches of the S.R.C.

IV

For student clubs, societies, and publications, S.R.C. recognition and support was of the first importance. It provided them with financial backing, as well as giving them access to University facilities. Recognition was not always easy to obtain. Not only was it a basic principle of the S.R.C. that all clubs and societies had to be open to all students before it would grant recognition, but in considering applications for recognition it sought to safeguard what it considered the best interests of the University, and also to avoid squandering the funds at its disposal. For some time the S.R.C. denied recognition to the Philosophical Club on the grounds that its constitution was unsatisfactory and that the club was in 'unsuitable hands'. The S.R.C. also initially refused permission for a soccer club to be established as 'such a Club would detract from the interest shown in Rugby football, this latter game being the recognised inter-collegiate sport'.[30] S.R.C. recognition was never extended to the A.N.S., nor the Democratic League.

Student societies were not only integral to the life of the University, but sometimes had a wider importance. Prior to World War II, the University, through its public lectures and exhibitions, and the dramatic and musical productions which it staged, was a major centre in the intellectual and cultural life of Johannesburg, and student societies contributed to this. From time to time student societies organized major public lectures, as when the Philosophical Society arranged one by the American philosopher, John Dewey, and several societies, notably the Bantu Studies Society and those with professional links, consistently attempted to interest audiences outside the University as well as within. The Dramatic Society, which initially included staff as well as students, generally aroused considerable public interest in its annual productions.

During the twenties and thirties the University's students established a wide range of societies. By the end of the twenties each of the professional faculties possessed student faculty societies; the Students' Medical Society, the Engineering Students' Society, the Law Students' Society, the Commerce Students' Society, and the Students' Dental Society. In 1930 the Medical Society was superseded by the Students' Medical Council, the first student faculty council in South Africa, to supervise and control all matters affecting the medical students, including their societies. In the late thirties students in arts and science established their own faculty societies, the Arts Students' Society and the Science Students' Association. Societies closely related to individual departments or groups of departments included in arts the Philosophical Society, the Afrikaans Taal en Kultuur Vereniging, the Musical Association, the Classical Society, and the Gubbins Society for 'the study of history for its own sake'; in science the Biological Society, the Geological Society, the Astronomical Society, and the Scientific Discussion Society for 'the study of natural science for its own sake'; and the Architectural Society. Two student religious societies, the Students' Christian Association and

Students' Jewish Association, were established in the twenties, and a third, the Students' Catholic Society, in the thirties. Societies which cut across disciplinary and religious lines, and involved students from all faculties, included the Debating Society and the Dramatic Society, and the more politically-oriented Bantu Studies Society, the Women's Political Discussion Circle, the International Study Circle, and the Diogenes Club. The Debating Society and Dramatic Society were popularly regarded as the two leading societies, though the standard of debate and performance might vary considerably from year to year.

Law, medical, and arts students generally dominated the Debating Society, which appears to have been at its height in the late twenties and in the thirties. In the University's first year, when Herbert Frankel was chairman, the society gained a certain notoriety for sponsoring a lecture by Mrs Knox Livingston, an American campaigner for prohibition, which produced an 'orgy of rowdyism'. On the night of the lecture Frankel was kidnapped to prevent him from taking the chair, and another student, who according to the press had recently stood for the S.R.C., was substituted in his stead. On a platform which had been adorned with illuminated advertisements for a certain brand of beer, and which had been liberally sprinkled with whisky, the new chairman mounted a beer barrel to introduce the speaker. Mrs Knox Livingston then proceeded with her address amidst interjections and interruptions from 'a small organised gang' in the audience. 'On the platform', according to the *Star* report, 'was Principal Hofmeyr, who during the evening never once raised his voice in protest, and it was left to a member of the public to offer an apology to Mrs Knox Livingston for the conduct of a section of the audience.'[31]

From 1923, Eddie Roux, as honorary secretary, took over the organizing of the Debating Society, and it rapidly gained in stature. 1925 proved a momentous year, with a visit from the Oxford Union, and a sparkling speech from Herman Charles Bosman that caught the attention of the local press. In opposing the motion 'That the emancipation of woman has made her less attractive', Bosman entertained the audience with an account of 'the fastest girl in Boksburg'. Following the introduction of an annual best speakers' competition in the late twenties, the Debating Society entered its most flourishing phase. Winners of the competition, many of them prominent in student affairs, included Phillip Heimann, George Colman, W. Gordon Murray, Maurice Millner, L.C.F. Turner, and Phyllis Orkin.

The Dramatic Society was formally established in 1923, its first production being Shakespeare's *The Tempest* at the Palladium Theatre. It was intended that the society should serve in 'uniting Professors and students in a common activity, and uniting University and town in a common enjoyment'. These aims it fulfilled with rather greater success in the twenties than in the thirties, when it became more strictly a student society, and the productions ceased to be as regular. Its policy was to stage major works that would not normally have been seen on the commercial stage. After 1923 the Standard Theatre was used to stage the productions of the University Players until in 1927 the assembly hall in the North West Engineering block came into use as a theatre as well as a venue for meetings. The first production staged in the assembly hall was Aristophanes' *The Clouds*. The set was designed by Stanley Furner, the architect, and Professor Kirby put the choruses to music.[32] Other members of staff often actively engaged in the productions of the Dramatic Society were J.G. Lawrie and A.D. Stammers, both accomplished amateur actors. Two student performers who were to have a future on the stage were Moira Lister, who made her first appearance in *The Vikings at Helgeland*, performed by the University Players in 1930, and Cecil Williams, for some time a local producer, who played Arkel in *Pelleas and Melisanda* in 1931. Dramatic productions were also sometimes staged by the medical school in the thirties, the most notable being *The Anatomist* in 1936. Staged in the dissecting hall at the medical school, it featured Professor Dart in the leading part of Dr Knox.

Of student publications, the *Umpa*, the University magazine, and *Wu's Views*, a fortnightly newspaper, were the direct responsibility of the S.R.C. Other official publications were the *Leech*, the journal of the medical school; the *Auricle*, published by the Students' Medical Council; the *Fulcrum*, the publication of the Engineering Students' Society; the *Scientific Discussion Society Journal*; the *Prattler*, the magazine of the men's residences; and *Wits Wits*, the rag magazine. Student publications which appeared briefly, but which did not survive for lack of financial backing, included the *Salamander*, published in 1931–2 and entirely devoted to literary and creative work; the *Philistine*, a more politically oriented journal edited by Jack Unterhalter in 1934; and *Wits Laager*, the journal of the Democratic League.

The publication with the longest ancestry was the *Umpa*. Since 1914 the School of Mines had produced a student magazine once or twice a year. With the founding of the University an attempt was made to bring out a monthly magazine, and for this purpose the S.R.C. invested in an Edison-Dick mimeograph machine. The experiment was rapidly declared a failure, and in the next year the S.R.C. decided to revert to a printed magazine, to appear twice a year and with some pretentions to literary merit. In 1925, following a competition among readers, it was decided to call the magazine the *Umpa*: "'The Umpa' was placed first on the grounds it is familiar to all students of the University, as well as to the wider public, through its place in the

University War-Cry, and it is equally suitable in both official languages.'[33] The magazine was initially sold, but as this limited circulation the S.R.C. undertook full responsibility for its financing, allocating a liberal share of its pages to advertisers.

The *Umpa* served a variety of purposes. It carried reports from the various student societies and clubs, provided editorial comment, and served as a vehicle for student creative and critical writing. It included critical articles, book reviews, short stories, and poems. Several of Vincent Swart's poems, including 'Casey Jones', were first published in *Umpa*, as were the earliest Afrikaans poems of Elisabeth Eybers. The *Umpa* sometimes achieved a high literary quality, but was never particularly popular among students.

The initial career of *Wu's Views* was erratic. It first appeared in 1927 as a mimeographed news and comment sheet, and in 1929 it began to be printed. In the next year, in which twelve numbers were issued, the cost of the paper was reduced from threepence to a penny, but considerable difficulty was experienced in finding sufficient advertisers and able contributors. In 1932 Cyril Adler, a former president of the S.R.C., sought to secure the closure of *Wu's Views*, then being edited by Max Gluckman, on the ground that it had proved 'an absolute failure'. He claimed that the paper served no useful purpose, and that the University would be better off without it.[34] *Wu's Views* was not then closed down, but in 1934 it ceased to appear. Advertising, it seems, was hard to come by, and the publication of the *Philistine* in that year caused a major furore in that it appropriated advertising revenue that the S.R.C. believed should be reserved for official student publications.[35] In 1935 *Wu's Views* made a brief reappearance as a duplicated comment sheet. Only in 1937 was it placed on a truly sound footing, with adequate advertising and an S.R.C. financial guarantee. Thereafter it was produced as a regular fortnightly newspaper, with liberal provision for opinion and gossip as well as news items.

The medical school journal, the *Leech*, first appeared in November 1928. It was not a purely student journal, but was directed at medical graduates as well as undergraduates. Indeed, according to the first editorial, the intention was that the journal should be 'of interest not only to the medical faculty of the University, but also to the entire medical profession of Johannesburg'. It was therefore to consist of a scientific section, including articles by senior members of the profession, as well as a 'social' section to satisfy student needs. Part of the problem experienced by the early *Leech*, which normally appeared twice a year, was that it could not make up its mind whether it was to be chiefly a scientific or a general and undergraduate journal. The complaint against the first number was that it was too scientific; against the second that it was too juvenile. In November 1933, on the fifth anniversary of the journal, when Dr Pericles Menof was editor, it was announced that in future years two numbers of *Leech* would be issued 'as a medical journal of general interest', and that a third would be 'coldly scientific in its outlook'. But in 1934 the *Leech* acquired a new editor in Joseph Gillman, and he proceeded to emphasize the serious and scientific nature of the journal. At the same time, he also increased the number of student contributions, a significant proportion of which focused on problems of health and disease in the African population. In 1935 the Students' Medical Council launched a new monthly publication, the *Auricle*, to provide students with the news, gossip, and humour denied publication in the *Leech*.

The *Fulcrum*, the journal of the Engineering Students' Society, was started in 1934 under the editorship of J. Drysdale, lecturer in the Department of Mechanical Engineering, having been preceded in 1932 by a mimeographed journal. Although students took over the responsibility for editing the *Fulcrum* in 1935, articles were provided mainly by staff and former students rather than students themselves. The journal covered the whole range of engineering, and by the end of the decade had established a high standard for its scientific and technological articles. Contributors included Professor W.J. Walker on turbine engines, Principal Raikes on coal and its by-products, V.L. Bosazza of the Minerals Research Laboratory, G.R. Bozzoli, R.L. Straszacker, and A.J.A. Roux, who wrote in Afrikaans. The *Fulcrum* made rather more of an attempt at bilingualism than did the *Leech*, and it enjoyed a wide circulation outside the University.

V

Apart from athletics, swimming, and rowing, where Wits teams excelled in the thirties, the University's record in sport was generally disappointing. Rugby, popularly regarded as the University's premier sport, was the cause of more complaint than congratulation, and the cricket and soccer teams languished in the lower leagues. Hockey, cricket, and tennis were hampered by the fact that the University did not allow sport on Sundays.

Sports facilities at Milner Park were established very gradually during the twenties and thirties, with the students themselves raising much of the finance for their construction. In 1920 a rugby ground and some tennis courts, provided by the Witwatersrand University Committee, were opened, but in the financial squeeze thereafter no further funds were forthcoming for the construction of sports facilities. In 1922 the students took the initiative, and organized a public campaign to raise £4 000 for sports grounds. The campaign fell far short of its target, but it was able to finance the construction of a hard hockey and soccer field and of a sports pavilion, which thereafter became a major centre for students at Milner Park. Teas and snacks were served there. In 1927 the S.R.C. under T.W.B. Osborn proposed the launching of a new fund-raising campaign for sports facilities, including a swimming pool. The result was the formation in the next year of the University Development Fund Committee, chaired by Principal Raikes but with a majority of student members. This committee organized the University Week and fund-raising campaign of 1928, and thereafter took responsibility for financing and developing sports grounds and facilities 'in accordance with the general layout plan decided on from time to time by the University Council'. In 1932 the committee was reconstructed as the Students' Development Fund Committee.[36]

By the end of 1928 the Development Fund had acquired a capital of £15 000, £4 000 from the public campaign, £1 000 from the additional levy of 15s per student in the S.R.C. fee, a £5 000 grant from Council in return for the use of the water supply from the swimming pool, and a £5 000 loan from Council at 5 per cent interest, repayable over ten years. The sum was considered sufficient for authority to be given for the construction of a swimming pool, at an estimated cost of £11 000, a new hockey field, another grass rugby field, and six more tennis courts. The swimming pool, which was opened in 1930, in fact cost £13 000, and the S.R.C. was shocked to discover that it was held responsible for its upkeep. The outcome was that in 1931 the S.R.C. fee was again increased, from £2 to £2 10s. In April 1933 an athletic track, constructed round the hockey field, was opened, and in 1935 a turf cricket pitch was laid. In 1939 soccer finally acquired its own field.

Until the developments of the thirties, limited facilities hampered student sports at Wits. Also restrictive was the ban on Sunday sport. Hockey suffered particularly, as all the local leagues were staged on Sundays, but cricket and tennis were also affected. The cricket and tennis clubs played in the Saturday but not the Sunday leagues, and the hockey teams depended on the willingness of league opponents to reschedule their matches on Saturdays. In the twenties the women's hockey club managed this with some success, while the men played friendlies and intervarsities only. In 1934 the women resorted to the expedient of turning out for the University Past Students' teams, and Wits itself ceased to enter the local leagues.

Another problem was that a significant number of students preferred to play for outside clubs rather than University teams. Inadequate facilities at Milner Park, the prohibition on Sunday sport, and the fact that in some sports, notably cricket and soccer, the Wits teams were confined to the lower leagues,

STUDENT LIFE

South African School of Mines 1st XV, 1912

Front row: M. Baumann, F. Long, E. Andrews
Second row: T. Leslie, C. Anderson, J.D. Mackenzie, W. Geerling, L. Taylor
Back row: W. Lindemann, G. Parry, J. van Belkum, C.A. Pratt, W. Galpin, B. Wade, J. Pocock

Johannesburg University College 1st XV, 1920

Front row: P. Geerling, T.D. Papenfus, C. Kemp
Second row: J.N. Lurie, W.H. Evans, E.H. Cluver, R.R. Robinson, B.O. Poynton
Back row: A.R. Mitchell, H. Clark, M.A. Thiselton, W. Clucas, B. Bovet, M. Rouillard, G. Russell

Wits Rugby Touring Team to the Eastern Province, 1923

Seated: P. Rankin, L.D. Adler, F.C. Gray, A. Lindenberg, D. Gien; Standing: T. Roos, E. Jooste, J. van Rooyen, A.L. Harington, M. Rostovsky, E.J.B. Shawe, S. van Aarot, G.M. Greef, E.J. Bam; Back row: F. van de Steen, F. Duthie, B.H. Ziervogel, H. Henning, C.J. Claasens; Inset: F.C. Hill, A. Adami, M.B.B. Salkinder

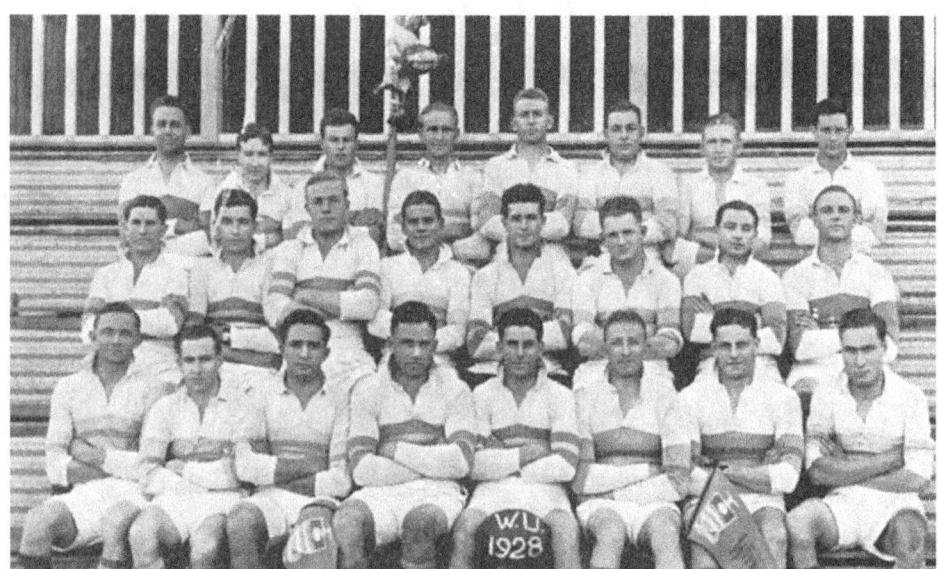

Wits Rugby Touring Team to Rhodesia, 1928

Front row: A.N. Sandenbergh, J.G. Kneen, P. van der Lith, F. Uys, B. Sieff, M.A. Cooper, H. Heydenreich, G. Mynhardt; Second row: H.B. Michalow, N.L. Murray, E.A. Faber, G.L. Burger, R.G. Weavind, A.D. Proudfoot, P. Kirsch, R. Brinton; Back row: Q. Ochse, T. Kneen, J. Freislich, C.J. Claassen, A.H. van Wyk, L. van Flymen, W. Heunis, F.A. Brandt

prompted several students to join outside clubs. Identification with local communities, particularly along the East Rand, and the maintenance of school allegiances through old boys' clubs, were in some instances even stronger factors inclining students to play for outside clubs. Although the problem of students playing for such clubs persisted throughout the twenties and thirties, no attempt seems to have been made to oblige students to play for Wits. In 1937 the S.R.C. did, however, resolve 'That registered students of the University at present playing for outside clubs, register next year for University Clubs under penalty of being refused University colours and membership to all Clubs and Societies of the University'.[37]

Of all the University's sports clubs, the rugby club was the least beset by these difficulties. The first sports field at Milner Park was for rugby, and the club was also the first to be given an additional field. All rugby leagues were staged on Saturdays, and it was more a cause for complaint in rugby that non-students or 'sham' students, who registered for courses but never sat exams, appeared for University teams rather than that genuine students played for outside clubs. Old boys' clubs tended not to possess rugby teams. By the end of the twenties the rugby club had a membership of almost 200 players, with seven teams entered in league competitions. The first fifteen competed in the first league, or Pirates Grand Challenge, throughout the twenties and thirties. Yet the rugby club was regularly regarded as a disappointment, primarily because the first fifteen was usually to be found in the lower rather than the upper half of its league, and because it lost more intervarsities against Pretoria than it won.

The rugby club's membership of the first league went back to 1913, but it was not to win the league until 1968. Before World War II, the club was at its greatest strength in the late twenties and the beginning of the thirties, due in some measure to the influx of engineering and medical students into the University. 1928 was memorable for the formation of an under-19 team, which promptly proceeded to win its league, as also for the achievements of the first fifteen. It defeated Pretoria in both intervarsities, came fifth out of twelve teams in the league, and undertook a tour of Rhodesia, winning four of its six matches, including one against the full Rhodesian team. In 1931 the first fifteen again won both intervarsities against Pretoria, came sixth in the Pirates Grand Challenge, and produced its first Springbok, H.M. Forrest, who was selected for the tour of the British Isles. By taking his rugby seriously, the rugby notes in *Umpa* commented, Forrest 'transformed himself within the space of three years from a mere soccer player into a rugby player of Springbok class'.[38] But thereafter the first fifteen went into something of a decline, and for five years failed to register a win over Pretoria in any of the intervarsities. 'I cannot leave the subject of sport', Principal Raikes complained in his review of University events in 1934, 'without a word as to the somewhat dismal fate which has overtaken Rugby football. In the past we have had sides second to none in the Transvaal, and one had hoped that we might go on to see more than a solitary Springbok selected from the University. But we have gone into a decline. It is time that we started to climb out of the valley of defeat and to show our colours again on the high tops.'[39]

Theoretically, rugby should have done well in the thirties. Engineering and medical students provided the club with its sturdiest recruits, and in the thirties enrolment in the engineering and medical faculties rose markedly. What was more, the traditional complaint that rugby at Wits was hampered because the English-medium schools in Johannesburg played only soccer, ceased to hold true. King Edward VII School, Jeppe High School, and St John's College all adopted rugby at the beginning of the thirties.[40] From the evidence of the student press, the chief complaint against the rugby club in the thirties was that it lacked commitment and spirit. In his S.R.C. president's reports for 1933 and 1934, F.R. Chamberlain claimed that the club's training methods were 'lackadaisical', and that the players were more interested in dancing on a Friday night than winning at rugby on a Saturday afternoon.[41] This refrain was still being repeated at the end of the decade. In 1938, when the first fifteen won only one league game and finished with the wooden spoon, *Wu's Views* commented: 'Lack of spirit is very marked in the Rugby Club; the general attitude of the players seems to be one of condescension when they do turn out.'[42]

Wits's main contribution to university sport in South Africa was probably in athletics. It was through the initiative of Wits athletes, notably Saul 'Pete' Suzman, that the annual South African intervarsity athletics championships were organized, and the South African Universities' Athletic Federation formed. The first intervarsity athletics championship was staged at the Wanderers Club, Johannesburg, in 1921. Three teams participated, representing the Transvaal University College, Grey University College, and Johannesburg University College, and at the end of the meeting a floating trophy donated by Sir William Dalrymple was presented to the victorious Johannesburg team. In the next year five universities and university colleges competed at the Wanderers for the Dalrymple cup, and in 1923 the number rose to seven, with only Stellenbosch University not participating. In the spring of 1923 Suzman also organized a tour of South Africa by the Oxford University Athletic Club, thereby pioneering visits to the country by overseas athletics teams. In 1929 the Achilles team, consisting of ex-Oxford and Cambridge athletes, toured, and they were followed in 1931 by an American team, and in 1935 by a combined Oxford and Cambridge team.

STUDENT LIFE

Lady Phillips presents the Dalrymple cup, 1921

Inter-University Athletic Team, 1925

Front row: A. Brink, J. Kneen
Second row: G. Stott, A.D. Macdonald, S. Suzman, J.C. Brink, R.L. Harris
Back row: A. Suzman, J.H. Gray, A.M. Snijman, H. Tucher, G. Eddy, T.L. Davis, J.H. Gear

In the twenties Wits athletes used the track at the Wanderers. It was with the opening of a track at Milner Park in 1933 that athletics at Wits truly came into its own. In 1939 the Wits team won the annual intervarsity athletics championships for the fifth successive year, thereby breaking the previous record of four successive victories established by Stellenbosch. Outstanding individual athletes who ran for Wits in the thirties included Lionel Melzer, who captained the S.A. Varsities team against the visiting Americans in 1931, H.A. Thompson and W. Botha, who both became Springboks, competing in the 1934 British Empire Games, and L.A. Fouché, who as a Wits student won the shot put title at the 1938 Empire Games in Sydney.

Following the opening of the swimming bath in 1930, the swimming club also enjoyed a series of outstanding successes. In 1929 the Wits swimmers had taken the initiative in organizing the South African Universities' Swimming Federation and the first South African intervarsity gala, held in Pretoria. In the thirties they dominated the intervarsity gala, winning it for seven successive years from 1933. Much of this success was due to the coaching of the swimming bath superintendent. Tom Ferguson. 'Fergy', as he was popularly known, was rated by one international list as the eighth best swimming coach in the world. He served as superintendent and coach at the swimming bath for 23 years, until his death in December 1952.

Swimming Team, 1933/4

Boat Club 'Four Crew', 1931
W.E. Marsh, E.G. Pringle, Professor O.K. Williamson, B.L. Bernstein, J.L. Parnell

Rowing was the only other sport at which Wits came to excel consistently. The initial career of the rowing club was, however, not at all promising. First formed in 1924, with A.D. Stammers as captain, the club used to row on the Wemmer Pan, but then faded out of existence. 'The Wemmer Pan began to dry up', it was commented in the *Umpa,* 'and with it the enthusiasm of the members.'[43] In 1930, due largely to the initiative of Professor O.K. Williamson, the club was revived under the new name of the Witwatersrand University Boat Club, and it was to go from strength to strength during the thirties. In 1937 the club acquired its own clubhouse at Rand Leases Dam, and celebrated by winning for the third time South Africa's premier rowing event, the Buffalo Grand Challenge at the East London Regatta.

It was not until after World War II that cricket, hockey, soccer, and tennis were to become major sports at Wits. In the twenties and thirties their development was severely restricted either by the ban on Sunday sport, or the competition of outside clubs for the services of student players, or a combination of both. In soccer, in fact, a South African Football Association regulation prevented many students, primarily from the East Rand, from playing for Wits by requiring that they appear for clubs in the districts in which they resided.[44]

None the less the University clubs in these sports were not without their

Women's Hockey Team, 1927

Front row: E. Bull, E. Shlom; Second row: B. Roe, I. Kowarsky, D. Kotze, J. Jacobson, E. Hartmann; Back row: B. Hartmann, J. Tierney, K. Knowles-Williams; Inset: M. Paine

Women's Tennis Team, 1934

H. Rheinallt-Jones, L. Strachan, E. Carr, W. Broadhead, M. Matheson, J. Sutherland, D. Loffell

STUDENT LIFE

Soccer Team, 1922

Front row: I. Carpel, E. van der Merwe; Second row: J. Glennie, T.L. Davis, G. Thomson, J. Gaw, W. Kerr; Back row: R. Stirling, M. Perlman, C. Forder, H.G. Durand, J. Leslie, L. Becker, A. Lomiansky; Inset: J.T. Morrison

Cricket Club 1st XI, winners of the Chauncey cup, 1932/3

Front row: W. Girdwood, W. Reichman, G. Christie, P. Bates; Second row: W. Meyers, M. Pringle, T. Fraser, A. Gyngell, C. Harington; Back row: G. Bozzoli, T. Staples, S. Stewart, M. Gluckman, M. Bryer, J. Smith

achievements. In the twenties, indeed, the women's hockey club, coached by the Springbok Mrs Yell, was a major power in the Southern Transvaal League, and produced its own Springbok in the person of Miss J. Jacobson, who toured England with the South African team in 1926. It was a major set-back to the club when in 1934 the league put an end to the practice whereby the Wits teams played their games on Saturday afternoons. It was claimed that this concession led to 'a great deal of inconvenience'.[45] At the end of the thirties Wits again entered teams in the local leagues, and in 1939 Miss Jackie Rissik was selected for the Springbok team to tour England. The cricket club, for its part, won the Chauncey cup in 1932/3, and in 1939 gained promotion to the top section of the reserve league. The Wits soccer club was confined to the junior leagues, but in 1939 became the first junior team to play in the Transvaal Challenge Cup, causing something of a sensation by defeating Brakpan 4–1 in the first round.

Other sports clubs at Wits by the end of the thirties included boxing and wrestling, golf, water polo, and even ice hockey. In 1936 an ice hockey club was formed, primarily through the initiative of Professor J.Y.T. Greig, himself an ice hockey referee.

VI

Rag, as an institution, is as old as the University, although it was not until 1929 that a rag was first staged to raise money for charity. The first organized rag in the history of Wits was on 4 October 1922, to coincide with the official inauguration of the University and its first graduation. It took the form of a mock funeral to bury the old School of Mines prior to the official ceremony and graduation to celebrate the birth of the new University of the Witwatersrand. The students marched from Plein Square to the Town Hall, where 'proper funereal honours' were accorded the School of Mines. Thereafter it became customary on graduation day, which was normally in March or April, for students to march from Park Station to the Town Hall, and in the twenties this was accompanied by a 'rag'. In 1923 the rag took the form of 'a procession of decorated vehicles' illustrating various student activities; in 1924 of a mock marriage between Mr Wu, the University's new mascot, and a large doll; and in 1925 Professor Dart and the Taung skull provided the main theme for rag. By 1924 the graduation rag was already regarded as sufficient of an institution for the S.R.C. to establish a committee to organize it and other 'public demonstrations' by students.

Rags were by no means limited to graduation day. Any important occasion

STUDENT LIFE

Graduation Rag, 1925

in the life of the University was regarded as adequate excuse to stage a rag. Perhaps the most famous 'rag' of all in the history of the University was on Tuesday 23 June 1925, when the Prince of Wales, the future King Edward VIII and Duke of Windsor, opened the central block. About 5 000 people had flocked to Milner Park for the occasion, and they were subjected to a massive hoax. Constable Gert 'Boet' Coetzee, a local policeman who regularly did traffic duty at the Twist Street tram terminus, possessed a remarkable likeness to the Prince, and at the instigation of the S.R.C. he was successfully passed off as the Prince. It was not till the Prince himself arrived that the hoax was uncovered.

The source of the hoax was Saul 'Pete' Suzman, then vice-president of the S.R.C. He had noticed Constable Coetzee on point duty, and suggested to Adam Backeberg, the S.R.C. president, that they pass him off as the visiting Prince at the ceremony for the opening of the central block. The two students approached the Principal, Sir William Thomson, and the Registrar, H.W.J. van der Brugge, who declared they were prepared to allow the hoax, provided the Prince himself approved. Suzman thereupon went to Pretoria to interview the Prince's aide-de-camp, Admiral Halsey, who was most unsympathetic. 'To impersonate His Royal Highness, as you propose to do', Halsey insisted, 'would be an offence to his Royal position, and I have no doubt whatever, that the Prince would object most strongly to your suggestion.' The Prince, apparently, had other ideas, and the next day Halsey cabled the Prince's approval to Sir William Thomson. A rag committee of Backeberg, Suzman, Michael Kam, the financial genius of the S.R.C., Lawrie Adler, Comyn Duthie, Seymour Heymann, and Joan Dietrich made the arrangements, which worked to perfection.

On the Tuesday, which happened also to be the Prince's birthday, a 'rag' cavalcade escorted Constable Coetzee from the Rand Club, where the Prince was staying, to the University. On arrival at Milner Park, the Royal Salute was sounded, the crowd cheered, and with 'great ceremony' the Registrar greeted the bogus Prince. 'The Prince' then carefully inspected the guard of honour provided by school cadets and made 'a dignified climb' to his seat of honour. While one of the songs for the occasion was being sung, a fleet of Crossley cars pulled up, and the real Prince stepped out to be greeted by another Royal Salute. Constable Coetzee quickly disappeared, and the Prince proceeded to open the building.[46]

The incident gained considerable press coverage, and the next day resulted in a major traffic jam at the Twist Street tram terminus as hundreds of motorists converged to see 'the Prince' on point duty. But not all in the crowd at Milner Park had appreciated the hoax, least of all those who had wasted

The Great Hoax, 23 June 1925

their camera film on the bogus Prince, leaving themselves little or none for the genuine article.

On Saturday 8 June 1929 the first rag for charity was staged. Its purpose was to raise money for the Johannesburg Radium Fund, for the treatment of cancer patients at the Johannesburg General Hospital. Women students were sent out collecting from early morning, and after 9.30 a procession of floats, illustrating cancer monsters and the wonders of radium treatment, was paraded through town. Bands of students, dressed variously as bandits, pirates, policemen, and cowboys, raided the pockets of the local citizenry. Events were concluded at the City Hall steps, where George Robey, the British comedian, sold by American auction a barrel of beer. Altogether the street collection raised £1 229. What was called the Hospital Rag thereafter became an annual event, with all moneys going to the General Hospital.

In 1931 a new feature was added; a humorous magazine in the form of *Wits Wits*. The first rag magazine in South Africa, the initial idea was to call it 'Witty Wits', and it was only after two and a half hours of 'violent discussion' in the rag committee that the name was changed to Wits Wits.[47] It was sold for one shilling, and raised nearly £500 in its first year. In 1932 it was

Hospital Rag

described as a magazine of 'lore, life and love', and in 1933 as a magazine of 'love, life and laughter'.

In the thirties the Hospital Rag proved enormously popular with the general public. It was a major occasion in the life of Johannesburg, and people would come in from miles around to watch the floats and make their donations. By the end of the decade the Hospital Rag was raising about £10 000. As a rule, rag won the approval of the University authorities, who welcomed the sense of goodwill it generally created for Wits. But the Hospital Rag was not without its critics. The boisterous and sometimes boorish behaviour of students always attracted critical comment from certain sections of the public, and among the students themselves there were those who rejected the 'group exhibitionism' of rag, and who questioned whether it was any part of the University's function to serve as a charitable institution, least of all for a hospital that was the responsibility of the provincial administration.[48] Such were the criticisms voiced after the rag of 1939 that the S.R.C., then chaired by Brian Bunting, earnestly discussed its purpose and future. The motion 'That the hospital Rag be not abolished' was carried by 14 votes to 5, but at the same time it was resolved to curtail the number of rag activities and to strongly recommend to the Johannesburg Hospital Board that £2 000 of the money collected by rag be 'allocated to the development of native clinics in Orlando Township'.[49]

VII

The residences were an important aspect in student life at Wits before World War II. The 250 or so students they accommodated in the thirties, following the opening of the women's residence at Milner Park in 1930, constituted a fairly significant proportion of the over-all student body, which numbered 1 609 in 1930, rising to 2 544 by 1939. But their influence on the general life of the University was often much greater than might be inferred from mere numbers. They formed a close-knit group, distinguished by their strong sense of loyalty to Wits as an institution. The University's cheer-leader was normally a residence man, and the sing-songs were attended largely by residence students. In the organization of the sporting and social life of the University, residence students were the most prominent.

The two men's residences at Milner Park, College House and Dalrymple House, together accommodated approximately 150 students. Once completed, the women's residence at Milner Park accommodated almost 100 students, as against the 30 Sunnyside had been able to house. The office of dean turned over rather more regularly in the men's than in the women's residences. Altogether there were seven deans of the men's residences in the twenties

Men's Residences, 1929

University Residence House Committee, 1928

Front row: Q. Ochse, Miss S. van Rensburg, I.D. MacCrone, Mrs M. Coetzee, O.G. Backeberg
Back row: S.C. Quinlan, P. van der Lith, F. Uys, W.E. Varrie, G. Wille

and thirties; J.H. Hofmeyr and C.W. Kops in 1922, E.L. Damant in 1923, I.D. MacCrone from 1924 to 1928, O.G. Backeberg from 1929 to 1930, G.E. Pearse from 1931 to 1938, and W.G. Sutton for 1939 and 1940. After Margaret Hodgson's brief tenure, there were but two deans of the women's residence; Miss M. Swansbourne, who served until the end of 1936, and Mrs Archie Pratt-Nickels, who was also an assistant in the Department of French and Romance.

While Miss Swansbourne maintained a tight control over the women in her residence, insisting on knowing their movements and meeting their escorts, discipline over the students in the men's residences was generally relaxed. As Johannesburg became increasingly suburban, so concern that students from out of town would be contaminated by its influences evaporated. The vices that the students in the men's residences indulged in were more the product of their own age, and the times they lived in, than of place. Their main vice was coarseness; others were swearing, dirty songs, occasional heavy drinking, initiation, and card games on Sundays when other forms of recreation were denied them. The prostitutes of Twist Street were sometimes talked about, but rarely visited. Religion was by no means absent, and in the thirties the evangelical Oxford movement had its followers in the residences as well as in the wider student body.

A certain formality was imposed from above on life in the residences. Dinners were formal, students were required to wear gowns, and Latin graces were said. These formalities were generally appreciated, not resented. Life in the residences was also comfortable for their student inhabitants. Under the supervision of a matron, the African staff made their beds, cleaned their shoes, cooked their food, and served it to them. The students were free to concentrate on their studies, and also their sports, and other extramural activities.

In the social life of the University, and more particularly of the residences, dances were of the first importance. It was the great age of the formal dance, and each residence organized two such dances a year. Other formal dances were arranged by the students' union, and were generally held at the Wanderers Club.

In material collected in 1935 for a history of the men's residences, the reminiscences from the twenties and thirties all give a central place to the sagas that surrounded Phineas II, the University mascot. The original Phineas was mascot of University College, London, and his namesake was a seven-foot, wooden, snuff-taking Highlander. In 1923 he was abducted by students from U.C.T., recovered, and then apparently abducted again. In 1930 he was recaptured in a daring raid by four Wits students, and brought back to Johannesburg. He did not remain in town for long as the students at Pretoria decided they would like possession of Phineas, and carried him off. This marked the beginning of a series of massive raids between the students of the two universities, with the men's residences as their targets and the capture or recapture of Phineas as their supposed object. The raiding parties would sometimes number almost a thousand, and they not infrequently caused substantial damage.

Phineas still exists, and is competed for annually by the men's residences at Wits. But outside of the residences few students are aware of him. He is a relic of a bygone age.

Phineas

Notes

1. 'Statistics: Medicine, Engineering, General', University Archives 211.
2. *Umpa*, March 1928.
3. *Wu's Views*, 9 March 1939.
4. L. Chisholm, 'The Early History of NUSAS: Leo Marquard's Presidency 1924–1930' (unpublished U.C.T. Honours dissertation, 1976), chap. 1.
5. *Natal Advertiser*, 11 July 1927.
6. J.C. Fick, 'Afrikaner Student Politics — Past and Present', in H.W. van der Merwe and David Welsh (eds), *Student Perspectives on South Africa* (Cape Town, 1972), 66.
7. S.R.C. minutes, 5 Sept. 1935.

8. N. Rubin, *History of the Relations between NUSAS, the Afrikaanse Studentebond and the Afrikaans University Centres* (Cape Town, 1960), 3.
9. Chisholm, 'Early History of NUSAS', 68.
10. S.R.C. minutes, 2 May 1933; Rubin, *NUSAS*, 8–9.
11. Ibid., 17.
12. Report on N.U.S.A.S., S.R.C. minutes, 6 Sept. 1938.
13. Ibid., 6 June 1935.
14. *Umpa,* Oct. 1936, 46; M. Legassick, *The National Union of South African Students: Ethnic Cleavage and Ethnic Integration in the Universities* (Los Angeles, 1967), 16.
15. *Wu's Views,* 23 Sept. 1937.
16. Ibid., 19 May 1938.
17. *Star,* 2 Sept. 1937.
18. *Wu's Views,* 13 Oct. 1938.
19. S.R.C. minutes, 5 & 14 June 1939.
20. Ibid., 25 Oct. 1922.
21. Ibid., 14 Sept. 1925.
22. Ibid., 7 Aug. 1934 & 26 Feb. 1935.
23. Raikes to the Secretary for Education, 28 March 1929, U.O.D. E68/6.
24. Council minutes, IV, 13 Nov. 1931.
25. Ibid., 4 April 1939.
26. Correspondence for Senate meeting, 2 Nov. 1925.
27. *Students' Handbook,* 1939, 21.
28. S.R.C. minutes, 26 Sept. 1938.
29. *Umpa,* March 1928, 52–3.
30. *Magazine, University College, Johannesburg,* June 1919, 76; S.R.C. minutes, 9 Oct. 1924.
31. *Star,* 17 June 1922.
32. For a fuller account of the productions of the University Players see Kirby, *Wits End,* chap. 17.
33. *Umpa,* March 1925, 32.
34. S.R.C. minutes, 7 June 1932.
35. Ibid., 8 May 1934.
36. Constitution for the Students' Development Fund, 27 April 1932.
37. S.R.C. minutes, 1 June 1937.
38. *Umpa,* March 1932, 31.
39. Ibid., March 1935, 4.
40. A.P. Cartwright, *Strenue: The Story of King Edward VII School* (Johannesburg, 1974), 93–5.
41. *Umpa,* June 1934, 3, & March 1935, 49–50.
42. *Wu's Views,* 22 Sept. 1938.
43. *Umpa,* March 1932, 26.
44. *Wu's Views,* 24 March 1938.
45. S.R.C. minutes, 5 June 1934.
46. See 'The Great Hoax' in Harry Zeederberg, *Down Memory Lane* (Johannesburg, 1972), 53–6.
47. *Leech,* Sept. 1931, 36.
48. *Wu's Views,* 8 June 1939.
49. S.R.C. minutes, 5 June 1939.

A NOTE ON SOURCES

FOR THIS VOLUME I was given unrestricted access to the relevant records of the University. These records, lodged mainly in the University Archives, include the minutes of Council, Senate, and the various faculties. In many respects, the records of the University for the period prior to World War II are disappointing. Very little of the University's general correspondence has survived, and the files for members of staff are extremely thin, often non-existent. The central block fire of 1931, and a flooding of the registry in 1934, were responsible for an extensive destruction of records. For the rest, the preservation of records in the pre-war period seems to have been somewhat less than systematic.

Fortunately, much of the University's correspondence with the government has been preserved in the Government Archive in Pretoria, and the files of the Union Department of Education (U.O.D.) have proved invaluable. Various organizations that have been connected with the University, and have preserved their records on a systematic basis, have also provided a fruitful source of material. These include the Witwatersrand Council of Education, the Transvaal Chamber of Mines, and Barlow Rand. The archives of the Standard Bank and the old National Bank, now Barclays, provided some relevant material, and they clearly constitute a major, but hitherto largely neglected, source for historians of modern South Africa.

Private papers that have proved valuable are those of three of the Union's first four Ministers of Education, F.S. Malan (South African Library, Cape Town), Patrick Duncan (University of Cape Town Archives), and J.H. Hofmeyr (Historical Manuscripts Department of the Witwatersrand University Library), and of the founder members of the University's Department of History, W.M. Macmillan (in the possession of Mrs M. Macmillan), and Margaret Ballinger (Historical Manuscripts Department of the Witwatersrand University Library).

Perhaps the chief difficulty experienced over sources related to the major *causes célèbres* that shook the early University, notably the Stibbe affair, the resignation of W.M. Macmillan, and the enforced retirement of Margaret Ballinger. For the Stibbe affair I did have the advantage of Alan Paton's masterly account in his biography of Hofmeyr, but I was unable to come up with much by way of new material. The main documentary evidence is provided by the minutes of Council and Senate, but, as is often the case in controversies of this nature, these were generally written to hide as much as they reveal. The papers and records of other parties involved include nothing substantial. There is no reference to the affair in the papers of Colonel C.F. Stallard, K.C., who was brought in as arbitrator, and his award has been lost. There is also little in the papers of Patrick Duncan, who as Minister of Education intervened in the affair. In his autobiography, Percival Kirby, the University's first Professor of Music, states that he kept a long-hand record of the Senate debates, but this has not been found. Most interesting of all is that there is barely a whisper of the affair in the files of the Union Department of Education in the Government Archive, though at the time there was certainly correspondence between the conflicting parties at the University and the Department, and Stallard's arbitration award was sent to the Department. The relevant file has presumably been destroyed, and it is possible that it was destroyed during Hofmeyr's own tenure as Minister of Education. One surviving file on Hofmeyr, concerning his first appointment as Principal, contains in it a scrap of paper with the information that the contents of the file were destroyed in 1940.

The University's own records on the resignation of Macmillan and the retirement of Margaret Ballinger are not very full; indeed there is no file on Mrs Ballinger. My material has consequently been derived mainly from the Macmillan and Ballinger papers, Macmillan's autobiography, and oral evidence.

INDEX

Aarts, W.H., 287
Accountants Designation Act 1927, 162
Accounting, Department of, 59, 234, 260, 263
Acheson, G.J., 148
Actuarial Science, Department of, 153–4
Adamson, J., 211–2
Adamson Committee on University Subsidies 1933, 75, 211–2
Adler, C., 252, 348, 356
Adler, L.D., 80, 252, 348, 370
Admission of Advocates Act 1921, 162
African Explosives and Industries Ltd, 226, 236, 282, 283
Afrikaans, Department of, 146, 234, 276–8, 281
Afrikaanse Nasionale Studentebond, 326, 340–2, 345, 353
Agar-Hamilton, J.A.I., 269
Aiken, A., 76, 87, 90, 200, 202, 207–9, 214–5, 256, 304, 328–9
Ainsworth, H., 66
Alexandra Health Centre, 249–50
Allen, A.L., 249
Allibone, T.E., 291
Alma Mater, 145
Anatomy, Department of, 179, 245, 251, 284
Anderson, P.M., 119, 209
Anglo-American Corporation, 138
Anglo-Boer War, 3, 7, 9, 12–13
Appeals
    1932, 222, 225
    1935, 225–6
    See also University Development Fund
Applied Mathematics, Department of, 106, 125, 136, 153, 159, 288
Archaeology, Department of, 290
Architects and Quantity Surveyors Act 1927, 162–3, 171–3
Architecture, Department of, 120, 162, 170, 234, 240–3, 280

Arthur of Connaught, Prince, 72, 109, 209
Arts, Faculty of, 19, 31, 33, 59, 93–4, 96, 120, 122, 125–6, 133, 143, 148–50, 158, 234–5, 264–8, 274–6, 278, 280–1, 327
Association of Transvaal Architects, 170–1
Athlone, Earl of, 224
Atomic Energy Board, 239
Attorneys, Notaries, and Conveyancers Admission Act 1934, 254
Australopithecine skull, 126, 181–3
Axelson, E., 281

Backeberg, A.C., 348, 370
Backeberg, O.G., 151, 153, 287
Bailey, A., 21, 66
Baker, H., 171
Balkin, I.J., 246, 321
Ballinger, M., *see* Hodgson, M.
Ballinger, W., 145, 270, 273, 329, 332
Balogh, E., 255–9
Bantu Studies, Department of, 120, 125, 136–9, 148, 234, 276, 278–80, 312
Barclays Bank, 226
Barnato, B., 21
Barrow, J., 105, 221, 223
Barry, T., 256
Bawa, I.M., 311
Beattie, C., 50
Becker, B.J.P., 245, 253
Becker, J.G., 184, 245
Beit, A., 3, 20–2, 47, 222, 282
Beit, O., 21, 45–6, 48–50, 66, 222
Beit bequest, 3, 22–7, 36, 39, 45, 46, 48–50, 54–5, 57–8, 60, 102
Bernard Price Institute of Geophysical Research, 227–8, 231, 281, 289–92
Bernstein, B.L., 260
Berry, T.B., 191
Beyers, C.F., 246
Biesheuvel, S., 276, 281
Biology Block, 71, 105, 111, 231

381

INDEX

Black, J., 246, 249
Bleksley, A., 155, 288
Bleloch, W., 153
Block, I.J., 321
Bloom, A., 246, 319, 321
Bosanquet, B., 132
Bosazza, V.L., 357
Bosman, H.C., 101, 150, 354
Botany, Department of, 59, 106, 111, 156–7, 159, 281–3
Botha, L., 3, 25, 39, 46
Botha, M.C., 325
Botha, W., 364
Botha Committee on Medical Training 1939, 243, 251, 317–8, 325
Boyce, C., 240
Bozzoli, G.R., 240, 357
Braun, L.I., 246, 319, 321
Brebner, I.W., 246–9
Breijer, H.G., 40
Breyer, J.H., 191
Breyer-Brandwyk, M., 178
Brinton, A.G., 320
British Association for the Advancement of Science, 224
Broederbond, 324
Brookes, E., 96, 126, 133, 138, 300, 311
Broom, R., 183
Brümmer, F., 275–6
Bryant, A.T., 138
Bryer, M., 242
Buchanan, G., 250
Buchanan, W., 40
Bunting, A.H., 282, 344
Bunting, B., 343–4, 373
Bureau of Archaeology, 289–90
Bushman Research Expedition 1936, 289
Busschau, W.J., 262
Buxton, S.C., 109
Byron, J.J., 150

Campbell, A., 320
Capelli, A.E., 231
Carnegie Corporation of New York, 219, 224, 227–8
Carpentier, F., 228
Cellier, J.S., 40, 44
Central Block, 73, 109, 112, 115–6, 216–9, 221, 227–8, 231
Central Mining and Investment Corporation, 66
Chamber of Commerce, 11
Chamber of Mines, 11, 62, 64, 66, 137, 164–5, 222, 226, 237, 239, 314
Chamberlain, F.R., 362
Chamberlain, J., 3, 16, 20
Charters, R.H., 40, 167–8
Chatgidakis, C.B., 245
Chemical, Metallurgical and Mining Society of South Africa, 239
Chemistry, Department of, 59, 125, 153, 159, 168, 281–2, 287
Chemistry and Physics Block, 105, 109, 112, 114–5, 231

Church of the Province of South Africa Central Record Library, 225
Cillie, P.M., 257
Civil Engineering, Department of, 167–9, 228, 235–7, 239, 240
Clarendon, Earl of, 224–5
Classics, Department of, 59, 146–8
Clinical Pathology, Department of, 250
Cluver, E., 86, 174, 176–9, 185, 244, 250
Coaker, N.E., 193
Coat of Arms, 173
Coetzee, A., 146, 278, 281
Coetzee, G., 370
Cohen, S.J., 253
College House, 42, 80, 104, 231, 373
Collett, H.O., 240
Commerce, Department of, 59
Commerce, Faculty of, 93, 163, 193–4, 234–5, 260–4
Consolidated Goldfields, 41, 44
Constancon, C.J.M., 155, 287
Convocation, 72–4, 77
Cooke, B., 242
Cooke, H.B., 286
Coplans, J.M., 187
Corstorphine, G.S., 32, 40, 44, 48, 51, 53, 58, 62, 65
Cory, G., 67, 130
Council, 72–7, 81–92, 207
Council for Scientific and Industrial Research, 292
Cowin, N.T., 223, 227
Cowin and Powers, Architects, 105
Craib, W.H., 246–9, 251, 315, 318–21
Creewel, P.A., 238
Cullen, W., 200, 222, 224, 255
Cursons, W.E., 99, 102
Curtis, L., 200
Cushny, A.R., 177

Dalrymple, W., 58, 60–2, 65–6, 76, 83, 201, 207, 221, 362
Dalrymple House, 104, 231, 373
Dalton, J.P., 84, 87–8, 132, 143, 153–5, 194, 200, 202, 204, 287–8, 329
Damant, E.L., 375
Dart, R., 110, 121, 126, 143, 145, 175, 179–84, 190, 204, 243–5, 292, 302, 305, 315–6, 319–20, 356, 358
De Beers Consolidated, 5, 45, 65, 165
De Kiewiet, C.W., 131, 149, 269, 326
De Kock, M.J., 285
De Meillon, B., 158
De Meillon, Commandant, 103
Dentistry, Faculty of, 185–91, 234, 253–4, 265
De Villiers, I., 240
De Vos, D.W., 240
Dewey, J., 353
Dietrich, J., 370
Dix, F., 194
Dobson, J.H., 18, 42

Dodds, D.A., 100, 206
Doke, C.M., 137–9, 145, 183, 276, 278–9, 312
Drennan, C.M., 84, 87, 148, 267
Drew, D., 57
Drysdale, J., 239, 357
Duggan, C., 145
Duncan, P., 53–4, 56–8, 66, 83, 87–90, 228, 290
Dunston, J.T., 184, 250
Du Randt, J.T., 302
Dutch, Department of, 59, 146
Duthie, C., 370
Du Toit, C.W.M., 313

East Rand Premier Mines, 41
Economics and Economic History, Department of, 59, 142, 149
Edelstein, J.M., 246
Education, Department of, 265
Edward, Prince of Wales, 109, 370–1
Einstein, A., 154
Elder, J.S., 291
Electrical Engineering, Department of, 109, 168, 170, 234, 237, 239–40
Electrotechnics, Department of, 167
Ellenberger, R., 279
Eloff, G., 285
Emley, W.H., 105, 109
Engineering, Faculty of, 93, 120, 162–3, 167, 216, 234–6, 240, 254, 264, 317
Engineering Buildings, 105, 109, 112, 116, 231
English, Department of, 59, 120, 148, 266–8
Evans, G.T.R., 156, 287
Evans, J.E., 76
Evans, S., 51, 53, 55, 62, 76, 207
Eybers, E., 277–8, 356

Fantham, H.B., 105, 121, 156–7, 281
Farrar, G., 21
Fassler, J., 242
Feetham, R., 57, 66, 208–9
Feldman, M.B., 253
Ferguson, A., 101
Ferguson, T., 364
Findlay, J., 88, 193–4, 200, 260
Fire 1931, 216–9
Fischer, P.M.S., 253
Fitzpatrick, P., 14, 21, 27, 30
Foote, H.J., 191
Forrest, H.M., 361
Fort Hare, 299–300, 308, 315–7, 341, 345
Fouché, L., 269–70, 330, 333
Fouché, L.A., 365
Frack, I., 252
Frankel, L., 348
Frankel, S.H., 142, 149–50, 251, 271–3, 344, 354
Frankenwald, 21, 26–7, 45, 58, 102, 282

Freer, P., 219, 224
French, Department of, 59, 145
Friel, G., 191
Furner, A.S., 173

Galloway, A., 245
Gane, P.G., 291–2
Gear, H., 252
Gear, James, 252
Gear, John, 248, 252
Geography, Department of, 59, 120, 158
Geology, Department of, 106, 125, 237, 239, 281–2, 285–7
Geophysics, Department of, 281
George, Duke of Kent, 224
German, Department of, 146
Gevers, T.W., 239, 282, 285–7
Gie, S.F.N., 120, 211, 308–9
Gilliland, H., 283
Gillman, J., 245, 253, 284, 357
Gimkey, S.F., 239
Girdwood, R.L., 321
Gluckman, I., 246
Gluckman, M., 139, 150, 341, 356
Goldblatt, I., 184
Gordon, G., 259
Gordon, M., 246, 321
Gorges, R.A., 240
Grant, W.G., 184, 246
Graumann, H., 54
Gray, J., 271, 273–6
Great Hall, 145, 228
Greenwood, H., 263
Gregorowski, L.F., 71
Greig, I.T., 339
Greig, J.Y.T., 225, 257, 265–9, 368
Grey University College, 45, 145, 277, 326
Groote Schuur Estate, 9, 45–6, 118
Gubbins, J.G., 220, 224
Gubbins Library, 220–1, 225

Haarhoff, T., 87–8, 146–7
Hahlo, H.R., 260
Hahn, P.D., 4–5
Hales, A.L., 287–8, 291
Hall, E., 240
Hall, T.D., 283
Halliday, E.C., 287
Halsey, L., 370
Hammond, J.L., 130
Hancock, W.K., 300
Hanson, N., 242
Harris, F.R., 5
Hartmann, E., 220
Hartog, J., 54
Hawke, F., 287
Hawke and McKinley, Architects, 105
Heather, H.J.S., 167–8
Hebrew, Department of, 148
Heiman, H.L., 246, 319, 321
Hele-Shaw, H., 18–19, 32, 166
Hellmann, E., 139
Hendrikz, W. de S., 280

INDEX

Herbert, G., 240–3
Herholdt, A. de V., 207
Hertzog, J.B.M., 97, 108, 115, 127–8, 130, 168, 199, 203, 277, 299, 324
Heyman, S.C., 246, 348, 351, 370
Higher Education Additional Provision Act 1917, 305
Higher Education Financial Provision Act 1931, 211, 214
Highfield Terrace, 41–2
Hill, F.G., 240
Hill, H.R., 209
Hillman, H., 228, 231
Hillman, W., 209, 228, 231
Hillman building, 170, 228, 231, 237
History, Department of, 59, 120, 271, 281, 332
Hodges, D.B., 291
Hodgson, M., 100, 127, 269–71, 273, 327–34, 375
Hoernlé, R.F.A., 92, 127–8, 131–6, 138–40, 199–200, 202, 270, 274–5, 300–1, 311, 320, 333
Hoernlé, W., 127, 132, 139–40, 150, 219, 279, 332
Hoffenberg, S.N., 165, 238–9
Hoffmann, L.C., 255
Hofmeyr, D., 78–80, 85
Hofmeyr, G., 113, 115–6, 120
Hofmeyr, H.J., 51, 53, 55, 62, 77, 85, 88, 200, 207–9, 304, 311, 320
Hofmeyr, J.H., 65–6, 76–92, 93–8, 100–1, 103–6, 113–5, 117, 122, 126, 132–3, 146–7, 174, 176, 186–8, 200, 202–3, 209–12, 227, 237, 273, 298, 304, 307, 315–6, 318, 320, 322–3, 325, 328, 332, 341, 354, 375, 379
Hollins, A., 55
Hooper, A.G., 266
Horton, J.W., 26
Hossack, F., 191
Houghton, D.H., 235
Howie, W.D., 242
Hubbard, C.W., 100
Huguenot College, 45
Hungerford, J., 209
Hunter, B.M., 187, 190–1
Hutcheon, J., 158
Hutchinson, G.E., 158
Hutton, C.W., 5–6

Imperial Chemical Industries, 224
Inauguration 1922, 71–2
Industrial and Commercial Workers Union, 129
Initiation, 348, 350
Institute of South African Architects, 162, 171
Iron and Steel Corporation of South Africa, 168, 236, 240, 262
Israelstam, S.S., 287

Jackson, S.P., 288
Jacobson, J., 368

Jaff, J., 344
Jameson, L.S., 49–50
Jameson Raid, 7
Janisch, E., see Plumstead, E.
Jansen, E.G., 130, 307
Jeffreys, F., 216–9
Jenkins, H.M., 266
Jennings, J.E., 240
Jensen, A.E., 239
Jeppe, C.W.B., 258–9
Jeppe, J., 76, 90
Jeppe Boys' High School, 40, 362
Johannesburg Consolidated Investment Company, 66
Johannesburg Dental Hospital, 187–8
Johannesburg Dental Society, 187–8
Johannesburg General Hospital, 175, 187, 246–7, 251–3, 302
Hospital Board, 102, 184
Johannesburg Municipal Council, 11, 102, 115, 121, 226
Johannesburg Public Library, 119
Johannesburg Training College for Teachers, 149, 265
Joint Councils of Europeans and Natives, 127–30, 138
Jones, J.D.R., 61, 65, 127–8, 136–8, 279, 300
Jones, W.H., 98, 100, 206
Jooste, G.F., 66

Kam, M., 370
Kannemeyer, J.C., 277
Kark, S.L., 253, 343
Karney, A.B.L., 201
Keiller, J., 291
Keith, A., 183
Keppel-Jones, A., 270–1, 273, 331
Kerr, A., 316
Kerr, P., 200
Kerrich, J., 155, 287–8
King Edward VII School, 18, 40
Kirby, P.R., 143–5, 183, 219, 228, 281
Kirkwood, W.E., 240
Klein, L., 184
Klenerman, F., 344
Kloppers, P.J., 253
Kops, C.W., 155, 375
Kotzé, R., 76, 85, 119, 208–9
Krige, C.F., 246
Krige, D.F., 240
Krige, E., 139, 149
Krige, G.J.R., 287
Krige, J.D., 140
Krige, U., 277
Kruger, C.M., 240
Krynauw, A.H., 209
Kuny, B., 184
Kuper, H., 140
Kuper, S.M., 259

Laburn, R.J., 240
Lance, W.F., 23, 33

Landau, J.L., 148
Lauf, G.B., 240
Laurence, P., 46
Laurence Commission on Universities 1914, 46–8
Law, Faculty of, 5, 19, 93, 125, 162, 191–4, 234–5, 254–7
Lawley, A., 18
Lawn, J.G., 7, 9, 32–3, 77, 85, 166
Lawrence, J.L., 5
Lawrie, J.G., 148, 281, 328, 356
Lehfeldt, R.A., 40, 77, 88, 125–6, 142–4, 163, 194, 261
Leipoldt, C.L., 97, 306–7
Le May, H., 40, 153–155, 209, 283, 288, 331, 333
Leonard, J.W., 220
Le Roux, A.P., 5
Le Roux, J.J., 146
Levin, J.J., 184, 246, 321
Lewin, J., 279
Lewsen, P., 267
Liberalism, Wits a centre for, 95–6, 102, 125–8, 273–4
Library, 118–20, 219–25, 231
   Church of the Province of South Africa Central Record Library, 225
   Gubbins Library, 220–1, 225
   Leonard Memorial Law Library, 220
   Reading Room and Library Committee, 119
   Seymour Memorial Library, 118–9
   Witwatersrand Library Appeal Committee, 224–5
   Witwatersrand Medical Library, 184, 219
Liddell, D., 261
Lindemann, W.C., 43
Lister, F., 245
Lister, M., 356
Livingston, K., 354
Loffell, B., 240
London Committee, 93
London School of Economics, 224
Loram, C.T., 302
Loram Committee, 302–3, 305–6, 308–9, 314
Louw, A.H., 319–20
Louw, W.E.G., 277
Lucas, F.A.W., 90, 201
Lyon and Fallon, Architects, 103
Lyttleton, A., 25

MacCrone, I.D., 127, 132–3, 140–2, 144, 150, 183, 276, 281, 375
McCubbin, D.A., 66
McEwan, M., 285
McGibbon, J., 184, 245
MacGregor, W.R., 140, 148
McIntosh, G., 242
McIntosh, W., 173
McKenzie, W.G., 209
McKerron, R.G., 192–3, 255, 157
Mackintosh, R.H., 250

Macmillan, W.M., 67, 84, 127–32, 142, 154, 220, 269–71, 273, 278–9, 305, 309, 330
Macmurray, J., 78, 84, 87, 132, 154
Madeley, W.B., 54
Maingard, L.F., 97, 143, 145, 183, 256, 258, 320
Maisels, I.A., 260
Malan, D.F., 97, 210–1, 214, 308, 312, 322, 324, 350
Malan, D.J., 291
Malan, F.S., 44, 46, 49–50, 53–5, 57–9, 66, 97, 173–4
Malcolm, D. McK., 139
Malherbe, E., 276
Marais, J.H., 50
Marais, J.S., 131, 269
Margo, C.S., 259
Marist Brothers' College, 40
Marquard, L., 340
Martienssen, R., 173, 241–3
Mathematics, Department of, 153, 155, 159, 287
Mechanical Engineering, Department of, 109, 168, 237, 239
Medical Association of South Africa, 302–3, 307, 325
Medical, Dental and Pharmacy Act 1928, 162, 186
Medical Library, *see under* Library
Medicine, Department of, 59, 248
Medicine, Faculty of, 66, 93–4, 96–7, 102, 108, 110–1, 114–6, 118, 162, 173, 175–85, 187–90, 216, 234, 243, 246, 264, 305–6, 309, 327
Melle, B.G., 246
Melzer, L., 364
Mendelssohn, E., 151–2, 286
Menof, P., 252, 356
Merriman, J.X., 24, 267
Metallurgy, Department of, 164–6, 237–8
Mettam, R.W.M., 184
Meyer, E.C.J., 77
Meyer, P.J., 341
Millin, D., 166
Milner, A., 3, 11–15, 20–2, 32, 47, 53
Minerals Research Laboratory, 166, 289–90
Mining, Department of, 5, 9, 11, 19, 109, 164–5, 228, 234, 235–40
Moffat, H.A., 301, 307
Molema, S., 301
Moss, C.E., 77, 88, 105, 156–7, 285
Moss, M., 283, 332
Mtimkulu, L., 308–9
Mulla, A.H.I., 311, 346
Muller, T.F., 240
Mullineux, J., 201
Munich Crisis 1938, 339, 345, 351
Murray, C.A.M., 252
Murray, I., 256
Murray, J.C., 191–3, 256–7
Murray, W., 45
Music, Department of, 93, 120, 145

INDEX

Natal University College, Pietermaritzburg, 45
Nathan, M., 15, 304
National Bank, 66
National Institute for Personnel Research, 276
National Research Board, 289
National Research Council, 288–9, 292
National Union of South African Students, 126, 326, 340–3, 345, 352
Native Recruiting Corporation, 75, 137
Neale-May, W.M., 240
Newman, S.C., 240
Nicholas, H.C., 260, 344, 345
Nienaber, P.J., 278, 341
North West Engineering Block, 109, 112, 116, 231

Ogg, J., 65, 155
O'Hara, J., 49, 51–7, 62–3, 102
Oliver, H.O., 288
Onderstepoort, 66
Orenstein, A.J., 246, 320
Orr, J., 7, 18, 34–5, 40, 64, 165–9, 237, 239
Osborn, T.W.B., 244, 338, 348, 352, 358

Paff, W.P., 145
Paine, H.H., 155–6
Papenfus, H.B., 54, 57
Park, T.M., 49
Passmore, J., 132
Paterson, A.C., 97
Paterson, N., 158, 284–5
Pathology and Bacteriology, Department of, 183–4, 245
Paton, A., 87
Pearse, G.E., 78, 105, 108, 170–2, 227, 239, 242, 280, 375
Pelser, O.C., 260
Penn, J., 253
Perry, J., 103–4
Pharmacology, Department of, 245
Philip, J., 129, 220
Phillips, J., 282–3, 285
Phillips, L., 45–6, 48–50, 52, 54, 57–8, 102
Philosophy, Department of, 59, 120, 136, 140, 149
Phineas, 375–6
Phonetics and Logopedics, Department of, 279
Physics, Department of, 59, 125, 155–6, 287
Physics and Chemistry Block, 105, 109, 112, 114–5, 231
Physiology, Department of, 245, 253
Pienaar, P. de V., 279
Pirie, J.H.H., 184
Pirow, H., 209, 308
Pirow, O., 130–1, 209
Plein Square, 15, 19, 30, 42–3, 71, 78, 83, 94, 103, 106, 111–5, 118, 237
Plumstead, E., 151–2
Pollak, H., 271–3, 344

Pollak, W., 193
Porter, A., 157, 184, 332
Porter, C., 16, 185
Pratt-Nickels, A., 375
Preventive Medicine, Department of, 179
Price, B., 76, 88, 207, 227
Prince of Wales, *see* Edward, Prince of Wales
Psychology, Department of, 140, 148, 234, 276, 281
Pugsley, F., 100

Quantity Surveying, Department of, 173
Queen Victoria Maternity Hospital, 247, 249
Quinn, J.W., 57

Rabinowitz, L., 350
Radcliffe-Brown, A.R., 139
Radloff, E., 244
Rag, 352, 368–73
Raikes, A.J., 204
Raikes, H., 93, 122, 131, 133, 153, 165, 190, 199–207, 209–10, 221–2, 224–5, 228, 231–2, 236, 255–8, 262–5, 267–8, 275, 284, 309–10, 312–3, 315, 317, 319–21, 323, 329–34, 339, 345, 350, 352, 357, 358, 362
Raikes, J., 203
Raine, R., 57
Ramsbottom, W.H., 126, 193
Randall, O.R., 168, 170, 239
Reedman, J., 263, 344
Reekie, J., 101
Research Grant Board, 152, 289
Residences, 41–2, 116, 338, 373–6
  College House, 42, 80, 104, 231, 373
  Dalrymple House, 104, 231, 373
  Sunnyside, 41, 80, 231, 373
  Women's Residence, 231, 373
Reunert, T., 20, 24, 47–8, 51, 55, 58, 62, 72, 76
Rhodes, C.J., 4–6, 39, 45
Rhodes University College, 45, 129, 193
Richards, A., 280
Richards, C.S., 225, 260–3, 271, 344
Rissik, H., 193
Rissik, J., 368
Roberts, A., 240
Roberts, D., 240
Roberts, H.M., 26
Robertson, J.B., 153, 287
Robertson, T.E., 18, 40, 42
Robey, G., 371
Robinson, J., 13, 21, 23, 30–2, 99
Rockey, W., 57
Roedean School, 80, 204
Routh, G., 343, 344
Roux, A.J.A., 239, 357
Roux, E., 151, 157, 283, 344, 354
Roy, F., 81, 92
Royal Institute of British Architects, 173

Russell, W., 250

St John's College, 40, 362
Salmons, J., 181
Samuels, L.M., 271
Sargant, E.B., 14, 32
Schapera, I., 150, 183
Scheepers, G.W.H., 253
Schonland, B., 290-2
Schreiner, O.D., 126, 193, 209
Schumacher, R.W.S., 30
Schuurman, J., 158
Schwartz, J., 348
Science, Faculty of, 20, 31, 59, 93, 111, 125, 150-1, 156, 158-9, 234-5, 281, 283, 285-8, 327
Searle, J., 271
Segal, B., 287
Selborne, Countess of, 83, 88
Selborne, Earl of, 23-5, 30
Senate, 31, 33, 41, 43, 72, 74, 76, 82-92, 100, 121, 238, 246, 249
Seymour Memorial Library, 118-9
Shand, H.S., 151
Shannon, H.A., 261, 272
Shapiro, M., 252
Shaw, G.D., 246
Shaw, J.C. Middleton, 189-90, 214, 253-4, 320
Sikakana, J.M.A., 139
Skeen, C., 240
Slade, G.F., 184
Smit, D.L., 301
Smith, A., 143
Smith, G.E., 179, 182
Smuts, J.C., 3, 24-30, 39, 45-6, 59, 71-2, 80, 97, 108, 113, 128, 137, 153-5, 228, 269-70, 282-3, 290, 292, 300, 312
Smyth, G.S., 246
Snyman, H.W., 253
Social Studies, Department of, 234, 273-6
Sociology, Department of, 234, 273-6
Solomon, R., 23
Sonnabend, H., 275
South African Association for the Advancement of Science, 136, 142, 158
South African College, 4-7, 9, 22-4, 48-9, 297
South African Council for Educational and Social Research, 266
South African Dental Association, 185-7, 189
South African Institute for Medical Research, 102, 111, 157, 175-6, 179, 183-4, 245, 250-2
South African Institute of Race Relations, 96, 128, 133-4
South African Institution for Engineers, 237
South African Medical Council, 162
South African Mining and Engineering Journal, 119-20
South African Mining Journal, 6-7, 19
South African Pharmacy Board, 162

South African School of Mines, 3, 5, 7, 9, 15, 19, 77, 237
South African School of Mines and Technology, 3, 30, 39-59, 64-7, 83, 118, 175, 297, 305
South African Student's Liberal League, 343-4
South West Engineering Block, 105, 109, 116, 231
Stallard, C.F., 86-7
Stammers, A.D., 244, 319-20, 356, 365
Standard Bank, 66, 226
Stanley, G.H., 40, 64, 166, 238, 290
Statistics, Department of, 142
Statutes, *see* University of the Witwatersrand Private Act
Staz, J., 253-4
Stein, H.B., 253
Stephen, H., 152-3, 239, 281, 283, 287
Steyn, S.J.M., 260
Stibbe, E.P., 62, 76-8, 81-7, 90-2, 111, 131, 133, 143, 173-4, 176-7, 179-80, 200, 203
Strachan, A.S., 245, 319
Straszacker, R.L., 239, 357
Stratford, R., 258
Strikes, 46, 71
Stucke, W.H., 105
Student Clubs and Societies
  Medical Students' Society, 319
  Sports Clubs, 41-2, 357-68
  Students' Christian Association, 319
  Students' Jewish Association, 319
Student Publications, 355-7
  Auricle, 355, 357
  Fulcrum, 355, 357
  Leech, 355, 356
  Philistine, 355, 356
  Prattler, 355
  Salamander, 355
  Scientific Discussion Society Journal, 355
  Umpa, 355, 356
  Wits Laager, 344, 355
  Wits Wits, 355, 371
  Wu's Views, 339, 355, 356
Students, 7-8, 11, 33, 35, 40-4, 59, 337-76
  Afrikaans, 96, 251, 299, 317-8, 321-7, 338
  Black Admission to Wits, 6, 96, 98, 204, 298-317
  English, 251, 337
  Jewish, 251, 299, 317-22, 337
Students' Development Fund, 222, 348, 358
Students Representative Council, 31, 265, 310, 318, 326, 342, 345-53, 361, 370
Stutterheim, N., 240
Sunday sport, 348, 350-1, 358
Sunnyside Residence, 41, 80, 231, 373
Surgery, Department of, 247
Surveying, Department of, 5, 228, 237, 239
Sutherland, L., 131, 149

INDEX

Suttie, D.P., 99
Sutton, W.G., 168-70, 207, 209, 239, 375
Suzman, A., 260
Suzman, S., 256, 362, 370
Swansbourne, M., 100, 375
Swart, V., 266-7, 356
Swiegers, J.U., 286

Tansley, A.G., 156
Taung skull, 126, 181-3
Tavaria, K.J., 316
Tawney, R.H., 130
Taylor, R.W., 71
Te Winter, J.B., 43
Theal, G.M., 130
Thomas, I. Glyn, 205-7, 272, 324
Thompson, G.R., 43-4, 184, 247, 320
Thompson, H.A., 364
Thomson, W., 93-4, 97-8, 116, 133, 145, 149, 200, 202
Thornton, E., 179, 250, 303, 314-5
Tillyard, H.J.W., 146
Tin Temple, 59, 105, 111
Transvaal Consolidated Lands and Exploration Company, 102
Transvaal Society of Accountants, 193-4
Transvaal Technical Institute, 3-4, 18-20, 22-3, 42, 170
Transvaal University College, 4, 20, 22-4, 26-8, 31-5, 40-1, 45, 58-9, 99
Transvaal Workers' Educational Association, see Workers Educational Association
Troost, N., 240
Tucker, W.K., 76
Tully, H.C., 173
Turner, F.J., 141
Turner, L.C.F., 281
Twala, J.S., 312

University College, Johannesburg, 59-60
University College, Potchefstroom, 326
University Development Fund 1928, 222, 348, 358
   See also Appeals
University of Birmingham, 74
University of the Cape of Good Hope, 4, 6, 19, 22, 31, 39, 45-7, 49-52, 54-7, 62, 98-9
University of Cape Town, 112, 117-8, 137, 140, 215, 236, 243-5, 297-9, 304, 315-7, 322
University of Pretoria, 324-6
   See also Transvaal University College
University of South Africa, 58, 100, 276, 299-300
University of Stellenbosch, 49, 117-8, 146, 324
University of the Witwatersrand Private Act, 73, 82, 90-1, 93, 112, 207
University Orchestra, 145
University Press, see Witwatersrand University Press
Unterhalter, J., 356

Van den Heever, C.M., 276-8
Van der Brugge, H.W.J., 98-9, 205, 308, 333, 370
Van der Horst, C., 282-5
Van der Horst Commission on University Finances 1927, 116, 122
Van Riet Lowe, C., 219, 290
Van Wyk, J.W., 291
Van Wyk Louw, N.P., 277
Verster, J.D., 314
Veterinary Anatomy, Department of, 184
Veterinary Science, Department of, 93
Victoria College, Stellenbosch, 5, 7, 47, 50, 129
Victoria Falls and Transvaal Power Company, 226-7
Vieyra, H.J., 259
Vilakazi, B.W., 139, 280, 311-3
Visser, W.H., 77, 88
Von Maltitz, A.A., 240

Wagner, A.I., 148
Walker, E., 130
Walker, S., 244
Walker, W.J., 168-9, 237-9, 357
Ward, C., 27, 76, 82-4, 90
Ware, F., 32
Ware Commission, 9, 14-18, 20-1
Wassenaar, T., 325
Watermeyer, G.A., 165-6, 238-9
Watkin, M., 145
Watkins-Pitchford, W., 183-4, 245
Watt, J.M., 87, 110, 177, 187-8, 209, 244, 319
Waugh, E.H., 103, 105, 112
Webber, W., 63
Weinbrenn, C., 158
Weintraub, D., 283
Weizmann, C., 152
Welchman, W., 246
Wellington, J., 158-9, 219, 288
Wells, L.H., 245, 253
Welsh, M., 286
Wernher, J., 30, 45-50
Wernher, Beit and Company, 21
Whyte, J.W., 184
Wiles, G.G., 287, 291
Wilkinson, J.A., 18, 40, 151-3, 168, 239, 281
Williams, C., 355
Williams, G.F., 7, 11
Williams, M.V., 148
Williams, T., 265
Williamson, F., 109, 223
Williamson, O.K., 184, 319-20, 365
Witwatersrand Council of Churches, 350

388

Witwatersrand Council of Education, 13–14, 19, 20, 30, 46–52, 60–2, 65, 72, 77, 114, 127, 137–8, 221–2
Witwatersrand Native Labour Assocation, 75, 137, 175
Witwatersrand University Committee, 58, 62–3, 65, 102–3, 106, 112, 114–5, 121, 185, 223, 357
Witwatersrand University Press, 138–9, 154
Wolfowitz, J., 252
Wolpe, J., 253
Woolf, E.B., 320
Workers Educational Association, 129, 154
Wyndham, H., 57

Xaba, R.J., 309

Yale Observatory Southern Station, 112, 231
Yale University, 112
Yates, J., 32, 34–5
Young, E., 283
Young, F., 155, 287, 320
Young, R.B., 18, 40, 42, 77, 82, 85, 151, 182, 201, 285

Zoology, Department of, 59, 106, 156–9, 281–5

www.ingramcontent.com/pod-product-compliance
Lightning Source LLC
Chambersburg PA
CBHW081707100526
44590CB00022B/3683